W9-CER-279

Who Speaks for the President?

Press Secretary James C. Hagerty sometimes gave President Dwight D. Eisenhower advice during press conferences. *Courtesy AP/Wide World.*

Who Speaks for the President?

The White House Press Secretary from Cleveland to Clinton

W. Dale Nelson

Syracuse University Press

First Edition 1998
98 99 00 01 02 03   6 5 4 3 2 1

The paper used in this publication meets the minimum requirements of American National Standard for Information Sciences—Permanence of Paper for Printed Library Materials, ANSI Z39.48-1984. ∞™

Library of Congress Cataloging-in-Publication Data

Nelson, W. Dale.
    Who speaks for the President? : the White House press secretary
from Cleveland to Clinton / W. Dale Nelson. — 1st ed.
        p. cm.
    Includes bibliographical references (p.   ) and index.
    ISBN 0-8156-0514-5 (cloth : alk. paper)
    1. Presidential press secretaries—United States—History.
    2. Presidential press secretaries—United States—Biography.
    3. United States. Office of the White House Press Secretary—
History.   4. Government and the press—United States—History.
    I. Title.
    E176.47.N45 1998
    352.23′2748′0973—dc21   97-40236

For Joyce

"The White House spokesman is the second most visible person in the country, which can be not only an honor but a headache."

—Larry Speakes
spokesman for President Ronald Reagan

"The only reason for the press secretary's job is that the president cannot deal with the press 24 hours a day. You have to have somebody to act as a stand-in for him."

—George Reedy
press secretary to President Lyndon Johnson

"I have been speaking of the press secretary's job as though there were general agreement on what it is. That is not the case."

—Jody Powell
press secretary to President Jimmy Carter

W. Dale Nelson spent forty years as a reporter and editor with the Associated Press. During twenty years in Washington, he won the Aldo Beckman Award for excellence in reporting about the presidency. He is the author of *The President Is at Camp David* (Syracuse Univ. Press, 1995). He and his wife, Joyce Nelson, live in Laramie, Wyoming.

Contents

x   *Contents*

Illustrations

Acknowledgments

RESEARCH FOR THIS BOOK was aided by grants from the Herbert Hoover Presidential Library Association and the Gerald R. Ford Foundation, to which the author gives grateful acknowledgment.

Other archives whose resources were utilized are acknowledged in the bibliography.

I am also indebted to the staffs and collections of the Library of Congress, the Washington County, Maryland, Free Library, the Albany County, Wyoming, public library, and the libraries of Shepherd College, Marshall University, Duke University, Princeton University, and the Universities of California, Iowa, Washington, and Wyoming.

Persons I interviewed for the record are identified in the bibliography. I am also thankful to colleagues in the journalistic community who shared their thoughts with me, but preferred not to be quoted.

Some fragments of this book were delivered as a paper at a conference, "The Carter Presidency: Policy Choices in the Post New Deal Era," held February 20–22, 1997, at the Jimmy Carter Library and Presidential Center in Atlanta.

Finally, I am grateful for the wise editorial counsel of my wife, Joyce Nelson.

Who Speaks for the President?

1

The Game

AS GROVER CLEVELAND PREPARED to enter the White House for his second term, a Washington journalist offered him some advice on the selection of a new private secretary.

"We were hoping," the president-elect's caller said, "that you will appoint a man who will be good to us newspaper men."

"I had a notion," said Cleveland, "of appointing a man who would be good to me."[1]

The story, which went the rounds in Washington in the spring of 1897, illustrates a truth that holds whether the president be Cleveland or Clinton.

His secretary, or in more recent years his press secretary, must try to serve both the president and the press, without doing a disservice to either.

Marlin Fitzwater, press secretary to Presidents Ronald Reagan and George Bush, put it bluntly: "The press secretary always fights with one arm behind his back, trying to serve two masters."[2]

The press does not have this handicap. Reporters work for only one master. Their objective is to get the story. But they, too, enter the fray with a hand tied behind them. They don't have the information. The press secretary, in most cases, does.

"It's a game here in Washington," veteran journalist Richard L. Strout said in an interview in 1976. "The executive has the sheep and we are the stealers—we're the poachers. We're trying to get the news and they are trying to keep it from us or select the news we get. And it's a game."[3]

Sometimes the game is played for high stakes.

On April 24, 1980, at a sandwich lunch in the Cabinet Room of the White House, Jody Powell had a lesson in just how high they can be.

President Jimmy Carter's press secretary had known for months that the administration had a contingency plan for a mission to rescue U.S. diplomats held hostage since November 1979 by the fundamentalist Moslem government of Iran.

He had learned details of the plan at a meeting at Camp David on March 22. On April 11, Carter told Powell the plan was on the agenda for a regular Friday foreign policy breakfast that the press secretary usually attended.

Did he think he should attend this one, or would it be better if he didn't know about it? Powell said he believed he should know exactly what was planned.

The secrecy of the mission would have to be protected, he argued, and that might involve misleading or lying to reporters. "If it did, I was the person to do it."

Carter agreed, and Powell sat in on the meeting. He was one of the few people in the administration who knew anything about the rescue plan. Chief of Staff Hamilton Jordan, responding to a question at a White House staff meeting on April 22, denied that any rescue mission was being considered.

Quickly, rumors of the staff meeting circulated in Washington. Jack Nelson, astute bureau chief of the *Los Angeles Times*, met with Powell and asked, "You people really aren't thinking about doing anything drastic like launching a rescue mission, are you?" No, said Powell, no decisions had been made on any military move and it would more likely be "something like a blockade" if undertaken.

Now the mission was under way, and Secretary of Defense Harold Brown was telling the president and his aides in the Cabinet Room that something had gone wrong, perhaps terribly wrong. Two of the eight helicopters sent to rescue the hostages were down in the desert. Within hours, the news became worse. Eight American servicemen had been killed in a crash of a C-130 transport and a helicopter. It would take nine more months of tortuous negotiations to free the hostages.

Powell's lie to Nelson was not the first time he had misled reporters about the rescue plans. Previously, however, he only "repeated false statements made by others." This time, the deception was entirely his own.[4]

That night, one of the first calls he made was to Nelson. "I just lied to you," he said.

Recalling the conversation later, Nelson said, "I couldn't raise any really serious concern about that, because lives were at stake."[5]

As he prepared to leave office along with the defeated Carter after the 1980 presidential election, Powell said:

> It is the only time in the past four years where I have faced that situation, which I suppose any press secretary could face any day, in which there was . . . a direct conflict between my obligation to be truthful on the one hand and my obligation—which I frankly consider to be a higher one—to the national interest and in this particular case to the lives of American citizens.[6]

In the early days of the Republic, there was no White House spokesman to worry about such problems. Each administration awarded government printing contracts to a friendly newspaper, which then served as a presidential mouthpiece. John Fenno, editor of the *Gazette of the United States,* won the initial Treasury Department printing contract and supported George Washington.[7] Andrew Jackson set up his own paper, the *Washington Globe,* and installed Kentucky journalist Francis Blair as its editor.[8] The *Globe* continued as the official organ for succeeding administrations as late as that of James Knox Polk in the late 1840s. It was supplanted by the *Washington Union* in the years leading up to the Civil War. By the time Abraham Lincoln took office, the practice had died out as government printing was handled by the newly established Government Printing Office.[9]

Presidents did not have any designated press functionaries. White House staffs were small. Not until the administration of James Buchanan, Lincoln's predecessor, did Congress authorize the hiring of even a single secretary to help the president with his duties.[10] Ulysses S. Grant had a White House staff of six at a cost of $13,800, although he supplemented this with help borrowed from the War Department. The staff had increased to forty-six people, with a budget of $93,500, under President Calvin Coolidge in the 1920s.[11] In fiscal year 1996, the cost had swollen to $21.7 million.[12]

President John Adams seldom mentioned administration relations with the press in his diaries.[13] Thomas Jefferson wrote to a friend that his aim was "to avoid attracting notice and to keep my name out of newspapers."[14]

Later presidents chose former journalists as aides. One of Andrew Jackson's lieutenants was former Kentucky editor Amos Kendall, described by an unfriendly congressman as "the president's *thinking* machine, and his *writing* machine—ay, and his *lying* machine!"[15]

Some presidents chose private secretaries with backgrounds in journalism. When Abraham Lincoln's secretary, John Nicolay, was in his teens he answered a help-wanted advertisement seeking an "intelligent boy . . . who can read and write, to learn the Printing Business." In eight years, Nicolay had become editor and sole proprietor of the Pittsfield, Illinois, *Free Press*. After leaving The White House, Nicolay served as American consul in Paris and spent forty years in historical research and writing. But his daughter, Helen Nicolay, said he "continued to regard himself, until well into middle life, as first of all a newspaperman."[16]

Nicolay was called upon, as modern presidential press secretaries have been, to separate the wheat from the chaff for journalists seeking guidance on stories they had heard. The editors of the monthly magazine *The Century*, particularly, consulted him about "anecdotes, reminiscences, and dark hints of startling disclosures" that had been sent to them.

Nicolay told the editors he did not think they would get anything worthwhile from one writer, who had offered them his reminiscences as a "personal friend of Lincoln's." The would-be contributor was "perhaps a good talker," he said, but this was "no qualification for a successful writer." Besides, the secretary doubted the writer's claim that he had taken notes on encounters with the president. Once in a while, his daughter said, Nicolay would be sent somebody's recollections and write back to the editors, "They are very interesting and historically important, and so far as I know, entirely new. . . . Print them by all means."[17]

As for the president, Lawrence A. Gobright, the Washington agent of the New York Associated Press, wrote, "While Mr. Lincoln was generally courteous to newspaper correspondents, it is not known that he gave to any of them his entire confidence."[18] A reporter calling at the White House would send in his card with a note saying what he wanted to ask the president about. Lincoln would then sometimes call the reporter into his office or join him in an anteroom.[19]

On a June evening in 1863, Gobright made such a call to ask the commander in chief how the siege of Vicksburg was going. Lincoln was anxious to know, too. The river city on Mississippi's western border was vital to Union hopes. The president asked Gobright to walk across the street to the War Department with him, and they climbed a flight of marble stairs to the second floor. A messenger raced after them from the telegraph office, tucked into a landing on the stairway, with a dispatch saying a report had been received in the Southwest that General Grant's army was in retreat from Vicksburg.

Lincoln, shaken, tried a little news management. As he read the telegraphed report by the dim gaslight in the cavernous War Department building, he urged the correspondent, "Don't say anything about this—don't mention it." The veteran journalist took the news more calmly, reminding the president that most rumors circulating in war zones were false. This cheered Lincoln up somewhat, but he remained "unwilling that such disheartening information should get into print." The rumor turned out to be as false as any, and on July 4, Vicksburg surrendered to Grant. The story, told by Gobright, may mark the only time a president asked a reporter along with him to check up on the progress of a war.[20]

Lincoln was not always as trustful of the press. Throughout his administration, said Gobright, he "acted on the fear that his annual messages might, if supplied to the press in advance, find their way into print in advance of delivery." Consequently, Nicolay would not give copies to reporters until he had delivered the manuscript to the Senate and the clerk had begun reading it. Even Gobright could not obtain a copy of a letter Lincoln had written to be read at the opening of the Illinois State Republican Convention. "I can't do it," the president said, "for I have found that documents given to the press in advance are always prematurely published." The next day, the letter appeared in an afternoon newspaper in New York. Gobright obtained a copy by telegraph from Philadelphia, and Lincoln read the letter the following morning in a Washington paper. The president rushed into Nicolay's office, with its stack of newspapers on a side table, and asked the secretary how Gobright got his copy of the letter. "Who gave it to him?" Nicolay said the AP agent had certainly not obtained it from him. As it turned out, and would turn out more than once in later administrations, the source of the leak was the president. He had sent a copy of the letter to a friendly editor, believing it would not be published until it had been delivered.[21]

On another occasion, first lady Mary Todd Lincoln seems to have been the culprit. Henry Wikoff, a correspondent for the *New York Herald,* acknowledged to a House committee that he had filed at the telegraph office portions of an undelivered message by the president but said he was "under an obligation of strict secrecy" as to how he obtained them. Wikoff was locked up in a room at the Capitol but was released after Lincoln reportedly appealed to committee Republicans to spare the president embarrassment. Benjamin Perley Poore, a correspondent for Boston newspapers, said, "It was generally believed that Mrs. Lincoln had permitted Wikoff to copy those portions of the message that he had published."[22]

More than anything else, it was censorship of war news that aroused Washington correspondents against the Lincoln administration. When reporters appealed to the president, he would tell them he didn't know much about it, and then change the subject.

Whether using the soft-lead pencils intended for some kinds of paper or the black-ink pens reserved for others, the censors did their work with a heavy hand. During the battle of Fredericksburg, one censor would not permit Gobright to send any report of the fighting or to say that wounded men had arrived in Washington from the Rappahannock. He did allow the correspondent to report that "a number of wounded men have arrived here," but not to say where they came from. "The rule was, we must not let the enemy know what was taking place, as if the enemy did not already know that he had fought a battle," complained Gobright.

The House Judiciary Committee, in its report of March 20, 1862, concluded that "the censorship was controlled by the Secretary of State" and that "despatches, almost numberless, of a political, personal, and general character, have been suppressed by the censor."

On the committee's recommendation, the House adopted a resolution directing that "the government shall not interfere with free transmission of intelligence by telegraph, when the same will not aid the enemy in his military or naval operations, or give him information concerning such operations on the part of the government." The only exception allowed was in case the government had to seize control of the telegraph, and even this would have to be approved by Congress. The resolution had little effect and the censorship continued, although many newspapers printed news of troop movements that they obtained from sources outside Washington.[23]

Andrew Johnson, who succeeded to the presidency on Lincoln's assassination, was the first chief executive to grant formal newspaper interviews. James Gordon Bennett of the *Herald* had published an account of a chat with President Martin Van Buren in 1839, but it was little more than an exchange of pleasantries in which the first presidential quote was "How do you do, Mr. Bennett?" Johnson's first interview was with Col. Alexander K. McClure, a Pennsylvania editor who, like many of his day, was as much politician as journalist. It appeared in the *Franklin Repository* of Chambersburg, Pennsylvania, on October 31, 1865. Johnson also granted interviews to J. B. McCullagh of the *Cincinnati Commercial.* McCullagh, later managing editor of the *St. Louis Globe-Democrat,* signed his pieces "MACK." They did not go over well with correspondents who were not granted similar favors. "The pernicious habit of 'interviewing' is a dangerous method of communication between our public men and the people," Poore wrote in his memoirs two decades later. Looking back over his long career, the journalist said, "Washington correspondents in those days were neither eavesdroppers nor interviewers, but gentlemen, who had a recognized position in society, which they never abused." [24]

After the Civil War, Congress became the prime source of news in Washington. Reporters paid little attention to a White House inhabited, one scholar has written, by men with "neither the personal spark nor the governmental leadership to inspire deep interest." [25] The journalists worked in the House and Senate press galleries. If a member of Congress ventured down Pennsylvania Avenue to visit the president, they would interview him on his return to get his report of what had happened. [26]

By the time Cleveland became president in 1885, however, the face of American journalism was rapidly changing. In 1776, there had been thirty-seven newspapers published for the approximately 2.5 million men, women, and children in the thirteen colonies that became the United States. In 1886, the country had more than quadrupled in area, to 3,612,299 square miles, the population had increased more than twenty-two times, to about 56 million, and one directory listed 1,216 dailies, or thirty-three times as many as when the Declaration of Independence was signed. In the previous year alone, there had been a gain of thirty-three over the year before. In New York, twenty-three monthly magazines had been founded. There were papers devoted to such arcane subjects as the silkworm and the honey bee. The day was vanishing when newspapers were adjuncts of political parties, so blatantly partisan that Charles G. Greene of the *Boston Post* could be one of Franklin Pierce's managers at the 1865 Democratic convention. They were becoming highly competitive business enterprises.

The education of journalists was also getting attention. Nicolay had glanced at the subject a few years earlier, only to ask: "After all, does the journalist absolutely need a high education? Does not the weight of facts hamper him—the contradiction of authorities bewilder him? . . . For him is neither the thinker's closet nor the chemist's laboratory. The journalist is a *popular teacher* whose true mission is to disseminate leading ideas, clear principles, prominent facts. To do this successfully strength is better than subtlety."

In the spring of 1886, the editor of the *Rochester Democrat* proposed that American colleges confer a degree of Bachelor of Journalism on graduates who took a course to prepare for newspaper careers. A writer in *The Critic* scoffed that graduates with such a degree "would be laughed out of the profession in a fortnight." In an argument that would continue a century later, *The Critic* maintained, "A young man can undoubtedly be fitted at college for a journalistic career, but it will be by obtaining a broad general education, rather than by taking a special course of studies." [27]

These changes in the journalistic landscape were unsettling for many politicians. Cleveland found them particularly so after he was married at the White House in spring 1886 to Frances Folsom, the daughter of a former law partner. The bridal couple left on a special two-car train for Deer Park in western Maryland, where Cleveland had rented a cottage with a view of the Blue Ridge Mountains. Reporters followed on an express train, arriving at daybreak and commandeering a pavilion several hundred yards from the presidential cottage.

When the new Mrs. Cleveland and her husband came out onto the porch of the honeymoon cottage at ten o'clock the next morning, a story was filed. Also when they took an afternoon drive and an evening stroll. Reporters lifted the covers of dishes sent from a hotel for their seven-course dinner. A reporter interviewed a stewardess on a ship aboard which the president's bride had traveled home after a stay in Europe.

Cleveland brought to Washington as his private secretary Daniel S. Lamont, former editor of the *Albany Argus,* who had also been his secretary when he was governor of New York. Poore summed up Lamont pithily in his memoirs: "Slender, with intellectual features and a dark red moustache, which lights up his pale face, Colonel Lamont has the mouth of a man who is silent and the ears of a man who listens, while the quick glances of his eyes take in what there is to be seen."

Evidently, Cleveland depended on this trusted aide to keep reporters at bay. "When President Cleveland rose at 10 o'clock this morning and looked from the front windows of his cheerful little domicile," one reporter wrote, "his first thought must have been: 'Dan wasn't as sharp as I thought.' " Cleveland wrote to Lamont complaining of "newspaper nuisances . . . sitting on a bridge, which marks one of the limits, waiting for some movement to be made which will furnish an incident."

Even some editors denounced such conduct. "The high position occupied by Mr. Cleveland renders his marriage a matter of public interest," conceded the *Toledo Blade,* "but it does not make it right or decent for every action or movement of the young girl who has been made his wife to be watched and made the subject of newspaper comment and criticism."

"Impertinent papers, like impertinent men, should be kicked," said *The Journalist*. One writer came up with the phrase "the new journalism," later to become current in the era of Vietnam and Watergate.

The *New York World,* on the other hand, protested: "The idea of offending the bachelor sensitiveness of President Cleveland or the maidenly reserve of his bride has been far from anybody's thought. . . . We must insist that the President is public property; that it is perfectly legitimate to send correspondents and reporters to follow him when he goes on a journey, and to keep watch over him and his family."

Cleveland entered the fray with a letter to the *New York Evening Post* saying the reporters had "used the enormous power of the modern newspaper to perpetuate and disseminate a colossal impertinence. . . . And they have done it, not to a private citizen, but to the President of the United States."

George F. Parker, an old newspaper friend who had no official status in the White House but advised Cleveland on his relations with reporters, summed up the president's attitude toward the press: "He was particularly wary of newspapermen . . . he had grown to have a strong aversion to them as a class."[28]

Benjamin Harrison, a former Indiana governor and senator who defeated Cleveland in the election of 1888, took a more lighthearted view. Harrison was the first chief executive to attend the annual Gridiron Dinner, at which reporters and officials trade good-natured insults. He had spoken at a conference on patents a few days earlier, and told the journalists, "This is the second time that I have been called upon this week to open a congress of American inventors."[29]

Harrison did become irritated when reporters, in silk hats and frock coats, followed him to Washington's Church of the Covenant on

Sunday mornings, interviewed him as he emerged, and fell into step with him as he returned to the White House along Connecticut Avenue. Fearful of having off-the-cuff responses quoted in the newspapers, the president persuaded a correspondent for Indiana papers, Perry S. Heath, to come to the church and walk back to the White House with him. The other correspondents sought Heath out to ask whether the president had given him any news. Heath always said that Harrison had not.[30]

By the time Cleveland unseated Harrison in 1892, winning a non-consecutive second term, Lamont had become wealthy through speculation and was no longer interested in being the president's private secretary. Cleveland made him secretary of war instead and chose Henry T. Thurber, a lawyer, as the private secretary he hoped would be good to him. A writer in *The Century Magazine* reported in 1897 that "news of finished business has been given by Mr. Thurber to the two press associations, and intimations of probable events have been withheld from everybody." Thurber, said Cleveland biographer Rexford G. Tugwell, "was neither as industrious nor as knowledgeable as Lamont had been."[31]

Early in his second term, Cleveland and his advisers faced a decision that would confront many of their successors: what to tell the public when the president is ill. Cleveland's answer was to tell them nothing. He did not confide in Thurber, but called on the trusted Lamont to protect his privacy when doctors told him he needed surgery to remove what they believed was a cancerous lesion in his mouth. The country was in a near-depression, and Cleveland feared political opponents would take advantage of his illness to attack his economic recovery program.

The surgery was performed July 1, 1893, on a yacht in Long Island Sound. Four days later Cleveland was taken by launch to Buzzard's Bay, where reporters saw him walk unassisted to his summer home.

Nevertheless, United Press was out the next day with a story that the president had been operated on for a "malignant growth." At a briefing in an old barn about two hundred yards from the house, Lamont told reporters the story was much ado about nothing; the president had gout and was "suffering from his teeth." Asked whether an operation had been performed, he said, "That is all," and ended the briefing. By the time an accurate account of the July 1 surgery was published in the *Philadelphia Press* on August 29, Cleveland had undergone a second operation. Still, his aides denied there was anything seriously wrong. The idea that the president's health was any of the American people's business had not taken hold. Cleveland died in 1908 at the age of seventy, and doctors have expressed doubt that the lesion was cancerous at all.[32]

In 1896, as Cleveland's final term was winding down, the White House came under a new form of journalistic scrutiny. William Price, called "Fatty" because he weighed nearly three hundred pounds, had come to the capital from the South and applied for a job with the *Washington Evening Star.* City Editor Harry Godwin offered to give Price a trial by sending him to the White House to see if he could find a story there. As editor of a South Carolina weekly, the ambitious Price, thirty-five, had met the two trains that passed through town each day and interviewed passengers. He thought maybe the same technique would work at the White House. So he stood outside the North Portico and questioned the president's visitors as they arrived and left. Soon he had enough news for a story that carried the headline "At the White House" in that evening's paper. Price got the job, and his column was a feature in the paper for two decades. Competitors quickly caught on, and the White House became a news beat.[33]

Now that there was a White House press corps, there was about to be a White House press secretary, or something very much like one.

2

The Confidential Stenographer

ARRIVING AT THE NEW YORK CITY POST OFFICE at 7:30 one morning in 1891, Colonel Estes G. Rathbone found a young man with piercing, nearly black eyes slipping his key into the lock of the door. Rathbone, chief inspector of the Post Office Department, was just off the train from Washington. He had not expected to find anyone at work so early.

The early arrival was George Bruce Cortelyou, private secretary to a top New York postal official. Not one to waste a secretary, Rathbone started dictating. He found Cortelyou a skillful stenographer as well as an early riser. A few months later, Rathbone was promoted to fourth assistant postmaster general and wired Cortelyou to come to the capital as his private secretary. At the age of twenty-nine, Cortelyou was off on a Washington career that would take him to the White House and the cabinet.

The reason the young secretary had been an hour and a half early that morning was that he had left early the day before. He did this three days a week, so that he would be on time for his second job, teaching at a New York business school.[1] Such industry was typical. When Cortelyou died in 1940, one of the items found in his wallet was a certificate signed by the principal of his grade school certifying that George had been "punctual, regular & obedient."[2]

He was a reserved gentleman of conservative tastes, a bird lover who was praised by acquaintances for his classical English writing style. After primary school, he attended a military school for boys on Long Island; went on at the age of sixteen to Westfield State Normal School in Westfield, Massachusetts; studied piano and voice at the New England Conservatory of Music in Boston for a year; then returned to

New York and learned stenography and typing. In 1883, he became stenographer to the appraiser of the Port of New York. He had ranked highest in the examination and was also a loyal Republican. When the Democrats took over two years later, Cortelyou became a medical stenographer and established a school in Roslyn, New York. The school failed, and he took the post office position in 1889.

In Washington, on a salary of $1,600 a year, Cortelyou bought a piano on the installment plan, went to school nights to earn a bachelor of laws degree from Georgetown University and a master of laws from Columbian University (now George Washington), and struggled to pay off debts incurred by the failed academic venture in Roslyn.[3]

With the beginning of the second Cleveland administration in 1893, Rathbone's successor, Robert Maxwell, kept Cortelyou on as his secretary. When Robert L. O'Brien, confidential stenographer to President Cleveland, resigned to become a newspaper reporter, Postmaster General William S. Bissell told Cleveland after a cabinet meeting that Maxwell had just the man to be his replacement. The next morning, Cortelyou put on the better of his two suits and went to the White House for an interview. The first thing he told the Democratic president was that he was a Republican and had voted against him. Cleveland said it didn't matter.[4]

According to one account, Cortelyou got this recommendation from Maxwell: "He is a mighty good man, efficient, close-mouthed, always on hand when you want him, never watches the clock or complains about long hours. He is a complete master of detail and never forgets anything."[5]

The description sounds like a list of the qualifications of a presidential press secretary but that position was not even thought of until decades later. Cortelyou's title, like his predecessor's, was confidential stenographer. Reporters soon saw him as a key player in the White House game. Title or no title, said McKinley biographer Margaret Leach, "he was the first of the presidential press secretaries."[6]

"Private Secretary Thurber never paid any attention to the real work of his office and Mr. Cleveland relied upon his confidential stenographer," Associated Press correspondent Arthur Wallace Dunn reported. Within three months, the confidential stenographer was promoted to executive clerk.[7]

As Republican William McKinley rode to his inauguration in 1897 with the outgoing president at his side, Cleveland is reported to have leaned over and told him, "Whatever changes you make in your office force, hang onto Cortelyou." McKinley reappointed the executive clerk but chose *Hartford Post* publisher John Addison Porter for the more important job of private secretary. This was, by all accounts, a mistake. A fashion plate in dress and a stuffed shirt in demeanor, Porter spent much of his time pursuing his political ambitions in Connecticut.[8] As office affairs fell increasingly on Cortelyou's shoulders, McKinley asked Congress to drop the word "private" from the secretary's title and create a new position of assistant secretary to the president. Congress complied, and Cortelyou was appointed assistant secretary in July 1898.[9] A year later, Porter's health was failing, and McKinley offered him the post of American consul general in Cairo. Porter declined and said he would soon "be back at the side of the president." He did return to work, but did not find presidential favor. In January, 1900, a social column in the *Washington Star* suggested administration officials were upset over informal attire of guests at White House receptions. McKinley railed at such snobbery and said he intended to have a talk with Porter. "I can stand anything around me but a fool," the president told Cortelyou. A month later, Porter was again ill, and McKinley told Cortelyou he wished his secretary would take a leave.[10] Shortly afterward, Porter resigned and Cortelyou became the president's secretary.

The attention of reporters was continuing to shift from the Capitol to the White House, particularly with the outbreak of the Spanish-American War in the spring of 1898. For the first time, work space was provided for reporters in the executive mansion. "Fatty" Price, invited inside from the pillared North Portico of the mansion, at first wrote copy by resting his paper against a wall. Soon there was a table with writing materials and chairs set aside for reporters on the second floor. They could write their stories there, catch visitors for interviews as they entered or left, or waylay the president's secretaries for tidbits of information. When the president himself occasionally strolled through, the reporters followed an unwritten rule and did not ask him any questions.[11]

Porter was little help. Peering at reporters through eyeglasses with a ribbon dangling from them, the president's secretary made no secret of his disdain for the press corps. He quickly became an object of ridicule.[12] He was, said a *New York Times* correspondent, "probably the extreme limit in the way of impossible secretaries."[13] Even the courtly Courtelyou confided to his diary that Porter's manners were "sometimes well-nigh offensive" and "detract from the good impres-

In the anteroom at the White House, showing a press table and the door into Secretary Porter's office, with the doorkeeper, Simmons, in the background.

1. William McKinley was the first president to provide working space in the White House for reporters. They gathered around a table outside Secretary Porter's office under the eye of a doorman. *Sketch from McClure's Magazine, July 1898. Photographic print by Timberline Photography.*

sion he should make on visitors and others, particularly representatives of the press." To avoid an open breach, the assistant secretary made it a practice to break off their conversation and leave when things turned unpleasant.

On the evening of March 21, 1898, as the White House and reporters awaited the report of a board of inquiry into the explosion that destroyed the battleship *Maine* in Havana Harbor, Porter went to the theater with friends and did not return to the office. On April 22, he was away much of the afternoon. On the twenty-fifth, he strolled in about 10:30 or 11:00 in the morning. The first week of June, he was absent from Tuesday to Thursday to go to the Cornell-Yale boat race. And so it went.[14]

Cortelyou was another matter. After his promotion from assistant secretary, newspaper correspondent Albert Halstead called him "the most popular secretary who has served a president in a quarter of a century." He had, said Halstead, the ability to "tell the newspaper correspondents what they should know without seeming to suppress information."[15] He often worked from eight or nine in the morning until midnight. Porter was said to have briefed reporters at noon and 4 P.M., but it was the conscientious Cortelyou who met with them at ten o'clock at night. He also wrote and handed out press releases, giving them to the three major news services first and then distributing them to all of the other correspondents. Sometimes he worked on the press releases at home. He developed a forerunner of the news summary that later presidents would receive, having clerks clip items from newspapers and making a selection to be brought to the president's attention.[16]

All of this, and other demands, prompted a tripling of the White House staff, from six persons to eighteen.[17] By the administration of President Bill Clinton, the staff had increased to about four hundred.[18]

Unlike Porter, his assistant had the advantage of being close to the president. "Porter sees him for a short time each evening, mostly on matters that pertain to his personal friends, sending in to me to be presented to the president papers and documents relating to other subjects," Cortelyou wrote in his diary.[19] A contemporary journalist recognized the importance of this relationship when he said that the ideal presidential secretary "must be fully in the confidence of his chief; he must, in a general way, be able to know just what his chief would do in any given case; he must understand his views about different men and measures. He should be able to decide quickly what to say and what not to say, and sometimes when to be a little indiscreet, so that certain things may become known without making the president personally responsible for the revelation."[20]

On presidential trips, Cortelyou provided the traveling press corps with advance texts of McKinley's speeches and had stenographers take down his extemporaneous remarks. Local reporters, as well as the carload of correspondents that accompanied McKinley, sought him out for information.[21]

When Charles G. Dawes resigned as comptroller of the currency in July 1901 to run for the Senate from Illinois, he suggested Cortelyou to McKinley as his successor. "While the appointment would mean a loss to the president of the most efficient secretary a public man ever had, it seems plainly an opportunity for Cortelyou, and I think he so regards it," Dawes wrote. Cortelyou, however, chose to remain at the White House and see McKinley thorugh his victorious re-election campaign of 1900.[22]

McKinley had recurring eye trouble and from time to time was kept in bed for days with influenza, then a serious disease that could easily develop into pneumonia. His secretary, however, dismissed reports of presidential illness as "foolish stories." He stuck by this pattern when the president, early in 1901, developed an even more serious case of the flu. All news of it was kept from the press. McKinley recovered, but it was an ominous beginning for his second term.

In September, McKinley attended the Pan-American Exposition being held in Buffalo to herald the new century. As at so many public appearances before, Cortelyou was at his side as he showed up for a reception in the exposition's Temple of Music, where hundreds waited to shake his hand. A man in the crowd extended his left palm and McKinley reached out to grasp it. The man, anarchist Leo Czolgosz, held a revolver concealed by a handkerchief in his right hand. As two bullets entered the president's body, he slumped forward, gasping, "Am I shot?"[23]

As the crowd began beating the assassin and an ambulance rushed the wounded president to a hospital, it seemed to Dawes that "the two clearest and calmest heads during all the excitement were first the president and then Cortelyou."[24]

Vice President Theodore Roosevelt had brought William Loeb, his secretary as governor of New York, to Washington with him. But when Roosevelt succeeded to the presidency, he retained Cortelyou as secretary, with Loeb as assistant. In February of 1903, seventeen months after he took office, Roosevelt tapped Cortelyou to be the secretary of the newly created Department of Commerce. Before leaving the White House and turning over his duties to Loeb, Cortelyou wrote out an outline of how the executive office should be run. Clearly, he had not lost the passion for promptness and diligence that won him praise in grade school. "Punctuality is required in morning arrival and return from lunch," he wrote. "Those clerks whose work is finished at 4 o'clock will be excused at that hour, but the character of the work of the executive office renders it impracticable to terminate the day at that hour, and clerks will be expected, whenever necessary, to remain as much later as required. . . . Arguing and other unnecessary and loud talking must be avoided."

Clerks were cautioned to "refrain from unnecessary newspaper reading during office hours," but told that they must "keep themselves posted on current events, and to this end should read at least one daily newspaper before coming to the office in the morning."[25]

Roosevelt later made Cortelyou his postmaster general and a key political adviser. Still later, he became secretary of the treasury before leaving government work.

If Cortelyou did deserve to be called "first of the presidential press secretaries," he also appears to have been the only one who had visions of becoming president himself. His wife said his former boss, Maxwell, urged him to run in 1908 and put $25,000 in the bank to serve as a campaign war chest.[26] In a rare wistful moment, Cortelyou once told an associate that Roosevelt had assured him that he, not William Howard Taft, was his choice for the Republican nomination. Others thought there must have been some misunderstanding. It does seem unlikely that the politically astute Roosevelt would have considered the earnest and colorless treasury secretary a preferable candidate to the genial, robust secretary of war. In any event, TR called Cortelyou to the White House and told him in no uncertain terms that he was backing Taft. That was the end of any political dreams for the former stenographer, who went on to become president of the Consolidated Gas Company of New York.[27]

•   •   •

Roosevelt and Taft were a study in contrast in their relations with the press. "I am not constituted as Mr. Roosevelt is," wrote Taft. "He talked with correspondents a great deal. His heart was generally on his sleeve and he must communicate his feelings. I find myself unable to do so."[28]

Among other things, Roosevelt established the first real White House press room. According to an often repeated story, the president looked out his second-story office window one rainy day, saw the reporters huddling around the marble pillars of the North Portico waiting to interview visitors, and took pity on them. He ordered plans for a press room to be included in the new executive office building, now called the West Wing, that he was having built.[29] Although Congress had long provided press galleries for journalists to work in, "the

presidents had remained aloof, some seeing an occasional favored reporter, some seeing none, but all looking with a measure of distrust
upon the correspondents as a whole," veteran Washington journalist
Delbert Clark wrote in his memoirs. There may have been calculation
as well as mercy in Roosevelt's decision to allow the reporters inside.
"Theodore Roosevelt took them in, literally and figuratively," said
Clark. "Roosevelt showed his successors how to make use of the
press." [30]

TR's shrewd assessment of the role the press would play in the
twentieth century was seen in one of his first moves as president.
Arriving in Washington a few hours after McKinley's funeral in Can-
ton, Ohio, he telephoned the capital bureau chiefs of the United Press,
the Associated Press, and the *New York Sun* press service—the three
dominant news agencies of the time—and invited them to a meeting
in the Cabinet Room. Roosevelt, who had seen reporters twice daily
in Albany, realized that the news columns of newspapers were what
mattered, as much as the editorial columns if not more. He promised
to be accessible to reporters and keep them posted, but said he would
"trust to their discretion as to publication." If a reporter filed a story
that the president did not think should be published, he said, he would
withhold news from the reporter's newspaper. TR seemed amused
when the *Sun*'s David Barry objected that it was unfair to withold
news because of one reporter's action. "All right, gentlemen, now we
understand each other," he said, and the meeting ended.[31]

The new press room was small, providing barely room for the
rotund Bill Price, with a little room left over for a running chess game.
An open door led to a waiting room where reporters could interview
presidential visitors. For the first time they had their own telephones
—three of them—to call in their stories.[32]

Cortelyou and Loeb continued the daily briefings for the press
that had begun under McKinley, but Roosevelt also met frequently
with reporters. Some thought the best way to get him to listen was to
see him as he was being shaved, just before lunch.[33] The truth seems
to have been the other way around: Roosevelt talked and the reporters
listened. The sessions, which came to be called presidential séances,
were not held on any regular schedule and were limited to a favored
few correspondents known to their colleagues as "the fair-haired."
They would get telephone calls early in the day inviting them to come
to the secretary's office at the specified hour. Loeb would usher them
into the president's office, or more frequently into a narrow reception

room where Roosevelt had his daily session with his barber. Reporters came to call it the barber shop.[34] "His comments on men and measures came blithely and briskly through the lather," said one of the favored correspondents.[35] His comments, however, could not be quoted or attributed to him. He often spoke off the record, meaning his remarks could not be used in any way. Other times, he would allow the reporters to use the information as long as they did not reveal the source.[36]

Army Captain Archie Butt, a former Washington correspondent for Southern newspapers who was TR's personal aide, wrote:

> Mr. Roosevelt understood the necessity of guiding the press to suit one's own ends. . . . He was his own press agent, and he had a splendid comprehension of news and its value. He saw the newspaper men freely, but they understood that they were only to print what he authorized them to use, and if they did anything else he would not allow them near the White House or office, and he has been known to have them dismissed from their papers. . . . Nothing went out from the White House except as the president wanted it.[37]

Roosevelt played favorites shamelessly. One favored reporter was Richard Oulahan, who as a correspondent for the *New York Evening Sun* had coined the phrase "rough riders" for the regiment Roosevelt led in the Spanish-American War. He was also the first writer to note TR's pronunciation of the word "delighted" by spelling it "dee-lighted."[38]

"Those whom he knew well had little difficulty in seeing him frequently," wrote Oulahan. "Usually it was not necessary to make appointments in advance. There were periods in the president's busy day when a correspondent could be slipped in for a conversation."[39]

For those who could not be slipped in, Loeb was the principal buffer between president and press during his more than six years as secretary. Starting as a stenographer for the New York State Assembly and secretary to the lieutenant governor, Loeb had joined Roosevelt's staff after his inauguration as governor of New York in January 1899.[40]

In Washington, he found that his duties did not end when he left the office. Often he would get a telephone call during the night from a reporter seeking details on a story the secretary thought he had covered adequately during the day. Nor were official matters his only concern. He accompanied the president to his home at Oyster Bay, New York, and was the major source of news about the Roosevelt children and family, sometimes a delicate task because of Roosevelt's zeal to protect their privacy.[41]

As to his own privacy, Roosevelt was less shy. When a photographer missed a shot of him jumping on horseback, he obliged by jumping again.[42] He willingly paused in his march up Kettle Hill in Cuba to strike a pose for newsreel cameramen. At a celebration of his birthday on a ship anchored in Long Island Sound, he interrupted a speech he was making, walked over to the rail, and doffed his hat to give cameramen a better shot. On inaugural day, as the parade neared the Treasury Building, he bowed and smiled to cameramen stationed outside.[43]

•   •   •

Taft, assuming the presidency in 1909 after holding various government posts in Washington, had none of TR's dramatic flair. "I will not play a part for popularity," the genial, rotund Cincinnati lawyer told Archie Butt, who stayed on from the Roosevelt administration to be his military aide with the rank of major.[44]

Reporters had found Taft cooperative when he was secretary of war and a candidate for the presidential nomination, welcoming them daily, sometimes twice a day, to his War Department office.[45] So when he visited Washington as president-elect, a small group called on him to offer congratulations, hoping also to get some news. They found none. When they left, said Oscar King Davis of the *New York Times,* "every one of us had the same queer feeling that something had happened to 'put us in bad' with the new president. The old cordiality and friendliness which had always marked his dealings with us . . . was wholly gone, and there was in its place a reserve that almost amounted to coldness."[46]

The "fair-haired boys" were in for a shock. "They went to the White House as before, but were not wanted," said AP reporter Dunn. "They did not get an opportunity to retail all of the tittle-tattle, offer advice, and come away with a load of alleged presidential secrets. They did not get anywhere." At times, they saw neither the president nor his secretary, Fred Carpenter.[47]

When Davis and a group of his colleagues called on Taft at the White House on inauguration day, the new president sent word through Carpenter that he did not wish to see them. Carpenter added that Taft would probably not see reporters as frequently as he did when he was in the cabinet, and that he would send for anyone he wanted to see. "For a minute or two the boys stood around, first on one foot and then on the other, and not much of anything was said," Davis recalled. Then one of them told Carpenter they were not looking for news, but just wanted to pay their respects. This apparently pleased the president, who emerged from his office beaming and shaking hands all around.[48]

Carpenter, a Minnesotan, was "a self-effacing, patient, painstaking little man" who did not become as friendly with the journalists as the more expansive Loeb had done.[49] In addition, said Davis, Taft "was not the man to permit the same sort of relationship between himself and his secretary that Mr. Roosevelt had fostered between himself and Loeb."[50]

Archie Butt tried to fill this void and smooth relations between the president and the press.

"I have noticed that when I ask him . . . if he wants to see the newspaper men, he will say, 'No,' but if I bring them to him he receives them and I think is glad to do so," he said.[51]

Taft at first held occasional news conferences, either in his office or in the Cabinet Room. Unlike Roosevelt, he provided chairs for the reporters. Sometimes there weren't enough, and latecomers had to stand.[52] Questions were not submitted in advance, as some later presidents required, but reporters complained that the president's answers provided little information.[53]

When a journalist told Butt over lunch that the press was getting angry at Taft for withholding news, the president's aide commented, "It is impossible for Mr. Taft to do as Mr. Roosevelt did and to keep the press fed with news every hour of the day. It would be unnatural for him to try to do it."[54]

Privately, Butt fumed.

"Neither the president nor his secretary gives out anything of any real interest, nor do they understand the art of giving out news," he wrote to his sister-in-law in Augusta, Georgia, during Taft's fourth week in office. "In consequence the papers seek their information from whatever source they can find and therefore print rumors which, if printed a month ago, would have resulted in a clean sweep of reporters from the executive offices."[55]

Away from the White House, Butt tried to overcome the impression of coldness that reporters had received. When Taft attended a baseball game in Pittsburgh, the military aide arranged for him to sit with the rest of the crowd in the stands. He told the president this was so he could see all the best plays, but he told the reporters that Taft wanted "to see the game where all lovers of the sport saw it, and where he could see the crowd and hear the comments of the fans."[56]

Taft soon abandoned press conferences. He did not give a reason, but Oulahan speculated he might be finding them "too large and too promiscuous to afford the value intended to be given them." In their place, the president held meetings with individual reporters or small groups.[57] Coming away from a session with Taft in April 1910, Davis complained that the president had not merely not made news; he had unmade it. "Only this afternoon, he killed four good stories," he told Butt. Taft had denied reports of a possible shake-up in the cabinet, a call from a cardinal about an incident in Rome, his plans to make a campaign speech in Ohio, and his worsening relations with Theodore Roosevelt.[58]

By 1912, the growing coolness between Taft and his predecessor had developed into open political warfare, posing a dilemma for Butt, who had close ties with both men. Under a strain, he showed signs of depression and fatigue. Taft sent him to Rome for a rest, with the official pretext of carrying a messsage to the pope.

For his return trip, Butt booked passage on the maiden and final voyage of the *Titanic*.

Survivors' accounts of the major's last moments varied. Some recalled him masterfully giving orders as the lifeboats were lowered; others did not remember seeing him or said that he stood aside quietly.[59]

President Taft sent an urgent message to the stricken ship asking for information about his aide, but the crew in the *Titanic*'s wireless shack, busy coping with the disaster that would send the vessel to the bottom, did not respond.[60] Taft said later he had no doubts about his loyal aide's conduct: "I knew that he would certainly remain on the ship's deck until every duty had been performed."[61]

3

The Inexhaustible Font

THE AUTUMN OF 1896 was a milestone for Thomas Woodrow Wilson. At the age of thirty-nine, the earnest, ambitious Princeton professor was chosen to speak for the university at its 150th anniversary celebration. Standing before a capacity crowd in stately Alexander Hall, Wilson took "Princeton in the Nation's Service" as his theme. From its modest beginnings as the College of New Jersey, he said, the school had evolved into "the perfect place of learning." The speech was met with tumultuous applause, but its impact was felt far outside Princeton's halls. Wilson, already acclaimed as a scholar and lecturer, began to be talked of as a leader among educators and perhaps a leader for the nation.[1]

Just forty miles northeast of Princeton, in Jersey City's Fifth Ward, seventeen-year-old Joseph Patrick Tumulty also made a speech that fall. It was his first, and it, too, was a milestone. Fired by William Jennings Bryan's polemics against the "cross of gold," young Tumulty helped his brothers celebrate the Democratic presidential candidate's visit to their city by setting off fireworks along the parade route. Then, as the son of a neighborhood Democratic activist, he had the honor of speaking at a Bryan rally. He admitted that the intricacies of the argument over the gold standard were beyond him, but attacked "the attempt of eastern financial interests to dominate the government of the United States." For him, as for Wilson, the speech was a marker on a trail that would lead to the White House.[2]

The two orators could not have been more unlike. Wilson was the son and grandson of Scots Presbyterian ministers. With his younger brother and two sisters, he shared a childhood of parsonage and seminary life in the South. It was an atmosphere of wide, tree-shaded

24

streets in the Savannah River city of Augusta, Georgia, of club meetings in the loft of a family barn, of neighborhood baseball games on the grounds of a private school.[3]

Tumulty, the fifth son and the seventh of eleven children of Irish American grocer Philip Tumulty, was born in the family living quarters behind and above their store. The store was at the heart of a poor Jersey City neighborhood, known locally as the Horseshoe, that boasted forty taverns. Young Joe's parents were second-generation Irish Americans, and better off than most families in the largely immigrant section. Philip Tumulty prospered in the grocery business, branched into real estate and gave his sons a parochial education. For Joe, it was St. Bride's Academy, St. Bridget's School, and St. Peter's College.[4]

Despite their differences, Wilson and Tumulty shared one passion that was to bring them together and, in the end, alienate them. They were fascinated by politics.

As an academic, Wilson wrote on political theory and jockeyed for faculty position, successfully enough to become president of Princeton in 1902. When his name began to be mentioned for public office, he made light of it but events soon showed that he was more interested than he let on.[5]

Joe Tumulty never concealed his taste for political life.

"No matter how far back my memory turns, I cannot recall when I did not hear politics discussed," he wrote in his memoirs. His father was an avid Democrat and twice campaigned for a seat in the state legislature, with the backing of party leaders. Sitting in the family grocery store, young Tumulty listened to gray-haired Uncle Jimmie Kelter, almost 100, tell of attending the House of Commons in Westminster and hearing Irish statesman Daniel O'Connell denounce English rule in Ireland.[6]

"Politics had me years before I could vote," he said. It was a rough game as it was played in what was then known as the Bloody Angle of Jersey City machine politics. Once Tumulty and his brothers followed an opposing gang into a stable "where the gang had a ballot box . . . intending to manipulate the returns." His athletic older brother, Philip, "went in at the gang leader and grabbed him around the legs. And we all waded in and punched right and left." They took the ballots to police headquarters to be counted.

Tumulty also marched in parades. One memorable night, he walked alongside a carriage in which his father, wearing a high hat, rode beside state legislator Jimmy Norton. Joe Tumulty kept thinking "what a grand thing it would be to be in the legislature." He made it, but he had to start at the bottom, joining the Fifth Ward Democratic Club and eventually becoming financial secretary. Once, a few nights before an election, he saw a club member making tabulations and asked what he was doing. "I am writing the returns," he was told.

After graduation from St. Peter's, where he won a gold medal for elocution, he began training to be a lawyer by clerking in a New Jersey law firm. He was admitted to the bar in 1902, married his childhood sweetheart, moved in next door to his parents, and built up a practice based largely on real estate. In 1907, Tumulty arrived at the state capitol in Trenton as a newly elected assemblyman.[7]

Before long, he was jousting with Woodrow Wilson. Princeton's president, his political ambitions no longer hidden, had permitted his name to be placed before the Democratic caucus in Trenton as the party's nominee for United States senator. The nomination was an empty honor, because senators were at that time elected by state legislatures and the New Jersey lawmaking body was under Republican control. But liberal Democratic legislators, regarding Wilson as a conservative southerner, feared the nomination was the opening wedge in a campaign for the White House. In a speech to the Democratic caucus, Tumulty assailed the educator as an opponent of labor. Wilson was persuaded to withdraw from consideration.[8]

When Wilson was nominated for governor in 1910, he accepted the nomination with a speech acclaimed for its ringing affirmation of progressive principles. Tumulty became a supporter. Wilson soon had his first taste of his future aide's advice, his first "dose of Tumulty," as he would later call it. The candidate opened his campaign with a speech in Jersey City, with Tumulty in the audience. Meeting with Democrats in Trenton, Wilson asked Tumulty what he thought of the speech. Tumulty told him he found it "most disappointing." Wilson urged him to be more specific. "Don't forget that I am an amateur at this game and need advice and guidance," he said. Tumulty obliged by telling the candidate he was the one who should be more specific —that his speech was too vague and general, and he needed to hit hard on such issues as regulation of public utilities and the need for employers' liability legislation. Before long, Tumulty gave Wilson a sample of the kind of oratory he had in mind. Arriving late for a rally in West Hoboken, the candidate found the ebullient legislator filling in for him.

Tumulty's remarks so held his listeners' attention that they did not even notice the arrival of the Princeton scholar. Wilson asked Tumulty to join him in his campaign tour. The legislator, impressed by now with Wilson and hoping for a judicial appointment, accepted.[9]

After his landslide election in November, Wilson asked Tumulty to be his secretary. The salary was meager for a rising lawyer, but Tumulty again accepted. Announcing the appointment, Wilson said the governor's secretary needed "a quick understanding of the demands and needs of the public."[10]

The two became increasingly intimate, Wilson often addressing his aide as "my dear boy." Tumulty called Wilson "governor," a practice he continued even after his chief became president. The new governor's wife, Ellen Axson Wilson, was also fond of her husband's secretary, finding in him not only a jovial Irish wit but a surprising taste for English drama and humanistic philosophy.

Press chores were part of Tumulty's duty. When *World's Work* magazine sent writer William Bayard Hale to Trenton to profile the new governor, already being mentioned as a prospective presidential candidate, Wilson recorded that besides spending hours with him, Hale "talked his fill with my secretary at such in-between times as there were."[11]

With Wilson's nomination for the presidency at the Democratic National Convention in Baltimore in 1912, it fell increasingly on Tumulty to be his link with the press. It was no easy task. Wilson did not like reporters. "Those contemptible spies, the newspaper men," he called them once. On another occasion, he complained that "the interest of the majority (of reporters) was in the personal and trivial rather than in principles and policies." "Always the newspapers! They make the normal and thorough conduct of the pubic business impossible," he exclaimed. "I have almost come to the point of believing nothing that I see in the newspapers," he once said.[12]

Reporters sensed Wilson's antipathy, but fortunately the candidate had a secretary who enjoyed the company of journalists and won their friendship. In the formal journalistic style of the day, news sources were generally referred to in print as "Mr.," but during the convention at least one reporter wrote of the candidate's aide as "Joe Tumulty."[13] After the convention, Tumulty arranged for Wilson to address the reporters at a dinner he gave in the newspaper men's cottage at campaign headquarters in Sea Girt, New Jersey. To Tumulty, it seemed that Wilson "opened his heart in a little talk of the most intimate and interesting character."[14]

Before long, the candidate was denouncing reporters for trying to find out who his cabinet appointees were to be. His face flushing and his hand banging his desk, he told a *New York Times* reporter, "I am doing what I believe to be best for the country and for myself. If the newspapers expect me to do anything else, I'll be damned if I will." Wilson was also angered by efforts to get human interest material about his family, especially any marital plans of his daughters. "I am a public character for the time being, but the ladies of my household are not servants of the government," he said.[15]

An even more personal issue threatened to come into the campaign at one point. In 1907, on a vacation in Bermuda without his wife, Wilson had met Mary Hulbert Peck, a woman six years younger than himself, widowed once, and living apart from her second husband. By 1911, Wilson was writing to her that his chief complaint about political life was that it robbed him of "the freedom to go to Bermuda" and recover "the most delectable suggestions of *you* and of the first time I had a real glimpse of you as I was to know you from that time on! Ah, how delightful it all is!" Replying to her "dearest, best of friends," Mrs. Peck wrote that "the best of me that is to be, is because of you." Wilson later described the relationship as "the contemptible error and madness of a few months." Now Tumulty said he had learned that a suit was about to be filed in Maryland that would expose his letters to her. "They won't use it," said the candidate. "They have been building me up as a cold, inhuman figure and to spring this would make me too human. They won't." The letters did not, in fact, become public until long after Wilson's death.[16]

With Theodore Roosevelt's Bull Moose candidacy siphoning off Republican votes, Wilson had little trouble denying Taft a second term. Tumulty gave the candidate the first definite news that he had been elected. The president-elect at first thought Tumulty too provincial to be his presidential secretary and was inclined to offer the job to Newton Baker, the reform-minded mayor of Cleveland who would later be his secretary of war. Mrs. Wilson was troubled by letters she had received complaining of Tumulty's Roman Catholic faith, a serious political liability at the time. Much as she liked the affable aide, she was undecided whether he should accompany her husband to Washington. In January, Wilson and Edward M. House, an honorary Texas colonel who was a close adviser, discussed the presidential secretary job. House predicted, correctly, that "this appointment will finally be given him."[17]

On inauguration day, March 4, 1913, Tumulty told skeptical re-

2. In one of the first photographs ever taken in the Oval
Office, Secretary Joseph P. Tumulty stood behind Pres-
ident Woodrow Wilson. *Courtesy Princeton University
Library.*

porters that the presidential secretary's office would be open to them
at any time. "You boys are great personages in public affairs, and in
Washington I will look after the publicity of this administration myself," he said. He then persuaded Wilson to do something no president
had ever done before and few have done since—hold press conferences
on a fixed schedule. The new president said he would meet reporters at
least once, and sometimes twice, every week, during business hours.[18]

At the first meeting, on March 15, 1913, more than a hundred reporters crowded into the president's office. Wilson was, said one observer, "plainly embarrassed" and "could not be as frank as he could have been with one." [19] The reporters, accustomed to only sporadic sessions with past chief executives, were heartened when Wilson promised "full and free discussion of all large questions of the moment." [20] But when a reporter ventured a question, it was answered, according to one of those present, "crisply, politely, and in the fewest possible words." One friendly reporter said his colleagues "came out of that room almost cursing, indignant." [21]

Wilson apparently was not satisfied with his performance. A week later, meeting reporters in the larger East Room of the White House, he said, "I asked Mr. Tumulty to ask you gentlemen to come together this afternoon, because the other day when I saw you, just after the fatigue of the morning, I did not feel that I had anything to say." This time, he said, he wanted to talk at more length but "just between ourselves." The journalists were provided with a text of his remarks, headed with the admonition, "It is understood that this speech is not to be published."

Wilson puzzled many of the correspondents by urging them, "Please do not tell the country what Washington is thinking, for that does not make any difference. Tell Washington what the country is thinking." "An excellent doctrine in theory," wrote Richard Oulahan, by then Washington bureau chief of the *New York Times*. "But how to translate it into practice was beyond us. . . . Our function, at least as we saw it, leaving aside our duty, was to inform the country what Washington was doing." The new president, Oulahan concluded, "had come to Washington with a distinct prejudice against the place and what he conceived to be its mental atmosphere."

What Oulahan believed the reporters could not do, Wilson was soon saying that his faithful secretary could do. During one of Tumulty's occasional absences from Washington, the president wrote: "I am happy to have him a good deal away—to pick up opinion,—which he does wonderfully well. Washington is no place to learn what the *country* is thinking about." [22]

The press conferences later returned to the Oval Office, where forty or fifty correspondents formed a crescent with its center about ten feet from the president's desk. Wilson stood at ease and answered questions in a low but clearly audible voice. To Oulahan, he "gave the impression that he was matching his wits against ours" in "sentences which sometimes, as he probably intended, left us confused as to his meaning." One reporter apparently tried to pass off one of these conferences as a private interview. John Callan O'Laughlin of the *Chicago Tribune* wrote that Wilson "received me in his office with the understanding that I was to quote him" in regard to banking and currency legislation that the president had proposed. O'Laughlin sent the "interview" to Tumulty for Wilson's approval, but it was never published.[23]

In July 1913, Wilson threatened to discontinue the conferences after the *New York Sun* published some of his comments on Mexico, which he had intended to be confidential. After E. A. Fowler of the *Sun* apologized in a letter to Tumulty, the correspondents suggested an agreement "that there shall be no further quotation of the president direct or indirect without his express consent or the consent of his official representative."

Wilson adopted this and other proposed regulations and the meetings continued, but not without friction.[24] In January 1914, responding to a question about U.S. relations with Mexico, Wilson lectured the correspondents:

> The foreign policy of the government is the one field in which, if you will permit me to say so, you gentlemen ought not to speculate in public. . . . I do not think that the newspapers of the country have the right to embarrass their own country in the settlement of matters which have to be handled with delicacy and candor.[25]

In July 1915, two months after a German submarine brought the United States closer to war by sinking the British liner *Lusitania,* with heavy loss of American lives, the president abruptly discontinued the news conferences. He cited increased pressure of foreign affairs, but one newsman charged that he had "abandoned his press conferences as soon as he could find a suitable pretext."

During the remainder of Wilson's first term, Tumulty periodically urged his chief to resume the sessions, but the president was adamant against it. After Wilson's reelection in 1916, the secretary wrote himself a memo to "take up with the President the question of resuming newspaper conferences after the convening of Congress." He brought up the question on December 6, and Wilson agreed. Oddly, although the president proposed having twice-weekly sessions, the reporters told Tumulty that once a week would be enough. The meetings were scheduled for Mondays at 12:30 P.M., but only one was held. "Why,

we never were fully informed," said Oulahan. Thereafter, press conferences were held only sporadically.[26]

At a press conference in January 1917, one writer, still puzzled
about the rules governing use of what the president said, asked
whether it was better to report that "the president told correspondents" or that "the president's opinion is such and such." Wilson said
neither one was acceptable—that his answers were "for the guidance
of your own minds in making up your stories." Understandably, the
reporters thought this was little help.[27]

In a considerable understatement, Fred Essary of the *Baltimore
Sun* wrote, "Mr. Wilson has no intimates among the Corps of Correspondents." Given Wilson's attitude, the burden of dealing with journalists fell largely on Tumulty. He seems to have relished the briefings
that he gave daily at 10 A.M., usually attended by about thirty reporters. "Before I came to the White House, I had read a great deal about
Washington correspondents and felt terrified at the prospect of being
interviewed by them," he said, "but after I had been in the White
House a few days they seemed quite human." The briefings were, he
said, "delightful interludes in a busy day."[28]

Cortelyou and Porter had met daily with reporters during the
McKinley administration, but Tumulty brought to the proceedings a
new stamp of combined formality and intimacy. Although he was addressed as "Mr. Secretary" throughout the meetings, he was "Joe"
afterward, and called the reporters by their first names. Manners would
change, but the general pattern for what would later be called White
House press briefings was set.[29]

Tumulty's dealings with the press did not end with his daily news
conference. After the United States entered World War I in 1917,
Wilson and Tumulty found, as Lincoln and Gobright had before them,
that rumors were rife. The president's secretary slept with a telephone
at his elbow, ready for the calls that would come in after newspapers
queried their Washington offices to check unconfirmed reports. "By
some trick of fate these false rumors would never be circulated until all
respectable people had gone to bed."[30]

On another front, Tumulty took steps to bring rules for the release
of confidential material more in line with evolving newspaper deadlines. A State Department press release marked "for publication in
regular afternoon editions, not noon editions" had caused confusion.
Tumulty decided that thereafter news embargoed for release would
carry the exact release hour.[31]

From early in the administration, war dominated the news from the White House, as elsewhere. About 2:30 of an April morning in 1914, Tumulty sat in his pajamas listening over the telephone as Wilson, with Secretary of State Bryan and Secretary of the Navy Josephus Daniels on extensions, discussed a new crisis in Mexico. The United States gunboat *Dolphin,* off Tampico, was involved in a curious dispute with Mexican officials arising from the jailing of members of the crew who had been sent ashore to shop for supplies. The Mexican officials had apologized, but the commander of the naval squadron, Admiral Henry T. Mayo, wanted more. He demanded that the Mexicans fire a twenty-one-gun salute to the American flag. Wilson backed him up and got the House to support his position by a vote of 337 to 37.

While the details were being worked out, a German ship arrived off Vera Cruz bearing arms for Mexican dictator Victoriano Huerta, whose government Wilson had balked at recognizing. Wilson ordered Mayo to seize the port. The engagement would lead to the loss of nineteen American lives, and damage Wilson's standing with the public. When Tumulty arrived at his office that morning, he gave reporters the first word of the presidential order. "They jumped, as one man, to the door," he said.[32]

By September 1916, Wilson, seeking a second term, was locked in struggle with former Senator and Supreme Court Justice Charles Evans Hughes. At a rented mansion in Long Branch, New Jersey, he met with reporters to give them the "inside of his mind." Asked about Hughes's campaign, he laughed and said, "If you will give that gentleman enough rope, he will hang himself. . . . His speeches are nothing more than blank cartridges." Tumulty said reporters left "with the firm conviction that the Democratic candidate was just 'playing' with Hughes and would pounce upon him at the psychological moment."[33]

It was not to be easy. At 9:30 on election night, Tumulty heard a noise outside his office. A small band of reporters burst in, led by a *New York World* writer with a bulletin from his office saying that Hughes had been elected. Tumulty steadied himself behind his desk and dictated a statement: "Wilson will win. The West has not yet been heard from. Sufficient gains will be made in the West and along the Pacific slope to offset the losses in the East."

A few minutes later, Wilson, who had also learned of the *World* bulletin, telephoned him from Long Branch. "Tumulty, you are an optimist," the president said. "It begins to look as if the defeat might be overwhelming."

The worried Tumulty got reassurance from David Lawrence, then

Washington correspondent of the *New York Evening Post*, who had prepared a table indicating the western states would elect the Democratic candidate. By two in the morning, the Far West returns began trickling in, and Tumulty's confidence turned out to be justified.[34]

Woodrow Wilson had won another term, but Joe Tumulty's future was in doubt.

Ellen Wilson, who had found Tumulty such a surprisingly charming addition to the Wilsons' New Jersey circle, had fallen ill in the White House. In August 1914, she died. Sixteen months later, Wilson married Edith Bolling Galt, widow of a wealthy Washington jeweler.

A week after his reelection, Wilson told his wife and Colonel House that he planned to retain all of his cabinet. "What about Tumulty?" asked Edith Wilson. Wilson replied that he was planning to offer his secretary the better-paying position of appraiser of the Customs House. His wife urged him to insist that Tumulty accept. The new first lady, though she said Tumulty's "explosive Irish wit" was "a lot of fun" on campaign trips, objected to his "commonness" and did not think him a fit associate for her distinguished husband. Wilson told her, "I share your judgment up to a certain point . . . *but* the majority, the great majority of the people who come to the office are not of our kind, and our sort of a gentleman would not understand them or know how to handle them . . . Tumulty does understand them and know how to deal with them—much better than I would, and I need the assistance of just such a man." [35]

The first lady was not Tumulty's only problem. During the Mexican crisis, Wilson had stopped allowing Tumulty to screen his mail, finding that he did not agree with his secretary's judgment of what was important. Tumulty's religion had continued to make him a target for bigots. A man in Mississippi sent a clipping raising fears of a "Spanish Inquisition" in the White House. Sending the clipping along to Wilson, a sympathetic correspondent added the bemused note, "I . . . did not know that Tumulty was your 'father confessor.' " Wilson defended his secretary against such attacks, but House was arguing that it was a mistake politically for the president to have a Catholic as his private secretary. The colonel said Wilson's close friends had been unable to work with Tumulty. House even went so far as to canvass for a successor. He told Wilson he was sorry he had originally pushed Tumulty for the White House job, and advised the president to shunt him to the Customs House. Wilson surprised him by responding, "I think you and I have agreed already to accept any resignation offered and not urge continuation in office." With Wilson's approval, House approached the assistant secretary of state, Frank Polk, about becoming the president's secretary. Polk agreed to consider it.[36]

Tumulty put up a fight, refusing to accept any position the president offered. However, three days after the offer of the appraiser's post, he wrote to the man he had followed from Trenton to the White House:

> I had hoped with all my heart that I might remain in close association with you; that I might be permitted to continue as your secretary, a position which gave me the fullest opportunity to serve you and the country. To think of leaving you at this time when the fruits of our long fight have been realized wounds me more deeply than I can tell you. . . . But despite these regrets, I feel that I can not do otherwise than leave you, if you really wish it. . . . I am heart-sick that the end should be like this.

Friends of Tumulty, including some in the press corps, rallied around him. David Lawrence concluded that Wilson had been persuaded to an unjust decision by the intrigues of a political cabal. After a forty-five-minute meeting in which Lawrence argued the case for Tumulty, the president sent for his aide and reinstated him.[37]

Still, the old intimacy between the two was gone. More and more often, Wilson would approach Tumulty with his hands thrust into the waistband of his trousers, a posture that the secretary came to recognize as a sign that his chief was displeased. Once, the president even forgot his aide's first name, greeting him with, "Well, John Tumulty, what are you here for?"[38] When Wilson sent a note to the neutral and warring nations of Europe calling for preliminary peace discussions, he gave his secretary no hint of what he was up to, fearing Tumulty would let the news slip out.[39]

Wilson frequently disregarded Tumulty's advice. From early in his administration, he had considered the establishment of a government publicity bureau to "handle the real facts, so far as the government was aware of them, for all the departments."[40] Tumulty is believed to have opposed the plan, and it was laid aside.[41] With the entry of the United States into the war, however, Tumulty's complaints were to no avail. When the House passed an administration-backed espionage bill, Tumulty warned against the measure's press censorship provisions, but Wilson told Senate conferees that the bill's enactment was "an imperative necessity" and it should include the restrictions on newspapers. Then, in April 1917, Wilson revived the publicity bureau proposal, naming western journalist George Creel chairman of a congressionally authorized Committee on Public Information.[42]

With the establishment of the Creel committee, Tumulty dropped his daily meetings with reporters. No longer was "secretary Tumulty" the "inexhaustible font of copy" from the White House, as he once put it.[43] His relative disappearance from public view gave rise to a renewal of anti-Catholic prejudice against him.

Rumors that he had been imprisoned at Leavenworth as a German spy cropped up in widely separated parts of the country and were even repeated from the pulpit by an itinerant Methodist minister in western Pennsylvania. In the Midwest, rumors were spread that he had been executed. Finally, Tumulty issued one of his now-infrequent press releases, blaming the rumors on "systematic and insidious propaganda."

Behind the scenes, Tumulty remained active, holding court for reporters at a table in Washington's Shoreham Hotel. He also gave the president advice for dealing with complaints of censorship. Tumulty suggested that the president tell his critics he could only be sure of his own motives and would "try to purge them of selfishness of every kind." Wilson, acting on his secretary's advice this time, wrote in response to one prominent critic, "I can only say that a line must be drawn and that we are trying, it may be clumsily but genuinely, to draw it without fear or favor or prejudice."[44]

Publicly, Creel's committee was the source of administration news. Creel urged Wilson to resume press conferences, but the president refused and instead gave occasional interviews to journalists of his choice.[45]

When Wilson traveled to Europe for the Versailles Peace Conference of 1919, Tumulty stayed in Washington. Ray Stannard Baker, a former newspaper reporter and magazine editor chosen by Wilson to work on peace conference materials, went to Paris. Baker got the impression that Tumulty "plainly disliked my entree at the White House." The president's secretary protested against Wilson's choice of Creel to handle publicity on the conference, citing the hostility of U.S. newsmen to the information czar. Wilson stuck to his choice, and Tumulty wrote to him, "I am sure that I can render better service by staying on the job . . . and keeping you in touch with affairs here." As Tumulty recalled the final moments before Wilson's departure from the White House, the president stepped close to him and said, "I know I can trust you to give me an exact size-up of the situation here. Remember, I shall be far away. . . . When you think I am putting my foot in it, please say so frankly. I am afraid I shall not be able to rely upon much of the advice and suggestions I will get from the other end."[46]

Whatever words passed between them, Tumulty was not shy about offering advice. On December 16, 1918, three days after Wilson's ship docked at Brest, he cabled Dr. Cary Grayson, the president's physician and adviser: "If the president visits hospitals, have the press representatives with him to get human interest story. Do not let his visits be perfunctory. Let him sit beside bed of common soldiers." Wilson did visit the bedsides of wounded soldiers at a hospital in Neuilly, but only his wife accompanied him. During a visit to Gen. John J. Pershing's headquarters at Chaumont on Christmas Day, he asked to eat outdoors with enlisted men, but was fed in the officers' mess instead. Tumulty, skeptical of Creel's public-relations skills, complained that the stories he was seeing showed the president only as "an official living in a palace and guarded by soldiery." He implored Grayson to "try to get newspapermen . . . to inject some emotion in stories" and to urge the president to meet soldiers "face to face." "President's smile is wonderful," he cabled. "Get this over in some way."[47]

On more substantive matters, Wilson had raised reporters' expectations with his talk of "open covenants, openly arrived at." When the newsmen found that they would be barred from the conference room where the substance of the treaty would be worked out, they filed a formal protest with the president. Tumulty sensed that such secrecy could doom Wilson's great hopes for a League of Nations. "In my opinion, if the president has consented to this, it will be fatal," he cabled Grayson. "He could have afforded to go to any length even to leaving the conference rather than to submit to this ruling."

Tumulty's rival, Baker, also raised his voice. "This is really very serious," he told Grayson. "Many of the men are sending hot despatches across—quite a number of which I have seen. They feel that a principle is involved." Wilson told Grayson he had fought for more openness, but had been overruled by his European colleagues. Tumulty then took his case to the president directly, arguing that the problem "could easily be remedied if you would occasionally call in the three press association correspondents . . . merely giving them an understanding of the developments as they occur."

Wilson, in a message to Tumulty, said the policy of the American commissioners at the talks was "to be very frank and give as much information as possible to the newspaper men, trusting that they will not publish any information that would in any way cause trouble or be indiscreet." "The president wants you to watch the press and cable him exactly the tone of the press and whether or not any particular papers are acting in an indiscreet way," Tumulty was told. As Wilson saw it, the trouble was with reporters who insisted on writing without knowing the facts. "We have won for the press all that is possible or wise to win," he said. Tumulty concluded that the real problem was the president's hostility to reporters.[48]

Back in America, Wilson gave mixed signals to journalists as he sought to sell his proposal for the League. Early on a western speaking tour, he visited the press car of the special presidential train, where, said one participant, "we would all gab and argue together—as though the president were one of the reporters himself." At times, the president would tap a newsman on the knee and say, "Now, look here," as he made his arguments. In Seattle, Wilson was less obliging. He invited the correspondents to sit along one side of a hotel meeting room at a conference with local officials and urged them to take notes if they wished. After the meeting, he told them, "Of course, everything that has been said here is in confidence. . . . I will expect my friends of the press, who have been my guests here, to observe that confidence." "By letting us in, the president had locked us of out of the story," said Hugh Baillie of the United Press.[49]

On the return trip east, Wilson experienced what is now believed to have been one of a series of disabling strokes and told Tumulty, "I seem to have gone to pieces." As the train stood in the station in Wichita, Kansas, Tumulty told reporters that the president was "very ill" and they would go directly to Washington. Grayson said, "The president has suffered a complete nervous breakdown." This was language often used at the time to describe someone suffering from fatigue. From the rear platform, Tumulty read a statement to the crowd awaiting Wilson's scheduled speech. The president, he said, was troubled with nervous exhaustion and must rest. On the return trip, Grayson issued bulletins saying that the president was suffering from overwork, that his condition was not alarming, but that he would need "rest and quiet for a considerable time." Reporters, who dropped the bulletins out of the train for station telegraphers to send to their papers, mostly accepted the soothing statements. A few believed the president was shamming illness.[50]

On October 2, 1919, Wilson collapsed in his bathroom in the White House residence. He had suffered a severe thrombosis that left him paralyzed on his left side. Grayson's bulletins took on a more ominous tone. The president was "a very sick man." His condition was "not at all good." But there were no details. The following Saturday, Mrs. Wilson was handed a note from Tumulty. His little daughters, he said, would offer their communion for the stricken president the following morning. Prevented by Mrs. Wilson from seeing his chief, Tumulty wrote, "Please let the president know that we all think of him every minute of the day." One day before, in tears, he had told Secretary Daniels, "We must all pray." [51]

Tumulty, operating in a secretive atmosphere alien to his nature, had no off-the-record information for reporters. Even when Wilson's condition so weakened that he realized he must consider resigning, press releases said the president was well on the way to recovery. The silence from the White House brought grumbling from Capitol Hill and spread rumors throughout the country. Wilson was mad. He had contracted syphilis in Paris.

Daniels, who had been a newspaper man before going into government service, argued for more openness. "If you would tell the people exactly what is the matter with the president, a wave of sympathy would pour into the White House, whereas now there is nothing but uncertainty and criticism," he told Grayson. The president's physician agreed, but said, "I am forbidden. The president and Mrs. Wilson have made me promise to that effect."

In the election year of 1920, Wilson's hopes for the League of Nations were dashed when the Senate rejected U.S. membership even with the crippling reservations that his foes had attached to the Versailles Treaty. Still, the desperately ill president nourished pathetic ideas of a third term. Tumulty, hoping to clear the air, persuaded his chief to grant an interview to a friendly journalist, Louis Siebold of the *New York World*. The resulting story, which won Siebold a Pulitzer Prize, bore all the signs of having been orchestrated. Wilson was pictured as walking around the White House freely, with only a slight limp, in far better health than he really was. One part of the script, however, had to be jettisoned. Tumulty and Siebold had worked out a set of questions designed to elicit from the ailing president a firm declaration that he would not run again. Mrs. Wilson stunned Tumulty with a letter agreeing to the interview only on the condition that political subjects were off-limits. Tumulty kept her letter and wrote a note in the margin. Edith Wilson, he said, could go to hell. Democratic party leaders saw to it that Wilson's name was not placed in nomination at the party's 1920 convention in San Francisco. The Democrats nominated Ohio Governor James M. Cox, with Franklin D. Roosevelt as his running mate. The Republicans chose Ohio Senator Warren G. Harding.[52]

Tumulty's task as Wilson's press spokesman was perhaps summed up best in a message he sent to Grayson after the death of Theodore Roosevelt in January 1919, as the Paris Peace Conference was about to get under way. "Roosevelt's death left great gap," he cabled. "We must from now on make the people not only admire but love the president." Perhaps he had read the then-current issue of the New York magazine *Life*, which contrasted Roosevelt with Wilson and observed that Wilson "loves his fellow men, but he has always found it hard to make them feel it."

Tumulty's last press duty for Wilson was performed on March 4, 1920, the day of Harding's inauguration. After the ceremony at the Capitol, the Wilsons were driven down Pennsylvania Avenue, past the White House, to the home they had chosen on S Street when they decided to remain in Washington. Tumulty invited a group of White House reporters to come into the house and say good-bye to the outgoing president. Wilson, overcome by fatigue and the emotions of the day, took their hands but said nothing.[53]

*   *   *

Reporters were soon to find a president as unlike Wilson as they could have wished. Long before Harding was nominated for the presidency, correspondent Charles Willis Thompson of the *New York World* paid a call at the Marion, Ohio, *Star*, of which Senator Harding had been both owner and star reporter. "What sort of newspaper man is Harding?" Thompson asked the managing editor. "He is an easy writer, a fine reporter, a good straight printer, the quickest and fastest make-up man I ever saw, can run a linotype, and in the business office he is one of the best buyers I ever knew." In fact, said the editor, the senator still wrote for the paper because "in his position news comes his way, and whenever he gets it he comes down here and writes it."[54]

With this background, Harding quickly made a hit with the Washington press corps. No longer were reporters being lectured for not asking the kind of questions a Princeton professor was used to. Harding resumed the twice-weekly news conferences that his predecessor had abandoned. On Tuesdays and Fridays, the days of cabinet meetings, he met reporters in the Oval Office. Contemporary accounts of the ritual have a flavor that today seems almost quaint. As the reporters filed into the office, each bowed to the president. Harding, standing behind his long, broad mahogany desk, bowed in return. The walls at that time were covered with rough green burlap and had two large built-in bookcases filled with books bound in buff-colored sheepskin. On one corner of the president's desk, a copy of the previous day's *Marion Star* lay at the top of a pile of newspapers.

Speaking in a soft voice as reporters in the rear strained to listen, Harding generally gave the fifty or so in attendance some idea of what the cabinet had discussed, in contrast to the secrecy in which previous presidents had shrouded cabinet proceedings. Like his predecessors, he made it a rule that he could not be quoted directly, but otherwise he answered questions freely. "He knows what is news and has an attractive way of communicating it to the press," said Oulahan.[55]

Harding's candor would get him in trouble, and end the easy give-and-take between him and the reporters. At the International Conference on Limitation of Armaments in Washington in the winter of 1921–22, the United States, France, Britain, and Japan agreed to respect each other's rights with regard to "insular possession and insular dominions" in the Pacific Ocean. A reporter asked Harding whether this applied to the homeland of Japan, and he said it did. This would have been the right answer at the time the treaty was signed, but second thoughts by the Japanese had led to a supplemental agreement excluding the main Japanese islands. The misstatement caused a diplomatic uproar and shortly afterward Harding decreed that reporters must submit their questions in writing. Most reporters thought the mistake about the islands prompted the change, although some said it was another misstep at about the same time. Harding had hinted to newsmen that the administration was interested in an Association of Nations, as an alternative to the League. The idea, floated in the 1920 campaign as a sop to internationally minded Republicans, was anathema to Charles Evans Hughes, now secretary of state. For whatever reason, it was generally agreed that Hughes sternly advised Harding to insist on written questions.[56]

In 1923, Harding became ill while returning from a train trip to Alaska. When he canceled a scheduled speech in Portland, Oregon, reporters began asking questions, but most accepted the official explanation that the president had indigestion from eating tainted crab meat. During an overnight stop in San Francisco, however, reporter Stephen T. Early of the Associated Press became skeptical of innocuous bulletins being put out about the president's health. Early remained on duty in the Palace Hotel, where Harding was staying.

When Florence Harding cried out for the doctor to come to her husband, the reporter rushed to a special wire the AP had installed in the hotel and filed a story saying the president had at the least taken a turn for the worse. Within minutes he flashed the first word that Warren Harding was dead. The cause of death was not announced, but it is now generally accepted that Harding had heart disease.[57]

A decade later, Steve Early would become the first person to hold the title of presidential press secretary. Not only was there no such functionary in the 1920s, but the president had nothing like the staff his successors would enjoy. "The fact is that the White House today is undermanned and its attaches are notoriously underpaid," a sympathetic journalist wrote.[58]

· · ·

As Harding's vice president, Calvin Coolidge had already been dubbed "Silent Cal," an inaccurate sobriquet that may have been pinned on him simply because vice presidents don't make much news, so he was seldom interviewed. In fact, after he succeeded to the presidency, reporters found him anything but silent. It was simply, concluded correspondent Louis Ludlow, that he "does not talk unless he has something to say." When he did, he could be loquacious. In sixty-seven months in office, Coolidge held 520 press conferences, or an average of 7.8 per month. Questions were still in writing. The president would rise from his chair with a sheaf of them in his hand and go over them one by one, answering some and saying he would have no comment on others. His first presidential press conference, held in his suite at a transition White House in the nearby Willard Hotel, lasted less than ten minutes. It struck United Press political writer Raymond Clapper that Coolidge "lacked the feeling of understanding which Harding, by virtue of his newspaper career, was able to maintain." Once he was in the White House proper, things went better. In his first Oval Office meeting with reporters, which lasted about half an hour, some of the approximately 100 attending were surprised to find that the new president had a sense of humor. He "cracked five distinct jokes," one writer said.[59]

In Coolidge's administration the term "White House spokesman" entered the political lexicon, although in a sense different from the one in which it would be used later. By deft use of the rules for presidential press conferences, Coolidge became the 1920s equivalent of the "senior administration official" who so frequently was quoted in the Nixon administration and who flew on the secretary of state's airplane. Reporters could not identify Coolidge as the spokesman, or say that his statements represented the president's views. Nevertheless, before long almost as many people knew that the spokesman was Coolidge as would later catch on that the senior official was Henry Kissinger. "He has come to be a prominent first-page character—this mythical spokesman for the president," wrote Charles G. Ross of the *St. Louis Post-Dispatch.* "Watch for him particularly in your newspapers of Tuesday afternoon and Saturday morning"—the first editions after the president's news conferences. In an even broader hint, Raymond Clapper, writing in *Editor & Publisher,* described the spokesman as "a thin, sandy-haired, small-mouthed, solemn little Vermonter." Little wonder that by mid-1927, Coolidge jettisoned the "spokesman" smoke screen, saying, "It has been used so long and there has been so much reference to it that one might as well say that the president said so and so." Thereafter, reporters used some such phrase as "those in a position to know the mind of the president revealed today."

The long-standing rule against direct quotation continued in force, but some found it ambiguous. "Considerable doubt prevails as to what is meant by indirectly," the author of an unsigned *Memorandum on Newspaper Conferences* complained to the White House.

The writer urged that the word be "explained at the first opportunity so that there can be no doubt of its application." For a while, reporters were allowed to check their notes against the transcript prepared by the president's stenographer, but the rules were changed and even this was withheld from them.[60]

The press mostly went along with the no-attribution rule. "Despite its evils, both sides derive advantages from it," wrote Clapper, the Washington correspondent for United Press. "Mr. Coolidge gets columns of publicity," he said, and the reporters could generally "rely on at least one good dispatch out of every White House conference." The *New York World,* the *Baltimore Sun,* and some other papers, notwithstanding, maintained that the president should not talk at all unless he was willing to be quoted. Frank Kent, writing in the *American Mercury,* said reporters had been "a great deal more than fair" to Coolidge. *The New Republic* went further, arguing that much reporting from the White House was "really pro-Coolidge propaganda disguised as news."[61]

The not-so-quiet president also recognized the growing competitiveness of a relatively new form of journalism, the newsreel. Films of

Harding's inauguration had been shown in New York theaters less than six hours after he took the oath of office.

Coolidge posed for so many newsreel pictures that correspondent Sherwin Cook wrote, "Cultured Americans wince at the thought of their president putting on a smock frock to pose while pitching hay and milking a bossy." And Kent complained, "We have been invited to vote for Calvin Coolidge because he knows his way around a barnyard."[62]

Coolidge's first secretary was C. Bascom Slemp, a former Republican congressman from Virginia. Slemp was believed to have taken the job in the hope of getting a cabinet appointment. When he came under Senate scrutiny because of his ties to some of the principals in the Teapot Dome oil scandal that tarnished the Harding administration, Coolidge replaced him with another former congressman, Everett Sanders of Indiana. Slemp had been popular with reporters, but Sanders crossed swords with the press over the rules governing quotation of the presidential spokesman. Carter Field of the *New York Tribune,* in an article on negotiations over settlement of France's war debt, wrote that Coolidge was in a "fighting mood." Sanders, acting on Coolidge's instructions, contended that Field's piece, "headlines and all, is a flagrant violation of the rules of the press conference." Field argued that the rules prevented him from writing, " 'It is very hot and will be hotter,' said President Coolidge today," but did not bar him from reporting, "President Coolidge believes it is very hot and will be hotter, a White House spokesman declared." Sanders solicited the support of speechwriter Judson Welliver, who charged that Field "has for a long time been taking a lot of liberties, not only with the proprieties of the White House, but with the standards of decent journalism." The reporter received a reprimand, but continued reporting.[63]

Meanwhile, journalists discovered one administration news source about whom they had no complaints. Coolidge's secretary of commerce was variously described as a "master of publicity," "the handy man of the administration," and "the best 'grapevine' in Washington." "An hour spent with him yielded enough news to give us a despatch a day for a week, with almost everyone of them sure to make page one," one reporter wrote.

This official would be heard from again. His name was Herbert Hoover.[64]

4

The Public Relations Secretary

AS THE GREAT DEPRESSION DEEPENED in the fall of 1931, Herbert Hoover went to a baseball game. A reporter who asked whether he enjoyed it was turned away without an answer. The cabinet member who was the Washington correspondent's best friend had become a president so hostile to journalists that he could fail to respond to the most innocent question.

Hoover refused to invite correspondents to White House festivities. He reluctantly allowed them to visit his hideaway in the Blue Ridge Mountains, but would not have lunch with them. He said he would "clean that bunch out" when he got the chance.

By 1932, the aide who handled his public relations was saying flatly in his diary that the president hated the press. Hoover was the first president to assign a secretary expressly to deal with reporters. Two men held the job in succession. Both assumed their duties with high hopes. Those hopes were dashed by a combination of economic forces, personality clashes, and presidential temperament.

George Akerson had spotted Herbert Hoover as a comer early on. Akerson, a former police and political reporter for the *Minneapolis Tribune,* became the paper's Washington correspondent in 1921, covering as his first assignment the Disarmament Conference about which Harding so grievously erred. It was the same year that Hoover became secretary of commerce. The two men did not meet, however, until the 1924 presidential campaign. Coolidge had succeeded to the presidency on Harding's death and was running, successfully as it turned out, for a full elected term. Akerson had returned to Minneapolis as his paper's assistant managing editor. The line between political parties and the press was not as clearly drawn as it would be later, and the assistant managing editor was serving on the side as a member of an advisory panel to the Republican National Committee.

His role was important. He used his extensive political contacts in the farm states to help turn aside the threat posed by Sen. Robert M. La Follette, a maverick Wisconsin Republican who had accepted the presidential nomination of the Progressive Party. La Follette had little chance of winning, but Republicans feared he might prevent either Coolidge or Democratic candidate John W. Davis from gaining an electoral majority. This would have left the election of the president up to the House of Representatives. Republicans controlled the House, but La Follette's support still worried the Coolidge forces, and Akerson's efforts won him the friendship of Herbert Hoover.

Akerson kept in touch with Hoover, bringing him up to date on the political situation in Minnesota and asking his advice when the *Tribune* offered to send him back to Washington. Whatever Hoover's reply was, Akerson returned to the capital as his paper's correspondent in June 1925. Four months later, he was named assistant to Secretary of Commerce Hoover. His duties included lining up political allies and getting favorable articles into national magazines.[1]

In 1927, Akerson accompanied the man he always thereafter called "the chief" to his home in Palo Alto, California, and to an annual end-of-summer encampment of pillars of the American establishment at the Bohemian Grove in the redwoods north of San Francisco. At about 11 A.M. on August 27, the two were sitting outside their tent smoking cigars and tinkering with fishing tackle when someone came and told them there was a telephone message for Hoover. The secretary sent his assistant scrambling half a mile up a rugged path to see whether it was important. A few minutes later, the long-legged Akerson, once described by a headline writer as a "Blond Minnesota Viking," dashed back through the trees. Yes, the message was important. In a mathematics classroom at a high school in Rapid City, South Dakota, where he had established headquarters while vacationing in the Black Hills, Calvin Coolidge had just handed reporters copies of a typed statement. It said: "I do not choose to run for president in nineteen-twenty-eight." "I'm sorry, George," said Hoover, "but it looks as if we'll have to go back to Palo Alto and get to work."[2]

In the ensuing Hoover campaign for the presidency, Akerson carried the title of "assistant to Mr. Hoover." "George's supply of applesauce was then a sorely needed commodity in Mr. Hoover's political cupboard," a writer in *Outlook* magazine observed. The genial Minnesotan's "airy manner, his Nordic bluster and his outstretched arm—or arms" helped win over skeptical Republican leaders and reporters who found Hoover too stern and forbidding a candidate.[3]

With Hoover's landslide election over Democrat Al Smith, Akerson found himself installed in a southwest corner office of the White House, a few steps from the president's desk. It was the same office where Joe Tumulty and his successors had sat.[4] This time, though, Akerson would not be the only presidential secretary. The growth of the modern White House staff was under way.

The new president had been accustomed to having a corps of assistants around him ever since his early days as a mining engineer in China. As secretary of commerce, he paid Akerson and other assistants from his own considerable wealth after Congress refused to grant him additional money for staff. Now he persuaded Congress to authorize three secretaries, each with a salary of $10,000, and an administrative assistant. Although the title of presidential press secretary was not yet in use, Akerson was officially detailed to speak for the president in dealing with the press. He also was in charge of the president's daily calendar of appointments. Walter H. Newton, a former congressman from Minnesota, was brought in on Akerson's recommendation as political secretary, handling appointments to government offices and relations with Congress. Lawrence Richey, a former private detective and Secret Service agent, had the most wide-ranging portfolio of the secretaries. One correspondent described him as "the official snooper." French Strother came from the Commerce Department as Hoover's administrative assistant.[5]

The de facto press secretary was a two-hundred-pound Norwegian American, a Presbyterian born in the heart of Minneapolis who played the organ in a Roman Catholic church to pay his way through Allegheny College in Pennsylvania. He went on to Harvard and just before graduation got a job with his hometown paper. His first assignment with the *Tribune* was to help cover the Democratic National Convention in June 1912. He never forgot the early morning scene in the dingy armory in Baltimore when Wilson reached the needed two-thirds of the delegates after an all-night battle with the forces of Missouri's Champ Clark.[6]

One of the first moves of the new men in the White House was to overhaul the executive wing, turning a basement storage area into office space and moving the press room to the opposite side of the entrance hall. In place of their old cramped quarters, they had what one writer described as a "ritzy loge," its amber walls hung with autographed photographs of Harding, Coolidge, Coolidge's C. Bascom Slemp, and "other departed immortals." There were a rich yellowish carpet and new typewriter desks. Akerson had a separate room set up for photographers, who had previously slouched on chairs in the public vestibule. Some objected that it was all too fancy, but it did provide more space.[7]

Hoover held his first press conference on the day after his inauguration. He said he wanted such conferences to continue "with the same understandings as those which you had with President Coolidge." Then, recalling the development of presidential-press relations beginning with Theodore Roosevelt, he asked the White House Correspondents Association to form a committee "to discuss the matter with me on some early occasion as to how we can further amplify these relations." Specifically, he said, "I am anxious to clear up the twilight zone as far as we can between authoritative and quotable material on one hand, and such material as I am able to give from time to time for purely background purposes on the other." In response to a question, he said that both direct and indirect quotation of his remarks would be prohibited unless a transcript was given out. When one of the reporters asked if they could have the text of his remarks on presidential-press relations, the president demurred, saying, "There is no very great public interest in it." The reporter persisted, saying, it was "a new point of view . . . and it will read very well." At this, Hoover agreed to provide a transcript. Similar requests to Coolidge had always been turned down, which encouraged reporters to believe this was a president they would be able to quote freely. These hopes were to be disappointed.[8]

Akerson assembled an eleven-member committee of Washington news bureau chiefs, which met with Hoover several times. The committee declined to put any rules in writing, arguing that it was up to the president to govern his own press conferences. Hoover then established three categories of presidential news. Either written statements or spoken announcements could be directly quoted if authorized by the president. Another category of spoken statements could be quoted indirectly and attributed to official sources, not to the president. Last came background information provided to keep the writers advised about governmental affairs. This, if published, was to be used by the correspondents on their own authority and put into their own

3. Herbert Hoover held an outdoor press conference during his 1928 campaign. After election to the presidency, he became less available to reporters. *Courtesy Herbert Hoover Presidential Library-Museum.*

words with no reference to the president or the White House as the source.

The conferences were held in the president's office. Reporters and photographers gathered in a shabby, bare-walled lobby outside until Hoover sounded a buzzer and an attendant clapped his hands twice to signal that it was time. Questions, as in the past, were submitted in writing. Hoover did not, as Coolidge had, hold them in his hand and leaf through them. Instead, he had either a prepared statement to be released for direct quotation or notes jotted on a pad. At his second conference on March 8, he appeared to be testing out his three categories. He answered a question about law enforcement with a statement, given out in mimeographed form, for direct quotation. The second question, on changes in government personnel, was answered in indirect fashion with a statement beginning: "The president said today that there were comparatively few changes contemplated." Other questions, on immigration, tariffs, and a revolt in Mexico, were answered "not for quotation, but for your information." To questions from the floor, he said the cabinet had discussed the Mexican situation and he did not believe the War Department was sending the government there any surplus aircraft.

From Mark Sullivan of the *New York Herald Tribune,* a member of the committee and a friend of the Hoovers, came words of warning.

"Category 1 will take care of itself, since it will appear in typewritten statements, or in dictated statements to be taken down verbatim and used verbatim," wrote Sullivan.

"It is the distinction between categories 2 and 3 that will give trouble. I anticipate recurrent difficulties on this point. Not only is there likelihood of the correspondents confusing these two categories. The president himself is likely to confuse them. In a running talk, or in amplifying something previously said, the president is apt to forget where 2 ends and 3 begins."

His words were prophetic. As one of Hoover's key advisers later noted, the system was "fine . . . in theory" but "did not work out in practice after troubled times arrived."

At first, Hoover's press relations were as good as they had been at the Commerce Department. *Editor & Publisher* headlined the lead story in its March 16 issue, "Hoover's Press System Best Instituted by Any President, Capital Writers Say."[9]

•   •   •

During Hoover's four months as president-elect, he had withdrawn from any contact with the press, except for a few correspondents who were close friends. Those not in the know speculated on whether the ghostly "presidential spokesman" that Coolidge had laid to rest would be revived. In a February radio talk, Oulahan said they did not know "whether he is dead or merely sleepeth." Now, however, *Editor & Publisher*'s Washington correspondent felt able to assure his readers, "That imaginary person, who never existed but was credited with talking a lot, will not be revived in the Hoover administration unless there is a complete breakdown in the system which now is working so satisfactorily."

Another Coolidge tradition also ended. Under Hoover's predecessor, one representative of each press association would dash for the door to file as soon as the president made a statement. The new president passed word through the grapevine that he might discontinue the conferences if this went on. Thereafter, reporters who wanted to leave did so surreptitiously. Less hurried reporters waited in the lobby for copies from balky White House mimeograph machines.

Akerson's twice-daily meetings with reporters, not yet dignified with the name of briefings, were held at 10 A.M. and 4 P.M. Like the briefings of some future press secretaries, it was said of them that they "sometimes have a delightful quality of banter, but are rarely productive of more than the most routine information." Often they were limited to such items of local needs as the appointment of postmasters. Hoover had a few favorite correspondents who, like the "fair-haired" ones of Theodore Roosevelt's day, got private background conferences with the president. Others, dubbed "assistant favorites," conferred with Akerson alone or in groups of two or three. "It is in the planting of a story that Mr. Akerson really excels," said the Washington correspondent of *The American Mercury*. "He is perfectly at home in the game and knows all the ropes." The same writer complained that Akerson "passed out only what the White House wanted known" in his formal press conferences.[10]

At his third press conference, on March 12, Hoover asked correspondents to submit their written questions twenty-four hours in advance, except for those "which have arisen on the crest of the day's events." He said he had not had time to give enough thought to the questions he had received that morning, and so would hold them over until the next session. Three days later, he answered what he said were several questions about oil conservation with a statement for direct quotation, and suggested reporters check his stenographer's shorthand notes to get it right. Few of the reporters knew shorthand, but a mimeographed version was issued later in the day. He also answered what he said were several questions about airmail service and several about a resignation. He said he was still considering one question about the Federal Radio Commission. He did not say whether any other questions had been received.

On March 19, he said he had "no very important questions this morning" and was not ready to make any announcements. He answered some questions in the second category, giving information that could be attributed to the White House, and provided some background on developments in Mexico. On March 29, he told reporters, "There is no use getting out your paper because the only questions I have today relate to matters that I am unable to make any announcement about."

On April 30, showing frustration with the system he had devised, the president opened his press conference by saying, "I haven't a single question from the press this morning. Apparently you have no curiosity whatever." After giving a brief, noncommittal answer about a U.S. attorney who was being removed from office, he told the reporters:

> I think you will have to take a part of this labor upon yourselves and indicate some directions in which you would like a little information. A press conference is a conference that works both ways, and I do not know that I can stand up here and deliver orations or essays or mandates or anything of that kind unless I have some suggestions from your side.
>
> So that is all I have on my mind today, I am sorry to say.

Then, as he generally did, he smiled pleasantly and gave a slight bow as the correspondents filed out. Some reporters charged that Hoover's statement was a subterfuge to conceal the fact that he was ignoring questions they submitted. Some even joked that he answered only questions he had written himself.[11]

Many questions on important issues that were submitted did indeed go unanswered. By the summer of 1930, some reporters had become so discouraged that they no longer submitted any.

At the president's 195th news conference on June 2, 1931, Paul Wooton of McGraw-Hill asked him in writing to comment on the recently passed Boulder Dam Act. Another reporter asked a question about disarmament. Neither matter was mentioned in the press conference, which consisted of brief statements on Army Air Corps maneuvers, the Agriculture Department budget, and the appointment of two U.S. attorneys. For Hoover's meeting with reporters three days later, there were questions on naval reductions and the opening of the border at Tijuana, Mexico. Again, there were no answers. The transcripts of the press conferences did not show how much time they took, but many of them could not have lasted more than five minutes. At one, he responded to a written question by denying a report that he planned to take a summer home in Gloucester, Massachusetts, but left questions on war reparations, federal patronage, and prohibition unanswered. At another, asked questions about narcotics, tariffs, and the possibility of lowering taxes, he responded only to the third, saying, "It is always a pleasant subject."[12]

Before long, both friendly and unfriendly columnists were agreeing that the news conferences were empty of news. The president was widely seen as floundering in the face of the economic depression that followed the stock market crash of 1929. The Missouri journalist

Charles Ross found Hoover "at a loss in dealing with large groups of correspondents," in contrast to his ease with smaller gatherings at the Commerce Department.[13]

Akerson also was coming in for some raps. While always genial, he didn't always get things right. One day, he was asked if Supreme Court Justice Harlan Stone was to be elevated to chief justice. He nodded in the affirmative. Half an hour later, he issued a statement announcing the nomination of Charles Evans Hughes to the position. Reporters complained that in posting the daily list of the president's appointments, the secretary could be counted on to include visiting high school classes, old Hoover friends from California, and diplomats presenting their credentials, but might overlook such significant callers as the secretary of war or the Senate majority leader. At one conference of journalists, he was blamed for a "cordon of duplicity" around the White House. Some said he was withholding reporters' written questions or censoring them before they got to the president. Ross found him less popular with reporters than either Slemp, who had served Coolidge as president, or Ted Clark, who had been his vice presidential secretary.[14]

It did not help that within the White House circle, Akerson was at odds with Richey, the member of the secretarial troika who was closest to Hoover. Their temperaments had clashed ever since they served together in the Commerce Department. Akerson was hard drinking, expansive, sometimes promising more than he could deliver. Richey was, in the words of one White House observer, "unobtrusive as a fleeting shadow and as smooth." The words were eerily reminiscent of Ben Perley Poore's description of Cleveland's Daniel Lamont, with "the mouth of a man who is silent and the ears of a man who listens." It was generally believed that Richey kept a watchful eye on everybody in the White House, including the three secretaries and the reporters, "and what he knows, Mr. Hoover knows." Writing less than a year after Hoover's inauguration, a Washington correspondent predicted a battle for dominance between the two secretaries and said that Richey, "being much cannier and cleverer than George . . . will doubtless succeed." Hoover, the engineer, might benefit from Akerson's affability, but he set great store by the kind of precise information that Richey could provide.[15]

It was Richey, not Akerson, who played medicine ball with Hoover at 7:30 in the morning. It was Richey, not Akerson, who went with the president to his fishing camp at Rapidan in Shenandoah National

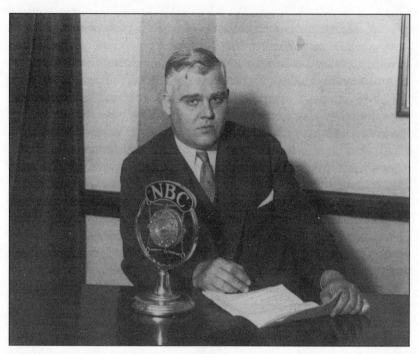

4. George Akerson, the first of President Hoover's two de facto press secretaries, took to the airwaves. *Courtesy Herbert Hoover Presidential Library-Museum.*

Park. And it was Richey who, after speculative stories appeared about a meeting Hoover had with Republican leaders at the camp, warned reporters that such speculation must stop or they would no longer be told who the president's visitors were.[16]

As Hoover's press relations faltered with the deepening of the depression, Akerson counseled more frequent contacts with reporters and urged the president to carry his message directly to the people through the new medium of radio. Hoover, however, heeded the advice of Richey, who argued that such public-relations gestures were beneath the dignity of the presidential office. When Raymond Clapper of United Press urged him to be more forthcoming with newsmen, the president replied, "We can't manufacture news for you."[17]

By October 1930, the *Outlook* was reporting that neither Hoover nor Akerson was satisfied with their relationship—that the president lacked confidence in his secretary and the secretary felt himself "reduced to the slavish state of a publicity man." There were stories of his heavy drinking in public. Publicist George Barr Baker became a frequent visitor at the White House. During a South American tour Hoover took as president-elect, reporters had angrily accused Baker of demanding changes in their copy before filing it. Now there were disquieting rumors that he would be the new secretary. At about the same time, it was noticed that Akerson, who had once so assiduously courted Hoover, now seemed to be courting the budding film industry. More and more, he expanded the privileges of newsreel cameramen at the White House in their bitter competition with the still photographers. It did not come as a surprise when Akerson resigned shortly after the new year to take a $30,000-a-year public-relations position with Paramount-Publix Corporation, one of the principal makers of newsreels. "I do greatly regret to lose an old friend out of my personal service," said Hoover. At Paramount-Publix headquarters at Forty-fourth and Broadway in New York, Akerson would not talk about his resignation. He told intimates, "The chief made the decision, and that was that."[18]

On March 16, Hoover announced the appointment of Theodore G. Joslin as his new secretary. Joslin, a Washington correspondent for the *Boston Evening Transcript,* had written a glowing review of Hoover's first year in office in the magazine *World's Work,* saying that the president was making an exceptionally good start and had accomplished much. He also said that sensitivity to criticism was perhaps one of Hoover's greatest handicaps. He wrote of informal White House dinners with the air of one who had been a guest. The gatherings, he said, gave Hoover "an excellent opportunity to get the point of view of others and information which he had been seeking." After dinner, he added, the companionable host escorted the men to the Lincoln Room, "of which he is extremely proud," while the ladies retired to an upstairs sitting room with Lou Hoover.[19]

Joslin got his first surprise when he reported for work. Hoover asked him if he had been sworn in. Although he had been in and out of the White House for fifteen years, it had not occurred to him that he needed to take an oath. In his diary that night, he wrote that he had "accepted the one and only appointive government position I would ever consider holding and under the only president in my time that I would care to serve." Joslin had turned down an offer to be Calvin Coolidge's secretary when the former Massachusetts governor came to Washington as vice president in 1921.[20]

On March 31, Hoover announced that Strother would be leaving his administrative assistant job on June 1 and that Joslin would, "at least for some time to come—carry on Mr. Strother's work as well as his own." When some papers reported that his principal task was to "humanize" the president, Joslin commented, "Would that were my only occupation. This is the hottest hot spot I was ever on." On April 6, a Monday, the president asked him how he liked his new work. "That office, Mr. President, every hour of every day, is like a newspaper office at edition time on election night," the new presidential secretary said. He repeated the remark in his diary and later, as an afterthought, came back and wrote in the margin that Hoover had replied, "There is only one desk in the world worse than that, Ted, and that is this one." [21]

The "Backstage in Washington" column in the *Outlook* noted that spring that "so far Joslin has done little except handle the press." He and Larry Richey were taking turns at Akerson's duties, the writer said, and Joslin's status was apparently undetermined. There was talk of a major White House reorganization, with a "heavy-pressure salesman" brought in to replace Strother. When George Hastings was announced as the new administrative assistant, however, his duties were chiefly confined to research and speech writing. [22]

Like others before and after him, Joslin found the job more consuming than he had expected. Even on Sundays, the president called him before breakfast to discuss the news in the morning papers. "The public relations secretary," he wrote, "is caught every waking hour between two powerful forces." The press wanted all the news; the president felt secrecy was often essential to success. "I sometimes wonder whether I ever will be able to tell the whole truth after serving through this position," Joslin confessed in his diary. [23]

By June 20, Hoover was working on a plan to foster economic recovery by declaring a one-year moratorium on foreign debts, provided the other countries granted the United States a corresponding year of grace. He planned to announce the program on the following Monday, but many newspapers had already published fragmentary accounts of it. All that afternoon, he met with key leaders of Congress and administration officials. Speaker of the House John Nance Garner and Senate Democratic leader Joseph Robinson were in their home states and did not attend. The secretary of the treasury, Andrew Mellon, was traveling abroad. At the *Herald-Tribune* office three blocks away, Mark Sullivan sat down at his typewriter and offered another of his frequent suggestions for his old friend in the White House:

Since it is given out and generally known that the president is carrying on important conferences with Democratic leaders, I think a good story might be made available to the press about the picturesque aspect of long-distance efforts to get in contact with Democratic leaders such as Robinson and Garner, who happened to be in remote spots. It would appeal to public interest to visualize the president as, for example, within one quarter-hour talking, perhaps, with Mr. Mellon in London, and with Garner in Texas, or Robinson in Arkansas—spanning a fifth of the earth's circumference in an effort to avert emergency in Europe.

Sullivan sent his suggestion to Richey with a request that it be passed on to the president. Nothing came of it. In view of the reports that had already appeared, Hoover announced the initiative at 4:30 that afternoon. Joslin experienced a curious sensation as he handed out the presidential statement. When his former colleagues dashed for the door to phone in the news, he wanted to run with them. "But I don't do that any more," he said. Joslin was apparently surprised at the frenzied response to the announcement, believing there was still plenty of time for reporters to make their deadlines for Sunday editions. He got into a row with Ray Clapper, arguing that morning paper release meant only papers published after midnight, which would have prevented Clapper's United Press wire service from supplying the story to many of its clients. Clapper convinced him that he was wrong. "The correspondents are not backward men; if they were, they would be in other pursuits," said Joslin.

"Ted, we've had a hard siege," said Hoover. He invited his secretary to bring his family and spend what was left of the weekend at Rapidan.[24]

Even at the camp in the Shenandoah, Joslin found himself faced with "incessant telephoning" about the announcement. He had already given orders to White House operators, or would soon do so, that he would not take calls from reporters at home after 11 P.M. Otherwise, he complained, his sleep would be disturbed every night.

On Sunday, July 6, as negotiations with other governments over the debt moratorium reached a crisis, Hoover cut short a Rapidan weekend and raced back to Washington, leaving behind the correspondents who were attempting to cover his activities from Orange, Virginia, or Panorama Resort, each of them thirty-three miles from the presidential camp. The next day, Hoover was angered by a *New York Times* story by Turner Catledge giving details of the sudden presidential trip down the mountain. Catledge said the president made the trip of more than a hundred miles, some of it over a narrow dirt road, in a little more than two and a half hours. It was a rapid, if not illegal, pace in 1931 traffic, but Charley Ross scoffed at Hoover's ire. "The president came back fast because he was eager to push forward the debt moratorium negotiations," Ross wrote in his diary. "There was nothing unfriendly in the Times story. Rather, it was calculated to put him in a favorable light. Very few Americans would object to the president's exceeding the speed limit in a good cause."

Hoover, however, feared the story would upset the French government, which was threatening to wreck the agreement. The report must have been particularly galling because Hoover had helped Catledge, when the reporter was with the *Baltimore Sun* in 1929, obtain his job with the *Times*. The story did no harm. The French capitulated and agreed to the American terms that afternoon. Announcing the agreement, Hoover said on the record that the moratorium would bring "the swinging of men's minds from fear to confidence, the swinging of nations from the apprehension of disorder and governmental collapse to hope and confidence of the future." He then answered a series of fifteen questions on background, for the reporters' guidance.[25]

Reporters still smarted over their problems in covering the president while he was at Rapidan. As soon as the camp was completed that April, Hoover had given orders that he was not to be trailed by journalists seeking the kind of human interest material they had been accustomed to getting on Coolidge's trips to the Black Hills. The reporters nevertheless followed him, but could not find accommodations any closer than Orange and Panorama resort. From these locations, they discovered that the best way to get information was to call the White House, which was in touch with Hoover by a direct telephone line. In the end, they concluded unhappily that they might as well stay in Washington.

Even there, the information they got was not always correct. On a June weekend in 1932, Joslin repeatedly told them that the president was resting at his camp. Actually, Hoover was on the telephone almost continuously over the weekend after getting word that a major bank was in serious trouble.

Reports of the Rapidan flap reached Alfred H. Kirchhofer, editor of the *Buffalo Evening News* and a publicity aide in Hoover's 1928 campaign, and he gave the president a lecture on the subject. Even opposition newspapers, he wrote Hoover, "can and will, and indeed must, carry . . . so-called human interest material." Kirchhofer went on:

> I am told you have an aversion to it. That you feel the American people want to pry too much into the privacy of the president; that you just don't like that sort of story. And yet it is often the most natural development in the world. You enjoy such incidents and, after all, whether our situation be high or low, we all seem to have a common denominator in that respect. Such stories were used time without number during the campaign of '28. They didn't detract from the lofty dignity with which you conducted the campaign. Some of them now again would act as the leaven that is needed to make people feel that the president, after all, is pretty close to the people. . . .
>
> The situation over Rapidan publicity is much the same. An effort to help the press association men and representatives of the larger papers who felt they had to cover the trips of the president there and back would have created an entirely different feeling.[26]

Hoover was keeping a low profile. Reporters nearly got left at the White House when the president took off early for an end-of-summer weekend at the Shenandoah camp. The writers had been told he would leave at 4 P.M. on a Friday, but George Drescher, the head of the Secret Service detail, was informed he was leaving two hours earlier. An aide spread word among the press corps and reported to Richey, "Tell the president if that is a leak then I am to blame, but we couldn't let the newspaper men be left that way." Richey told the man he should not have passed the word because Newton was doing so. Newton, however, had not.[27]

At his afternoon press conference on July 9, Joslin announced that the White House would conduct an investigation to determine the source of some fifteen human interest stories, including Catledge's account of the wild ride from Rapidan, that did not come through official channels. Thereafter, Joslin said, news was to be confined to announcements "from a stated source," meaning the president or himself. Oulahan, by now the *New York Times* bureau chief, said, "Ted, I think you are making a big mistake." The distinguished looking elder statesman of the press corps then emphasized his remark by walking out. In his diary, Ross exclaimed, "What a commentary on the publicity notions of the Chief! . . . A man in the White House can have a decent regard for public opinion without taking notice of every pinprick." The White House questioned correspondents and Secret Service agents, but after eight days, Joslin closed the investigation without finding the sources of the stories.[28]

* * *

Joslin appears to have realized he was in trouble. A week later, he asked Ray Clapper to submit hunches to him whenever he had any. He struck Clapper as very friendly. Late in July, he was reported to be hanging out at the National Press Club trying to rehabilitate himself with newspaper men. He asked one of them whether it was true, as reported in a magazine article, that he was in bad with correspondents. "If you don't know it, you are the only one who doesn't," he was told.[29]

Meanwhile, the president was meeting almost nightly at the White House with industrialists and others about the unemployment crisis. On August 7, he told reporters that local, state, and federal agencies, as well as private relief and charitable organizations, would put together a coordinated effort to deal with the widespread hardship expected when winter came.

Joslin said the announcement might result in "premature" publication of stories about the conferences he was holding, but they would not be as sensational as the stories that would crop up if he made no statement. At the same time, he said, "As a newspaper man, it is amazing to me that the press does not watch the White House itself more closely in such a time as this." A few days before, a top telephone company executive had been in. Another day, it was automobile tycoon Henry Ford. "Yet they come, confer and go without the press ever getting wise, even coming in as early as five in the afternoon. . . . The present day correspondents seem to think all the news [ought to] be given to them without any effort on their part and are continuously crabbing because they don't get more."[30]

Some of Joslin's friends in the press corps told him there was "a concerted effort to 'get' me, not because of anything against me, but because of hostility to Mr. Hoover." As Joslin saw it, there was a conspiracy to discredit the administration, fueled by "wets" in the press corps who wanted an end to prohibition and by "pinks" who felt Hoover was not acting aggressively enough to deal with the depression.[31]

One day Joslin telephoned Byron Price, conservative Washington bureau chief of the Associated Press, and asked him to come to the White House and talk to "the chief." "He is in a state and maybe a talk with you will do him good," Joslin said. Price found Hoover, his hair rumpled, crouching behind his desk and denouncing political opponents and foreign governments "with absolutely unbridled language." He did not direct any of this vituperation against journalists although a year later Joslin would be writing, "How the president hates the press!"[32]

When the *New York Herald-Tribune* reported in September 1931 that the government was trying to help banks with frozen assets, Joslin issued a confidential statement asking that such stories be checked with him before printing. Asked whether the story was true, he had nothing to say. He later told reporters that if he had commented he would have disputed the story. In the meantime, Secretary of the Treasury Mellon and other administration officials had confirmed it. Reporters charged Joslin with censorship and he issued another statement saying he had no such intent. United Press carried both statements on its wires on a confidential basis.[33]

When three steel companies announced wage cuts on September 22, Hoover told his aides he would make no comment. Joslin and Newton argued that the press should be given some guidance to avoid erroneous speculation. Hoover finally agreed to let them say, "The president's anxiety for maintaining the standard of living in the country has been constant and is unaltered." "It was something" at least, said Joslin. But no sooner had Joslin made the announcement than Hoover regretted it.

"A few more days like this and I will be a nervous wreck," said Joslin. "Yet I argue with him, especially when I am convinced I am right." The next day, he reviewed press coverage of his statement, and concluded that it "was not entirely satisfactory, but it could have been worse." Rather than make any clarification, he decided that "a policy of silence is by far the best." A week later, before making background statements on a couple of unrelated issues, the president told reporters, "I think we need a reunderstanding of what background consists of— it is the desire on my part to help the correspondents with the facts about various things on which I do not desire to be quoted. There seems to be a little departure from that idea." After he left the White House, Joslin would write, "The president should see the press only when he is willing to speak for quotation. . . . I often have believed that much of the background data given by Mr. Hoover and his predecessors would have been in quotation without any harm being done."[34]

On October 6, Hoover scheduled an evening meeting with bipar-

tisan leaders of Congress "to advance a program of national unity in
setting up of constructive forces in place of destructive forces now
working in this depression." At his noon press conference that day, he
told reporters he would like to talk with them "perhaps even more
confidentially than background." He said he recognized that their job
was to "find out anything you can find out," and appealed to them to
"bear with me if I don't discuss these matters with you."

"I propose to make a statement tomorrow," he said.

Oulahan, as dean of the press corps, broke in, "Mr. President,
cannot you, after tonight's conference, give us some rather definite
statement? It is coming out piecemeal if you don't."

"I would like to make an arrangement, but I don't think it is
possible," said Hoover. Then he went further: "It would be helpful in
this very difficult situation if you were prepared to just leave this
generally alone and forbear any attempt to pry into what may take
place tonight and allow me until tomorrow, that I may have at least a
few hours to formulate the conference into a program."

This was too much for Jay G. Hayden, the correspondent of the
Detroit News. "I don't have a morning paper," Hayden said. "But no
individual newspaper can do that. You cannot effect an agreement
among newspapermen on that."

Reporters then sought a more specific statement of the purpose of
the conference. Would it deal with domestic issues only or with the
international situation as well?

"Largely domestic," said Hoover. "It has bearings and roots from
abroad. So that is all I am able to say to you at the present time."

Reporters pressured Joslin for a statement immediately after the
conference, and late in the afternoon he agreed that one would be
issued.

Disregarding the presidential injunction, about a hundred correspondents gathered at the White House during the conference and
interviewed departing participants when the meeting broke up at midnight. Joslin issued a lengthy statement, mimeographed and handed
out to reporters in one-page "takes." The last take was received about
1:30 A.M.

Late editions of Wednesday morning papers did thus get a detailed
report of what the government proposed to do, but only after a struggle. Although Hoover's action was consistent with his general attitude
toward the press, the blatancy of it startled the journalistic community.
"Correspondents were obviously shocked at being virtually ordered

by the president of the United States to 'lay off' a story of this magnitude," said *Editor & Publisher*.[35]

Calvin Coolidge took a different view. Talking with the former president at his home in Northampton, Massachusetts, Clapper mentioned "that there had been a good deal of trouble with the press at Washington." Coolidge answered, "You have a good publicity president . . . I used to wake up in the night and think of something that would have been a good thing to have given the newspapermen, but I was never very good at it. But he seems to know just what the newspapers want and to be able to give it to them in just the way they want it."[36]

Many of the correspondents' written questions continued to go unanswered—questions about stock market speculation, about a proposal for a canal through Nicaragua, about negotiations for a naval accord, about Japan's role in a five-power conference. It was on October 15, 1932, that the president even declined to say whether he had enjoyed the ball game he had gone to the day before. Reporters could not miss the contrast with Harding, who answered a similar question in 1920 with nearly two hundred words ending, "Smith pitched a wonderful game, and the teamwork in his defense was a bit of baseball glory." The glory had faded for Hoover. Edward T. Folliard of the *Washington Post* noticed at press conferences that "Mr. Hoover's eyes were bloodshot, as if he had gone sleepless during the night."

On June 8, with an army of veterans encamped in Washington demanding early payment of a soldiers' bonus, Elsie Robinson of International News Service submitted this question: "The Bonus Marchers have a one-day supply of food left. They are forbidden to beg. They can not find work. What plan would you support to feed the Bonus Marchers? If they are not fed, what shall they do?" As in the past it was not clear whether all questions reached Hoover. A handwritten memo survives reflecting a conversation between someone designated "J," perhaps Joslin, and an unidentified person designated as "D." The memo reads: "J. Why submit that question? D. Dunno, had no answer. J. Then it's a just question? D. Well, it comes from Miss Robinson, who is covering the marches."[37]

Whatever the outcome, the subject of the Bonus Marchers did not come up at any of Hoover's three news conferences that month. On Saturday night, June 18, he handed Joslin a statement asking the marchers to leave Washington. "It left me cold," said Joslin. The next day, he told the president his statement was neither strong enough nor opportunely timed. "Well, I have got to do something," Hoover said. Joslin argued that the marchers would probably begin drifting out of the city in a day or two anyway, and the president agreed to withhold the statement for another day. Many of the marchers did leave, but others stayed. "I am not at all sure but the president will have to act before this emergency is over," Joslin wrote in his diary. On July 28, Hoover acted. Marchers were evicted from a cluster of government buildings scheduled for demolition, touching off a riot in which two veterans were killed and three policemen sent to the hospital. The president asked the army to assist District of Columbia authorities in ending "violence which no government can tolerate." He ordered Army Chief of Staff Douglas MacArthur to confine himself to moving the marchers out of the downtown district and back to their camps. General MacArthur, defying the orders, followed the veterans across the Anacostia River to their encampment, where some of them burned their ramshackle huts in protest and MacArthur's soldiers torched the rest. The next day, Hoover told reporters, "A challenge to the authority of the United States Government has been met, swiftly and firmly." He took no questions and offered no rebuke to MacArthur for his insubordination, leaving his political opponents to capitalize on the image of a heartless administration burning the squalid shacks of the needy.[38]

Attempting to thaw the cold war between his chief and the press, Joslin tried to persuade Hoover to invite White House reporters to a garden luncheon on August 11. The president, his eyes flashing, replied, "Don't mention it again. That is one thing I won't do. They have no respect for the office I hold. I don't mean all of them, but I do mean the character assassins among them. Once I am reelected, I am going to clean that bunch out whatever the consequences may be."

On the day of the luncheon, Hoover accepted the Republican presidential nomination with a nationally broadcast speech in Constitution Hall. The *Sun*'s Fred Essary ran into Republican campaign publicist Henry Allen on the street the night before and cautioned him that late release of the text would be folly. Allen, a longtime Hoover ally and former Kansas senator, said he knew it but was unable to budge Hoover because the president felt some newspaper men were not to be trusted. The text was made available to the press about 10:30 A.M., an hour after it was delivered. "I continue to marvel at the ability of the White House to do everything wrong when it comes to handling press matters," wrote Clapper.[39]

From July 1 to November 8, election day, Hoover held seven news conferences, a far cry from his original two a week.

On August 20, he reluctantly agreed to let reporters and photographers into Rapidan, describing them as "necessary nuisances." He posed stiffly for pictures of himself fishing, walking with Mrs. Hoover, playing with his dogs, and riding horseback. "He is no showman," said Joslin. "He wanted to get it over." He begged off having lunch with the journalists, and Joslin substituted for him. "It hurts, but he doesn't and will not see it," the presidential spokesman wrote in his diary.[40]

About this time, Ted Clark, Coolidge's secretary as vice president, showed up at the White House during an absence of Joslin. "Situation vague and mysterious, as to whether permanent or not," mused Clapper, who followed up with a story detailing Clark's activities as a lobbyist. By mid-September, Joslin was back and the former Coolidge aide was gone. "Hoover has managed to run without Clark—due to publicity as a lobbyist—most of which I gave him," Clapper boasted.[41]

No matter how he ran, Hoover was not going to be able to make good on his bluster about clearing out the White House press corps once he was reelected. "The president, as of Sept. 15, was hopelessly defeated," Joslin jotted in a space for memoranda at the end of his diary's October section. "If I were making my usual newspaper survey now as I did in the last four presidential campaigns, I would have to say that the president would be able to carry only eight states."[42]

He carried six.

5

"The Early"

ONE OF THE RESPONSIBILITIES of a presidential press secretary is to see that reporters get where they need to be to cover the president. One of the responsibilities of local police during a presidential visit is to keep away unauthorized persons who might harm the president. On October 28, 1940, at Pennsylvania Station in New York City, these responsibilities came into conflict, as they often do.

Stephen T. Early, a secretary—or, as he was beginning to be called, the press secretary—to President Franklin D. Roosevelt, was trying to persuade a police detail to admit thirty-five reporters and White House aides to the president's special train. In the ensuing argument, Early either kneed or kicked a policeman named James M. Sloan. It depends on whose story you believe.

The scuffle might have attracted little attention outside the White House press corps, except for one thing. Sloan was black, one of the few African Americans then serving on the New York police force. Early was a white southerner who had been notably reluctant to admit representatives of what was then called the Negro press to White House press conferences. He was believed by some to have helped stall antilynching legislation in Congress for fear of southern retaliation at the polls.[1] Roosevelt, facing a challenge from liberal Republican Wendell Willkie in the election the following Tuesday, was not satisfied that New York's crucial black vote was solidly in his camp.

As it turned out, FDR was easily reelected, commanding the vote of Patrolman Sloan among others, and the policeman and the press secretary patched up their differences. But the incident cast a not entirely flattering light on the talented, hot-tempered former newsman whom Roosevelt had chosen to be his bridge to the press.[2]

Steve Early was the first White House secretary to be officially assigned to handle press duties exclusively, and would become a public figure in ways that no previous presidential secretary had been. The era of the true White House press secretary had arrived.

One of eight children of a railroad mail clerk, Early was an old Washington hand and one of the few presidential secretaries who never went to college. His family had moved from Crozet, Virginia, to the nation's capital in 1898, when Steve was nine. Nine years later, the new United Press wire service also arrived in Washington. By 1912, Early was a reporter for UP covering the Democratic National Convention in Baltimore that nominated Woodrow Wilson for president on the forty-sixth ballot. The reporter met Franklin Roosevelt, a delegate from New York who was working for Wilson's nomination. "I got to know him because I liked him as a personality and for the additional reason that he always was 'good copy' for a newspaper reporter," Early recalled years later.

Roosevelt's reward for his support of Wilson was an appointment as assistant secretary of the navy. By this time, Early had left UP for its older and more prestigious rival, the Associated Press, and his beat was the State, War, and Navy building, across the street from the White House. Roosevelt continued to be good copy. A flamboyant personality who designed his own flag to be flown on ships during inspections, he also was an outspoken proponent of preparation for war. His views brought him into conflict with Wilson and the secretary of the navy, Josephus Daniels, and gave Early a number of exclusive front-page news stories.[3]

Early, who shared Roosevelt's convictions on the need for preparedness, was a reserve officer in the army, and was called to active service when the United States entered World War I. After serving as an infantry captain and an editor of the American Expeditionary Force paper *Stars and Stripes,* he returned to the AP and covered the San Francisco Democratic convention that nominated Ohio governor James Cox for president with Roosevelt as his running mate. FDR then asked Early to join his staff as an advance representative. Traveling two or three days ahead of the campaign train, Early interviewed political writers and party officials. His background and contacts enabled him to arrange good coverage for the candidate, but his reports, drafted late at night on hotel stationery and transmitted to the candidate by telephone or telegraphic code, made it clear that the campaign was, in words he used later, "a hopeless quest."[4]

Roosevelt was looking to the future. In a gesture that would bind key aides to him, he presented Early, Louis Howe, Marvin McIntyre, and Marguerite LeHand with gold cuff links. One side of each link was engraved "FDR"; the other bore the recipient's initials. As long as they lived, the members of the "cuff links gang" held an annual reunion to celebrate the birthday of the man they were already calling "The Boss."[5]

Meanwhile, Early returned to the AP. In 1923, he covered the first presidential speech to be broadcast over a national radio hookup, a St. Louis address by Warren G. Harding on the World Court. The experience may have planted the germ of an idea that would come to fruition in FDR's "fireside chats." The experience also got Early arrested. As he pushed his way through a crowd to reach the speaker's platform— with no presidential press secretary to clear the way for him—St. Louis police took him into custody on suspicion of being a Communist agitator. The AP bailed him out and sued the city for false arrest, claiming its reporter's professional standing had been damaged.

Early's fortunes took another turn after he overheard Florence Harding screaming for a doctor in a corridor of San Francisco's Palace Hotel. He scrambled down a fire escape to a telegraph operator in the hotel basement, and the AP was six minutes ahead of its opposition with the news of President Harding's death. Early received a bonus and the AP dropped the lawsuit. Lawyer John W. Davis told news service officials, "No jury could be convinced that a reporter who had been given a bonus had suffered any substantial damage."[6]

When Roosevelt next ran for national office, it was not a lost cause. The New York governor was confident enough of defeating the unpopular Hoover that he began shaping his White House staff in his mind before the election. To handle press relations, he first considered McIntyre, a former *Washington Times* city editor whom he had met as a member of George Creel's wartime propaganda bureau, assigned to the navy department. McIntyre handled publicity for FDR's 1920 vice presidential campaign, then freelanced and drifted from job to job in journalism until he again landed on the Roosevelt campaign train in 1932. He was an ineffective press agent and was shifted to the role of business manager while Early, who had left the AP in 1927 to join the new Paramount Newsreel Company, served as the candidate's "eyes and ears in Washington." Advisers persuaded Roosevelt that Early was the better choice for the press job. FDR telephoned him the day after the election and invited him to Warm Springs to offer him the position.

Early, who liked his job as Washington editor for Paramount, told the president-elect, "You don't need me, and after all, in 1920, I helped you to be the worst defeated candidate in Democratic history."

Nevertheless, he accepted the offer quickly, saying later, "It was much like the bugle call I heard in 1917 when I resigned from the AP to go into the Army."[7]

Four weeks after the election, Early was at the president's Georgia retreat again, outlining how he thought the press secretary's job should be handled.

He wanted to be able to see the president at any time, and said that his own door would be open to correspondents. He wanted his comments to be attributable to him as the president's press secretary, not to some anonymous spokesman. Roosevelt agreed to most of Early's demands and he and Early worked out a twice-weekly schedule for presidential press conferences, 10 A.M. on Wednesday for afternoon papers and 4 P.M. on Friday for reporters whose papers came out in the morning. When Early said he wanted to give reporters as much factual information as possible, Roosevelt agreed to this also. FDR later gave a more candid assessment when, praising his press secretary, he said, "He has carefully avoided conveying to the press any information; but he has been able to give the information necessary to keep the correspondents from printing inaccurate stories."[8]

On March 1, three days before what was then the constitutional date for presidential inaugurations, Early told Raymond Clapper of United Press that he did not plan to hold regular press conferences of his own, but would come into the news room with announcements of news as it broke. As it turned out, the New Deal made so much news that Early was soon holding regular press conferences after his morning meetings with the president in FDR's bedroom. He was making good on his promise to Clapper to "make the White House assignment an important one and not a watchdog affair." Early also assured Clapper he would be available to correspondents at all times, and told him, "I may even take the door of the office off." He didn't, but reporters were soon crediting him with being open and available, although surly. Unlike most of his successors, he had a listed telephone number.[9]

The same day that he talked to Clapper, Early asked Hoover's Theodore Joslin if he could grind out the inaugural address on the White House mimeograph machine so that Roosevelt's memorable "only thing we have to fear" speech could be distributed before delivery. Joslin refused. The tone had been set by Hoover, who would not admit photographers when FDR visited him at the White House. Early had to report for work on inaugural eve at Washington's Mayflower Hotel, long a favorite with Democrats. He was in for another disappointment. He had been led to believe that FDR would follow the Hoover precedent of three secretaries of equal rank. Instead, he learned at the last minute that Louis Howe would be the president's secretary, with a salary of $10,000 a year, while he and McIntyre would be assistant secretaries at $9,500.

He acquiesced on condition that he would serve only two years. He ended up staying for thirteen.

Early disdained the large room next to the Oval Office that Joslin had occupied, choosing an office in the front of the West Wing, still a short walk from the president's desk but closer to the press room. McIntyre, who was put in charge of the president's daily schedule of appointments, used Joslin's office. Howe moved into the office formerly occupied by Richey.[10]

The new press secretary moved in on Sunday morning, March 5, the day after the inauguration. With the help of his two secretaries, he prepared a news release on the president's proclamation calling for a special session of Congress to deal with the depression. He also worked with Harry Butcher of CBS preparing for Roosevelt's radio broadcast at 11:30 that night of an appeal to restive war veterans for cooperation in the emergency. The White House had no facilities for radio broadcasting, and they had to improvise to get the president on the air. On Monday, Early learned that administration officials are not always cooperative with the president's press secretary. Scrambling to answer reporters' queries about the complexities of FDR's proclamation calling for a bank holiday, he turned to Secretary of the Treasury William Woodin, but Woodin refused to help him. Early solved the problem by talking to Roosevelt.[11]

Reporters eagerly awaited Roosevelt's first press conference, held four days after his inauguration. White House news conferences had fallen into such low esteem in the latter days of the Hoover administration that correspondent Henry Suydam of the *Brooklyn Eagle* suggested they be abolished. This would change. As about 125 reporters filed into the Oval Office, they were introduced to the president by John Russell Young, a former president of the White House Correspondents Association. Roosevelt shook each by the hand and offered a few words of greeting. Then it was down to business. "I am told

5. President Roosevelt's Stephen T. Early talked with reporters in the office still used by presidential press secretaries six decades later. *Courtesy Franklin D. Roosevelt Library.*

that what I am about to do will become impossible, but I am going to try it," Roosevelt said. "We are not going to have any more written questions." His answers could not be quoted unless specific permission was given. Most of what he said was background material to be used by the reporters without attribution to the White House. Some was strictly off the record.[12] Interestingly, a *New York Times* reporter found this category to be "the most important . . . as it furnished much information on the administration's attitude and enabled reporters to separate truth from chaff in reports that go the rounds." Roosevelt asked the reporters not to repeat this off-the-record information even to their own editors, and said, "I think you will go along with me." He was wrong in this prediction. As Raymond Brandt of the *St. Louis Post-Dispatch* observed, "Reporters consider their first allegiance is to their newspapers and their editors." The rule was scrapped.[13] Early, as would be his custom, stood against the wall behind FDR during his freewheeling discussion of the banking crisis. Reporters, unaccustomed to so much news from a president, broke into applause after Roosevelt signaled that it was time to wind it up. The custom of the senior wire service correspondent ending the conference with the words "Thank you, Mr. President" did not take root until several months later.[14]

More than any previous White House secretary, Early took an active role in helping Roosevelt prepare for the conferences. On each press conference day, he would bring up possible subjects and answers during his morning meeting with the president. Occasionally, he would write out a suggested answer. He also prepared by planting questions with reporters—suggesting that they bring up issues that the president wanted to discuss. Roosevelt was often late, keeping reporters waiting in a double line in the lobby until he pressed a button to sound a buzzer in Early's office. Early would pass the word to doorman Pat McKenna, who would give the traditional double clap with his hands and open the doors to an anteroom where the reporters would wait again until a door opened to a corridor leading to the president's office. No cameras or recording devices were allowed without presidential permission, which was rarely granted.[15]

Roosevelt held 337 press conferences in his first term alone. Occasionally, they were held at his home in Hyde Park, New York, outside his Georgia cottage, or on the presidential train, but most of them were in the Oval Office.

There were usually 75 to 150 reporters in the 546-square-foot office, although the number was said to approach 300 at times. At two square feet per person, the room was estimated to barely accommodate 273. Although there were a few chairs for guests, the reporters stood while the president sat at his desk. It was a notoriously uncomfortable assignment. Richard L. Strout of the *Christian Science Monitor,* just back from his doctor's office after getting shots for an overseas assignment as a war correspondent, fainted in an Oval Office press conference. "I never hit the ground and I woke up on a sofa outside," Strout said.[16]

Despite the unpleasant working conditions, Roosevelt won over many reporters with his chummy manner and always gave them something to write about. When the Oval Office was enlarged as part of a rebuilding of the White House West Wing in 1934, he saw to it that the press quarters were also enlarged and card and chess tables provided. He called reporters by their first names, laughed at their jokes, and might ask for details if one of them seemed a bit hung over. One writer, perhaps less awed than his fellows, described the dozen or so reporters immediately in front of the presidential desk as a "giggle chorus" whose guffaws at FDR's sallies sometimes drowned out the president's more serious replies.[17]

There were not to be follow-up questions in the Oval Office. When a reporter suggested at an early press conference that his first question had not been satisfactorily answered, Roosevelt sternly announced, "No cross-examination."[18] Some, also, complained that the conferences were short on real content. One said that for the average reporter they were "not worth the time consumed getting to the White House or the discomfort he goes through after he gets there." Author John Gunther described one such meeting with reporters:

> In twenty minutes Mr. Roosevelt's features had expressed amazement, curiosity, mock alarm, genuine interest, worry, rhetorical playing for suspense, sympathy, decision, playfulness, dignity, and surpassing charm. Yet he *said* almost nothing. Questions were deflected, diverted, diluted. Answers—when they did come—were concise and clear. But I never met anyone who showed greater capacity for avoiding a direct answer while giving the questioner a feeling he *had* been answered.[19]

Gunther's comments strikingly echoed reporter Oulahan's observation that Wilson "appeared to show a ready appreciation of our endeavors and a sympathetic attitude toward them" while at the same time "answering in sentences which sometimes, as he probably intended, left us confused as to his meaning."[20]

Roosevelt did not make Wilson's mistake of asking reporters to keep him posted on what the country was thinking. "I am more closely in touch with public opinion in the United States than any individual in this room," he told a group of newspaper editors. "I get a better cross section of opinion."[21]

Not long after beginning his new job, Steve Early wrote to his old boss at Paramount: "I have learned in the past few months how different the view is when seen from the inside." Each day, he was picked up at his home by a White House chauffeur at about 8 A.M. and driven to the White House, where he stopped briefly at his office. Then he conferred with FDR while the disabled president ate breakfast in bed. Next it was back to his office to brief reporters at 10:30 A.M., usually from memory. He seldom took notes in his meetings with Roosevelt. The sessions with reporters were informal and punctuated with bursts of profanity when a question aroused the Early temper. Nonetheless, at the end of the first two weeks, one correspondent was satisfied that "the White House lay-out is functioning fine from our point of view, better than I have ever seen it." [22] A year and a half later, *U.S. News* was reporting that "the machinery for getting and giving the news runs about as smoothly as could be wished by either side." [23]

Early encountered stiff criticism, as later press secretaries would also, when the administration moved to control, or at least coordinate, the information activities of governmental departments and agencies.

The report of the Committee on Administrative Management that was created early in the New Deal and headed by management expert Louis Brownlow is best remembered for four words: "The president needs help."

The words touched off decades of growth in the White House staff, which consisted of eleven assistants, secretaries, and clerks when Roosevelt took office. The staff mushroomed with the establishment by Congress of the Executive Office of the President in 1939, and there was a corresponding growth in the bureaucracy throughout Washington. Early in the administration, the press secretary was placed in charge of an Executive Council that was supposed to coordinate the public relations of executive agencies. The responsibility was later shifted to a larger group, the National Emergency Council, which proved too cumbersome. The Brownlow committee then proposed that "a division of information should be established to serve as a central clearing house for the correlation and coordination of the administrative policies of the several departments in the operation of their own informational services." Some administration officials came up with similar ideas. [24]

Within the White House, Early responded to one such proposal by pledging to "oppose the project with every ounce of energy and power I have." Outside the White House, however, the press secretary got the blame for what was seen as increasing White House control of government information. From the start, he had sought closer coordination among departmental press officers.

He was instrumental in the appointment of experienced journalists to these positions, rather than handing them out as rewards to the party faithful as had been the custom in the past. Some of the new press officers were hired directly from newspapers. In many cases, however, Early was giving a helping hand to journalists who had lost their jobs during the depression. Sometimes he even created jobs for them.

He told his recruits, "Do your job just like you were working for a newspaper." He also sent memoranda to their bosses on such subjects as "How to Call a Press Conference."[25]

By 1935, a writer in *The Nation* was saying that Early had created "a propaganda machine without precedent in American government." The writer added, however, that most of Early's handpicked press officers were "scrupulous about stating the facts when properly questioned."[26] The less friendly *Chicago Tribune* likened Early to Dr. Joseph Goebbels, Hitler's minister of propaganda. "The man whose position most nearly approximates that of an American Goebbels," wrote Chesly Manly of the *Tribune Press Service*, "is Early." Even Manly conceded that in instructing his press officers the president's secretary "cautioned them against attempting to put over any propaganda."[27]

More thoughtful criticism came from Ted Joslin. The former Hoover public-relations secretary, speaking in January 1935 to an audience of friendly newspapermen, conceded that more press officers were needed in view of the burgeoning of the executive branch. But, he said:

> The present administration is using to the ultimate every known agency of publicity—the newspapers, magazines, the radio and the movietone. Its purpose is to get before the people such information as it wants them to have. . . . Trained newspaper and magazine men, editors and correspondents, have been employed to disseminate this propaganda through your columns. . . . It is the multiplicity of writers whom this administration has brought into the government service that has quickened public interest and caused concern.

A Senate committee investigating the executive branch would say two years later that 146 persons were engaged in full-time publicity work in fiscal 1936, with an additional 14 working part-time.

Joslin, on the other hand, said he had compiled an incomplete list of approximately one hundred writers brought into the government and believed there were several hundred more.[28]

Early responded, "Mr. Joslin is talking through his hat."

"I know something about the Washington corps of correspondents," the press secretary said. "From that standpoint I defy any administration to feed them with propaganda, or even undertake such a thing. Believe me, they are not babes in the woods."

Early also contended, "President Roosevelt takes the newspaper men as they come. There are no favorite groups who are called into private seance because they are friendly to the administration."[29]

This was not entirely true. During Roosevelt's bank holiday speech, Raymond Clapper was given a telephone in the north corridor of the second floor of the White House with a direct view into the study from which the president was speaking. Other correspondents surely would have liked to be similarly favored.[30]

Professor Betty Houchin Winfield, a close student of Roosevelt's press relations, believed that "for at least part of the time, Clapper had a special relationship with the White House, serving as a conduit for the president." *New York Times* columnist Anne O'Hare McCormick met about once a year with the president and was permitted to report his views without quoting him or saying directly that she had talked to him. Roosevelt also gave an exclusive interview to *New York Times* bureau chief Arthur Krock about his 1937 plan to pack the Supreme Court. Krock agreed to submit the story, including the headlines, to the White House for editing. He incorporated into it material inserted and added by Early and his assistant, William Hassett. The interview helped win Krock his second Pulitzer Prize, but infuriated other correspondents. Roosevelt, accused of favoritism by Fred Essary of the *Baltimore Sun,* said, "Fred, off the record, Steve laid his head on the block and so did I. It won't happen again." There were no more exclusive interviews with Washington-based correspondents. "Roosevelt . . . left them with a feeling that he was very sorry," said Krock. "He wasn't sorry at all, of course. He just wanted to get out of trouble, because he told me later that the interview helped him a lot."[31]

Joslin was certainly correct in arguing that Roosevelt sought to make maximum use of the radio, which Hoover had used reluctantly. Unlike his predecessor, FDR was at ease with the relatively new medium.[32] Watching from the hallway as the president took to the airwaves, Clapper found the setting "quiet, calm, congenial, pleasant, no atmosphere of tension." Early later detected "a strange but subdued excitement" as Roosevelt and his aides prepared for a broadcast.[33]

Roosevelt's best-known use of radio was his series of "fireside chats." Early may have got the idea for these talks from George Akerson, who was a friend of his and who tried unsuccessfully to persuade Hoover to make such talks.[34] Roosevelt and Early did not say which of the president's many radio talks they considered fireside chats, so estimates of the number of them vary from twenty-four to thirty-four.[35] There is general agreement that the first took place on March 12, the beginning of the president's first full week in office. "My friends," said the president, "I want to talk for a few minutes with the people of the United States about banking. . . . I want to tell you what has been done in the last few days, and why it was done, and what the next steps are going to be." Unlike most politicians of his day, Roosevelt did not speak into a microphone as though he were haranguing a multitude in Madison Square Garden. The direct, informal approach exactly suited a radio audience many of whom had a few minutes before been listening to columnist Walter Winchell's popular NBC broadcast to "Mr. and Mrs. North and South America and all the ships at sea."

Early assiduously promoted the fireside chats, sometimes announcing them two to three weeks ahead of time, but usually not disclosing what the president would talk about. He then skillfully built up interest by giving out information a bit at a time until the speech transcript was released. Sometimes he had a hand in the final rewriting of these and other speeches. He avoided working on first drafts so that when reporters asked him what was in a forthcoming speech, he could truthfully say he didn't know.[36] As he gave out the texts, he might tell reporters, "I think you will find your lead on about the 4th or 5th page." The NBC journal *Broadcast Merchandising*, reviewing one of the chats, said it "could never have been so immediately effective if it had not been merchandised properly beforehand."

The chats were by no means the only Rooseveltian use of radio. Network microphones were allowed into the room for live broadcast of Early's announcements after the attack on Pearl Harbor. Beginning in 1943, the president's meetings with reporters were entitled "radio and press conferences" instead of just "press conferences."[37]

Early drew the line at government efforts to establish its own radio stations. When Commissioner of Education John Studebaker proposed a broadcast studio in the Interior Department building to produce educational programs, he won the backing of Secretary of the Interior Harold Ickes, but Early argued that a panel of experts should study the proposal before anything was done. "This government has adopted and pushed the policy of allowing private initiative to operate radio in the United States," he said. He also complained of unnecessary expense. Roosevelt shelved the proposal until after the 1936 election, then approved it. Ickes used the "educational" station effectively to trumpet the accomplishments and policies of the Interior Department. He went too far, however, with a broadcast advocating federal control of the oil business. The House voted in 1940 to end most appropriations for the station.[38]

All this activity made Early the most visible presidential secretary ever. He was the subject of a six-page picture spread in *Look* magazine, caricatures in the *Washington Post* and Chicago *Daily Times,* and admiring profiles that noted his sturdy frame, bluff demeanor, and penchant for horse races, golf, and poker. One writer noted that Roosevelt, who had private names for various members of his staff, called his press secretary "The Early."[39]

Little noted was his adamant opposition to the admission of black reporters to either the president's or First Lady Eleanor Roosevelt's press conferences. Early had insisted from the beginning that only regular Washington correspondents be admitted. The restriction was designed to keep out visiting editors and publishers and representatives of government agencies. Its effect was also to largely limit attendance to writers for daily newspapers. Because most black newspapers were weeklies, Early could tell representatives of the Negro press that they were excluded by the rules. When black reporters for dailies applied, he told them they must first get accreditation from the congressional press galleries. This, too, proved an obstacle.

In 1935, Mrs. Roosevelt was pressing Early on whether "a colored girl newspaper reporter" could be admitted to her meetings with female journalists. She got nowhere. Even six years later, after a reporter for a group of black weeklies in Pittsburgh called at his office to seek admission, Early advised the first lady that the reporter could be allowed to attend only as an occasional visitor. "I made it plain to her that this arrangement was a 'courtesy'—not a right, because the papers she wanted to represent were printed as weeklies, not dailies," he wrote. Not until 1944 did members of the Negro press gain admittance to White House conferences by demonstrating that twenty-five representatives of weekly trade journals were attending regularly.[40]

Early's politically embarrassing encounter with patrolman Sloan occurred as security-minded policemen refused to admit a White House press contingent to Penn Station even after Early identified himself. When the angry press secretary began to force his way down a stairway into the station, two policemen pushed him. Sloan then joined the fray and was struck painfully in the groin. He had been operated on for a hernia only three months before. Early maintained that he had kneed Sloan accidentally when his leg was lifted upward by a policeman pushing him back. Sloan said he had been kicked. Republican candidate Willkie condemned the "irresponsible act." District Attorney Thomas E. Dewey ordered an investigation. Roosevelt asked aide Sam Rosenman to look into the facts of the matter. Some presidential advisers thought Early should be fired. Harold Ickes said he should resign. Heavyweight champion Joe Louis, one of the most popular African-Americans of his day, visited Sloan at his home while on a visit to New York to campaign for Willkie. The campaign event went awry when one of the reporters who tagged along asked Sloan whom he would vote for. The patrolman replied, "I will vote for Mr. Roosevelt."

Time magazine called the incident "Steve Early's greatest mistake," but White House reporters defended the press secretary and *Editor & Publisher* concluded that he "was victimized when he attempted to perform a service to the newspapers of the U.S." Columnist Doris Fleeson blamed the fracas on the "goose-step efficiency" of the police.[41] Early issued a statement denying that he attacked or kicked any officer, but adding that "since one officer believes I was responsible for hurting him, I wish to apologize."

Sloan, for his part, wrote Early a handsome letter after the election.

> I regretted as much as you did the incident at the Pennsylvania Station when you were seeking to join your chief, the President of the United States, as it was your duty to do. On the other hand, the sergeant of the New York police, under whose direction I was performing my duty, had orders which left him and his men, among the latter me, no discretion. The misunderstanding was not your fault, nor was it ours.

Sloan said he would forget the whole thing "in the midst of the joy that has come over me and my family over the reelection of President

Roosevelt." Early reflected that the incident "did leave its scars" but "this is life."[42]

Early imposed strict rules on photographers. They were not allowed within twelve feet of the president, or, in large gatherings, thirty feet. Candid shots within the White House or aboard the presidential yacht *Sequoia* were generally barred. In June 1935, the barriers were lowered temporarily and pictures were taken on one yachting trip. Early found them "decidedly poor" and ruled that photographers needed to get permission from the Secret Service before taking pictures. There was a strict taboo, described by one photographer as a "gentleman's agreement with the Secret Service,"[43] against taking photographs that showed the president's withered legs or his braces. Even before his inauguration as governor, Roosevelt had imposed an unwritten ban on such pictures, not without reason. Although most Americans knew that Roosevelt had been stricken with polio, few realized how crippled he was. Even editorial cartoonists depicted him as a strong, vigorous man, perhaps riding a bucking bronco or going over a waterfall in a rowboat.[44]

Reports circulated in the 1932 presidential campaign that news photos of Roosevelt being helped out of a car were sent to the White House with the suggestion that the Hoover campaign might want to use them. Apparently, nothing was done.[45]

Some newspapers and magazines did violate the rule. On October 6, 1937, the *Chicago Tribune* printed an Associated Press picture showing the president's braces. The *New York Times* also carried the photo, but cropped everything below the trouser cuffs. About the same time, *Life* magazine published a distant shot of FDR in his wheelchair, being trundled into a Washington hospital to visit an ailing cabinet member.

"This should be investigated and steps taken to prevent any repetition," Early wrote to the president's physician, Dr. Ross McIntire. The identity of the photographer, believed to have been an amateur, was never discovered.[46]

Early also controlled the use of other photos. During a 1944 campaign trip, a picture taken during a San Diego appearance showed Roosevelt with his mouth open, looking "weary, sick, discouraged and exhausted." It was seized upon by the president's political opponents to argue he was no longer up to his job. Rosenman blamed the president's "tragic-looking" appearance on the fact he had his head bowed over a printed page and his mouth open to pronounce a broad vowel.

"Unfortunately, Steve Early was not aboard the train, for he always took great pains to see that that kind of unfair and distorted picture was not distributed," the presidential counselor wrote in his memoirs.[47]

Although stern with still photographers, Early could be cozy with his old friends in the newsreel business. When Ambassador-at-Large Norman Davis was preparing to leave for the 1933 Disarmament Conference in Geneva, the president's press secretary tipped his former employer, Paramount News, enabling the cameramen to catch Davis leaving his home. William Montague of Paramount told Early that "we . . . delayed him so long that the other newsreels did not get him at the boat." Roosevelt repeated radio speeches for the cameras immediately after delivery or, in some cases, gave the newsreels a preview.[48] W. French Githens of Movietone News said Roosevelt's fireside chats "brought hundreds of patrons to the theater. Anti-New Dealers came to hiss."[49]

As in so many other administrations, war news soon began to take up more and more of the press secretary's time. On the night of September 27, 1938, at his home, Early received a telephone call to come to the White House. The president was getting ready to send a final plea to Hitler in an effort to avert war. Shortly after 9 P.M., reporters and photographers were summoned to his office, told only that "something very important would be given out."[50]

As August turned into September in 1939, Early planned a two-week vacation in the mountains of North Carolina. It turned out to be one week. At 6 A.M. on September 1, he received a call from the president's military aide, Gen. Edwin M. Watson. Three hours and ten minutes earlier, the president had received a telephone call from Ambassador William Bullitt in Paris. Germany was invading Poland and four cities were being bombed. "The 'Boss' wanted me back at my post." Early flew to Washington in an army plane. Arriving at the White House, he "found the feeling tense." At the regular Friday news conference, the president was asked whether the United States could stay out of the European war. Roosevelt said, "Only this, that I not only sincerely hope so, but I believe we can; and that every effort will be made by the administration so to do."[51] By September 25, one of Roosevelt's advisers was admonishing Early to urge the president to "drop the term WORLD WAR" and call it a European war instead.[52]

In the early days of his administration, Roosevelt had half-jokingly told reporters he would have a sign put up over his desk saying "Don't

6. Drawing by Gluyas Williams; © 1942 by The New
Yorker Magazine, Inc.

interpret." Now, as the international crisis deepened, he was increasingly concerned that reporters would put a wrong spin on his words. Asked what interpretation should be placed on a 1941 foreign policy speech, he responded, "I wouldn't try to interpret, because you know it is a grave question as to whether interpretation is news."[53] It was the same "grave question" that Woodrow Wilson had raised in the same room when he admonished reporters that foreign policy was a field in which they "ought not to speculate in public."

About the same time, Roosevelt said questions of ethics, morality, and patriotism were raised by the action of newspapers that printed secret testimony by Army Chief of Staff Gen. George Marshall before the Senate Military Affairs Committee.[54] Marshall had testified that army and navy planes were being dispatched to the Pacific fleet because of the worsening situation in the Far East.

Ray Clapper, by now a columnist for the *Washington Daily News,* wrote a friend that Roosevelt appeared to be laying the groundwork for wartime censorship. "Seeing that he may wish to take action, Mr. Roosevelt is probably trying to develop an atmosphere of public suspicion toward the press that will give him the leverage with which to operate," Clapper told Cranston Williams, general manager of the American Newspaper Publishers Association.[55]

In April, Roosevelt spoke out again after newspapers carried stories about a British battleship putting into New York for repairs. To questions, he said some newspapers had themselves suggested government censorship, but added, "I much prefer to go along with the overwhelming majority of newspapers at this time." He permitted direct quotation of the sentence. Early, asked to elaborate, said the president believed most newspapers favored cooperative control of news. "This is not censorship but an effort to avoid censorship," he said. "It has got to work out on voluntary grounds."

In November, another revelation by Marshall broke into the news. The chief of staff had told a group of correspondents in confidence that the United States was prepared to defend the Philippines indefinitely in the event of war with Japan. Among those pledged to secrecy at the meeting was a *New York Times* reporter. Arthur Krock, who was not at the meeting, confirmed the story with another War Department official and published it. "From then on there was no possibility that an outright censorship system could be avoided," Kenneth G. Crawford of the liberal New York daily *PM* wrote later.[56]

Lowell Mellett, a former Scripps-Howard editor, was already in place by this time as director of the Office of Government Reports, which supervised federal press agencies. Mellett sent the president a weekly summary of editorial response, which he had requested.[57] The week before the Japanese attack on Pearl Harbor, the report ran five pages.[58]

Early was reading the Sunday papers in his library at home when the president called him on December 7. As he recalled, FDR said, "Steve, I have a bulletin here I want you to give to the papers. Got a pencil?" Early had a pencil, and wrote from Roosevelt's dictation:

"The Japanese have attacked Pearl Harbor from the air and all naval and military activities on the Island of Oahu, the principal American base in the Hawaiian Islands."

Then, oddly, the president asked his press secretary, "Have you any news?" Early said he had none to compare with what he had just been given.[59]

Early arranged a conference call with the three principal news services, and read the statement over the phone to them at 2:25 P.M. It was on the wires by 2:26. At 2:30, he was back on the phone: "A second air attack is reported. This one has been made on Army and Navy bases in Manila." He left his home about 2:35. At 3:10, he was seated at a leather desk chair in his office, giving reporters what scant details were available. NBC and CBS were allowed to bring microphones into the office for the first time. Five minutes later, he issued a statement that the attacks were believed to be still in progress. After meeting with the president and his secretaries of war and the navy, he came back to his office and announced that FDR had called a cabinet meeting for 8:30 P.M. and invited congressional leaders of both parties. At 4:30, he told reporters the president was in his study dictating a draft of a message to Congress to his secretary, Grace Tully. Reporters wanted to know what time the attack was, what time the White House received word, and so on through ten questions. Early answered most of them, but ducked one on whether Japanese correspondents would be arrested. "That is an activity of the Department of Justice," he said. As the conference broke up, he said, "I want to ask you before you leave if there are any of you reporting for Japanese agencies. If there are, I am giving you no information and I have asked the Secret Service to take up the credentials of Japanese correspondents." The transcript indicates no one spoke up.

Sunday's last announcement was made by William Hassett at 7:40 P.M.: "Preliminary reports from the War Department showed that the losses in the Army only on the Island of Oahu were about 104 dead and over 300 wounded." On Monday, Early held a morning briefing and another at 7:45 P.M. A reporter said there were rumors on Capitol Hill that the Japanese had sunk four battleships at Pearl Harbor. "Is there anything that can be said here?" The press secretary made a slight change in the verb: "Nothing that will be said here."[60]

Nine days after the United States was plunged into the war, Roosevelt appointed Byron Price director of censorship. The sturdy executive news editor and former Washington bureau chief of the Associated Press was suggested for the job by Early, who had worked with him as an AP reporter in the 1920s.[61] Most reporters applauded the appointment, but the liberal *PM* predicted Price would be "the George Creel of the Second World War." Ken Crawford of *PM,* unhappy among other things because Price had once threatened to resign from the AP rather than negotiate with the American Newspaper Guild, wrote Early that he was "heart-sick" about the New Deal president's choice. Price, he said, stood for "the old deal in Washington journalism." Roosevelt sought to quiet fears by saying newspapers would be free to publish any news they could get, but would be trusted to refrain from publishing troop and ship movements. Price's job, he said, would be to prevent government agencies from releasing military secrets.[62]

Early resisted censorship, saying he was "principally concerned . . . that there not be set up anything comparable to the old Creel Committee." "Those here will remember what that was," he told reporters in his office on the day of Price's appointment. "Everything ran from the Committee of Information headed by George Creel. He had his own reporters who went into the departments and covered those departments." Under the new plan, he said, "the information sources in the departments remain open to you."

"You won't have to get a story cleared," Early said. When Price announced his censorship guidelines a few days later, they did call for reporters to clear with Price's office any information not obtained from an "appropriate authority," although compliance with the guidelines was voluntary.[63]

The censorship applied to presidential travel. Since mid-1939, Early had asked reporters not to publish exact times of the president's travel schedule. Now he began withholding any information at all about presidential trips, including a tour of inspection of a West Coast shipyard in October 1942.

Correspondents were barred from accompanying the president on that trip or writing about it until it was over. They complained that crowds who gathered at the shipyards knew where the president was, but they could not report it. The press corps, said Early, "is mad— mad all through and the over-all picture is worse than it has been in many years."

Early stood fast, telling reporters there were "mechanical reasons" for not taking them and that they would not be allowed to go on the next trip, either.[64]

During other wartime trips, Roosevelt allowed three wire service reporters to accompany him, but they could not release their stories until he had returned. On a trip to Hawaii, one of the reporters complained that Roosevelt "put on and took off security like winter underwear" by placing restrictions on legitimate reporting while posing for photographs with the troops that could be used in his 1944 reelection campaign. Early sympathized with the argument. He had long been "pounding away without result" at the president to abandon politically inspired "inspection" trips. Now he advised FDR to take heed and avoid using a baseball park or live civilian audience for a radio speech he was delivering from Seattle on his return trip. "If you appear before people of Seattle at ball park and conceal yourself elsewhere, reaction certainly will not be good," he said. Roosevelt spoke aboard a destroyer at the Puget Sound Navy Yard in Bremerton, Washington, with only shipyard workers as his audience.[65]

In March 1944, Washington correspondents for the *New York Times, Chicago Sun, Philadelphia Inquirer, New York Herald-Tribune,* and *Washington Star,* writing on behalf of their newspapers, petitioned Early for the right to be advised of the president's travels "so that they may, acting upon their own, if necessary, stay within reasonable distance of him." Writing on the stationery of the White House Correspondents Association, they said that their editors "are motivated by the knowledge that the President's health has not been good in recent months, and that this is not only a Presidential election year, but probably the decisive year in the European war."[66]

Other presidential visits were cloaked in even greater secrecy. Late in August of 1944, a part-time correspondent for the *Newark Evening News* tipped the New Jersey paper that Roosevelt had visited Tranquility Farms, some thirty-five miles from Newark. According to an internal White House memo, Roosevelt's private train had been shunted onto a siding so that he could spend a few hours at the farm because his father had once visited it and he had always wanted to see it. This was a transparent cover story. Tranquility Farms was the estate of Lucy Mercer Rutherford, an old flame of Roosevelt's, now widowed, whom he had resumed seeing without his wife's knowledge. White House reporters knew of the relationship, but agreed not to mention it. Lawrence Woodruff of the *News,* however, badgered the Office of Censorship as well as both Early and Hassett, seeking a way to break the story. Early believed it was bound to break in any event and suggested that the reporters traveling with the president be permitted to write it on their return to Washington. FDR, however, kept the lid on.[67]

On New Year's Day, 1945, Roosevelt granted a request from Gen.

Dwight Eisenhower to have Early sent to Paris for sixty days to make recommendations on how Supreme Headquarters, Allied Expeditionary Forces could improve its public relations.[68] Early refused a private office and spent thirty days at a pine table in the office of Eisenhower aide Harry Butcher, the CBS man who had helped him wire the White House for radio for Roosevelt's first presidential broadcast. While Early was in Paris he received word that his son, Stephen T. Early Jr., known as Buddy, had been wounded in the leg while serving at the front under Gen. George Patton. The wound was not serious, and Early was able to fly to England to visit his son. After Early returned to Washington, Butcher wrote in his diary, "He has made at least one contribution that I think will help greatly in our press relations. Henceforth, whenever security requires that news be delayed, the correspondents are to be given sufficient quotable information to write a story so not only they but the public at home will know, in general, the reasons for the delay." Early also suggested that the SHAEF press office avoid the use of the term "blackout." [69]

On his way to his assignment in France, Early accompanied FDR to the conference of Allied leaders at Yalta. Before departing, he told associates he planned to leave the White House soon. The press secretary, who at FDR's suggestion had been supplementing his meager government paycheck by writing magazine articles, was angling for, and eventually achieved, a well-paid executive position with the Pullman Company.

Also, there were signs of increasing friction between Early and FDR. One of the reasons was that Early would stand up for White House reporters when he thought they were right, even if "The Boss" thought they were wrong.[70]

Jonathan Daniels, the son of the Josephus Daniels who had been Roosevelt's boss as secretary of the navy in World War I, acted as press secretary in Early's absence. Early returned on March 22, but did not come into the office until two days later. Although Early had been saying as long ago as 1939 that he wanted to return to private life, he appears to have had trouble making the break when the moment came. "He was in a bad mood and said some rather shocking things about the president," an assistant, Eben Ayers, wrote in his diary. Early went to the Oval Office, where it was agreed that he would leave, probably in June. Daniels would be press secretary. Early would stay on temporarily as appointments secretary, succeeding Watson, who had died on the way home from Yalta. When Early returned to the press office, he was still in a foul mood. Ayers and Daniels "gained the impression that he was upset that the president had accepted his resignation."

The two men argued heatedly about who was to draft a statement announcing the changes. Early finally agreed to do it, but balked when Daniels suggested he take it to the president for his approval. Daniels also balked, not wanting to propose to the president a statement announcing his own appointment. The White House executive clerk, Maurice Latta, fortunately wandered by and resolved the crisis by agreeing to carry the announcement to the Oval Office.[71]

On April 12, 1945, Hassett was at Warm Springs and Early at the White House when Roosevelt was stricken by a coronary thrombosis. Hassett was among aides in the sitting room of the president's cottage when Comdr. Howard Bruenn, a navy cardiologist, emerged from the bedroom with the word that the president had died. White House physician Ross T. McIntire called Mrs. Roosevelt. Hassett did not call the new press secretary. Instead, he called Early. They agreed to make simultaneous announcements.[72]

Before he made the announcement, Early performed one other duty. He called Vice President Truman at the Capitol and told him, in a voice that showed the strain of the moment, "Please come right over."[73]

6

Scholar in the Press Office

"MY ADVICE TO ALL PRESIDENTS is not to put up a newspaper man to meet the press," said Charles G. Ross. "Choose a politician."

Ross wrote the words in 1931, when he had been Washington bureau chief for the *St. Louis Post-Dispatch* since the waning days of Woodrow Wilson.[1] On April 18, 1945, he received a summons from an old schoolmate, now suddenly the president of the United States. Harry Truman wanted him to be his press secretary.

Charlie Ross was about to prove himself wrong.

Truman could not have chosen a spokesman more unlike Roosevelt's Steve Early.

Like Early, Ross was a member of the press corps that accompanied Warren Harding on his fateful West Coast trip in 1923. But while Early scampered down the fire escape of a San Francisco hotel to break the first news of Harding's death, Ross was asleep in his room on the floor just below the president's. Earlier in the day, he had filed an optimistic report based on bulletins from Harding's doctors.[2]

Once alerted, Ross turned to what he did best, writing an analysis and appraisal of Harding's presidency. After reviewing the president's accomplishments and the scandals that scarred his administration, he wrote: "He was a product of Main Street and was proud of it, for he believed that the virtues of Main Street were the chiefest virtues of America, the qualities that had made the nation great."[3]

The episode illuminates the strengths and weaknesses that Ross brought to the White House press office. "Early suggested a man perpetually poised to cover an exciting story," wrote one Washington journalist. "Ross suggests a scholar, a deliberative mind which delights in undertaking research." For most of his professional career, he was a

89

specialist in what the trade calls "think-pieces," thoughtful analyses and in-depth reports such as the eighteen-thousand-word article on the depression that won him a Pulitzer Prize in 1931. His work often appeared on what *Post-Dispatch* staffers called "the dignity page," the front of the editorial section.[4] He was the kind of reporter who gets called "one of the ornaments of the profession."[5] He had little experience of the day-to-day hurly-burly that was the stock in trade of most White House reporters, and seemed not to understand why it was so important for a Steve Early to be six minutes ahead of the opposition. He was well-informed, however, and few reporters ever complained that he tried to mislead them.[6]

Ross had one other asset that was important for a presidential press secretary. He was very close to Harry Truman.

In high school in Independence, Missouri, Ross, the better scholar, had been something of a hero to Truman, who "always looked up to Charlie."[7] Together, the two classmates, both more interested in books than sports, found a description in Caesar's *Commentaries* of a bridge the Roman emperor built across the Rhine. They spent most of a month building a replica of it. The two also collaborated for a while on a translation from Latin orations of Cicero. The work was never finished, but it contained the memorable phrase "The good of the people is the chief law."[8]

In 1945, Ross was at first unsure that the good of the people required him to become a press secretary. When he did accept the job, his and Truman's thoughts turned to Independence and they agreed that the first person to call was their high school English teacher, Tilly Brown. Miss Brown had often lectured them on Tennyson's poem "Merlin and the Gleam," in which the wizard of Arthurian legend gives a young mariner the advice he has followed all his life, saying, "After it, follow it, / Follow the Gleam."[9] Ross was so impressed that when he was called on to edit the senior class yearbook, with Harry Truman as a member of his staff, he called it *The Gleam.* It was the start of his journalistic career.

Charlie's father, J. B. Ross, was a mining engineer temporarily turned deputy town marshal because there were no mining jobs in Independence. For a while, the family lived in the marshal's quarters next to the county jail. Ross's biographer, Ronald T. Farrar, says the boy's mother, Ella Ross, a piano teacher, "gave him her concern with detail, as well as her penchant for having things thoroughly correct."[10]

Unlike his classmate Harry Truman, Ross went on to college from

Independence High, graduating as valedictorian and winning a scholarship that paid the modest fees charged by the University of Missouri in Columbia. To cover his food and shelter, he became a campus correspondent for the *Columbia Herald*. After graduation, at which he was named class poet, he joined the *Herald* as a full-time reporter, but soon went on to the more prestigious *Post-Dispatch,* where city editor O. K. Bovard taught him a lesson that he would long remember. When the young reporter turned in a story about a painter who had fallen from a smokestack, Bovard read it over and demanded: "How tall was the smokestack?" Ross didn't know. It was "quite tall," he said. Bovard sent him back to the scene of the accident, a long streetcar trip and a tiring hike. When he returned, he had the smokestack's height, in feet and inches.[11]

In 1907, Ross moved across town to became a copy reader, and soon chief of the copy desk, on a rival St. Louis newspaper, the *Republic*. A year later, he went back to his alma mater as an instructor in the newly established University of Missouri School of Journalism. He was promoted to assistant professor, and wrote a textbook, *The Writing of News,* that showed he remembered his city editor's lesson. "If your story is pathetic it is not necessary to tell the reader so," he wrote. "Let him find it out from the simple, human facts. In describing a pretty girl, don't stop with saying she is pretty; tell how she is pretty —tell the color of her hair and eyes. Strive always to be specific."[12] Ross later made full professor, and remained at the journalism school ten years, including a sabbatical year in Australia as subeditor of the *Melbourne Herald*. Back from down under, he tired of teaching. One day, he became so irritated by a young woman in his class who was sucking on a piece of sticky candy that he walked out, headed for the Western Union office, and accepted a standing offer to return to the *Post-Dispatch*. The young woman, ironically, was one of his brighter students. Her name was Pauline Pfeiffer. She became a writer for fashion magazines and the second of novelist Ernest Hemingway's four wives.[13]

The *Post-Dispatch* was opening a Washington bureau, and made Ross its chief. At first, he was chief only of himself, and was instructed to write only hometown news items, but both the bureau and its scope soon expanded. On February 24, 1919, Ross had "a big day," covering President Wilson's arrival in Boston from peace talks in Paris and then boarding the presidential train for the return trip to Washington, interviewing Wilson aide D. R. Francis en route.[14]

The Harding and Coolidge presidencies found Ross increasingly skeptical. He admired Harding personally, but lamented "the failure of the country to become aroused" over corruption in his administration. He was disappointed in Coolidge's cabinet choices and wrote in the *Post-Dispatch*, "The president no longer feels the need of making the faintest gesture of conciliation toward the progressives of his party." The country was keeping cool in the face of scandal and graft, he complained. "What will make us hot I don't know."[15]

What made him hot was injustice. In 1923, he mounted a crusade in the *Post-Dispatch* for freedom for fifty-two Americans being held in prison for leftist and antiwar views they had expressed in 1918. They had been jailed under wartime emergency laws that Ross argued no longer applied. His columns prompted formation of a citizens' committee to seek amnesty for the prisoners. Harding pardoned twenty-eight of them and Coolidge the rest. Ross was also involved in his paper's campaign to reopen the case of Nicola Sacco and Bartolomeo Vanzetti, the two anarchists whose prosecution for murder became a worldwide cause célèbre in the 1920s. After the pair were executed, despite doubts about the evidence against them, he wrote, "The fight was lost, but it was lost in distinguished company."[16] Muckraking reporters Robert S. Allen and Drew Pearson saluted Ross as "a keen and fearless analyst and writer."[17]

Although he covered the White House, he preferred the Senate. Returning to his alma mater in 1926, he told journalism students that the not-for-quotation presidential press conference system was "useful to the newspapers, but it has one serious drawback from our point of view. It enables the president to put out his views without accepting responsibility for them." By contrast, he said, covering the more open proceedings in the Senate "is a fascinating and a stimulating job."[18]

He appeared to have no plans to give it up. "A newspaper man ought to be that and nothing else," he wrote in 1931. "A public official ought to be that and nothing else. Newspaper men turned public officials try to be both, and they rarely succeed. Sooner or later, they will have the 'chief' on their backs for giving out too much information, or the newspaper men on their backs for giving out too little."[19]

Ross's Pulitzer Prize–winning essay on the depression, which filled twenty-four columns of type in the paper's editions of November 29, 1931, was headlined "The Country's Plight—What Can Be Done About It?" One thing that he said could be done about it was for the government to take a more active role; mere budget cutting was not enough. He traveled with Hoover during the 1932 presidential campaign, but believed FDR had one powerful asset to offset the advantage of Hoover's incumbency. "Mr. Roosevelt had, and still has, the Depression," he wrote. "It appears at this writing . . . that the Depression will win." [20]

In 1933, Ross received a gold medal for distinguished service from the Missouri School of Journalism. As the prize-winning bureau chief of an influential newspaper, he was often invited to Washington parties, which he attended with soft-leaded pencils and folded-up sheets of newsprint in his pocket, just in case he ran into a story. His reporting days were coming to an end, however, at least for a while. Publisher Joseph Pulitzer Jr. thought the newspaper was moving too far to the Left. Pulitzer wanted a good man to take over the editorial page and steer it to a more moderate course. His choice was Charlie Ross. [21]

The job brought Harry Truman back into Ross's life in a way neither of them had anticipated. In 1934, Truman, then an official of his native Jackson County, ran for the Senate. Ross did not think it was a good idea. In a telegram to Pulitzer at the publisher's summer home in Bar Harbor, Maine, the new editorial page editor described his old schoolmate as "the candidate brought out and supported" by Kansas City's corrupt Pendergast political machine. "He is Pendergast's creature," said Ross. Although the *Post-Dispatch* did not ordinarily make primary endorsements, Ross believed the three-way race presented "the vital issue of whether Pendergast through his control of the Kansas City machine and the state house is to be allowed to extend his influence through the naming of a senator." He urged that the paper endorse one of Truman's opponents, Rep. John J. Cochran of St. Louis. [22]

Pulitzer replied that he feared endorsing Cochran would "lend color to the charge that he is a quote creature unquote of the Post-Dispatch." He thought the paper should make clear "the disqualifications of Truman as a boss-picked and boss-controlled candidate" but stop short of endorsing anybody, because no candidate appeared to be of outstanding ability. [23] Ross, after talking with others, responded that he now wanted to hold off on any endorsement but "leave the way open to denunciation of Truman as boss-controlled if on further thought you believe it desirable." [24]

The matter rested there until after Truman's victory in the primary. Then Pulitzer and Ross decided that denunciation was indeed desirable. "County Judge Truman is the nominee of the Democratic

Party for the United States Senate because Tom Pendergast willed it so," the paper said in an editorial. "The result demonstrates the power of machine politics." [25] In November, Truman defeated his Republican opponent by more than a quarter of a million votes. The *Post-Dispatch* made no endorsement.

In his account of the campaign in his memoirs, Truman did not mention the *Post-Dispatch* or Ross. Discussing his 1940 reelection, he said only that the newspaper "disapproved of me because of my Democratic background in western Missouri." [26]

A year after taking over the editorial page, Ross had still not moved it far enough to the Right to please his publisher. In July 1935, Pulitzer complained of "our policy of pretty general acquiescence in everything the New Deal does, and the consistent absence of outspoken criticism, with only the mildest occasional disagreements." This, the publisher demanded, "should be changed in both tone and tempo." [27] Ross demurred, citing what he said was "a considerable sum of outspoken criticism over the course of a month or so." But he wrote an editorial, and airmailed it to Pulitzer at Bar Harbor, criticizing Roosevelt for "taking his constitutional responsibilities too lightly." [28]

In June of that year, at Pulitzer's suggestion, Ross had interviewed prominent Americans including Republican Senator William E. Borah of Idaho, Supreme Court Justice Louis D. Brandeis, and Felix Frank-furter, then a Harvard law professor and adviser to the president. Reporting on his conclusions, he told Pulitzer, "We should view with skepticism all current proposals for enlarging the federal power over wages and hours of industry." [29]

By 1936, Ross had come to share Pulitzer's view that the paper should support Roosevelt's opponent, Republican Alf Landon. He wrote the editorial himself, denouncing "the building up at Washington of a government not of laws but of men" and declaring that the Democratic Party "today, under Mr. Roosevelt, burns its incense before strange gods." The Constitution, he said, "must not be amended by subterfuge and indirection." [30]

In 1940, the *Post-Dispatch* again opposed Truman, saying his renomination would cause "shrill rejoicing among all the forces of evil in Missouri." [31] By this time, however, Ross was free of editorial page duties. In January 1939, he had returned to Washington as a contributing editor, assigned to write the interpretive pieces at which he excelled. An unusual feature of his new assignment was that he was free of editing. The editors could withhold his copy and ask him for clarification, but they could not change it. [32]

It was a great job, and he relished it. In a column in the spring of 1940, he wrote that the "boomlet," as it then was, for Wendell Willkie "might conceivably develop into a sizable boom." He backed up his prediction by making some small bets with skeptical colleagues, and collected when the hitherto little-known Willkie captured the Republican nomination to oppose FDR.[33] His column, "Washington Letter," was soon syndicated.[34]

One of his avid readers was Harry Truman. Despite Ross's pivotal role in the *Post-Dispatch*'s opposition to him, they renewed a cordial relationship after Ross returned to the capital. First lady Bess Truman had been a classmate at Independence High also, and Ross became a friend of the family. He forged a close bond with the Trumans' daughter, Margaret, and took an interest in her aspirations for a career as a concert singer. To Margaret, he was "Charlie."[35]

The day after Franklin D. Roosevelt died, Ross sat down at his typewriter and wrote an article for the Sunday *Post-Dispatch* about the vice president who was moving into the Oval Office. "The Republic," he said, "is in no danger from the accession of Harry Truman. . . . He is no nonentity and no Harding. He may not have the makings of a great president, but he certainly has the makings of a good president."[36]

Three days after the article appeared, Truman asked Ross to come see him at Blair House, the presidential guest quarters where he was staying while Eleanor Roosevelt packed up. With Steve Early unavailable and Jonathan Daniels leaving, Truman had announced at his first press conference that J. Leonard Reinsch would assist him on press and radio matters, but did not say whether Reinsch would have the rank of presidential secretary. This ambiguous announcement created consternation in the press corps. Reinsch, thirty-six, was managing director of radio stations owned by former Ohio governor James M. Cox, the 1920 presidential candidate who had picked FDR as his running mate. Reinsch had helped Truman with vice presidential campaign speeches.

"He is a radio technician and has never been a newspaperman —a fact which raised some additional question as to his status," said *Editor & Publisher*. Although a handful of radio reporters, equipped then only with pencils and note pads, had joined the representatives of the print media in the White House press corps, they were still viewed with suspicion. Print reporters blanched at the thought of a broadcasting executive as press secretary.

"I already knew that the press corps traditionally held anyone in radio in bitter contempt," said Reinsch. "What I didn't know was how deep that bitterness ran." By Reinsch's account, reporters for the three wire services tried to have him replaced after his first briefing. By other accounts, the briefing had been a disaster. "The press secretary," Reinsch complained, "was expected to be the president's alter ego, in a sense—to be knowledgeable about every thought and action of the president—in advance!" *Broadcasting* magazine said pillars of the Washington journalistic community pressured the White House and the Democratic National Committee for Reinsch's removal. Both Reinsch and Truman said later that his appointment was never intended to be permanent.[37]

Wherever the truth lay, Early suggested to Truman that he appoint Ross. The new president's response was, "Do you think he'd take it?" Early suggested there was only one way to find out. In their meeting the next morning in his study at Blair House, Truman sensed that his old schoolmate was interested, but Ross asked time to think it over and discuss it with his publisher. The job's $10,000-a-year salary was less than a third of what he received from the *Post-Dispatch,* he liked his work in the Washington bureau, and Pulitzer was reluctant to lose him. That night, talking it over with his wife, Ross decided. After all, Louis Brownlow had said, "The president needs help." Ross told Florence Ross, "This man needs help."[38]

He returned to Blair House the next evening and told Truman he would take the job. He asked that he be allowed to go ahead with plans to cover the forthcoming organizational conference of the United Nations in San Francisco for his paper. Truman agreed. Announcement of the appointment would be withheld until May 15, after the UN conference. The two classmates' thoughts turned to Tillie Brown, the only one of their high school teachers still living. On the spur of the moment, Truman put in a call to her. As soon as the president hung up, Steve Early shrewdly warned that the story would leak. Sure enough, their former teacher no sooner got off the phone in her kitchen in Independence than she told a friend. The friend told someone who told the Independence *Examiner,* which tipped off the wire services, and the White House phones started ringing. The next day, Truman made it official. At a hurriedly called news conference, he read a telegram from Cox asking to have Reinsch back, and said Pulitzer had agreed in a telephone call to let Ross go for two years. "Mr. Ross will be the press secretary?" a reporter asked. "Press secretary," said the president. No ambiguity this time.[39]

Ross was sworn in on May 15, placing his hand on the same Bible on which Truman had taken the oath a little more than a month earlier. The man now moving into the press secretary's office, with its thick red carpet, pea-green walls, and black desk, was fifty-nine years old, a year and a half younger than Truman. He looked older. Tall and stooped, he had pronounced pouches under his blue eyes and suffered from arthritis and heart trouble. One writer said he looked like a veteran character actor playing a denizen of the old homestead in a country opera. His naturally mournful face made some believe that he was unhappy in his job. Ross, however, once said, "Sometimes it seems to me as if I'm just playing a game with my former colleagues."[40]

He did not have the rooms full of assistants that press secretaries were later to enjoy. A week before he was sworn in, he asked Eben Ayers, a former wire service and newspaper reporter and executive who had recently come to the White House as an assistant press secretary, to stay on. His only other staff consisted of four women who performed clerical duties. Reinsch continued to advise Truman on radio matters from the Cox broadcasting office in Atlanta, but had no official role.[41]

Truman had received good marks from the press in his debut. Copies of his first presidential address to Congress were ready almost an hour before delivery, instead of a few minutes before as usual under FDR. His first press conference drew a record crowd of 348 correspondents, and Truman opened it precisely on time. He had replaced Roosevelt's gadget-bedecked desk with a simpler one topped with only a few papers and some writing materials. He announced that he would hold press conferences once a week, instead of twice as FDR did, and they would not be on fixed days. He would call them when there was news, and would notify the correspondents sufficiently in advance. This announcement may not have pleased anyone, but many reporters found the blunt-spoken chief executive a welcome change from his wily predecessor. There was, said one, "no double-talk."[42]

Nevertheless, the new team in the press office had its work cut out. When a press conference was late starting, one reporter was heard to ask another, "What are they doing? Why do we have to wait?" The not very comforting reply was, "They are trying to get his foot out of his mouth."[43] By early 1946, Ross and others were urging the president to answer "no comment" to tricky questions. He occasionally took the advice.[44]

Ross was criticized by some reporters because he did not, as Early

7. Charlie Ross showed eager reporters the announcement of President Harry S. Truman's seizure of struck railroads on May 17, 1946. *International News Service photo courtesy Corvis-Bettman.*

did, interrupt the president and correct him when he made a misstatement. "On such occasions, Ross stands by silently, a stooped, lean, tired figure, with sad spaniel eyes," one such account said.[45]

In private, however, Ross did not hesitate to correct his old schoolmate. On May 24, 1946, facing the threat of a railroad strike, Truman sat down at his desk with a pen and wrote a blistering attack on union leaders winding up with an appeal to World War II veterans: "Let's put transportation and production back to work, hang a few traitors and make our country safe for democracy. Come on boys, let's do the job!" Truman dropped the twelve pages of lined tablet paper on his press secretary's desk and told him to get it typed up. Ross, probably the only White House aide who sometimes called the president "Harry" in private,[46] told him the speech could not be given as written. As redrafted by Ross and Clark Clifford, the address was tough, saying the rail crisis was "caused by a group of men within our own country who place their private interests above the welfare of the nation." It said the government would take over the railroads if necessary. But it made no mention of hanging.[47]

One of Ross's first big tests as press secretary came when Truman traveled aboard the navy cruiser *Augusta* to a meeting of the Big Three —Britain, the Soviet Union, and the United States—at Potsdam, near Berlin, in the summer of 1945. The war in Europe was over, but hostilities with Japan continued. The *Augusta* was accompanied by an escort ship, the *Philadelphia*. Hoping to withhold any news of the meeting until the president and his party had safely arrived in Antwerp, Ross limited the traveling press contingent to a pool of four reporters and three photographers, who would transmit no copy until after the ships docked. A few hours after the *Augusta* sailed from Newport News, Virginia, Drew Pearson broadcast a story that the president was on his way to a secret meeting with Britain's Winston Churchill and the Soviets' Joseph Stalin. He didn't say where, but Clement Attlee, the British Labor Party leader, released a letter accepting Churchill's invitation to attend the meeting "in Berlin." With the cat out of the bag, Ross allowed the pool correspondents to file, angering reporters back in Washington who had been left in the dark. Ross instructed Ayers, who had remained at the White House, to tell them that the shipboard pool "represented the entire American press and nobody was scooped by the action permitting them to file." Ayers, a quiet-spoken New Englander, told his boss, "I've learned a great many things about the men with whom I associated for 25 or 30 years, in the months on the opposite side of the desk. The mildest thing I would say is that they can be a bit irritating." From a list of a dozen correspondents seeking credentials to join the Potsdam party, he selected three, eliminating "the men who complained the loudest." On the *Augusta* one afternoon, Truman talked informally with wire service reporters as they watched a shuffleboard game on the forward deck. He struck Merriman Smith as far more "willing and frank" about his hopes for the conference than Roosevelt had been in going to previous Big Three meetings. "We went to Potsdam understanding what it was all about," the United Press correspondent said.[48]

On August 6, 1945, Ayers, still tending the store in Washington in the press secretary's absence, conducted one of the shortest, and oddest, press briefings in White House history. "I have got here what I think is a darned good story," he told reporters. He then read the first three sentences of a statement by the president. "It's a hell of a

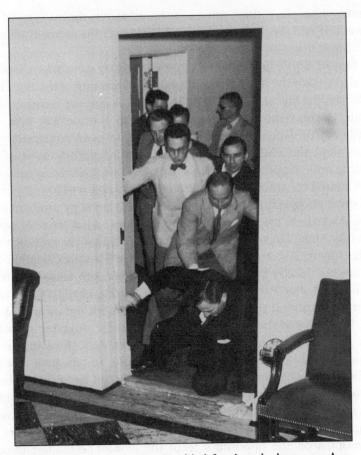

8. White House reporters scrambled for the telephones on Aug. 14, 1945, with the latest news about the imminent Japanese surrender ending World War II. *International News Service photo courtesy Corvis-Bettman.*

story!" said a reporter. The first atomic bomb had been dropped on Hiroshima while the Big Three were meeting. "Go to it," said Ayers.[49]

Truman cut short his stay in Europe and returned to Washington. On August 11, with the capitulation of Japan expected momentarily, he approved a recommendation by Byron Price that wartime censorship be lifted as soon as the surrender was announced.[50] On August 12, Ross told reporters that coded messages intercepted that morning by the Japanese legation of neutral Switzerland "do not contain the answer awaited by the whole world." The transcript of Ross's briefing ends:

"(There was a rush for the door—Bump! Thud! Bump! Bump!) VOICE: Ouch."

On August 15, it was all over, and the president officially lifted censorship. That day's briefing transcript began: ("The reporters came in very quietly.)"

The bomb continued to be, in Ayers's words, "a darned good story." The British and Canadians argued that as allies of the United States in the war, they were entitled to more information about the new weapon. The subject came up during a presidential fishing vacation in Tennessee in 1946. Truman invited reporters to a cocktail hour in his cottage and one of them seized the chance to ask him about the Canadian and British demands. Quickly, Truman answered, "No. We're not going to give it to them. You wouldn't expect General Motors to give away its production secrets, would you?" Vainly, Ross reminded reporters that the session was supposed to be off the record. Truman's remark was too good a story to sit on.[51]

In 1947, the bomb was the subject of a Metro-Goldwyn-Mayer movie, *The Beginning or the End?*, in which Ross became the first presidential secretary to be portrayed on the screen while he was in office. Edward Earle portrayed Ross in a scene about a fictional conversation in which Truman tells him that the bomb has been developed and will be used against Japan. More and more, the president's press secretary was becoming a public figure.[52]

As in FDR's day, the Oval Office was an inconvenient place to hold crowded press conferences. Reporters standing against the wall in the back had trouble hearing. Some were shaking their fountain pens and getting ink on the carpet. At the suggestion of Leonard Reinsch, Truman asked White House architect Lorenzo S. Winslow to draw up plans for expansion of the West Wing to include an auditorium with facilities for radio and television broadcasters. The auditorium was to seat 375, compared with the estimated maximum of 273 who could stand in front of the president's desk.[53]

The West Wing addition also included fifteen thousand feet of office space so that presidential assistants and clerical workers in other buildings could be moved into the White House. By one compilation, the White House staff had grown to 503 persons, up from 72 in the last year of the Hoover presidency.[54]

The Commission of Fine Arts approved the plan on November

30, 1945, reserving the right to alter details. A $1.65 million appropriation for this and other White House improvements was tacked onto a pending bill in Congress four days later. Controversy erupted after architect Winslow outlined the plans in a radio interview on January 20. Winslow told the interviewer the extension was not an addition to the White House and Truman insisted it not be visible to passersby on Pennsylvania Avenue. Nevertheless, the president was flooded with telegrams protesting "the defacing of our White House." Secretary of the Interior Ickes joined the fray, urging Truman to consult leading architects "before such a drastic change in policy." Wilting before the opposition, the House amended the appropriation bill by removing the $883,660 specified for the West Wing expansion. Truman persisted, but the project was dead. In 1950, Truman moved his press conferences and some staff offices to the old State Department building across Executive Avenue.[55]

As usual, there were complaints from the press about the press secretary. He was not always aware of everything that was going on.[56] He was not alert to the needs of the wire services.[57] He did not run his office well.[58] He failed to coordinate news releases with the government departments and agencies.[59] Some correspondents said they "received a run-around and have been understandably exasperated at prolonged delays in getting answers to questions."[60] On top of all this, he was hard to hear.[61]

Ross's reaction was summed up in a memo he wrote to Ayers after the Potsdam conference:

> I am not clairvoyant. I cannot tell precisely what the President is going to do. At every step of the way, I have sought, however, to give the newspapermen, for their guidance, my idea of the probabilities. It would have been easier to impose a complete blackout, but we—you and I—have tried to be helpful. It seems that the more we try, the more hell we get.[62]

One of Ross's greatest strengths was his ability to give reporters authoritative information on background, a basis that permitted them to use it without naming him as the source. Edward T. Folliard of the *Washington Post* learned the value of this after letting slip while having lunch with colleagues at the National Press Club that he did not believe Truman would run for reelection in 1952. *Life* magazine heard about Folliard's hunch and offered him $1,000 to write an article about it. Folliard, worried that he might be wrong, dropped in to see

Ross. The press secretary told him that Truman had privately been against Roosevelt seeking a third term and believed that for him to run again would, in effect, be seeking a third term himself. "Why don't you write it?" he suggested. Folliard did, earning $1,000 and some laurels as a prophet.

"What a strange job is that of the press secretary," Ross jotted to himself in 1948. "There is no other in the world, I am sure, that is even approximately like it."[63]

It became even stranger after Truman's secretary of commerce, Henry A. Wallace, paid a call at the White House. Wallace privately opposed Truman's get-tough policy regarding the Soviet Union, but had not made his views public. On September 10, he showed Truman the text of a speech he was to deliver two nights later at a rally in Madison Square Garden in support of Soviet-U.S. friendship. Truman thumbed through the manuscript, and raised no objections to it. By the time of the president's 4 P.M. news conference on September 12, most reporters had advance copies of the speech. It said in part: "I am neither anti-British nor pro-British; neither anti-Russian nor pro-Russian. And just two days ago, when President Truman read these words, he said they represented the policy of his administration." Truman was asked for comment on the speech, and said he could not comment on a speech that had not been delivered. "If the president had only stopped there!" Ross said later. But he did not. Raymond Brandt of the *Post-Dispatch* asked whether his approval of the paragraph mentioned by Wallace extended to the whole speech. He said it did. In fact, the speech departed drastically from the policy being pursued by Truman and Secretary of State James Byrnes by advocating a hands-off approach to Eastern European affairs and the abandonment of the postwar arms buildup.[64]

Ross, standing at the president's side at the news conference, was apprehensive, but said nothing, as he had not seen the speech. Back in his office, he got calls from two cabinet undersecretaries, Will Clayton at the State Department and John L. Sullivan at the Navy. It was still fifty-five minutes before the speech was to be delivered, and they thought Wallace should be headed off. Ross called Truman, who said that the speech would have a good political effect in New York and "while it might ruffle Byrnes, he did not think it would do any permanent damage." When the wire stories started coming over the news ticker in the press office, Ross realized that Clayton and Sullivan were right and the president was wrong.

At the next morning's staff meeting, Truman conceded that he

had made a serious blunder. Ross favored making an immediate statement, but others counseled against it. On Saturday, Ross won Clifford
to his point of view. He, Clifford, and Clayton then drafted a statement
for the president saying he did not mean to approve the contents of
the speech, but only Wallace's right to deliver it. Truman read the
statement at a hurriedly called news conference in his office that afternoon. It was greeted as a lame excuse and called "a clumsy lie" by
Time magazine. Byrnes, who was in Paris, sent a teletype message to
the president saying he would resign immediately if Wallace could not
be curbed. Ross told the president "that it was impossible for him to
keep on driving two horses going in opposite directions." On September 20, ten days after their chat in the Oval Office, Truman fired
Wallace. The awkward incident severely damaged Truman's already
declining popularity.[65]

When Ross was hospitalized for four weeks after a painful bout of
arthritis, rumors circulated that he was about to resign.[66] Back at the
White House, he called the *Post-Dispatch* to assure his former colleagues that he was in good health, "was not 'a rat' and certainly
would not 'run out' under present circumstances."[67] On November
10, a radio commentator repeated the resignation rumor. Asked about
it at his news conference the next morning, Truman said, "Mr. Ross is
not going to resign."[68]

Ross was sometimes faulted in later years for not developing a
strategy to bolster Truman's fading image. He himself said, "I only
wish I could get the public to appreciate the Harry Truman I know."
But it is likely, as Truman scholar Alonzo Hamby has pointed out, that
it never occurred to him that image-mending was part of his job.[69]
Biographer Farrar wrote that Ross "knew little and cared less about
the techniques of modern press agentry" and "did not always judge it
necessary to place the president in a favorable light." His position was
that the president's words and deeds spoke for themselves. Farrar, who
interviewed Truman, said Ross followed this policy with the president's knowledge and consent.[70]

Ross did make one important suggestion in Truman's 1948 election campaign. He was among those who encouraged the off-the-cuff
speaking style that helped propel him to victory.[71] He was also involved
in one of the campaign's most embarrassing moments. Ross enjoyed
having a few drinks occasionally, but his wife did not look kindly on
alcohol.[72] So as the president's campaign train made its way through
southern Idaho, the press secretary took the opportunity for a conviv-

ial evening with reporters in a Sun Valley bar. The next morning, he learned that an airport dedication at the little town of Carey had been added to the president's schedule. Feeling the worse for drink, he asked a Secret Service agent to pinch-hit for him in checking out the details. The agent passed the information on to Maj. Gen. Harry Vaughan, who briefed the president. Among Truman's first words were: "I am honored to dedicate this airport and present this wreath to the parents of the brave boy who died fighting for his country." There was a gasp from the audience. The information had become a little garbled in transit. The airport was being named the Wilma Coates Airport in memory of a sixteen-year-old girl killed in the crash of a small civilian plane piloted by her boyfriend. Truman apologized to the girl's parents.[73]

A far more serious embarrassment arose from Truman's remarks at a press conference in an ornate room in the old State Department building on November 30, 1950. For months, the country had been mired in an unpopular war in Korea. Now it had become clear that China was intervening in support of communist North Korea. Truman opened the conference with a carefully prepared statement, couched in general terms, on the gravity of the crisis and the administration's plans to meet it. An hour before the press conference, as usual, Ross and others had met with the president and discussed questions that might come up. Korea, of course, was mentioned. So were jobs, a forthcoming conference with congressional leaders, and Truman's status as a lame duck president. Nobody said anything about the atomic bomb.

At the press conference, reporters pressed for more detail on what steps would be taken to counter the Chinese intervention. Truman replied that, subject to United Nations approval, the United States would take whatever action the military situation required. "Will that include the atomic bomb?" Jack Doherty of the *New York Daily News* asked. Truman said it could include every weapon in the U.S. arsenal. Paul R. Leach of the *Chicago Daily News* followed up: "Does that mean that there is active consideration of the use of the atomic bomb?" The president said there had always been active consideration of its use, adding that he did not want to see it used. A few minutes later, Merriman Smith of United Press gave Truman a chance to get out of the morass he was leading himself into. "Did we understand you clearly," Smith asked, "that the use of the bomb is under active consideration?" Truman repeated that it always had been. Frank Bourgholtzer of NBC then asked, "Mr. President, you said this depends on United Nations action. Does that mean that we wouldn't use the atomic bomb except on a United Nations authorization?" No, Truman said. If action against the Chinese were approved, "the military commander in the field will have charge of the use of the weapons, as he always has." This statement was particularly inflammatory because Gen. Douglas MacArthur, the colorful and impetuous commander in Korea, had made no secret of his desire for more aggressive action.

By the time the Associated Press moved its first lead on the news conference—a wrap-up after the initial bulletin series—the story had taken shape: "President Truman said today use of the atomic bomb in Korea has always been under consideration—and whether it is used is up to American military leaders in the field."

Ross, watching the Teletype machines in his office, rightly feared that a wrong impression was being created. He called in White House correspondents and told them the president had not meant that there was any *new* consideration of using the bomb. Ayers wrote in his diary that for reporters to say that MacArthur had authority to use the bomb "reflected complete ignorance, apparently, of the law which provides that only the president can authorize . . . the use of the bomb." But if hurried wire service editors were expected to be familiar with this fine point of law, surely the president and commander in chief should have known it. The reporting, however imperfect, accurately stated what the president had said, even though direct quotations were not permitted. It was Truman who made the mistake.

Whoever was to blame, response was swift and intense. To his scheduled 12:30 P.M. appointment with the president, the secretary of state, Dean Acheson, brought a draft of a clarifying statement. Ross went to the Oval Office and picked up the draft, but felt it would not do. Acheson and George Elsey, a young officer detailed from the navy as a White House aide, accompanied the press secretary to his office and collaborated with him on the statement that was released. The statement said the president had not authorized using the bomb, and there had been no new consideration of doing so. In his notes, Ross wrote, not entirely accurately, that Truman had "said nothing that he has not said before."[74]

Abroad, there was dismay. The *Times of India* ran an editorial headed *NO NO NO*. In Rome, *Il Momento* reported that the U.S. bomber command in Tokyo was ready to take off with the bomb. In London, where it was about 5 P.M., the news arrived during a two-day parliamentary debate on foreign policy. More than a hundred members rushed from the House of Commons to sign a letter of protest. Clement Attlee, now prime minister, called a cabinet meeting and said, "I shall have to go to Washington to see the president."[75]

In Washington, Truman and Attlee conferred first at the White House and then, on December 5, during a Potomac River cruise on the presidential yacht *Williamsburg*. Ross went along so he could brief the press. He took notes on a lined tablet as Truman told the British leader, "We can't voluntarily back out of Korea. South Koreans would be murdered if we did that. I can't bring myself to face that situation," and Attlee replied, "We are in with you. We stand together." The two-hour meeting, which dealt with a resolution on Asian policy that the United States and Britain wanted to introduce in the United Nations, broke up about 4:45 P.M. Back at the White House, Ross told reporters, "There will be nothing to cause a mad rush from the room, so . . . please relax." Then he gave a briefing that Raymond Brandt described as "masterly . . . complete in every detail." The press secretary denied a London story that Truman and Attlee had discussed a possible "re-invasion of Korea" if UN forces should be pushed out. He gave the menu for the lunch served on the *Williamsburg*. He said the two leaders would meet again the next day at 11 A.M. He also talked about the concert that Margaret Truman, winding up her debut tour as a professional singer, was giving that night in Washington. Ross had brought his dinner jacket so that he could change and get to Constitution Hall to hear his young friend sing.[76]

An NBC team asked Ross to repeat some of his remarks for broadcast, and set up a microphone, attached to a recorder, on his desk. Ross, a chain-smoker, lit a cigarette. "Don't mumble," his secretary, Myrtle Bergheim, chided him. "You know I always speak very distinctly," he said. Then he slumped sideways in his chair. NBC's Bourgholtzer thought it was a joke—a humorous gesture to show how tired he was. Myrtle Bergheim grabbed the telephone. In moments, White House physician Wallace Graham was bounding up the stairs from his office a floor below. He administered a stimulant and began administering oxygen. But it was too late. Charlie Ross's heart had failed.[77]

There was, after all, occasion for "a mad rush" by reporters to file the news, but the *New York Times* reported that "it was a most difficult bulletin for them to articulate on the telephone."[78] Truman wrote a statement in longhand paying tribute to the friend he had known "as a boy and as a man." He walked to the press lounge, but couldn't read more than a few words. "Aw hell!," he said. "You fellows know how I feel anyway."[79]

The concert Margaret Truman gave that night is best-known for an ill-tempered letter her father wrote the next morning to a *Washington Post* critic who said she did not sing very well. As he and Bess Truman prepared to go to the gala affair, however, they were preoccupied with whether to tell their daughter of Ross's death. They decided not to. "The atmosphere was charged not only with grief, but mystery," Margaret Truman wrote later. "I think I should have been told that my friend had died."[80]

7

"Tell Jim to Take Over"

JAMES C. HAGERTY, napping on a couch after a morning of golf and a long lunch, was awakened by the White House telephone in his den. It was ringing continuously, a signal that the call was urgent.

The telephone call to Hagerty's twelve-room, two-story brick home on Washington's Reno Road, at 4:30 P.M. on September 24, 1955, was the beginning of his finest hour as President Eisenhower's popular but controversial press secretary.

Murray Snyder, the deputy press secretary, was on the line from Eisenhower's vacation working quarters at Lowry Air Force Base in Denver. The president had suffered a heart attack.

Hagerty's candor in the days that followed reversed decades of secrecy and deceit about presidential illnesses. The precedent he set would make it difficult for press secretaries in the future, including himself, to dissemble when the president for whom they speak falls ill.

Within twelve hours of receiving Snyder's call, after alerting Vice President Richard Nixon and others to the crisis, Hagerty was on an Air Force plane to Denver. For three weeks, he held news conferences three or four times a day to keep reporters up to date on the president's condition. He persuaded reluctant doctors to hold a news conference of their own. He even issued a report on the patient's first bowel movement.[1]

The decisiveness and efficiency with which Hagerty acted had propelled him from the reporters' gallery at the New York state capitol in Albany to a decade as Gov. Thomas E. Dewey's press secretary and then to the Eisenhower campaign of 1952 and the White House.

Eisenhower, who had spent most of his career in the army, wanted efficiency, and from Hagerty he got it. What he did not get—and probably did not want—was a Charlie Ross who could knowledgeably provide reporters with background on public affairs.

A few months after Eisenhower left office, twenty Washington correspondents agreed to answer questions from a journalism student writing a master's thesis on Hagerty's performance as press secretary. Two words, "superficial" and "technical," occur over and over again in their replies.[2]

Hagerty had an encyclopedic knowledge of deadlines, lighting, acoustics, and television camera problems. He knew when to break up a news conference to meet the deadlines of eastern seaboard newspapers. To one writer, he seemed even to have a grasp of deadlines in Calcutta.[3]

When it came to substance, many newsmen thought him thin. "I sense that Hagerty had never read nor thought about some policy matters," said one correspondent. "This was particularly glaring at international conferences, where he was out of his depth."[4]

Change in the White House press office had begun with Ross's death. For reasons that are not clear, Truman, stunned at the loss of his friend, chose Joseph H. Short Jr., a hot-tempered correspondent for the *Baltimore Sun* who had feuded with Ross, to succeed him. By most accounts, Short ran the press office more efficiently. He expanded the staff by naming two assistants instead of one. Roger Tubby, who had been with the press office at the State Department, was given responsibility for foreign affairs. Irving Perlmeter, a press officer for the Bureau of Internal Revenue, handled domestic matters. Eben Ayers, who had been Ross's lone assistant, quit the press office in a huff, but remained at the White House as a special assistant, doing odd jobs for Truman. Ayers characterized Short as "one of the nastiest" of White House correspondents and had refused to accredit him to go to Potsdam.[5]

Tubby imported from the State Department a new system of preparing the president for his press conferences, collecting material into a notebook two or three days in advance instead of relying on a discussion group only a few hours ahead of time.[6] Perlmeter brought new efficiency to arranging for press buses and hotel accommodations on out-of-town trips, about which reporters had grumbled for years.[7] Army Signal Corps magnetic tape was substituted for stenographic notes at presidential press conferences.[8]

All this efficiency seems to have come at a price. Despite denials by Perlmeter, reporters complained that their access to news sources was being cut off. International News Service correspondent Robert Nixon spoke of "a flat order to all members of the White House staff that they could not have contacts with or give information to newsmen about *anything,* even the time of day or the state of the weather." [9]

In September 1952, less than two months before Eisenhower's election, the intense, driven Short died of a heart ailment, as Ross had done before him. "I feel as if I killed them," said the sorrowing Truman.[10] Tubby and Perlmeter became acting press secretaries for a brief time. When Perlmeter had a heart attack that removed him from action, Tubby became press secretary. Hagerty met with Tubby to go over press office operations before moving into the White House.

The new press secretary came to the job steeped in politics. He cherished a dim recollection of meeting Theodore Roosevelt on the front porch at Sagamore Hill when his father, *New York Times* political writer James A. Hagerty, took his family for a summer visit while covering the former president.[11]

Later, young Hagerty joined the *Times* himself, covering politics in New York City and Albany for eight years before joining Republican Dewey's staff in 1942 as executive assistant in charge of press relations. He handled press duties in Dewey's 1944 campaign against Roosevelt and again in 1948, anticipating that he would become the presidential press secretary after Dewey's defeat of Truman.[12] Truman's upset victory sent him back to Albany.

Hagerty found a new presidential hopeful to coach in the art of public relations when Dewey introduced him to Eisenhower at a dinner at the Waldorf-Astoria Hotel in New York. Eisenhower was then president of Columbia University, but being drawn increasingly into politics. He and Hagerty met frequently in the months that followed. Eisenhower called him "Jim" and he called Eisenhower "General."

Hagerty's years of experience served Eisenhower well. According to an often-told story, the sometimes imperious former general blew up at his new press aide early in the 1952 campaign. When the candidate's rage had run its course, he noticed Hagerty standing calmly by, saying nothing. "You don't scare easily, do you?" Ike remarked. "No, sir," said Hagerty.[13]

When a crisis arose over a potential fund scandal for running mate Richard Nixon, Hagerty told a newsman and Nixon confidante, "Look, have Dick make a full report. That's what the general's waiting for."[14] Nixon's subsequent television speech persuaded Eisenhower to keep him on the ticket. After the election, Hagerty accompanied the victorious candidate to Washington, a city where he had never worked.

After being briefed by Truman's Tubby, he decided to make no changes in the three-room physical arrangement of the office. He and Tubby discussed rumors that Eisenhower intended to move reporters from the White House press room to another building. A prospective White House aide, visiting the West Wing, had looked askance at the coats and hats piled untidily on a large table in the lobby and said, "I can't see why you fellows need so much space. The general is going to require more for his staff." Besides, he said, Eisenhower would not like having his visitors questioned right outside his door. Hagerty concluded that moving the press "would make more trouble than it would actually be worth." [15]

At his first meeting with reporters the day after Eisenhower's inauguration, he told them, "I am here to help you get the news. I am also here to work for one man, who happens to be the president." He said he would have one assistant, Murray Snyder. He had received a memo from conservative journalist David Lawrence suggesting that written questions be revived, [16] but he told the reporters, "That will not happen." [17] It did not. Dismissing rumors that Eisenhower would abandon regular press conferences, he said the president would probably hold them "more than weekly." [18]

But Eisenhower did not meet with reporters until February 23, more than a month later. After that, he usually held news conferences at intervals of one to three weeks, with a couple of months off in the summer. In January 1954, he groused that "having a press conference in the middle of getting up a legislative session is damn silly," but agreed to hold one after Hagerty pointed out that he had not done so for nearly a month. [19]

Hagerty prepared for the first session a two-page suggested schedule and a brief outline of procedures. Each reporter would arise and identify himself before asking a question. There would be no direct quotation unless authorized by the president or his press secretary. Hagerty suggested that after welcoming the correspondents the president announce he was rescinding an unpopular order on security control issued by Truman. "Many departments and agencies have hidden behind this order in an attempt actually to suppress legitimate news," he said. Eisenhower did not follow this advice, but opened the conference by talking about farm prices. [20] The administration later relaxed the security order by limiting the power of government agencies to put a secrecy label on documents.

Press conferences were held across Executive Avenue from the White House in the Old State Deparment Building, a nineteenth-century structure later to be called the Executive Office Building and still later, after a new one was built, the Old Executive Office Building. One wag dubbed it the Edna May Oliver Building, for the prim, spinsterish character actress of many 1930s movies. After ascending to the fourth floor, the press and the president assembled in the Indian Treaty Room, a high-ceiling chamber that drew its name from the many solemn pacts with Native American tribes that were initialed there.

Despite the splendor of the room's gilt and marble, Hagerty called it "a terrible place, but . . . the only room available."[21] Others shared his assessment. Beth Short, wife of Truman's second press secretary and a former Associated Press reporter, objected to the "staid old room" after Truman moved his press conferences there on August 27, 1950. Like many reporters, she missed the intimacy of the crowded Oval Office sessions, in which, as INS's Nixon recalled, reporters standing in front of the president's desk "could see every expression on his face, every movement of his hands."[22] The Old State Department building was not air-conditioned, and Paul Wooton of the *New Orleans Times-Picayune* noted that when 311 reporters crowded into it "the space was utilized as it is in the canning of sardines."[23] Reporters showed up at 8:00 A.M. to start lining up for a 10:30 A.M. press conference.

There were compensations. The room was larger than the Oval Office, and it had seats, even if they were only temporary wooden chairs. Despite the lack of air-conditioning, the two-story height of the ceiling made the room cooler, even in Washington's sweltering summers, than one would expect on the fourth floor of an old building. Eisenhower stood behind a large mahogany desk, usually topped with a blotter, a pen-holder, and two microphones. He usually brought in a single sheet of paper and placed it on the desk. On one such day, a reporter noticed that the sheet bore grease pencil lettering—by Murray Snyder, the reporter learned—listing five topics: "Red Cross . . . Italians . . . Farm Bill . . . Upper Colorado . . . Personal."[24] If the president had an opening statement, Hagerty saw to it that mimeographed copies were placed in the telephone booths of wire service reporters so they could begin dictating as soon as the press conference ended.[25]

The news conferences were ordinarily held on Wednesdays. On Monday, Hagerty would have made a list of questions that he thought would be coming up and sent them to the various government departments. By noon Tuesday, the departments would supply him with their responses. At 9 A.M. on Wednesday, Hagerty would run over the assembled material with other White House aides. The aides might suggest additional questions that they had heard raised, and Hagerty would add these to the list. An hour before the press conference, the press secretary, his deputy, a few senior White House officials, and sometimes a cabinet member or two would review the questions again, this time with the president.

Arriving late at one such meeting, Eisenhower's secretary, Ann Whitman, heard him wondering "how was a person supposed to remember all the details of disarmament . . . and farming . . . and everything." At the same session, an argument arose about a proposed statement on civil rights sit-ins at southern lunch counters, and the president said, "There is no use of you fellows trying to get me to say things I don't believe—you might as well go on to the next subject." Hagerty did so.[26]

The press secretary was at the president's side in the press conferences, and did not hesitate to help him out. At a conference in 1958, for instance, Eisenhower told a questioner that he had urged Soviet Premier Nikolai Bulganin to make public a letter he had written him. Quickly, Hagerty was on his feet whispering in the president's ear. "Sorry, I have apparently made a goof," said the president. "Isn't that in the letter?" "No, sir," said Hagerty.[27]

The greatest change Hagerty wrought in presidential press conferences was the introduction of television.

In a report to Sherman Adams, the chief of staff–designate, a month before inauguration day, he said, "The radio and TV companies will make a special effort again this year to try to get conferences opened for broadcasting, but I would recommend that they again be turned down."[28] By the day after the inauguration, he had apparently changed his mind. "I would like to work out with television representatives and with you gentlemen a system whereby the president could give talks to the people of the country—possibly press conferences to the country—on television," he told reporters. He said such sessions might be held monthly, with nontelevised news conferences in between. Direct quotation would be permitted when the press conference was televised.[29]

In New York, CBS president Frank Stanton issued a news release greeting the proposal warmly and calling it "a logical development of news coverage." Two days later, Hagerty met with representatives of

CBS, NBC, ABC, and the Mutual Broadcasting Company to "start working out with the radio and television industry a suitable arrangement to carry out the plans we have in mind." Hollis M. Seavey, Washington representative for Mutual, was named chairman for the industry and suggested the news conferences be held "in the upstairs study in the White House" with the president and reporters "seated in comfortable chairs, casually grouped, to convey a relaxed, homey atmosphere."[30]

Newspaper representatives were less enthusiastic. Paul R. Leach, Washington bureau chief of Knight Newspapers, argued that the best way for the president to use television would be "in the form of the Roosevelt fireside chats, rather than to have a press conference televised." The New Bedford, Massachusetts, *Standard-Times,* although it was building a television station of its own, editorialized that a televised news conference Eisenhower held in Abilene, Kansas, as a candidate, had "revealed the distractions that are bound to arise in the use of a medium of communication so closely associated with entertainment."[31]

As "a first step in opening up the news conference to other media," the White House permitted radio broadcast of Eisenhower's thirty-three-minute news conference of December 16, 1953. Ray Scherer, in his 6:40 P.M. evening news broadcast on Washington's WRC, exulted, "Today is a significant milestone in radio journalism" and noted that permitting direct quotation "will make, we should think, for more accurate, that is, verbatim reporting." Besides portions on the evening news, WRC and other network and local outlets carried the full press conference later in the evening. Live broadcasting was not permitted.[32]

In January of 1954, the urbane movie star Robert Montgomery came aboard as an unsalaried adviser on television. The *New York Times* described him as "the first man in professional show business to have a permanent office in the White House." Like the second such official, Ronald Reagan, he was a Republican who had served a stormy term as president of the Screen Actors Guild. He coached Eisenhower in such tricks as using smaller prompt cards and "being aware of talking to people rather than into a camera."[33]

Hagerty delayed televising press conferences because with the slow film then in use, "you'd have to light it up like a Hollywood premier, and that would destroy it." In October of 1954, Eastman Kodak and network representatives told him they had developed faster film that could be used with less intense lighting. He went to a studio with them, saw a demonstration, and told Eisenhower, "I think this is going to work." At the president's suggestion, he held a ten-minute mock press conference in the Indian Treaty Room, casting himself as the president and television correspondents as reporters. The results were screened in a basement room in the White House, with Eisenhower and Sherman Adams in the audience. At the end, the president just said, "Thank you." Hagerty told the television people he would let them know the decision. A few days later, Hagerty caught up with Eisenhower as the president headed back to his office after lunch and told him he was convinced that the lights would no longer be a problem. The president okayed letting the camera into the next day's news conference. Hagerty announced the decision at his briefing that afternoon before the conference. The response was vociferous, with the loudest protests coming from reporters for the three wire services. Years later, Hagerty remembered such questions as "Who's going to sponsor him? What beer is going to sponsor him?" Knowing that the networks were high-paying subscribers to the wire services, the press secretary suggested that the television people put in some calls to wire service executives. It worked. UP's Merriman Smith, the most adamant of the protesters, heard from his main office in New York and told Hagerty, "I'll shut up." [34]

The next day, January 19, there were 218 reporters in attendance, up from 177 and 194 at the previous two press conferences. Thirteen of them had to take seats in a high balcony that surrounded the room on four sides. In the glow of six lights from a scaffolding in the rear of the room, Eisenhower opened by saying, "I see we are trying a new experiment this morning. I hope it doesn't prove to be a disturbing influence."

With the rule against direct quotation scrapped, Hagerty hired a stenographic firm to provide quick transcripts for reporters. He reserved only the right to edit the transcripts. Fourteen answers were edited out, including one in which the president could not recall the name of the commissioner of labor statistics and one in which he referred to Indochina as Indonesia. NBC filmed the conference on a pool basis for all the networks. Reporters in the back of the room found the whir of the cameras a minor background noise; for those in the front, it took an effort to hear them at all. Eisenhower told Hagerty afterward that they had not bothered him. The *New York Times* found the president less openly irritable than usual and "plainly conscious

. . . that he was, so to speak, 'on the air.' " More reporters than usual seemed to be wearing blue shirts, favored over white by television technicians.[35]

A few hours after the news conference, Hagerty watched a show-ing of it in a Washington television studio. CBS was the first network to broadcast the conference, relaying it to stations throughout the East from its Washington affiliate, WTOP-TV, at 7 P.M. EST. ABC carried the program at 9:30 and NBC from 11:30 to midnight, with West Coast stations refilming it for broadcast later in the evening. The broadcasts were not sponsored. "All in all it was a good day," said Hagerty, emphasizing the thought in his diary with four exclamation points. Reading the *Times* the next morning, the press secretary, not noted for his sense of humor, found the paper's main story on the conference "sort of a snide one." He was cheered by the more favor-able columns of Washington bureau chief Arthur Krock and television critic Jack Gould. Krock wrote that Eisenhower "discussed a wide range of subjects with the ease of a man who knew what he was talking about" despite "the glaring and unforgiving eyes of motion-picture cameras." Gould said fears of a circus atmosphere had proved unjusti-fied and the program had given "a new insight into President Eisen-hower's personality on the TV screen." "There could be some unhappy Democrats this morning after last night's TV program," the television critic added.[36]

Hagerty would continue to resist live television, arguing that the Treaty Room was too small for the necessary equipment.[37] Before each conference, he would check every camera to make sure it was not too noisy.[38] James Reston of the *Times* would question "whether the presidential press conference, as now conducted, can be reconciled with the complexity and menace of the events of today."[39] But tele-vised press conferences, in one form or another, had become a fixture of White House life. Actor Montgomery, reviewing the transcripts of televised and untelevised conferences and comparing them with the news coverage, concluded that coverage was better when all media were represented. "Apparently," the television adviser said, "reporters made a greater effort to be accurate when the cameras were making a visual record." Four months after the first televised meeting, the edit-ing was abandoned and complete tapes and transcripts were released.[40]

Hagerty held two press conferences of his own each day and put out the president's list of engagements a day in advance, a practice later press secretaries were to follow. He and Snyder alternated, a week at a time, in taking night calls at home. He attended weekly meetings between the president and Republican congressional leaders. He sat in on cabinet meetings "whenever I thought I had to," but most of the time he did not. He avoided National Security Council discussions of government secrets because "if I know about them too soon, there's always the chance I might give something away by a hint or a suggestion."[41] His office was thirty steps from Eisenhower's, with another seven steps to the president's desk. "Don't hesitate to walk in on me," Ike told him.[42]

He was adept at providing such trivia as details of Eisenhower's golf game, listing the sixteen courses he had played while president and providing his score and the par score for most of them.[43] Reporters often felt, however, that they were being shut out from more important information. "Jim Hagerty holds a lens ground to his own prescription over the White House—and outsiders have little choice but to look through it," said one.[44] Another criticized "his narrow concept of his job—to make his boss and the Republicans look good" without considering "the interests of the country and his duty to the public."[45]

No one could deny that Hagerty was a master of logistics. Eisenhower traveled abroad far more than any previous president. His mileage for 1959 alone was more than seventy-seven thousand miles. On all trips, Hagerty preceded him to make arrangements for press coverage. He checked to see whether the telephones were good enough for broadcast use, whether reporters would need transformers to use their electric shavers, where the cable offices were, whether correspondents would have to pay cash to move their copy, where they could get their laundry done, and what kind of clothing would be suitable for the climate. "Any press secretary who has gone through that experience could very easily handle the Barnum and Bailey circus anywhere in the world," he said. For a trip to India, he gave reporters a mimeographed brochure of thirty-seven single-spaced pages giving the president's schedule hour by hour.[46] It was not much different on domestic trips. Riding into Philadelphia with Hagerty on one campaign visit, the former World War II commander looked over the itinerary his aide had prepared and cracked that it took up seven times as many pages as the plan for the invasion of Normandy.[47]

Perhaps because he had far more political experience than Eisenhower, Hagerty became a more dominant force in the White House than any previous press secretary. If a crisis arose during the night,

Hagerty decided whether the president should be awakened. If a statement was to be made, he would often read it in front of the cameras. "It was sometimes a little hard to tell whether he was president or whether Eisenhower was president," said Richard L. Strout.

The *Department of State Bulletin,* a weekly collection of important statements on foreign affairs, quoted Hagerty five times in the first eighteen months of the administration. Short had a statement published in the bulletin only once and Ross never did, although both were more knowledgeable than Hagerty on foreign policy.[48] More and more, the president's spokesman began sentences "We do not believe" or "We never thought," establishing a pattern that his successors would follow as the press secretary became increasingly a voice of the administration.[49] Hagerty advised Eisenhower on fiscal policy, urging, against the advice of other administration officials, that the president should veto appropriation bills and insist spending be reduced. In an eight-page memo as 1958 drew to a close, he advised his boss to "follow the old Roman idea of 'The Tribune of the People,' " and said that Lyndon Johnson and his allies in the Senate "should be slapped down hard—whenever they try—for political purposes—to encroach on the president's prerogatives." In advice that the president was to follow, he urged Eisenhower to "personally participate more in foreign affairs" by taking trips outside the United States. He outlined "sort of a schedule of 'trips' I would like to see you make as president." It included India, the Philippines, Formosa, Japan, Korea, Europe, Russia, Africa, the Near East, and what Hagerty called "South and Latin America."[50] Eisenhower visited all of them except Russia, the Middle East, and Japan. A planned trip to Tokyo during Eisenhower's last year in office was canceled by the Japanese after an advance party including Hagerty was surrounded and pelted with stones by anti-U.S. demonstrators. A widely distributed picture showed Hagerty taking pictures with a small camera as the crowd rocked his car. Eisenhower was amused to learn later that the camera had no film in it.[51]

Discussing the question of presidential illness with Hagerty, the president dwelt on the near-paralysis of government that followed Woodrow Wilson's hushed-up stroke in 1919. "Jim, don't let that happen to me," his press secretary remembered him saying.[52]

When the issue became a reality with the 1955 heart attack, Hagerty was at home on vacation from the Denver White House. In that afternoon's *Washington Star,* he read a two-column box near the bottom of the front page quoting his deputy, Snyder, as saying the president had a "digestive upset." He thought little of it, knowing that Eisenhower had a sensitive stomach. Receiving his deputy's call saying it was a heart attack, he was at first skeptical, and questioned Snyder about the change in diagnosis.

The president had felt ill during the night, Snyder said. On instructions from White House physician Howard Snyder, who was no relation, he had told reporters it was an upset stomach. Besieged by reporters seeking more details, Murray Snyder had telephoned the president's secretary, Ann Whitman. She called the doctor, who said to tell the journalists the president's condition was not serious. Murray Snyder did so. Dr. Snyder had been giving Eisenhower standard emergency treatment for a heart attack, but said he withheld the truth to give the president rest and quiet and avoid emotional turmoil, thus limiting the heart damage. That afternoon, as Murray Snyder and Ann Whitman were having lunch with other White House aides at a Denver restaurant, the doctor called again. The president had suffered a "mild anterior coronary thrombosis."[53]

Snyder assured Hagerty that a cardiogram had confirmed the heart attack. He said he was rounding up reporters to make the announcement to them. "How long have I got?" asked Hagerty. "I think you have half an hour." "Go ahead," Hagerty said.[54]

Leaving his radio tuned to *Monitor,* the NBC weekend news program, Hagerty started making telephone calls. The first person he called was Vice President Nixon. "Dick, you'd better sit down," he said. On the phone at his home in the nearby Spring Valley neighborhood, Nixon was silent for several seconds—so long that Hagerty thought they had been disconnected—and then suggested withholding the announcement until they were sure. "We are absolutely sure," said Hagerty. "Let me know where you can be reached at all times." A few minutes later, continuing to make calls, he heard Ray Scherer announce the bulletin on the radio.[55]

After a very early morning call to Nixon to tell him the situation was unchanged, Hagerty boarded a Military Air Transport Service Constellation for a 4 A.M. flight to Denver. Dr. Thomas Mattingly, a Walter Reed Army Hospital physician carrying Eisenhower's medical records, joined him. Merriman Smith, one of many newsmen who called him during the night, had asked to go along, and was invited. Hagerty appreciated the fact that Smith, although an aggressive newsman, refrained from grilling Mattingly about the president's physical condition during the five-hour flight.[56]

The plane was scheduled to land at Lowry, but was diverted to Denver's Stapleton Airport because of torrential rain. After a rough landing, Hagerty was taken in a waiting car to Fitzsimons General Hospital.

"Look, I've got to have a bulletin right now," he told the doctors. They objected, but agreed after Hagerty put it as an order from the president and told them what Ike had said about Wilson. There was also an argument, which went on for "quite some time," before the doctors agreed to hold a press conference.

Eisenhower later said that when he saw Hagerty, two days after being stricken, he instructed him, "Tell the truth, the whole truth; don't conceal anything." Hagerty, in his diary for that day, recounted their conversation but did not mention any such instruction.[57]

At any rate, Hagerty answered reporters' questions in the Lowry pressroom every day at 7:00 and 11:30 A.M., and usually again around 3:30 P.M., with a final wrap-up at 9:00 P.M. He had the eminent heart specialist, Dr. Paul Dudley White, mark 500 pertinent pages of his 1,128-page book *Heart Disease* in red, bought twenty copies, marked them similarly, and put them in the press room.

On the second day, at White's suggestion, he included in his bulletin the fact that Eisenhower had a bowel movement. The president thought this was carrying realism too far, and many members of the public agreed with him, but White told a news conference it was an important first sign of recovery.[58]

Hagerty's sterling performance was marred only by his inability to resist doing a little stage-managing to boost the boss's image. When the attorney general, Herbert Brownell, visited the president at the hospital, Hagerty scheduled a news conference for Brownell to announce approval of an ambitious program of federal court reform. Much of the program had been announced earlier, and skeptics doubted that the stricken president really went over it in detail in a twenty-five-minute bedside visit. One reporter spotted Hagerty handing a cabinet member a statement on the president's appearance before the man entered the hospital room. "The president was getting better and we wanted to show he was taking up the reins," said his press secretary.[59]

Eisenhower indeed bounced back from his heart attack, and announced on February 29, 1956, that he would be a candidate for reelection. But two months before the Republican National Convention, he fell ill again.

This time Hagerty was less forthcoming. About 7:45 in the morning of June 8, Dr. Snyder called Adams to say the president had digestive problems and the scheduled cabinet meeting should be canceled. At 8:50 A.M., Hagerty told reporters the president had an "upset stomach and headache." At noon, he said the illness had been diagnosed as ileitis, an inflammation of an intestinal valve. Eisenhower was taken by ambulance to Walter Reed Hospital, followed by Hagerty and a press contingent that kept vigil into the night. A bulletin said there was a partial obstruction of the small intestine. At 2:15 A.M., Hagerty announced that surgery would be performed immediately. Hagerty, Adams, and Gen. Andrew Goodpaster, the White House staff secretary, stood in a hospital corridor watching through an open door as surgeons operated on the president. At 5:11 A.M., Hagerty said the president was in excellent condition after an hour and fifty-three minutes on the operating table. Subsequent bulletins were reassuring.[60]

Hagerty bombarded reporters with encouraging minutiae. The president had taken his first steps. He had signed twenty-seven papers. He had eaten a soft-boiled egg and buttered toast. Hagerty's reports were so soothing that Richard Strout, writing under the pseudonym "T. R. B." in the *New Republic,* dubbed them "the ileitis-is-good-for-you pitch." John S. Knight of the Knight papers, a staunch supporter of the Eisenhower-Nixon ticket in 1952, editorially denounced the White House's "Ike's-as-good-as-ever" theme. Hagerty, on the defensive, said, "A presidential heart attack is the property of the people. But we did not consider the ileitis something that endangered the president's life."[61]

On November 25, 1957, just a little more than a year after his reelection, Eisenhower became dizzy while trying to sign papers at his desk. Unable to hold his pen, he summoned Ann Whitman, but found himself unable to summon the words to tell her what had happened. She called Goodpaster, who guided the president to the White House residence and got him to bed. Doctors concluded he had suffered an occlusion of a small blood vessel in the brain, a condition commonly called a stroke.[62]

Hagerty was in Paris making arrangements for coverage of Eisenhower's planned attendance at a NATO meeting. In charge in his absence was his deputy, Ann Wheaton, a former political reporter for the *Knickerbocker Press* in Albany who had succeeded Murray Snyder six months before. Despite the diagnosis of a minor stroke, she told reporters that "the president suffered a chill and the doctors have ordered him to bed." It took repeated questioning to elicit from her that Eisenhower was under mild sedation. At 8:55 a.m. the next day, she announced that the president was resting comfortably, had a good breakfast, and was progressing very well. She couldn't say whether he had a fever or what he had for breakfast. An hour and a half later, she said the doctors were making a further evaluation. Asked if it were anything more serious than a chill, she said, "I don't know anything about it now."

At 2:58 P.M., facing what the official transcript described as "an avalanche of reporters," Wheaton handed out a medical statement by Dr. Snyder and Gen. Leonard Heaton of Walter Reed Hospital. The statement said their further evaluation "confirms our original diagnosis that the president suffered an occlusion of a small branch of the middle cerebral artery." Asked to interpret the medical language, Wheaton first said it referred to "a form of heart attack, as I understand it," but later said the heart was not involved. To repeated questions, she said she did not know whether it was a stroke.

Whatever it was, she said she was not aware of the original diagnosis when she described it as a chill. That night, Charles Roberts, Washington bureau chief for *Newsweek,* called Wheaton to ask who was in charge during the president's illness. He said she could not answer.[63]

Adams, noting that Wheaton was trying to pacify reporters "without a definitive medical report to give them," told Goodpaster to summon Hagerty home from Paris.[64] The press secretary returned at midnight and told reporters the president had a light supper and watched television for two hours before going to sleep. At 8:15 A.M., he told them that the president was up and had shaved himself, that he normally used a safety razor, and that he breakfasted on a half grapefruit, creamed chipped beef, toast and honey, and Sanka. He declined to go into detail about Eisenhower's difficulty in speaking. He would not call the president's illness a stroke, although other doctors consulted by reporters did not hesitate to do so.

There was confusion about whether Eisenhower would go to the NATO meeting. A State Department announcement seemed to indicate he would not, but Hagerty said no decision had been made. By 10:45 A.M. Hagerty could say that the president had signed twelve documents and initialed one. He produced a photograph of one of the signatures. *Newsweek's* Roberts commented that a "few simple facts from a man who had talked to the president—a man we knew to be truthful" were "better than a 1,000-word medical communiqué."[65] Eisenhower attended the NATO meeting as scheduled and held a press conference, his first since the stroke, after his return. The Associated Press reported him "ruddy as of old," but the United Press said he was pale and "occasionally appeared to be having trouble finding the right word."[66]

The old pro was in charge again when Hagerty returned to replace the inexperienced and flustered Wheaton. Still, although there was ample information about the president signing papers, eating breakfast, shaving himself, and walking around, there was little in the way of detail about his illness. In this as in other matters, one reporter may have spoken for many when he said he found himself being told more and more about less and less.[67]

8

Entertaining the Press

PROMPTLY AT THIRTY SECONDS AFTER 6:00 P.M. on March 23, 1961, John F. Kennedy walked briskly from a State Department waiting room onto an auditorium stage and looked out over row upon row of reporters.

Over them, not at them. Kennedy's gaze was fixed intently on the red lights of a television camera on a platform between the twelfth and fifteenth rows of coral and black-trimmed plastic seats. There were two cameras on the platform, but he knew the glowing lights meant that this one was running.

The new president, barely two months into his administration, had a statement to make about the "potentially dangerous" situation in the little-known Southeast Asian kingdom of Laos, where combat specialists from North Vietnam were assisting communist insurgents. He was making it, not to a select group of Washington journalists, but to the American people.

CBS correspondent George Herman, seated in the auditorium, was struck with admiration and astonishment at seeing "for the first time . . . a president of the United States do something that was so professional, from a television man's point of view."

A few seats away, Peter Lisagor of the *Chicago Daily News* got an entirely different impression. To Lisagor, the president's demeanor meant that print reporters "became spear carriers in a great televised opera. We were props in a show, in a performance."[1]

The responses of the two seasoned newsmen to that performance were symptomatic of a debate that raged in both the administration and the journalistic fraternity, and would persist for years.

Pierre Salinger, the chubby former San Francisco newspaperman who was Kennedy's press secretary in the 1960 presidential campaign and followed him to the White House, first broached the idea of live television a few weeks after the election.

Salinger was something new in presidential press secretaries. Brash and irreverent, he made headlines as a roly-poly epicure who, ordered by his boss to set a good example by taking part in a fifty-mile hike to promote physical fitness, dropped out with aches and blisters after the first six miles. He was the figure of fun who showed up in Bermuda shorts to brief reporters in Palm Beach and was told by Kennedy, "Get back into long pants," who wore colorful vests and party hats in his White House office, who hit the clubhouse with his drive when he and the president played golf.

Inside the White House, the picture was different. Salinger was a press secretary who, in two major crises involving Fidel Castro's Cuba, was kept in the dark by his boss, at least until the last minute. Reporters, accustomed to the brisk efficiency of Hagerty, described Salinger in such terms as "an amiable water boy . . . sloppy with a glass," "poor on details," "imprecise," "often unsure of his facts," "mediocre," a "sort of a peripheral guy" who was responsible for "numerous clerical and factual mistakes." Even the *New York Times*'s hard-bitten Bill Lawrence, who came to like Salinger and admire his wit, conceded that he was "sloppy after a mechanical marvel like Hagerty." The historian Arthur M. Schlesinger Jr., serving as a special assistant to Kennedy, summed up the press secretary's job in a terse sentence: "Pierre Salinger entertained the press with jocular daily briefings."

Sometimes, the press was not entertained. After too many of Salinger's answers started with, "I believe," a veteran of the White House press corps barked at him, "I don't want to know what you believe, I want to know what the facts are."[2]

Salinger was not a Kennedy insider, neither one of the intellectuals the president recruited from academia nor one of the "Irish Mafia" who followed him from the rough-and-tumble political wars of Boston. He was born in San Francisco in 1925 to a Jewish mining engineer who died when he was fourteen and a French American journalist of the Roman Catholic faith. The future press secretary became a child prodigy on the piano, giving his first concert at the age of six. After wartime service in the navy, he became night editor of the *San Francisco Chronicle* at twenty-five. He broke into politics as a press agent in California campaigns, then moved to *Collier's* magazine. In 1956, he was working on an article about corruption in the Teamsters Union when he got a call from his editor telling him not to bother; *Collier's*, a leading American magazine in decades past, had fallen on hard times and was folding. From major investigative work for the once-proud *Collier's*, the down-on-his-luck journalist went to a lackluster job as assistant news editor for *House and Home*. During his Teamsters investigation, however, he had crossed paths with Robert Kennedy, then chief counsel of the Senate Rackets Committee, which was also looking into the Teamsters. Kennedy offered him a job, and Mr. Salinger came to Washington. He got along well with Kennedy, but it was quickly clear that his laid-back California manner did not fit with the lifestyle of Massachusetts millionaires. Invited to dinner at the Kennedys' Virginia home, he was asked what he would like to drink and startled his host by asking for wine. Kennedy did not keep any on hand, and was startled again when Salinger went to his car and brought back a bottle of a good California red.[3]

When Sen. John F. Kennedy began building his 1960 campaign staff, Salinger was tapped for the press secretary's job, working in a leased office over a garage on Constitution Avenue. "I felt very much like an outsider during those first months," Salinger said. After a letter about Kennedy's campaign plans got out before he was ready to announce as a candidate, a colleague remembered the press secretary shaking his head and saying, "I don't know if I'm going to be around here much longer." On the road, he gained confidence, introducing instant transcripts of speeches and installing telephone cars in motorcades so that wire service reporters could file running accounts of the candidate's reception on arrival at campaign stops. Still, he was unsure whether he would get the White House assignment, and troubled by rumors that Kennedy would choose a big name from the news media. He jumped at the job when Kennedy casually offered it to him in a walk across the lawn at the Kennedy family compound on Cape Cod the day after the election. As his second in command, Salinger chose Andrew Hatcher, former editor of an African American newspaper in San Francisco, who had assisted him in the campaign. Hatcher was the first African American to serve as an assistant White House press secretary.[4]

When Salinger came up with the idea of live television for press conferences, Kennedy had his doubts about it. He feared overexposure, was worried that the networks might not provide time that was worth up to $100,000 an hour, and correctly anticipated stiff opposition from the pencil press. Finally, he told Salinger, "Start it moving with the networks. But let's hold off on the announcement until we know they'll buy it."[5]

Kennedy didn't need to worry about the networks, but his other concerns were nothing compared with those of some of his advisers in the weeks ahead. Dean Rusk, the secretary of state–designate, was particularly vehement against live television, fearing that a mistake or slip of the tongue could trigger an international crisis. The national security adviser, McGeorge Bundy, and Theodore Sorensen, who at the time was in line to be CIA director, agreed with Rusk. Appointments Secretary Kenneth O'Donnell, a longtime Kennedy aide often to be at odds with the upstart Salinger, was also "not wildly enthusiastic about it."[6]

Kennedy was confident of his ability to handle tricky foreign policy questions, and told Salinger in Palm Beach, Florida, two days after Christmas, "This is the right thing. We should be able to go around the newspapers if that becomes necessary. But, beyond that, I don't know how we can justify keeping TV out if it wants in." Salinger met with network representatives for ninety minutes that afternoon and told reporters, "There was agreement . . . that there will be live television and radio coverage of some White House press conferences."[7]

Print reporters, lounging around the pressroom in the Palm Beach Towers in bathing trunks and shorts, responded with the anticipated scorn. What about the long-standing rule that nobody was to leave a press conference until it was over? After all, millions would now be watching on television, so reporters should be free to go file their stories in a timely manner. The press secretary stood fast. It would be disruptive to have reporters walking in and out during the question-and-answer period. The *Times*' gravelly-voiced Lawrence told Salinger he was getting "deeper and deeper into matters about which you know absolutely nothing."[8]

Columnist James Reston, sharing Rusk's fears of a catastrophic slip of the tongue, called live television in the press conference room "the goofiest idea since the hula hoop," a fad of the 1950s in which people twirled their hips to rotate a plastic circlet. His paper, the *Times,* ran a cartoon of Kennedy and Salinger, against a backdrop of an FDR fireside chat, saying, "It might succeed even better on live TV." Some journalists said that with press conferences on live television, reporters would cover them by watching the tube. In fact, many news organizations did write running accounts of the conferences this way, but most also sent reporters to ask questions and do follow-up stories. Salinger dismissed the gripes, predicting, "TV is here to stay."[9]

William Wilson, a New York television packager who produced Kennedy's campaign appearances, was now to advise on televising press conferences. He scouted three other government auditoriums before settling on the 75 x 100-foot theater in the new State Department building, five minutes from the White House. Salinger had already decided that the Indian Treaty Room was too small, and Wilson reported that the General Services Administration auditorium was also. He rejected those at the Commerce and Interior Departments as "dingy and poorly arranged." [10]

The TV adviser recommended keeping the Eisenhower-Hagerty rule that reporters must identify themselves, arguing that viewers would want to know what newspapers the questioners represented. Salinger scrapped the rule, saying there was "no good reason for permitting reporters to advertise their affiliation on television." [11]

The one thing Wilson didn't like about the gleaming State Department auditorium was its size. With a seating capacity of eight hundred, it was about five times as big as the Indian Treaty Room. Wilson proposed a permanent curtain on a ceiling track, masking the back half of the room to "help recover some of the intimacy" of the old-fashioned chamber Truman and Eisenhower had used. This did not wash with reporters. True, the president's platform would be a low, arena-style stage, unlike the high proscenium-arch stages Wilson had turned down. Still, it was a stage; even reporters in the front row would be separated from the president by a wide well. Although not as cozy as the Oval Office, the Treaty Room had, they argued, enabled reporters to "feel the heat of Mr. Eisenhower's anger," required them to brace themselves "against the glint in Mr. Truman's eye," and put them close enough to the president "to reach his pulse." [12]

Pulse or no pulse, Kennedy made the State Department setting his own; future presidents would choose to hold their news conferences in the White House instead.

In the weeks after the election, Salinger visited the White House for three transition meetings with Hagerty. When he arrived again, in a rented morning coat about two hours after Kennedy's inauguration, he encountered, as all White House staffers in a new administration do, empty desks and file cabinets. "It's a place without a history," he thought.[13]

Across the West Wing lobby from his office, the fastidious press secretary found the White House pressroom "a disgrace." Paper littered the floors and desks, and the odor from the ancient spittoons was rank. He told White House carpenters to partition the room into small compartments. Disdainful reporters put up signs reading "Pierre Salinger Loan Company." [14]

A more popular Salinger initiative was his announcement that the White House would be an "open beat," with reporters free to make their own appointments for interviews with presidential aides. Under Hagerty, such calls had been screened by the press office, and the press secretary sometimes sat in on the interviews. Most correspondents applauded the change. Salinger said those who were unhappy were lazy and wanted the press office to do their work for them. Sometimes the beat was too open for his liking; he was heard to complain that Appointments Secretary O'Donnell and others in the inner circle arranged interviews with the president behind his back. [15]

Despite their objections, 418 reporters, 107 more than had ever attended an Eisenhower press conference, crowded into the auditorium for Kennedy's premiere at 6 P.M. on January 25, five days and six hours after he had been sworn in. He fielded thirty-one questions in the thirty-eight-minute session, about half again as many as Eisenhower, primarily because his answers were more succinct. He surprised reporters with a reply about a Portuguese cruise ship that had been seized at sea in an act of piracy. His questioner had not asked exactly where the ship was, but Kennedy said that at 4:10 in the afternoon, less than two hours earlier, it had been about six hundred miles north of the mouth of the Amazon River, at 10 degrees 35 minutes north, 45 degrees 32 minutes west, proceeding at fifteen knots on a course of 117 degrees. At another point, he talked about resuming nuclear "tests" when he meant "talks," but newsmen passed it off as a slip of the tongue. Riding back to the White House in the presidential limousine, Kennedy told Salinger, "I thought that went very well. How many people do you think saw it?" The answer was about 60 million. [16]

Kennedy's mastery of detail was the product of both a keen mind and an elaborate system of preparation. The afternoon before a conference, Salinger met with departmental information officers and produced a list of twenty to thirty questions most likely to be asked and, on the touchier ones, a suggested answer and background briefing. He gave this material to Kennedy to study before going to bed. Next morning, at an hour-long breakfast with key presidential advisers beginning at 8:30 in the family dining room of the mansion, Salinger sat across the table from the president and fed the questions to him. Sometimes the president would say, "I can handle that one—let's move on." More often he gave his answer and invited the relevant aide

9. John F. Kennedy was the first president to hold regular live televised news conferences. Press Secretary Pierre Salinger and his deputy, Andrew Hatcher, joined Kennedy in the State Department auditorium. *Courtesy John F. Kennedy Library.*

or cabinet member to respond. If the adviser suggested he answer with a "no comment," his response was usually along the lines of "Hell! I'm having a press conference, and I've got to say something!" Sometimes, he gave irreverent replies that would not have been suitable for television. He once joked that it was dangerous to have these in the back of his mind, but if he was tempted to use one at a real-life press conference he never gave way to the temptation. If he needed more information, Salinger would look it up for him and fill him in after lunch. About ten minutes before press conference time, they would arrive at the State Department, where Rusk and his top aides would brief the president on the latest State Department cables.[17]

Kennedy had a special interest in foreign policy, and his press secretary, who spoke passable French as well as good English, paid increased attention to foreign reporters. He added Agence France-Presse and the British agency Reuters to the domestic wire services

monitored in his office. He broke new ground by including a correspondent for the Soviet agency, Tass, in the pool of reporters covering
the visit of a Soviet official with the president. He hired Jay Gildner, a
United States Information Agency press officer in Toronto, to work
with the foreign press. After Gildner failed to satisfy the demanding
Jacqueline Kennedy with his handling of coverage of her trip to India,
he moved back to USIA and was replaced by State Department information officer Malcolm Kilduff.

Gildner was not the only White House aide to have his troubles
dealing with Mrs. Kennedy, who called female journalists "the har-
pies" and said her policy toward reporters was "minimum information
given with maximum politeness." Salinger found that "handling Mrs.
Kennedy's press was not the easiest problem." She graciously acknowledged the difficulty, presenting him with an autographed photograph
inscribed "To Pierre, from the greatest cross you have to bear." [18]

Twice each day, Salinger met in his office with newsmen in what
came to be called by the military term "briefings"; previous press
secretaries had called such sessions news conferences or press conferences. Salinger's were scheduled for 11 A.M. and 4 P.M., but frequently
were late. Up to a hundred would attend, jostling for room amid the
desks, filing cabinets, and bookcases that crammed the meager space.
The new press secretary earned a reputation for guessing at answers,
and sometimes guessing wrong. An aide in the press office, required
to attend the briefings to keep abreast of what was happening, was
frustrated because Salinger would promise something and then the
staff would "spend an awful lot of time explaining why we didn't have
it ready." [19]

Kennedy was the first president to assign to his press secretary
the official responsibility for setting the information policies of the
government. Like Steve Early, Salinger was influential in the naming
of departmental information officers. Unlike Early, he met with them
weekly "to agree on the form and procedure" for releasing information about their departments. The practice got both the press secretary
and his boss into trouble. Two weeks into the new administration,
Editor & Publisher listed Salinger's weekly coordinating meetings as
part of a "disturbing trend" toward tighter control on government
information. Salinger added fuel to the fire on January 25 with his first
speech as press secretary, telling the National Press Club, "We intend
to have an open information policy within the confines of national
security." At the president's first press conference five hours later, a

reporter asked about Salinger's indication that "there might be a need for tightening of information" on security matters. Kennedy backed up his press secretary, telling reporters, with millions watching on television, "We just have to wait and try to work together and see if we can provide as much information as we can. . . . It's a question of trying to work out a solution to a sensitive matter."[20]

Kennedy also was accused of news management for announcing at the same press conference that the Soviet Union had released two United States Air Force pilots held for six months after their reconnaissance plane was shot down over Soviet territory. The president commended the *New York Herald Tribune* for withholding the story because the airmen's departure from Moscow had been delayed, and publication could have jeopardized their safety. "In doing this," he said, "the *Herald Tribune* prevented the violation of an agreement between the United States and the USSR which might have had regrettable repercussions." Assuming this agreement dealt with publication of the news, *Editor & Publisher* asked, "On what ground and by what right does this administration commit the press and communications media of this country to any particular performance in the handling of information?" Salinger replied that the Russians insisted on simultaneous announcement of the story as a condition of the release.[21]

On a less momentous matter, Salinger raised hackles in the press by telling reporters that he would not always disclose when Kennedy was leaving the White House or where he was going. He maintained the president was entitled to his privacy and reporters could maintain a twenty-four-hour watch if they wished to. Salinger suspected that the president had mistresses, as later came to be known. He has said he did not know who they might be.[22]

Far more serious disputes over the administration's handling of news were in the offing. On a mid-April afternoon in 1961, Kennedy telephoned his press secretary from Glen Ora, the country home he was leasing in the Virginia hunt country. "I want you to stick close to home tonight, Pierre," he said. "You may have some inquiries from the press about a military affair in the Caribbean. If you do, just say that you know only what you've read in the newspapers." That, Salinger was to say later, "was to claim an enormous amount of knowledge." But he could say it truthfully. Despite newspaper stories suggesting that something was afoot, he had not been told of any of the meetings that led to the disastrous invasion of Cuba by a fourteen-hundred-man U.S.-trained emigré force at the Bay of Pigs. His first firm word came from George Herman of CBS, who called him at 6:30 in the morning and asked if he knew that Cuba had been invaded. When he got to the office, he told reporters, "Our only information comes from the wire service stories we have read." Later, he responded to questions with "I wouldn't have any comment on it" or "I have no idea." When the invasion collapsed after only three days, Salinger protested vigorously to the president that he should have been informed of what was going on.[23]

At his next news conference, Kennedy told reporters, "I do not think that any useful national purpose would be served by my going further into the Cuban question this morning." When one reporter raised a question anyway, he replied that the facts would come out in due time. Back in his office, he raged, "What do they want me to do —give them the roll call vote? . . . The publishers have to understand that we're never more than a miscalculation away from war and that there are things we're doing that we just can't talk about." Salinger had a suggestion. Kennedy was to speak six days later to the Bureau of Advertising of the American Newspaper Publishers Association in New York. "Why not lay it on the line there?" The timing could hardly have been worse.[24]

Even before the failed expedition in Cuba, there had been grumbling about administration information policies. At a meeting of the American Society of Newspaper Editors, Indianapolis publisher Eugene Pulliam told Salinger, "We honestly feel that much information is being withheld, not for security reasons, but to protect individuals' mistakes." At the Pentagon, an admiral had been ordered to revise a speech questioning the usefulness of negotiations with the Soviets. Information about U.S. tracking of a Soviet man-in-space shot was restricted. Usually available details about the defense budget were withheld. "There's an air of secrecy, of censorship, of arbitrary rulings," the privately published weekly *Navy Times* complained.[25] The publishers gathered at the Waldorf-Astoria were in no mood for the lecture Kennedy gave them.

Kennedy said he had no intention of establishing an Office of War Information, as in World War II, "to govern the flow of news." But he added: "Every newspaper now asks itself, with respect to every story: 'Is it news?'. . . In the absence of open war, they are considering only the tests of journalism and not the tests of national security, and my question now is whether additional tests should not now be adopted."

The answer was no. In editorials throughout the country, the president was accused of advocating wartime censorship in peacetime and of trying to blame the failure of the invasion on reports some newspapers had published on the training of the rebel brigade. Even Jonathan Daniels, the one-time Truman press spokesman, now editor of the Raleigh, North Carolina, *News and Observer,* said, "President Kennedy should be thinking more about how the free, informed American people can contribute to the struggle, not how 'greater official secrecy' can be imposed upon them with the connivance of reporters and officials together." [26]

When Kennedy invited eight top newspaper executives to meet with him May 9, he found them unyielding. Felix McKnight of the *Dallas Times-Herald,* president of the American Society of Newspaper Editors, said there was no agreement on the need for greater restraint in covering national security affairs, and he saw no need to set up machinery to deal with the problem, as Kennedy had suggested in his speech. Salinger told reporters the seventy-minute meeting had been "a healthy discussion," but later pronounced it "a total failure." [27]

Salinger's relations with the president were businesslike, but informal. "I never wrote him a memo the whole time I was press secretary," he said. "I never got one from him either. We would see each other six or eight times a day." The relationship hit a rocky spot late in February when Salinger, attempting to smooth over a minor flap concerning a White House chef, blurted out that the seventy domestic servants in the mansion had signed pledges not to write about their experiences with the Kennedys. The story made headlines suggesting that the first couple were imposing unreasonable conditions of employment on their servants, and the press secretary was summoned to the Oval Office for a forty-five-minute tongue-lashing. [28]

A graver slip of the tongue got Salinger into hotter water on May 31, 1961. The day before, Gen. Rafael Leonidas Trujillo Molina, the absolute ruler of the Dominican Republic for more than three decades, had been shot to death while being driven to a tryst with his mistress in Ciudad Trujillo. Early in the morning, the first report of his death reached Washington, which had severed diplomatic relations with the Trujillo regime in August because of human rights abuses and aggravation of tensions in the Caribbean. Other reports came in from the still-functioning United States consular office in Ciudad Trujillo, and from other governments, intelligence sources, and travelers who had stopped briefly at the Dominican capital's airport. But still, there had been no official announcement. Kennedy, in Paris for meetings with European allies, was kept informed.[29]

Salinger was struggling into white tie and tails for a state dinner when the telephone rang in his suite at the Hotel Crillon. It was O'Donnell, who was with Kennedy at the president's guest quarters at the Quai d'Orsay. Rusk would not be arriving the next day as expected, he told Salinger, "because of the situation in the Dominican Republic." "What situation?" asked Salinger.

"General Trujillo has been assassinated," O'Donnell replied. He apparently did not add that the report was unconfirmed. Salinger, assuming it had already been announced, did not check it out further. When he stopped by the press room and was asked whether Rusk was coming on schedule, he repeated what O'Donnell had told him.[30]

When Salinger arrived at the Quai d'Orsay to join the presidential party and told Kennedy what he had done, the president exploded in anger. "We now have later intelligence that Trujillo may not be dead," Kennedy said. Salinger, realizing that his job was on the line, said, "Mr. President, if he's not, I am." His next telephone call was from Rusk. The secretary of state, in his own words, "gave Pierre Salinger hell." Salinger recalled Rusk shouting over the transatlantic line, "Are you out of your mind? You have to straighten this out—and right now."

Rusk feared that Trujillo's son, Ramfis, who was in Paris, might hear the announcement as coming from Salinger and believe that the United States had something to do with the assassination. Moments later, Salinger got another call, from the press room. The Dominican government had announced the assassination. The crisis in the Dominican Republic continued, but the crisis for the president's press secretary was over.[31]

His stature in the White House rose as the months went on. "On balance, Salinger is functioning well in a difficult spot," said Merriman Smith. "He takes more telephone calls from working newsmen than any press secretary I've known." "This is a very important job, and not merely an automatic one," Kennedy told an interviewer. "He has to use a good deal of judgment."[32]

The job took on an unprecedented dimension after Salinger was asked by a television producer, a month before Kennedy was to meet with Soviet leader Nikita Khrushchev in Vienna, if he would take part in a debate about press freedom with top Russian journalists including Alexei Adzhubei, Khrushchev's son-in-law and the editor of the Soviet government organ *Izvestia*. Salinger agreed without much thought, believing the Soviets would never allow it to happen anyway. As it turned out, the suggestion led not only to a debate, but to plans for a series of Kennedy-Khrushchev television exchanges. Khrushchev canceled the exchanges after Kennedy announced that the United States planned to resume nuclear testing.

Meanwhile, at a lively party at his debate opponent's home in Virginia, Adzhubei had invited Salinger to visit him in Russia. Salinger thought he was just being polite, and made no commitments, but suggested to the president that he invite Adzhubei and his wife to lunch at the White House. At the lunch, Kennedy, knowing that "a meeting with Alexei Adzhubei was an indirect meeting with Nikita Khrushchev," announced that Salinger would be happy to accept the invitation. Conservative Republican Rep. Bruce Alger of Texas promptly denounced the notion of sending "a young and inexperienced White House publicity man" on a mission to Moscow. Ken O'Donnell told Salinger, "The announcement that you're going has already been a political minus for the president." There was also grumbling from middle-level officials at the State Department, and the president had doubts about the trip himself, particularly after Khrushchev's cancellation of the TV exchanges. He finally agreed to it after consultation with the State Department's top Soviet expert, Charles Bohlen. Defending the mission in a news conference, the president said, "I know there are some people who feel that Americans are always young and inexperienced, and foreigners are always able and tough and great negotiators. But I don't think the United States would have acquired its present position of leadership in the free world if that view were correct. . . . I don't think we should worry so much about Americans traveling abroad; I think they've acquitted themselves well and so will Mr. Salinger."

When the press secretary arrived at the Moscow airport on May 11, 1962, U.S. Ambassador Llewellyn Thompson told him he was going to meet not only with Adzhubei, but with Adzhubei's father-in-law. Khrushchev had invited him for a visit at his *dacha* outside Moscow. Their fourteen-hour meeting made Salinger the first press secretary ever to be a top-level diplomatic emissary, and provided Kennedy with useful insights into Khrushchev's thinking.[33]

The president needed the insights five months later when the Cuban missile crisis presented the Kennedy administration, and its press secretary, with their severest test.

On Tuesday, October 16, Kennedy told Salinger he anticipated that Rusk, Secretary of Defense Robert McNamara, United Nations Ambassador Adlai Stevenson, and the joint chiefs of staff would be visiting the White House throughout the week. "If the press tries to read something significant into it, you're to deny that anything special is going on," he said. Salinger did not pursue it.

On Friday, Kennedy left for a five-state political swing, to be capped by an appearance at the Seattle World's Fair. During a stop at Chicago's Sheraton-Blackstone Hotel, Salinger took a call from Carleton V. Kent of the *Chicago Sun Times*. Kent wanted comment on a report that the Eighteenth Parachute Corps was standing by for a jump into Cuba. Salinger went upstairs to see Kennedy. "Call Kent and tell him the report is all wrong," said the president.

The press secretary also went to O'Donnell, whose room was on the same floor as the president's; Salinger, the outsider, was one floor below.

"You're going to have to cut me in pretty quick," he told O'Donnell. "I'm flying blind with the press." O'Donnell advised him cryptically that the president might have to develop a cold. The next morning, Kennedy instructed his press secretary to tell reporters he was returning to Washington on the advice of the White House physician, Rear Adm. George C. Burkley, because he had an upper respiratory infection and was running a temperature of 99.2 degrees. Salinger relayed this word, but said to Kennedy on the flight back, "Mr. President, you don't have that bad a cold, do you?" "I've had worse," the president replied. "Then there's something else?" Kennedy's reply was curt, uninformative, and chilling.[34]

On the day Kennedy first alerted Salinger, he had just learned that a U.S. surveillance flight had taken photographs of Soviet medium-range missiles in Cuba and more advanced missile sites under construction. On Saturday, the day the president broke off his trip, he and his advisers decided to impose a naval quarantine, or blockade, to prevent shipments of arms into Cuban ports.

When the presidential helicopter arrived back at the White House, Kennedy took Salinger by the arm. "You'll be around?" he asked. Salinger nodded, and sent the rest of the staff home "to create the impression of routine Saturday activities." Still, Salinger had not been filled in on all the details. He saw McNamara and Attorney General Robert Kennedy slip in through a side door to converse with the president, but did not know until later that there were other callers from the State and Defense Departments and the White House staff. When David Wise of the *Herald Tribune* called to ask him why Rusk was canceling his speaking engagements for the week, he could honestly say, "I don't know." When an editor at the *Washington Post* noticed that the vice president, Lyndon Johnson, was flying back from Hawaii because of a cold and asked Salinger to explain the coincidence, he had no comment. Once again, Salinger had to dance a Cuban tango without having been taught the steps.[35]

On Sunday, he was finally briefed by Bundy. "The president's mood and events of the preceding week were no longer mysteries." That night, in a telephone call from his home, he set up a system by which he and the top information officers at the Pentagon and Foggy Bottom could all be on the telephone together at any time. "We were on the phone eighteen, twenty, twenty-two times a day during that thing," he said. He was now in on strategy sessions, but still answered questions with a "no comment." "I am not in charge of speculation," he told reporters. "That's your job."[36]

On Monday, October 22, in a televised address, the president told the nation that the purpose of the Soviet bases was clearly "to provide a nuclear strike capability against the Western Hemisphere" and the missiles were capable of striking Washington or any city in the southeastern United States. In the most chilling phrase in a speech fraught with menace, he said, "It shall be the policy of this nation to regard any nuclear missile launched from Cuba against any nation in the Western Hemisphere as an attack by the Soviet Union on the United States, requiring a full retaliatory response upon the Soviet Union."[37]

The press office went on twenty-four-hour duty. Salinger moved into the Claridge Hotel, near the White House. Either Hatcher or Kilduff spent each night in the office, catching naps on a cot. The day after the president's speech, Salinger, accompanied by top information officers of the State Department and the Pentagon, met with news executives in his office. He handed them a memorandum asking newspapers, magazines, and broadcasters to "exercise caution and discretion" in reporting twelve categories of information "considered vital to our national security." The memo listed such things as plans for employment of the armed forces, estimates of U.S. capability, intelligence information, details on troop movements, and the degree of alert of military forces. Salinger said he detected "a certain hostility on the part of some of the press representatives there," particularly AP General Manager Wes Gallagher and William McAndrew, news director of NBC. The National Security Council had refused to allow reporters to sail from Norfolk on ships destined for the blockade, and the newsmen proposed as a compromise that one pool reporter be allowed on each vessel. "They just simply refused to have any correspondents anywhere," said Gallagher. "They thought they could run a private war."

The next day, when Salinger issued a general release of the twelve points, a White House official said the memo was not a request for "voluntary censorship." The *New York Times,* however, said reporters who were in Washington during World War II could see little difference between the Salinger rules and those enforced by Byron Price, the wartime chief of censorship. On October 25, despite the restrictions, the White House let it be known that strict security measures had gone into effect in an eight-state region from Raleigh to New Orleans and from Memphis to Key West, that the Louisiana National Guard was stepping up patrols, and that the Florida National Guard was on twenty-four-hour alert. "It is self-evident that as long as Soviet ships continue to sail toward Cuba with unknown cargoes, the blockade by United States naval forces will continue," Salinger said.[38]

The executive committee of the National Security Council refused to release the aerial photographs of the missiles, but Kennedy, pressed by Salinger and Don Wilson of the United States Information Agency, agreed to their release after they were shown on television and published in Britain. In one of the most memorable moments of the thirteen-day crisis, the pictures were shown at the United Nations by Ambassador Adlai Stevenson, who challenged his Soviet counterpart to explain them and said he would wait "until Hell freezes over" for the answer.[39]

With the Office of Emergency Planning, Salinger worked out plans for a pool of White House correspondents and photographers who would accompany the president if he had to evacuate Washington. He prepared instructions to be relayed to the journalists when the time came. It never came. On October 28, Khrushchev announced that construction of the military sites on the island would be stopped and those in place would be dismantled.[40]

On November 7, the Pentagon cleared the first group of reporters into Guantanamo, the United States naval base on Cuba. On November 20, the guidelines request was withdrawn, and Kennedy pledged that "if the procedures which have been set up . . . are being used in a way inimical to the free flow of news, then we'll change those procedures." Privately, White House aides said the president was little concerned about the barrage of criticism from news groups.[41]

Many reporters felt the secrecy had continued long after it was no longer needed. In December, newspaper organization representatives met and issued a statement saying in part, "We are concerned lest government go beyond the legitimate suppression of strictly military information and look upon news of what the government is doing not as an honest report of what has happened, but as a means to some desired end." In a *Newsweek* poll of forty-three top Washington correspondents in April 1963, thirty-one of them said they got more access to news from Kennedy than from Eisenhower. By a margin of twenty-nine to six, they said the Kennedy White House worked harder at news management than Eisenhower and his aides did, but they split almost evenly on which was the more successful at it. Asked which president had the better press secretary, thirty-five of the forty-three answered, and the count was twenty-eight to seven in favor of Hagerty.

At the White House, Salinger's stock had risen enough by the fall of 1963 that the president asked him to accompany a high-level mission to the Far East, headed by Secretary of State Rusk. He was officially the spokesman for the delegation, but Kennedy gave him the assignment so that he could make preliminary soundings for a trip to Japan that the president planned to make early in 1964.

As the Rusk party flew over the Pacific Ocean about an hour and forty-five minutes west of Hawaii on November 22, the secretary's assistant for public affairs, Robert Manning, tapped Salinger on the shoulder. Rusk wanted to see him up forward. In the private cabin reserved for Rusk as the senior official aboard, Salinger saw the secretary holding a yellow piece of paper that he recognized as a United Press International bulletin. Looking over Rusk's shoulder, he read it: "Three shots were fired at President Kennedy's motorcade today in downtown Dallas."

Within ten minutes, Rusk ordered the pilot to turn around and return to Honolulu. A message came from "Stranger," a code name for an aide with the president's party in Texas, saying all cabinet officers were to return to the White House. About half an hour later, Salinger was called to the telephone and returned saying there were "conflicting reports." He said he was to get another call clarifying the matter.

After ten minutes passed, he came back from the forward part of the plane and said, "He's dead."

Rusk announced the news over the airplane's public address system. "We have a new president," he said. "God bless our new president and our nation." A presidential aide, doing his best the next day to set down a chronology of events on the flight, could say only, "The plane fell into complete grief-stricken silence, for a period that no one can measure by the clock."[42]

In Washington, press office assistant Barbara Garamekian was shopping in a department store when she heard the news. A colleague, at work in the office on that quiet Friday, received a call from a reporter who wanted to be cleared into the White House. "Well, yes, we'll clear you, but there is nothing going on here at all," she said. "There is really no reason to come in." At this point, she was told of the bulletin that had just come over the wire.[43]

In Dallas, the new president, Lyndon Johnson, directed Associate Press Secretary Kilduff to hold up the announcement of Kennedy's death until he could reach *Air Force One* at Love Field. As he arrived, the television in the presidential stateroom was on and the room was crowded with listeners. Within moments, the local television station they were watching interrupted the CBS news with the bulletin from Parkland Hospital. The president had died thirty-five minutes earlier.[44]

Listening to the announcement in a small room at the hospital, the *Washington Post*'s Ed Folliard, a reporter in the capital since the days of Woodrow Wilson, would remember for the rest of his life how much the setting "looked like some sort of a classroom" with reporters sitting at "a lot of little desks."[45]

By this time, the White House press room was crowded with reporters. As the afternoon wore on, they could hear helicopters going and coming on the South Lawn. Who was being picked up? Andrew Hatcher, the other associate press secretary, was taking the afternoon off and missed the terrible news from Dallas, so there was no senior press officer on hand to provide answers. Finally, Garamekian decided it was foolish to keep the reporters in the dark any longer. A helicopter had been sent to pick up the president's brother, Sen. Edward M. Kennedy, and one of his sisters, who were flying to the Cape Cod compound to be with their father.[46]

From the room full of little desks at the Dallas hospital, reporters went by bus to Love Field, and waited for a press plane to return them to Washington. Morning paper reporters had their stories to write.

"They wrote it on the bus, some wrote it in the plane, and some wrote it in the terminal." When they got back to Washington, said Lisagor, "we all went to the White House out of some instinct. The story had long since left us. But we all went to the White House. . . . I sat there for a while and wondered what was I doing there."

The airplane carrying Salinger and the rest of the Rusk delegation arrived back at Andrews Air Force Base shortly after midnight. Salinger went directly to the White House, but found there was little he could do there either and went home to find solace in sleep.

In the morning, a White House telephone operator called: "Mr. Salinger, the president wants to speak to you." For a brief groggy moment, he may have thought it had all been a dream. Then another voice came on the phone.

"Pierre," said Lyndon Johnson, "I want you to stay on the job."[47]

9

The Disposable Press Secretary

WHEN PIERRE SALINGER REPORTED TO WORK on November 23, 1963, he found an empty office, just as he had on the day thirty-four months earlier when he first put his feet on a White House desk.

This time, the office was the president's, not the press secretary's. Noticing a door of the Oval Office ajar, Salinger peeked in. All of President Kennedy's belongings had been removed, as is always done when the presidency changes hands.

The transition had begun, thought Salinger. He sensed it would be a difficult one.[1]

A memorable photographic image from the Johnson presidency, showing the tall Texan picking up one of his beagles by the ears, drew complaints of presidential cruelty from dog lovers. He did not treat his press secretaries much better, running through a record four of them in less than two full terms.

After Salinger, the spiffy boulevardier, came George Reedy, the kind of man who has to be reminded to get a haircut or straighten his tie. Third was the savvy Baptist seminarian Bill Moyers, followed by George Christian, a veteran of the Texas political wars who kept his head down and let the president speak for himself.

Through it all, Johnson made their job more difficult by trying to do it on his own.

Early in 1964, the pool of reporters accompanying Johnson on a flight from his Texas ranch to Washington was startled when the president suddenly appeared at the press table. What followed was one of the most bizarre encounters in all of presidential press relations.

"I need your help," said the president. "I'll tell you everything.

You'll be as well informed as any member of the Cabinet. . . . Of course, I may go into a strange bedroom every now and then that I won't want you to write about, but otherwise you can write everything. If you help me, I'll help you and make you all big men in your profession."

The suggestion that journalists should write their stories as the president suggested, and be rewarded for it, did not sit well with the AP's Frank Cormier. "Mr. President," he asked, "don't you know that sooner or later every reporter around this table is going to write something that will make you mad as hell?"

Johnson responded by denying that he ever became angry with reporters, and pounding the table to emphasize the point.[2]

Clearly, Salinger had his work cut out for him.

The new president, said his press secretary, "had come into office with his own distinct way of dealing with the press, and while it was not what you might call high-handed, it was perhaps a bit imperious."[3]

Personally, said Salinger, Johnson was "wonderful to me." He even came to dinner one evening at the Salingers' home, something the elegant Kennedys had never done.[4]

A few months after Johnson took office, the traditional honeymoon for new presidents ended and damaging leaks from the White House began appearing in the press. Johnson became less communicative. At first Salinger was one of the few aides with free access to the Oval Office. Then one day, when he started to walk in as usual, the president's secretary told him that in the future he should call for an appointment. He knew he would not be around the White House much longer.[5]

Although not a member of Johnson's inner circle, Salinger was included in critical meetings. He was among those in the Cabinet room, along with top officials of the State Department, Pentagon, and CIA when anti-U.S. rioting in Panama City heightened tensions between the United States and Panama in January 1964. It was Salinger who got Panamanian president Roberto F. Chiari on the telephone for the president. [6] Obviously, the press secretary was more tuned in than he had been during Kennedy's Cuban crises.

In another respect, Salinger found the new regime an improvement over the old. Lady Bird Johnson hired Liz Carpenter, a reporter with experience in Texas and Washington, to deal with eighty-five female reporters who covered the White House East Wing, where her offices were located. No longer would West Wing press briefings on international crises be interrupted with questions about the first lady's clothes.

"I worked out a clear division of powers with Pierre," said Carpenter. "The president's press secretary would worry about all the news from the president, Kosygin, Vietnam and De Gaulle. I just had to worry about women, dogs, old brocades, Luci changing the spelling of her name, Luci becoming a Catholic, Luci having her ears pierced, Luci getting engaged, Luci getting married . . . and forty Lady Bird trips covering 20,000 miles."[7]

More and more, however, Salinger felt out of place. He had made history by persuading Kennedy to face his questioners on live television, but Johnson was no John Kennedy on the video screen. Former journalist Douglass Cater, serving as a Johnson aide, suggested that the president all but abolish the televised news conference and rely on FDR-like meetings with reporters in the Oval Office. It was an idea that Salinger had scorned when reporters brought it up in the Kennedy days. Cater added that the televised press conference format might be used on special occasions but that, all in all, periodic pooled network interviews with TV reporters "ought to mollify the television industry."[8]

In fact, most of Johnson's press conferences were held in his office, usually on short notice. LBJ also followed up on the television interview idea, but the first such interview, conducted in March 1964, was widely rated a flop.[9]

Salinger was offended by the crudity of some of Johnson's behavior, especially his habit of summoning cabinet members and others to his bathroom while he was on the commode.

More seriously, the bon vivant Pierre, who had preferred sipping wine during his visit with the Robert Kennedys at Hickory Hill, now was drinking a bottle of scotch a day. "I had to leave the White House because I could not overcome the memory of JFK," he said.[10]

His opportunity came as a prospective opening for a Senate seat from his home state of California in the 1964 elections. Democratic Sen. Clair Engle was ill with a brain tumor and not expected to live. Salinger began to to consider entering the race even though O'Donnell, still skeptical of the press secretary's abilities, told him, "I don't think you've got the guts."

On March 19, twenty-four hours before the filing deadline, Salinger called Gov. Pat Brown in Sacramento and told him he was flying to California to file as a candidate. That afternoon, he submitted his resignation to the president, taking Hatcher with him as his campaign press secretary. Johnson cordially assured him, "I hate to see you go," but later was quoted as complaining to a political associate that he received "not one minute's notice" of Salinger's intentions.[11]

The Kennedy aura gave Salinger a narrow victory over the less colorful State Controller Alan Cranston in the primary, and Brown appointed him to the Senate seat when Engle died on August 3. Salinger's Republican opponent was George Murphy, a movie song-and-dance man who was a good friend of another actor with political aspirations, Ronald Reagan. Murphy filed a protest with the Senate, contending Salinger was a carpetbagger who had not met California's residency requirement. The new senator was seated anyway, and served 148 days before losing to Murphy in the November election.[12] Salinger went on to success as a businessman, journalist, author, and public-relations executive.

His departure from the White House was, as the *New York Times* observed, "one more indication that the Washington of John F. Kennedy's day was slowly, surely disappearing."[13]

•   •   •

When Johnson asked him to stay on after Kennedy's death, Salinger at first demurred, arguing that the new president would be better served by someone he had worked with before. He suggested Reedy, who had worked for LBJ in the Senate and the vice president's office for a dozen years. After Salinger left, Johnson halfheartedly offered the post to Philip Potter of the *Baltimore Sun*, who turned it down. The president then considered other high-profile media figures, but in the end turned to his longtime aide.[14]

Reedy, who was in the hospital with gall bladder trouble when the offer came, didn't want the job. "I had been Johnson's adviser on not only the press but also labor issues and civil rights issues, and there he would listen to me. I knew that we were going to get separated if I became press secretary because he had such absolutely wild ideas about the press." Still, Reedy got his doctor's approval to leave the hospital and go to the White House. When he walked in, he was told, "You're elected." Twenty minutes later, he was standing in front of cameras and microphones discussing his new job.[15]

Reedy was a rumpled, pipe-smoking liberal intellectual who looked like a casting director's idea of the college professor he later became. He was so careless of his appearance that the natty Johnson instructed a doorman to report in the morning if Reedy needed a haircut or was otherwise disheveled. If so, the press secretary would get a telephone call from the president telling him to spruce up.

Born in Chicago in 1917, Reedy was, like Salinger, a child prodigy, one of the original Whiz Kids on Chicago radio. He went on to study at the University of Chicago in the palmy days of President Robert Maynard Hutchins, who made the urban campus a magnet for liberals and a target for the right wing. After graduation, he followed his father, a crime reporter for the *Chicago Tribune,* into journalism and became a congressional reporter for United Press. He left the press gallery in 1951 to handle press relations and other chores for Johnson.[16]

LBJ, often ill at ease with intellectual graduates of elite institutions, abused Reedy mercilessly. According to some accounts, he once addressed him in front of others as "you stupid sonofabitch." Reedy said he recalled no such incident and "I would have quit if that had happened; but if they mean he was pretty much a savage tongue-lasher, yes, that's true." Another time, at the Johnson ranch while Johnson was in the Senate, a political associate visiting the senator heard him telephone Reedy and call him "every filthy name in the book and some that aren't." Then Johnson showed his visitor an expensive new station wagon he was giving Reedy, who was staying in a guest house at the ranch, as a present. "You never want to give a man a present when he's feeling good," said the wily Senate majority leader. "You want to do it when he's down."[17]

Reporters saw Reedy as "highly intelligent, kind of one of nature's philosophers," "probably too nice to be a press secretary," cowed by Johnson, and lacking Hagerty's toughness or Salinger's humor. "He was liked by reporters, but was more a philosopher than a generator of news," said Liz Carpenter.[18]

In briefings in his office, Reedy would look down at his desk or at someone's shoes while listening to a question. After answering, he would thrust his pipe into his mouth and stand to one side, looking down while he waited for the next question. If he thought he had been thrown a verbal curve, he would blink, widen his eyes, and shoot his bushy eyebrows up.[19]

Not long after Reedy's appointment, Johnson told him he was going to abolish the pool of reporters that traveled with the president on *Air Force One.* The president said the reporters were "spies" trying to ferret out embarrassing secrets. Reedy tried to persuade him that

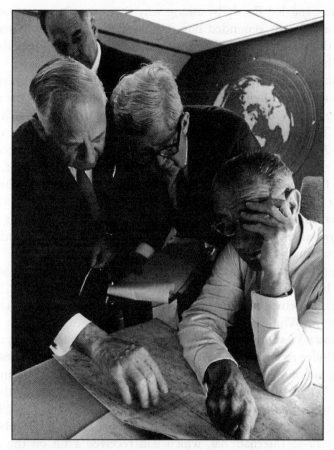

10. George F. Reedy, President Lyndon B. Johnson's second press secretary, joined him in studying a map aboard *Air Force One* on June 25, 1965. In San Francisco that day, Johnson appealed to the United Nations for help in settling the Vietnam war. *Left to right:* unidentified, Glenn Seaborg, Reedy, the president. *Courtesy Yoichi R. Okamoto, LBJ Library Collection.*

the practice, begun by Eisenhower's Jim Hagerty, was only "protective" coverage designed to assure that correspondents were on hand in the event any real news occurred. LBJ said his press secretary was being naive. The incident soured already strained relations between Johnson and the press.

Later, on a flight to inspect flood damage in the Southeast, the president startled Reedy by asking why there wasn't a press pool on the plane. Reedy reminded him it was by his orders. By November 1965, the pool reporters were back and Johnson was jawing with them about his health as they flew toward Texas.

Johnson was given to rambling background sessions with reporters, much like the ones he had held, with his feet up and the drinks flowing, under the Brumidi ceilings of the Senate majority leader's office. The sessions seldom lasted less than two hours, and one ran for seven. A reporter complained that Johnson seemed to expect journalists to read his mind as to what could be quoted and what not. Cater urged the president to let reporters know "that when you discuss a subject off the record this does not mean that they can turn it over to another member of the bureau to publish." Reedy argued that everything possible should be put on the record, and background information given only to explain facts already announced.[20]

In October 1964, Reedy had what he called one of the saddest duties he had ever performed. A little more than a week before, Walter Jenkins, a former Senate aide to Johnson who was now his chief of staff at the White House, had been arrested in a men's room of the downtown Washington YMCA for making advances to a sixty-year-old man. Police reporters did not recognize his name when they saw it in a long list of arrests, as he was identified only as a clerk from Jolly, Texas. When Washington newspapers did learn his identity, they acceded to pleas from Johnson intimates Clark Clifford and Abe Fortas not to carry the story so long as no one else did. On October 14, United Press International, which had received a tip on the arrest, moved an account on its wires. With the presidential election only a month away, the story became an instant political sensation. Johnson was in New York to speak at a Democratic dinner when the news broke, and it fell to Reedy to confirm it in a briefing at the Waldorf-Astoria. Trembling and tearful, he told reporters that the resignation of his longtime colleague had been accepted.[21]

As United States forces plunged deeper into the war in Vietnam, the war between correspondents and the White House also intensified, and the president's press secretary bore the brunt of it. When reporters asked about escalation of the war, Reedy replied, "That's an operational matter, not a policy matter."

Reedy would long remember Douglas Kiker of the *New York Herald Tribune* greeting a new White House reporter with, "Welcome to Credibility Gap." Kiker's paper had been one of the first, if not the first, to use the phrase, running a story by its Washington bureau chief on May 23, 1965, under the title "Dilemma in Credibility Gap." The words soon became so familiar that by 1967 the Amherst Game Company was advertising "Play Credibility Gap," a board game in which the objective was to overcome bureaucratic hurdles and reach the Truth Vault.[22]

The words were a catch-all phrase for statements by the president or his spokesman that the press found uninformative or misleading. "I myself thought that it wasn't really justified," said Reedy. "I thought what he was really doing was changing his mind, and I hate to think that a president cannot change his mind." Justified or not, the catalogue of misstatements continued.

On January 22, 1965, two days after Johnson's inauguration, a reporter asked whether the president had made an agreement with the vice president, Hubert H. Humphrey, about procedure in the event of presidential disability. "No, we just haven't gotten to that," Reedy replied. A few days later, when Johnson was hospitalized with a respiratory infection, the press secretary was asked again and replied that the two had executed such an agreement "sometime before the inauguration." The contradiction led to briefing sessions at the hospital and the White House that were, *Newsweek*'s Charles Roberts said, "as bitter and acrimonious as any I can remember since the days when Hagerty used to blow his top."[23]

Reedy derided a *Los Angeles Times* report that Johnson was preparing to ask Congress for a $4 billion reduction in excise taxes, saying the figure had no relationship to any decision that had been made. Johnson asked for a reduction of $3.964 billion.

"Rarely does any news come out of the press-secretary's twice-daily briefings," said James Deakin of the *St. Louis Post-Dispatch*. Many correspondents felt that the real trouble with Reedy was that Johnson was not leveling with him.[24]

In Reedy's view, Johnson "did not understand the objective of journalism" and regarded newspapers as "arenas in which contending politicians battled for dominance." To gain dominance in the arena, he sought to reward reporters for writing favorable stories about him and punish them for writing unflattering ones. In vain, Reedy tried to convince him that "stories are usually written because they have happened." LBJ appeared not to have a glimmering of what TR had grasped so quickly six decades before—that newspapers were no longer primarily partisan organs but business enterprises competing vigorously in getting the news. He considered them his friends or his enemies—and usually the latter. "I think they want to hurt me," he once said.[25]

On a back-country road in the Texas hill country near his ranch, Johnson took correspondents for a high-speed ride with one hand on the steering wheel of a Lincoln Continental and the other grasping a beer can. When the reporters wrote stories about it, he thought his hospitality was being abused. "He just can't understand how a reporter can write a critical story after he's been down on the ranch," one correspondent said. Reedy told Johnson the best way to avoid such stories would be to observe the speed limit.

While he was convalescing after his 1965 heart attack, the president got the exercise his doctors had prescribed by taking evening walks, trailed by reporters, to visit his Cousin Oriole, an old woman with a few acres next to his ranch. Helen Thomas of UPI wrote a story that, to Reedy, was a touching evocation of "Johnson's rough, but somehow tender, sensitivity to the loneliness of an elderly widow." To Johnson, however, it was "a story inspired by Bobby Kennedy with the purpose of telling the United States that the Johnsons were nothing but a Tobacco Road family." He was particularly incensed by the words "bare feet."

During a visit to Cyprus, Johnson got a warm reception from Turkish Cypriots but the island's Greek inhabitants, unhappy with U.S. policy, virtually ignored him. As Reedy recalled it, Johnson flew into a rage and had to be dissuaded from summoning reporters for a showdown. He told Reedy the journalists were allies of Robert Kennedy trying to show that the president was unpopular abroad.

Tensions between the president and his press secretary were exacerbated by Reedy's doubts about U.S. policy in Vietnam. Once, while Defense Department experts at a National Security meeting were presenting their estimates of Vietcong casualties, Reedy slipped the president a written question designed to challenge some of their assumptions. With a piercing look at his press secretary, Johnson tore the paper in pieces and discarded it. Reedy had privately told Johnson he thought Vietnam would be a disaster, but now realized that the subject was off-limits.[26]

"Our relationship became more and more tenuous . . . and I looked for a graceful exit," said Reedy. On July 8, 1965, he took a leave of absence to undergo surgery for hammer toes, a painful hereditary condition in which shrinking tendons curl the toes and lock them

into a downward cramp. The leave was widely expected to be permanent. Reedy returned to the White House in 1968, but did not handle
press relations. He later became a writer and lecturer and dean of the
School of Journalism at Marquette University.[27]

.   .   .

To replace Reedy, Johnson considered three of his White House
aides: Jack Valenti, Horace Busby, and Bill Moyers, who had succeeded
Jenkins as chief of staff. Valenti took himself out of the running. Lady
Bird Johnson lobbied her husband for Moyers, whom she had liked
ever since he worked as a teenage summer intern in Johnson's Senate
office in 1954, answering mail. The first lady's urging, among other
things, led to this conversation in the Oval Office.

> LBJ: "I think you should take the job."
> MOYERS: "I don't think I can do it."
> LBJ: "Well, I want you to do it."
> MOYERS (after a pause): "Yes, sir. Let's try it."

The trial was supposed to be for a year. It turned out to be a year
and a half.

Part of Moyers's hesitancy may have been because he already had
a big job. No White House aide had ever tried to serve as both chief
of staff and press secretary, as Johnson was asking him to do.[28]

Johnson told him: "Your first loyalty is to your country, your
second loyalty is to me, your third loyalty is to the press. I don't
anticipate that there will ever be serious contradictions between those
three basic loyalties." Moyers said there never were.[29] His critics said
Johnson overlooked another possible loyalty: loyalty to Bill Moyers.[30]

Moyers was born in Oklahoma in 1934 but the family moved to
Marshall in east Texas while he was an infant. In Marshall, his father
worked as a timekeeper at an ordnance plant and his mother as a clerk
in a funeral home. He enrolled at North Texas State College in his
teens, but after his summer stint in Johnson's office, Lady Bird hired
him to work a three-hour morning shift as assistant news editor at her
television station in Austin, and he transferred to her alma mater, the
University of Texas.

Later came a Rotary International Fellowship to study ecclesiasti-
cal history at the University of Edinburgh and a degree from South-
western Baptist Theological Seminary. Deciding for politics instead of

the pulpit, he came to work as a staff assistant for Majority Leader Johnson in 1959 and lived in the Johnsons' basement for five months during the 1960 election campaign.

After Johnson became vice president, Moyers served as associate director and later deputy director of the Peace Corps. On November 22, 1963, he was having lunch in Austin while on a political mission for Kennedy when he heard of the president's assassination. He chartered a plane to Dallas, and sent in a note to the new president on *Air Force One:* "I'm here if you need me." Johnson decided he did, and Moyers became a White House assistant.[31]

The young man with the polished manner and the horn-rimmed glasses quickly became a key member of the president's staff. "That boy works like a dog for me and is just as faithful," Johnson once said. When United Nations Ambassador Adlai Stevenson had trouble getting a chance to talk to the president, Vice President Humphrey told him his best chance was to work through the thirty-year-old Moyers. Moyers was recommended by Fortas, a Johnson adviser even after he became a Supreme Court justice, for undersecretary of state. The president, one morning as he was shaving, told Moyers, "Bill, I don't want you over there. I want you here with me."[32]

"Moyers, articulate and canny, became the darling of the top name columnists," recalled Liz Carpenter. He lunched with them in fancy restaurants. It paid off. To television newscaster Chet Huntley, he was "the most interesting of the whole lot and one in whom I would put more trust than any of them."[33] Three and a half months after his appointment, *Time* said he was "widely rated as the best White House press secretary in memory."

Inside the White House, there were differing views. One colleague, generally admiring of Moyers, wrote: "Around him he built a loyal staff which was virtually a White House within the White House, and this was bound to cause conflicts in the tightly structured environment of 1600 Pennsylvania Avenue." Another less admiring staffer said, "He was a good press secretary for Bill Moyers, in my opinion."

Moyers continued to have an impact on foreign and domestic policy and speech writing after he became press secretary. He still attended the Tuesday luncheon group on foreign policy along with the president, his national security adviser, and Secretaries Rusk and McNamara.[34]

Ten minutes before his daily 11 A.M. briefing for reporters, he telephoned Johnson for final instructions. For forty-five minutes after

11. Press Secretary Bill Moyers, who succeeded George Reedy, shared a laugh with President Johnson. *Left to right:* Moyers, Clifford Alexander, the president. *Courtesy Yoichi R. Okamoto, LBJ Library Collection.*

the briefing, he kept his door open in case any reporters had further questions. Preparing for his second briefing at 4 P.M., he typed his own notes. He was a good typist, producing neat copy at a hundred words per minute.

Like most press secretaries, Moyers occasionally planted a question that he wanted asked at a presidential press conference. While Reedy was press secretary, Johnson had proposed that the idea be carried a step further and all the questions and answers for a televised conference be written out in advance. Reedy called the idea "apocalyptic in its looniness" and talked Johnson out of it. On August 25, 1965, a little more than a month after Moyers moved into the press office, the apocalypse took place in the ornate East Room of the White House. After days of advance preparation and question planting, the president opened with prepared statements on ten issues, ranging from home rule in the District of Columbia to the rule of law in outer space. These were followed by a dozen questions and answers. The first questioner asked if the president had any comment on the threat of a steel strike. Naturally enough, he did, and he obliged with a previously prepared statement. Asked whether Republican congressional critics of his position on Vietnam were guilty of undue partisanship, he replied loftily that war and peace issues transcended personal and party differences. The show went on before a huge blue canvas backdrop and under a newly installed portable lighting system that one writer likened to the lights around the star's mirror in a theater dressing room. The whole proceeding, wrote columnists Rowland Evans and Robert Novak, "was very nearly as carefully staged as a Broadway play." Johnson's deftly timed announcement of a go-ahead on the Air Force's long-planned manned orbiting laboratory made banner headlines, but the press response to the experiment was derisive. Chalmers Roberts in the *Washington Post* called it "a virtuoso views conference performance." It was not repeated.[35]

The White House, meanwhile, was trying to keep tabs on reporters. In January 1966, Moyers had to acknowledge that telephone operators were taking reporters' names when they called staff members, on the orders of presidential assistant Marvin Watson. The press secretary said the checks were designed to measure the work load of the staff, but reporter Jim Deakin thought this could have been accomplished by keeping track of the number of calls, without the names. State Department officials were asked to submit weekly reports on their meetings with journalists.[36]

Despite his expressed reluctance to take the job, Moyers seemed to be enjoying it. He "relished the spotlight," said Carpenter.[37] But soon the spotlight was again on the credibility gap.

On November 3, 1966, a reporter asked Moyers about a report that the president was undergoing a health checkup. At the moment Moyers was scanning a proposed statement by White House physician George G. Burkley saying in part that Johnson's general health continued to be excellent. Moyers told the reporter the president was in excellent health. He did not tell him that the rest of the statement said the president needed follow-up surgery from his gall bladder operation a year earlier. When Burkley read his statement to reporters later in the day, Moyers said the apparent conflict was a coincidence, but conceded, "I wanted to keep the lid on for two more hours."[38]

Sometimes the transcripts of Johnson's news conferences failed to coincide with what he said. Once, Johnson told reporters that lawmakers "were" involved in spreading cabinet resignation rumors; the White House transcript said "could be." Journalists were not satisfied with the White House explanation that such changes were designed to clarify.[39]

Just before the mid-term congressional elections of 1966, word sped around the country that Johnson planned a four-day campaign trip through as many as fifteen states on his return from a seven-nation tour of the Pacific. Boston had eleven hundred uniformed policemen stand by to protect the president. Officials in Memphis, Chicago, and Los Angeles built grandstands and hired bands. Hard-pressed by reporters, Moyers took time on the way home from Asia to give them a detailed background briefing about the planned trip. No sooner had Johnson arrived back at the White House, however, when he announced that he was merely going to his ranch to rest up for the surgery. Plans for the campaign trip, he said, "primarily involve the imagination of people who phrase sentences and write columns." Discarding a statement the embarrassed Moyers had written to explain the change in plans, the president said, "We don't have any plans, so when you don't have any plans, you don't cancel plans." Reportedly, the president had changed his mind, but didn't tell Moyers because "Bill would have leaked it to the press." Johnson was also said to have been angered by the background briefing Moyers gave.[40]

On New Year's weekend in 1967, at the vacation White House in Texas, Deputy Press Secretary Robert H. Fleming told reporters no announcement was imminent about the proposed supersonic transport plane. The next day, the Federal Aviation Administration announced that Boeing had been selected as the contractor.[41]

"The list of outright prevarications, half-truths, concealments and misleading denials by the administration is almost as long as its impressive list of achievements," columnist Charles Roberts wrote in *Newsweek* in December 1966. Among other things, Roberts cited the administration's failure to disclose peace feelers reportedly made by North Vietnam through the United Nations Secretary-General, U Thant. The State Department at first denied U Thant had relayed any offers, then later said the offers were nebulous and not to be taken seriously. They had come to light only when U Thant referred to them in a speech.[42]

A few days after the Roberts column appeared, National Security Adviser Walt Rostow told a *Newsweek* White House reporter, "You guys are a bunch of Goddam liars. That article in *Newsweek* was just like the Communist line . . . What is your magazine, a Republican outfit? Are you trying to elect a Republican president in 1968?" Rostow said the overtures relayed by U Thant contained nothing but "the same old four points" Vietnam had offered before.[43]

As it had with Reedy, the war in Vietnam played a role in the deteriorating relationship between Johnson and the press secretary who had once been called almost a son to him. One newspaper account described Moyers as the "informed doubter in the president's circle, not a dove on Vietnam as such, but a man with solid connections to the less militant circles."[44] Other published reports said he had developed a network in the government, operating independently of the National Security Council, that questioned the administration's conduct of the war. Bromley Smith, who was executive secretary of the NSC under Johnson, said, "I think there was quite a bit in that."[45]

Johnson also may have felt that Moyers's ties to Robert Kennedy were too close. "He became part of the Hickory Hill group, and I think he had a feeling that Bobby was the wave of the future," said Charles Bartlett, a columnist who was close to the Kennedys.[46] At the dinner table in the White House, the president began dropping remarks showing displeasure at Moyers's frequent contacts with Kennedy. Lady Bird Johnson was still loyal to Moyers, whom she called "slim, quick, so very intelligent." But Mrs. Johnson bit her tongue and remained silent.[47]

Johnson also knew that Moyers had talked with William Manchester, whose book about the Kennedy assassination gave an unflattering portrayal of Johnson's conduct in the crisis. He told Moyers that he believed Manchester and presidential campaign chronicler Theodore H. White were among "the people who want to destroy me, and I hate to see them use my friends to do it, but they do do it." The president was particularly offended by Manchester's account of his addressing the widowed Jacqueline Kennedy as "honey." When Moyers suggested he say he had no recollection of such an incident, Johnson exploded, "Oh, hell no! I have a recollection. It didn't happen. I think it's a God damned lie!"[48]

Moyers's ambitions for a larger role in government may also have played a role in his departure. Bartlett, one of a group of journalists who lunched with Moyers shortly before he left the White House, got the impression that the press secretary wanted to try his hand at foreign policy. "I think that Johnson got the feeling slowly that Moyers was really working harder for Moyers than he was for Johnson," the columnist said.

Moyers himself said, "If I stay in the executive branch of government, I would like to work someday in the Defense-State complex." Johnson was quoted as saying that Moyers quit because he wanted to be secretary of state and Johnson didn't consider him qualified. James Reston, one of the correspondents with whom Moyers frequently talked, said the press secretary had wanted to go to the State Department as a roving ambassador.[49]

Late in 1965, Moyers had asked three White House TV correspondents if they would be interested in taking the press secretary job if it were offered. Robert Pierpoint of CBS and William Lawrence of ABC said no, and Ray Scherer of NBC was noncommittal. None was offered the job. When news of his overtures broke in the press in January 1966, Moyers smilingly denied that he was looking for a successor.[50]

He stayed on for nearly a year. In December 1966, he resigned to become publisher of the New York daily *Newsday* at better than triple his $30,000-a-year White House salary.[51] Later he became a familiar figure on public television. On Moyers's departure from the White House, Reston commented that Johnson seemed to have invented "the disposable press secretary."

• • •

For his fourth and final spokesman, Johnson did not turn to any of the media stars Moyers had sounded out, but picked a low-key, soft-spoken veteran of political public relations in Austin. George Christian was born in 1927 in the hill country district that Johnson later represented in Congress. His father was district attorney, known by reputation to the future president, who liked to attend trials as a boy. After seven years as a political reporter for International News Service in Austin, Christian became press secretary to Democratic governor Price Daniel and later to Daniel's successor, John Connally. In 1966, he joined the White House staff as an aide in the National Security Council office. Unlike Reedy and Moyers, and to a lesser extent Salinger, he was scarcely acquainted with Johnson when he took on the press office job.[52]

Also unlike the others, he showed no reluctance. Johnson asked Christian if he was willing to become press secretary at one of the frequent morning meetings he held with aides in his bedroom. Christian said he was. "Do you think you can handle it?" asked the president. "I think I probably can." The appointment was announced that day. Christian served two years, longer than any of his predecessors.[53]

Johnson told Christian there was too much loose talk around the

White House, too many people talking to reporters and telling them things that might or might not be accurate. Christian got the impression that the president believed Moyers "was leaking a lot of things that he had no business leaking." It was causing Johnson grief, and he wanted it stopped. He wanted nobody but the president and the press secretary to speak to the press. Christian realized that was impossible, so he set up a system requiring all White House aides to report to him on what they were telling the press. He then relayed these reports to the president. "They didn't always tell the truth," he said afterward. "I didn't pay any attention to them to speak of."[54]

Johnson also felt that too much confidential information was lying around on secretaries' desks in the press office, where reporters could see it. One evening, he walked down the corridor from the Oval Office to the press office and paced off a space in the hallway that he wanted converted into an anteroom for the secretaries. "He just made the decision himself to create an extra office for my operation," said Christian.[55]

The president promised him generous access. "He said if there were more than two people in his office and I was curious about what was going on, to walk in, and if he didn't want me there, he would throw me out." In practice, Christian usually sent in a note asking if the president wanted him to come in. Most of the time, he was invited. He was never thrown out.

Johnson also said the press secretary could come as often as he wanted to the presidential bedroom, where the president did much of his work under doctor's orders. Christian ended up coming there more often than he might have liked. "He wanted me over in the bedroom early in the morning," he said. "I sometimes couldn't get there as early as he wanted."[56]

With the press corps constantly expanding, Johnson suggested that Christian brief reporters in the Fish Room, so-called because Roosevelt had stocked it with fishing trophies, instead of in the crowded press secretary's office. Toward the end of the Johnson administration, Christian began doing this, establishing for the first time a setting in which reporters could be seated while questioning the press secretary.[57]

Journalist Deakin, who was to feud with Christian many times, derided him on his appointment as a "bland import from the Italianate political world of Gov. John Connally, where as little as possible is done in the open."

Within the White House, Christian was given credit for improving coordination with departmental press offices and getting them to handle more of their own business instead of having it announced at 1600 Pennsylvania Avenue. He also encouraged Johnson to have impromptu press conferences. "I tried to minimize the value of the briefings," he said. "I did it deliberately. I wanted him to make the major announcements, not me."[58] Christian harbored no desire to be the "inexhaustible font" of White House lore that Wilson's Tumulty had boasted of being.

The "clear division of powers" that Liz Carpenter worked out with Salinger began to show signs of strain. "Liz got her feelings hurt a time or two about the president's press office butting into her business," said Christian. "But he [Johnson] would order me to do certain things when he wasn't happy with what the East Wing was doing."

In May 1967, the president and first lady became unhappy with aggressive questioning by reporters at White House social events. Responding to a request from Mrs. Johnson, Carpenter said reporters had been free to wander about at such affairs at least since the Truman administration. Beginning with the Kennedys, reporters at the social events were divided into two groups—guests, who had been sent invitations, and pool reporters, who were there on assignment. Carpenter said she was not always successful in curing the pool reporters of a tendency to "cover the president and not the party." Some of the reporters invited as guests couldn't resist being reporters also. In conclusion, Carpenter cautioned the first lady, "Even though the election is a long way off, I do not think we should turn the water faucet off now and expect to turn it on next year."

A few weeks later, at the president's instruction, Christian asked Carpenter to make clear that journalists invited to social affairs were there "as guests, not as working reporters." He also proposed that members of the pool, who would cover the event, not be allowed to remain throughout the evening.

Carpenter objected, and she and Christian worked out a memorandum saying that "to drastically change the longtime social coverage at the White House will result in ill will for the president and a series of bad stories." The memo suggested inclusion of ten guest couples at each event, two each from the Washington area print press, the foreign press, editorial pages, Washington radio and TV, and non-Washington radio and TV. Carpenter and Christian said the pool should stay throughout the event but not try to question the president or his guests. Reporters would be asked to leave if this rule was broken.

Johnson turned down the ten guest couples idea. "He will invite as guests only those that he wants to invite, and not by category," Christian told Carpenter. "On the other hand, he has consented to permit a small writing pool to stay all evening at each event. He is opposed to this, but says he will go along." [59]

On November 17, 1967, Christian and his deputy, former ABC Washington bureau chief Fleming, engineered the exact opposite of the stagy August news conference that had brought such ridicule two years earlier. Many in the press office had long thought that Johnson needed to free himself from the formality of the podium. "When he stands behind the podium, he looks like he's fresh from a taxidermist's shop," said one. Christian said, "We devised this idea that we leave the podium there in the East Room, but try to hook it up so he could step out from behind it." The "new Johnson," walking around the room with his lapel microphone, got rave reviews. "Pounding his palms together for emphasis, dry-washing his hands, milking his fingers and sawing the air with extravagant gestures, this was the LBJ of the congressional cloakroom coming to the nation live on television," exulted *Newsweek*.

A month and a half later, when Johnson resumed his series of fireside chats with television newsmen after a hiatus of four years, he was still glowing from the good notices. Seated in a rocker, he told his interrogators he would like to wander around, as he did in the East Room. He was dissuaded when a network man told him, "Mr. President, you can rock as much as you want, but if you walk around you'll walk out of range of the cameras." The president never did it again at a news conference either. "I think it was just pure obstinacy," said Christian. "He didn't like the idea that he needed some kind of razz-ma-taz news conference to get attention." [60]

Although he dismissed talk of a credibility gap as an invention of journalists, Christian had troubles with it, too, drawing scoffs when he said in a radio interview that Johnson was a candid man who had been "rather open in his discussions with the press and with the public." [61]

In September 1967, at the ranch, the president told Christian he was considering not running for reelection. He asked his press secretary to confer with Governor Connally and prepare a statement in which he could make the announcement.

On October 3, Johnson shared his thoughts with Rusk, McNamara, and others at a meeting in the Cabinet Room. He thought about including the announcement in his State of the Union message to Congress in January, and asked aide Horace Busby to prepare a statement.

Busby's draft, which arrived two days before the State of the Union address was to be delivered, contained the sentence, "I shall not seek—I have no desire to accept—the nomination of my party for another term in this great office of all the people."

Lady Bird suggested changing "I have no desire to accept" to "I will not accept," strengthening the statement as well as giving a textbook example of the correct uses of "shall" and "will" in the first person. Johnson accepted the suggestion and asked his wife to write a version of her own.

Meanwhile, he asked Christian to write a draft combining what the press secretary had written earlier and what Busby had written. Christian brought it to the White House about noon of State of the Union day. Mrs. Johnson found his face "calm, unrevealing, as it always is." She thought her own draft feeble compared with his. Johnson was still uncertain whether he would include the momentous announcement in his speech. "He keeps looking from one to the other of us—those close to him—for an answer," his wife wrote in her diary. "But there isn't any answer." Only LBJ could decide.[62]

That night at the Capitol, Christian kept waiting for the president to pull the folded statement from his pocket and read it. Johnson never did. He had not brought it with him. "It just didn't fit," he told Christian. "I couldn't go in there and lay out a big program and then say, 'Okay, here's all this work to do, and by the way, so long. I'm leaving.' " Johnson told Christian to keep the statement up to date.[63]

Early in 1968, the president told aide Joseph Califano, "Only Bob McNamara and George Christian knew how close I've come to announcing that I would not run." Late in March, he asked Busby to make a new try at a statement. It reached him on March 30, as he was in the Cabinet Room, going over the speech he was to make on television the following night, announcing a pause in the bombing of North Vietnam. He read it and handed it across the table to Christian. As usual, Christian's face betrayed no emotion as he read the words, "I shall not seek, and I will not accept, the nomination of my party for another term as your President."[64]

12. Press Secretary George Christian joined LBJ in watching television news reports and analysis of the president's speech Mar. 31, 1968, announcing he would not seek reelection. *Left to right:* Clark Clifford, Christian, Horace Busby, Leonard Marks, the president. *Courtesy Yoichi R. Okamoto, LBJ Library Collection.*

In the Oval Office the next night, Johnson detected "a look of shocked surprise" when Deputy Press Secretary Fleming, supervising the 9 P.M. broadcast, read the final words on the teleprompter. He glanced at the press pool Christian had brought to the door of the office to watch, and thought, "They're in for a surprise, too."

After the speech, Johnson went to the residential part of the White House. A little before 11 P.M., Christian escorted about thirty-five reporters over and Johnson came downstairs to the Yellow Room for a press conference. "George, you better get yourself a drink," he told Christian. After the press conference they went to the West Hall, the living room for the president and his family, and watched television news and analysis of Johnson's bombshell announcement.

For Lyndon Johnson and for George Christian, the White House days were drawing to a close. The next January, Johnson went home to his ranch. Christian, as he had always said he would, returned to Austin, where he became a partner in a public-relations firm.[65]

"The Christian era was more inhibited and less inspired than the Moyers reign," said Liz Carpenter, "but while there were fewer hits, there were also fewer errors."[66]

10

No Longer Operative

IN THE ANNALS OF THE NIXON ADMINISTRATION, Ronald Ziegler is remembered as the press secretary who dismissed the Watergate break-in as a "third-rate burglary attempt" and then ten months later said that all previous statements on the subject had become inoperative. He is the press secretary who declined comment twenty-nine times in a row when asked about possible administration involvement in the bungled crime,[1] and who likened congressional impeachment hearings to a "kangaroo court."[2]

Under Richard Nixon, relations between the press secretary and the press became embittered as they had never been before. There was none of the "air of conspiratorial amiability" that one reporter detected as a hallmark of Pierre Salinger's reign.[3] Ziegler has gone into the books as the grim-faced stonewaller of Watergate.

But there is another Ronald Ziegler. A classic chronicle of the 1968 presidential campaign portrayed him as an enthusiastic neophyte who quickly grasped the needs of reporters.[4] Once he reached the White House, he was the subject of newspaper stories about "Ziegler's boyish charm and his winning smile and how it was impossible to get mad at him."[5]

The husky, dark-haired object of these accolades was born in 1939 in the Ohio River town of Covington, Kentucky, where he became a star running back at Dixie High School, married his favorite cheerleader, and won a football scholarship to Xavier University in Cincinnati. When his father, a rising star in the Magnus Metal Company, was transferred to Los Angeles to accept a promotion, young Ziegler moved west too. At the University of Southern California, he cut his teeth at public relations by handling press arrangements for the Miss

USC contest. He was excited when he got a chance to do the same thing for campus visits by the two candidates in the 1960 presidential campaign—Democrat John F. Kennedy and Republican Richard Nixon. For three summers, Ziegler piloted a "jungle cruise boat" at Disneyland, making thirty-three trips a day in which he cautioned passengers that the natives on the bank had "only one aim in life and that is to get a-head."

After graduating from USC as a B-minus marketing major, he was recruited by the soap company Procter and Gamble for a coveted job in sales development. About three weeks later, he was offered a job handling press relations for the Republican caucus in the State Assembly, with an office in the Capitol dome in Sacramento. People at Procter and Gamble "just couldn't conceive of anyone who would want to do that, but I did it, and that was the step that changed the direction of my life," Ziegler said. He said he never looked back and had no regrets. Ziegler moved on to being press coordinator for the state Republican Party, based in Los Angeles. His boss was Herb Klein, a former newspaper editor whom he first met while at USC.

In Nixon's disastrous 1962 campaign for governor, Ziegler was a junior aide who passed handouts around and saw that reporters' luggage was on the bus. After the election, he went to work for campaign manager H. R. Haldeman at the Los Angeles office of the J. Walter Thompson advertising agency, handling the Disneyland and Sea World accounts. When Haldeman left again to manage Nixon's 1968 campaign for president, he took Ziegler to serve as a sometime spokesman, a sort of second fiddle, under Klein's supervision.[6] As Nixon later reflected, Ziegler was "a superb mechanic, but not a designer."[7]

Shortly after the election, a Nixon aide told reporters that the president-elect did not plan to have a press secretary "in the traditional sense."[8] Recalling his days as Eisenhower's vice president, Nixon did not want a spokesman in the image of Jim Hagerty, who he thought had too much influence on administration policy.[9] The president would be the spokesman for his own programs. Ziegler was to be called "press assistant" or "spokesman" at first, but by inauguration day he had been given the traditional title. He had the big office and gave the day-to-day briefings, while Klein was put in charge of the newly created Office of Communications.[10]

Klein said his job was to coordinate information activities of the government departments, deal with news organizations not represented in Washington, and "be an overall spokesman, particularly with the emphasis on national television."[11] Like Early and Salinger, he got many of his handpicked people into the top departmental information posts.[12] Some cynics in the news media dubbed Klein the "czar of information," but the consensus was that he had been kicked upstairs, away from the center of power. Klein gradually lost stature in the White House hierarchy and resigned early in 1973.[13]

Ziegler was bright and ingratiating and knew how to banter with reporters. But he lacked any journalistic experience, so he hired as his deputy Gerald L. Warren, assistant managing editor of the *San Diego Union,* whom he had met while visiting the newspaper on campaign trips.[14] Warren's main job was helping Ziegler dig up the facts to use at briefings. His office was right outside the press briefing room, and the door was always open, as Ziegler's was not. Philomena Jurey, White House reporter for the Voice of America, found him "patient and cordial, even though he had little to say."[15]

Ziegler furnished his office with a deep royal blue rug, a sofa, comfortable arm chairs, bookshelves, and a telephone with a silver receiver. He also had a Western Electric Videophone on which he could call up the likes of Henry Kissinger and see the person he was talking to. Reporters listened to him because they knew he had access to the president, whom he usually saw two or three times a day. But the reporters were not always impressed with what they heard. The terms "Zieglerism" and "to Ziegle" entered the press corps vocabulary as synonyms for what would later be called stonewalling. A favorite was "I can only be as factual as the facts permit."[16] Confronted with especially tough questions, the kind that caused LBJ's George Reedy to study the top of his desk or a reporter's shoes, Ziegler had the habit of pursing his lips and puffing furiously on a cigarette.[17] Once, Ziegler had trouble with the controls in a White House shower and was doused with alternately scalding and near-freezing water. Emerging, he said, "Jesus, it was just like the daily briefing."[18]

One of the new administration's early steps in press relations was to try to move the White House press corps out of the White House. The first plan called for a press room on the ground floor of the Old Executive Office Building, to be connected to the West Wing by a tunnel. The dean of the press corps, UPI's Merriman Smith, said he believed his colleagues would object vehemently to the change. Ziegler and Warren "fought long and hard," Ziegler recalled, against the change. When Ziegler reluctantly submitted to Smith an alternative proposal to build a sunken press room into the lawn facing Pennsylvania Avenue, the veteran correspondent thought this was better, but advised White House officials to check with the Commission of Fine Arts. William Walton of the commission told them the group would never approve such "monkeying with the White House."[19]Nixon, still unhappy with the cluttered press quarters just off the lobby where his visitors arrived, pushed an alternative plan to move reporters into an area within the West Wing occupied by FDR's swimming pool, a sauna bath, three rubdown rooms, some dog kennels, and a place where flowers were prepared for social functions. The president took Smith and two other reporters on a tour of the proposed facility and, Haldeman wrote in his diary, "they basically bought the idea. . . . Now it's a fait accompli except for the details."

The new half-million-dollar press headquarters formally opened April 2, 1973. Instead of the nine small booths and twenty-three desks in the space the press had used since Theodore Roosevelt's day, they got forty writing desks, some in glassed-in booths, and twelve broadcast cubicles. Between this working space and the press office was a briefing room with a platform from which the press secretary could hold forth, instead of having reporters crowd around the big desk in his office. The room was furnished with four beige sofas and a number of Elizabethan straight-backed chairs, and lighted by lamps shaped like ginger jars and hunting horns. It also had piped-in music.[20] One writer said it had been "decorated to resemble a high-class mortuary."[21] Nixon considered naming it the "Merriman Smith Press Lounge," but it remained nameless.[22] There would be changes, but the basic setup would continue in at least five administrations to come.

There was little grumbling by reporters about leaving the cramped quarters TR and his successors had set aside for them, although some were unhappy that they would no longer be in the strategic entrance way where the president's visitors came and went. In the succeeding Ford administration, reporters continued to sit in the West Lobby while waiting for their appointments, but this practice was banned after some White House aides complained that the journalists were interviewing or eavesdropping on them and their callers.[23]

Immediately after the new administration took office, a flurry of activity began aimed at humanizing the often stodgy-appearing Nixon. Haldeman, installed as chief of staff, instructed speechwriter Pat Buchanan five days after the inauguration to take notes on "anything unusual or offbeat" in the president's meetings with legislative leaders. Four days later, Haldeman said the president wanted any particularly poignant item in the daily news summary flagged "as a potential human interest story to be further followed up." [24]

In June of his first year in office, Nixon suggested to Ziegler that he tell columnists the president had "become a regular bowler at Camp David on weekends," with an average of 130 to 140 and a best game of 204. [25]

Throughout 1969, Haldeman summoned Klein and Ziegler to meetings to discuss "the need for more effective work on the president's color and image." By the end of 1970, these had evolved into an arm of the White House known at first as the "anecdotalist program" and later as the "color reporter program." [26]

The president, it was said, wanted "an assigned anecdotalist in attendance" at almost all his meetings. This functionary was to go immediately to the press office and relay colorful tidbits to Ziegler or Warren, who might either tell reporters about them or wait for a written report in twenty-four hours. The report was to include what the anecdotalist planned to do with the tidbit, such as "drop it casually to a reporter at lunch the next day." Speechwriter William Safire was considered a star anecdotalist and was assigned to cabinet meetings and other big doings. By early 1973, Safire had left the White House and the program had largely fallen by the wayside. Ziegler more and more often declined to pass the nuggets of color on to the press. Haldeman decided there was "a basic question of whether or not the program really is worth continuing." [27]

The program was, in fact, backfiring. Pat Buchanan warned that for every color story they got into the media, there was probably one major story about the "new effort to humanize the president." Ziegler told Buchanan that his efforts to pass on the anecdotes in the pressroom generated stories, not about what a jolly good fellow Nixon was, but about his aides' efforts to make him appear one. Bob Pierpoint of CBS said in one broadcast that there were "22 image-makers" on the White House staff. John Pierson wrote in the *Wall Street Journal,* "The humanizing of Richard Nixon . . . won't work: Mr. Nixon is simply not a very humorous, relaxed, fun-loving man." [28]

This was not the only time Ziegler and his staff resisted efforts of Haldeman and others to manipulate the press. "There are many, many instances where we simply did not proceed with the directives that came to our office," Ziegler said.

In ordering a list of reporters who "are out to get us," Nixon told right-hand-man John Ehrlichman to ignore the objections of Ziegler and Klein. Decreeing that no one in the White House should talk to any reporter for the *Washington Post,* he said, "Ziegler and Klein . . . will not agree with this policy but . . . I want it carried out." Again, in ordering the *Post* excluded from his historic trip to China in 1972 because he was angered by a *Post* editorial, he told Haldeman that "Ron is not to come simpering and arguing about it."[29]

When ABC's Tom Jarriel derided the White House's "low-key" handling of a presidential statement on school desegregation, Ziegler cautioned Haldeman not to assume that Jarriel's broadcast represented "an overall attitude among the press corps" and urged that the implied criticism "should be taken in stride."[30]

He resisted Nixon's plan to limit photo opportunities for journalists to one a day.[31] He objected to Buchanan's suggestion that televised news conferences be announced only a few hours before they were held.[32]

As Vice President Spiro Agnew headed for Birmingham, Alabama, with a speech continuing his running attack on reporters and saying that "the time for naive belief in their neutrality is gone," Ziegler said in the briefing room that Agnew's speeches were his own to give and no curbs would be placed on him by the president.[33] Behind the scenes, however, he sought to tone down the vice president's rhetoric, telling Haldeman that Agnew's text was "defensive, negative in tone and full of quotes that can be used to ride the story forcefully against the administration and the presidency." He said it was "not only essential, but imperative" that a "more thoughtful, less provocative, antagonistic address" be delivered. He submitted one, arguing that a healthy creative tension between the government and the news media "serves to raise the level of performance on both sides, and . . . serves the people by serving the truth."[34] Agnew, said Haldeman, was determined to give his original version "and won't listen to Ziegler, or Klein."[35]

When Haldeman aides became upset over a Hugh Sidey column in *Life* saying Nixon had a credibility problem caused by "careless language and . . . arrogance," Ziegler wrote back: "Mr. Sidey is a very sensitive, perceptive man and my only thought would be that as each member of the White House staff reads the Sidey article he take a good look at himself. Perhaps a change in attitude amongst the staff could eliminate this type of disservice to the president in the future."[36]

The 190-pound, 6-foot press secretary, code-named "Whaleboat" by the Secret Service,[37] was a profoundly conservative man and a

Nixon loyalist to the core. When government expenditures on the
president's California and Florida retreats were challenged, he said
such complaints were irrelevant "to our way of life in this country."[38]
He also worked hard, probably harder than some of his detractors in
the press. "Working in a press office is much more demanding than
working on any newspaper I've ever heard of, or ever experienced,"
said Jerry Warren.[39] At 6:30 each morning, at his Alexandria, Virginia,
home, Ziegler jumped into a black Chrysler New Yorker from the
White House motor pool that pulled up stocked with copies of the
Washington Post, Baltimore Sun, Wall Street Journal, New York Times,
and the president's news summary. He read the newspapers in the
car and went through the approximately forty-page mimeographed
summary at the office, taking notes on a yellow pad. He attended
an 8:15 staff meeting and then started making telephone calls to
cabinet members and White House specialists or taking the few
steps to the Oval Office to check something with the president. He
briefed twice a day, at 11 A.M. and 4 P.M., usually wearing a blue suit
and a pastel shirt—a tiny revolt from the white-shirt pattern set by
the starchy Haldeman and followed by most other White House
aides.[40]

"We felt that our role was to be a direct spokesman on behalf of
the president and that we had to work to maintain our credibility and
our legitimacy," he said. "Obviously during Watergate that all fell
apart because we were given false information that we conveyed, and
we lost our credibility together with the administration."

Even before Watergate poisoned the briefing room atmosphere,
many found Ziegler's responses too larded with such phrases as "to
the best of my knowledge" and "I won't take that question." A wire
service correspondent said, "I don't expect much out of him, so I
don't get disappointed." Another reporter, noting Ziegler's advertising background, said, "He's the kind of press secretary I'd probably
have if I were president."

Besides briefing reporters, Ziegler dealt with such momentous
issues as press parking. When Bill Lawrence covered the White House,
first for the *New York Times* and then for ABC, he had a parking spot
on West Executive Avenue, a short walk from the press room, for health
reasons. When Lawrence left the beat, ABC kept the parking spot and it
was used by the healthy Tom Jarriel. CBS's Pierpont and NBC's
Richard Valeriani had to park farther away, on the ellipse. They wanted
equal status. When a memo on the matter reached the press secretary,

13. Ronald Ziegler briefed reporters in the new quarters President Richard Nixon provided for them. Ziegler's once-cordial relations with the press were soured by Watergate. *Courtesy National Archives.*

it was just filed away and, for the moment anyway, the parking remained as it was.[41]

Nixon's attitude to the press was spelled out in his memoirs:

I knew that as president my relations with the media would be at best an uneasy truce. . . . The majority of New York and Washington newspaper and television reporters, news executives, columnists, and opinion-makers are liberals. I am not. . . . I considered the influential majority of the news media to be part of my political opposition.

This viewpoint was reflected in extreme sensitivity to the press's treatment of him. When he visited Manila in August 1969, newspaper reports said he got a "friendly, but restrained" reception, not as enthusiastic as Johnson had received in 1966; Nixon passed the word to Ziegler that this was obviously a "deliberate job" designed to discredit him.[42]

On another occasion, Haldeman asked Ziegler to compare AP photo coverage with UPI's to check suggestions that AP photo editors also had been tending to "job us" to make the president look bad.[43]

The chief of staff insisted on approving pool assignments before each *Air Force One* trip,[44] and Nixon personally approved all of the approximately eighty reporters who covered his China trip.[45] Three weeks before departure, Haldeman told Ziegler "not to tell any press people they're going until the President reviews the China list again." The list excluded newspapers such as the *Boston Globe* and *Newsday* whose previous stories had raised hackles at the White House. The *Washington Post* made the trip despite the president's objection. Ziegler said the other papers were passed over because they had not regularly covered the White House or presidential travel.[46]

Nixon had not been in office a month when, planning a trip to his Florida retreat at Key Biscayne, he started "worrying about whether Ziegler has gotten out the story of how hard he's been working, long hours, etc."[47] Haldeman, who recorded the president's worries in his diary, passed them on to the press secretary and repeatedly complained that the point was not being made pointedly enough. Once, he checked Ziegler's briefings for a full month and said that only once did he find "even a hint that the president was working hard."[48] John Ehrlichman said that actually meetings on affairs of state were rare at Key Biscayne and Nixon spent most of the time relaxing with his friend Bebe Rebozo.[49]

Nixon held seventeen news conferences in his first twenty-two months in office, compared with forty-six for a comparable period by the last previous Republican president, Dwight Eisenhower. When a reporter asked him why, he said, "I try to have press conferences when I think there is public interest—not just a press interest or my interest. . . . I am not afraid of them, just as the press is not afraid of me." A committee of Sigma Delta Chi, the professional journalism organization, said Nixon's use of the news conference provided "little to inspire confidence that he actually believes in full and free accountability to the public."[50]

After the *Wall Street Journal* ran a column criticizing press coverage of one news conference, Ziegler was asked to post the column in the press room and check on the response. He reported that "most of the discussion focused around who posted the article in the press room and why."[51]

Late in 1970, with his popularity in the polls beginning to slide,

Nixon asked the White House Correspondents Association for suggestions on how to improve his press conferences. The correspondents' answer, boiled down to its essence, was: Hold more of them. In all 1971, however, he held only nine, compared with an average of twenty-four to thirty-six by presidents over the previous quarter of a century.[52]

What happened in the meantime was a series of meetings aimed at using television appearances, without the White House press corps, to bolster the president's image. As he had once before, Nixon agreed to a "conversation" with four network reporters on January 4, 1971, much like the ones Johnson held with mixed success. Somebody in the White House suggested letting each of the four question the president on a single subject of his choice for ten minutes, then allow a twenty-minute free-for-all at the end. The reporters seemed to like the idea, but Nixon did not.[53]

Next in line was Barbara Walters of the NBC "Today" program, who had been pestering Ziegler for months for a Nixon interview. She got it on March 15. A week later, Nixon gave an hour-long interview to ABC's Howard K. Smith, one of the TV correspondents most friendly to the president even though he had written his political obituary after his defeat for governor of California.[54]

Polls showed that Nixon received at least a brief bump-up in popularity after each of these television appearances. On December 6, 1971, NBC cameras were back for the filming of a special called "A Day in the Life of the President." A script prepared in the White House called for the president to walk out of his bedroom at 7:40 A.M., pick up a newspaper from a table and glance through it briefly, then walk to the Oval Office for a series of meetings. The schedule called for his secretary to bring an old friend in at 12:10 P.M., for a handshake and photo, but noted this event was "dependent upon a friend being in town." Treasury Secretary John Connally was advised to submit a memo in advance on what he thought the president should bring up in what was sardonically referred to, in quotation marks, as their "spontaneous" meeting. In a last-minute change in the script, it was decided that the Nixon family's setter, King Timahoe, would not make his entrance in the morning, but in the evening, permitting a shot of the president and his dog strolling back to the residence together.[55]

In the East Wing, Constance Stuart, First Lady Pat Nixon's staff director and press secretary, held briefings for reporters on Monday mornings and Thursday afternoons[56] and relaxed the ground rules for coverage of state dinners.[57] Notebooks were permitted, but tape recorders banned.[58] Still, there was kibitzing from the president's staff in the West Wing. Orders went out in the spring of 1970 that no one from the AP, *Time, Newsweek,* the *Washington Post,* or the *New York Times* was to be invited to social events for the next three months. Ziegler was told to talk to Mrs. Stuart about clamping down on the organizations "in any way she can without lousing up her basic operation on the social side." Haldeman once suggested that reporters cover a state dinner while standing behind velvet stanchions, but Mrs. Nixon overruled the idea.[59] During the 1972 Christmas season, *Washington Post* reporter Dorothy McCardle was excluded from the pool of reporters covering social events, in which Washington newspapers had routinely been represented. Ziegler denied that the action was retaliation, but the *Post* noted that it followed the newspaper's aggressive coverage of the burglary at Democratic National Committee headquarters in the Watergate building.[60]

Ziegler was at Key Biscayne with Nixon on June 16, 1972, when five men tried to break into the party offices in Washington and got nothing but trouble. Two days later, police said two of those arrested had the home telephone number of former CIA employee Howard E. Hunt in their address books with the notation "White House" or "W.H." The White House personnel office confirmed that Hunt was a consultant with an office in the Old Executive Office Building. Ziegler, asked about this information, said, "I am not going to comment from the White House on a third-rate burglary attempt. It is as simple as that."[61]

It wasn't as simple as that. Almost all the questions Ziegler got the next day were about Watergate. He and Pat Buchanan wrote a memo to the president saying, "Ziegler's objective was to keep the thing out of here; our view is that it should be kept away from White House association." They urged Nixon, if asked whether he was satisfied that there was no White House involvement, to reply merely that "nothing has been reported or charged . . . that has diminished my personal confidence in any of my assistants." Nixon believed that "reporters would pounce on any modifiers or qualifiers in my answer, so . . . I should just state unequivocally that there was no involvement whatever." He talked to Ziegler about it. Ziegler and Buchanan then suggested he deny involvement and decline any other comment. This is what he did.[62]

During the steamy Washington summer, coverage of Watergate

continued to escalate. On October 10, the *Washington Post* reported that Nixon's campaign committee had hired Donald Segretti, a West Coast lawyer, to conduct political spying and sabotage. Nixon told Ziegler to "quit trying to pander to those who are philosophically against us" and to "just stonewall it." On the plane to Florida a few days later, he instructed Ziegler, in Haldeman's paraphrase, that reporters were "to be used as enemies, not played for help."[63]

The unpopular war in Vietnam, although winding down, still had to be dealt with as the Watergate crisis deepened. On January 4, 1973, the president told Ziegler that sensitive negotiations were under way in Paris and he was to reply to all questions with no comment. On January 9, the day the basic elements of a settlement were agreed to in Paris, the president told his press secretary to play it "very cool" and show no indications of optimism. He said he would speak with national security adviser Kissinger, given to background sessions with reporters,[64] and "pound into him that he must not talk to the press and that we're going to do all possible to be sure that people think that nothing happened in Paris." "In other words," Haldeman translated, "we need to mislead them."

On January 23, the day Kissinger flew to Paris, the president told Ziegler to leak word to the *Washington Post* and to CBS correspondent Dan Rather that the agreement would be initialed on Friday, "so that we can throw them off balance." That day, Secretary of Defense Melvin Laird hinted that the initialing might come as early as Wednesday. It took place on Tuesday, as had been anticipated.[65]

As the Senate Watergate committee cranked up its investigation, Ziegler urged that senior White House aides not be sent to Capitol Hill to testify, to avoid what Haldeman described as "a complete circus, difficult for us to live with." Secretary of State William Rogers told the president that his press secretary had a good point. In the end, executive privilege was waived and the aides did testify. Ziegler still did not seem to be in on the most sensitive discussions. On March 23, the president and Haldeman conducted a long review of strategy, but only after the press secretary had received his instructions and left the Oval Office to give his briefing.[66] That month, Ziegler got 478 questions on Watergate. To reporters who openly scorned his responses, he said, "You can giggle if you like."[67]

On April 17, 1973, Nixon announced that he had begun an investigation of Watergate "as a result of serious charges which came to my attention."

Ziegler told reporters this was now the operative statement.

R. W. Apple of the *New York Times* asked a question that made a bit of history. Did this mean the other statements were inoperative?[68] The answer was yes. "This is the operative statement. The others are inoperative."

The remark was greeted by stunned silence in the briefing room and intensified criticism of the press office's handling of Watergate. Connally, Laird, and Alexander Haig, all of them now in key positions at the White House under a shakeup ordered by Nixon, believed Ziegler should be replaced. Nixon was loyal, however, to the spokesman who had loyally defended him. Ziegler was promoted to assistant to the president. Warren took over most of the briefing duties. Ziegler, though still holding the title of press secretary, largely retreated behind the scenes. The president who had not wanted a Jim Hagerty at his side now, in a sense, had one. He did not say, "Tell Ron to take over," but Ziegler became perhaps his closest confidante and adviser.[69]

Three days after his "inoperative" statement, Ziegler left with Nixon to spend the Easter weekend at Key Biscayne. Calling on the president at his home at the Florida retreat, he said he believed Haldeman and Ehrlichman should take leaves of absence. Nixon asked him to call Haldeman, who was spending the weekend at Camp David, and tell him this. Afterward, Ziegler told the president Haldeman seemed thoughtful when he received the message.[70]

On Monday, April 23, Nixon decided the two aides must resign. Buchanan recommended that Ziegler give Haldeman the word because of their longtime close association. Ziegler stared out the window and said nothing. When he called Haldeman at his home that evening, he was clearly in an emotional state. Dutifully, he read from his notes of what the president had told him. Haldeman and Ehrlichman had done no wrong, but they would be in the thick of controversy if they stayed, and they must go. Ehrlichman, receiving the word, thought, "The presidency is in some lot of trouble if Ron Ziegler has become Lord Chamberlain."[71]

Ziegler continued to argue against requiring the two to resign, but the president's mind was made up. On the Sunday after Easter, the two men were summoned to Camp David. When their helicopter arrived, Ziegler met them and took them to Laurel Lodge, one of the larger cabins at the Maryland hideaway. When Ehrlichman went into another room to prepare notes, Ziegler asked Haldeman to go for a walk with him in the oak woods. He told his old friend and boss that he was alarmed because Nixon had told him that he, too, was going to resign—more than a year before he did so. Haldeman said to forget it, it was just talk.

After Haldeman and Ehrlichman had agreed in separate meetings at the presidential lodge to submit their resignations, the president told Ziegler, "It's all over, Ron, do you know that?"

"No, sir," said Ziegler.

"Well, it is, it's all over."[72]

On April 30, Nixon went on television to announce that Haldeman, Ehrlichman, and White House counsel John Dean had resigned. He said new information he had received in March had persuaded him "that there was a real possibility" that members of his administration or campaign committee might be implicated.[73]

On May 3, four days after the forced resignations, the president met privately with Ziegler for thirty-one minutes.[74] "Someone had to sit there across the desk from Nixon and listen to his rambling, instruction-studded conversation for hours on end," said Ehrlichman. "Ziegler filled the vacuum."[75] It was Ziegler who argued that the expletives in tapes subpoenaed by the House Judiciary Committee should be deleted. The lawyers wanted to keep them in, saying they would give the tapes more verisimilitude. They stayed out.[76]

In August, as Nixon was preparing for another Watergate speech, Kissinger advised an expression of contrition. "Contrition is bullshit," said Ziegler. "No apologies." Sen. Barry Goldwater of Arizona, who had carried the Republican banner to overwhelming defeat in the 1964 presidential election, said, "I just can't believe he [Nixon] would listen to Ziegler. . . . Ziegler doesn't understand politics."[77]

Despite their close relationship, Nixon's irritation with what he saw as Ziegler's pampering of reporters erupted in public. Arriving at a hall in New Orleans where he was scheduled to speak to the Veterans of Foreign Wars on the U.S. incursion into Cambodia, the president saw his press secretary following him with a pack of reporters. He gave Ziegler a sturdy shove and cried out, "I don't want any press with me, and you take care of it." The episode was played twice in slow motion on CBS news. Nixon apologized to Ziegler, and the White House said the president was "under a strain."

Aside from this incident, said Ziegler, "Richard Nixon was always very considerate of me. He was always completely understanding of the intensity of the job I held."[78]

At 8:25 P.M. on Saturday, October 20, a grim-faced Ziegler appeared in the White House pressroom and announced what came to be known as the "Saturday Night Massacre." Nixon had fired Archibald Cox, the special prosecutor hired by the administration to investigate the Watergate affair. The attorney general, Elliot Richardson, and his deputy, William Ruckelshaus, had resigned. The office of special prosecutor had been abolished. Nixon had not anticipated the intensity of the response to this action. The television bulletins struck him as "breathless, almost hysterical," the commentary as "apocalyptic."[79]

On April 29, 1974, Nixon released edited transcripts of the tapes sought by the Judiciary Committee. Even with the expletives deleted, the blunt talk on them aroused a furor, and there were demands for Nixon's resignation. Ziegler issued a statement, approved by Nixon. The president would not resign. "He is up for the battle, he intends to fight it, and he feels he has a personal and constitutional duty to do so." Nevertheless, Nixon talked several times with Ziegler and Haig about resigning. They advised against it.[80]

Under congressional pressure, Nixon had agreed to the appointment of a new special prosecutor, Leon Jaworski, who subpoenaed tapes of sixty-four presidential conversations. On July 24, the Supreme Court ruled unanimously that the tapes must be turned over to U.S. District Judge John Sirica. Two days later, the Judiciary Committee voted 27 to 11 for an article of impeachment charging Nixon with obstruction of justice. Ziegler called him with the news as he was dressing in his beach trailer at San Clemente after a swim in the Pacific Ocean.[81] On Sunday, as Nixon flew back to Washington, Haig told reporters on *Air Force One* that the president might consider resigning if it were in the national interest.[82]

On July 31, Haig read the transcript of the June 23, 1972, tape— the one that came to be called the "smoking gun"—in which Nixon instructed Haldeman to have the CIA step in and halt the FBI's Watergate investigation. "I just don't see how we can survive this one," he told the president. "Once this tape gets out, it's over." Ziegler either listened to the tape or read the transcript the same afternoon. "I could tell that he too now felt the situation was all but hopeless," said Nixon.[83]

The next day, at his hideaway office in the Old Executive Office Building, Nixon told Ziegler that he had decided to resign. He said he wanted to do so immediately, but Ziegler persuaded him to take time to prepare.

At 12:30 P.M. on August 8, Ziegler stood in the briefing room, out of breath and near tears, and said, "Tonight, at nine o'clock Eastern Daylight Time, the president of the United States will address the nation on radio and television from his Oval Office."[84]

Before making the announcement, he called Bob Hartmann, chief of staff to Vice President Gerald Ford. Ford had been picked by Nixon when Agnew pleaded guilty to income tax evasion and resigned. Tomorrow, he would be President Ford.

"I never cared much for Ziegler," said Hartmann, "but I murmured something like, 'I'm sorry, Ron.' "[85]

11

A Matter of Conscience

ON AUGUST 8, 1974, Jerald F. terHorst was one of a horde of journalists asking questions about the resignation of President Nixon. On August 9, he stood nervously at the podium in the pressroom as spokesman for President Gerald R. Ford.

Thrust into the presidency in midterm, Ford turned, as Truman had before him, to a home-state journalist.

In 1948, as a twenty-six-year-old reporter for the *Grand Rapids Press,* terHorst covered Ford's first campaign for Congress. Ford, thirty-four at the time, won it, and terHorst soon was hired by the *Detroit News,* covering state and local politics and then moving to the newspaper's Washington bureau.

Along the way, the congressman and the journalist became friends. By the time Ford became president, terHorst was chief of his paper's five-member Washington bureau and had been covering the White House for sixteen years.

He had thirty-six hours notice that he might be offered a White House job. The first call came from Republican Sen. Robert Griffin of Michigan, a member of the "kitchen cabinet" that counseled Ford as vice president. Nixon was still president, but his resignation was becoming increasingly inevitable. TerHorst expressed interest.

Philip Buchen, the new president's legal counsel, was from Grand Rapids, as were Ford and terHorst. Buchen recommended to Ford that their fellow townsman be tapped.

"The moment I heard he might be available, I told Phil to call and offer him the job," said Ford. After talking to his wife and his editors, terHorst called back and accepted.[1]

"The Michigan mafia is taking over," groused Robert Hartmann, the former *Los Angeles Times* correspondent who had been Ford's chief of staff as vice president.[2]

To UPI's Helen Thomas, terHorst was "the reporter's ideal of a press secretary. . . . He believed the public was entitled to the facts from the White House."[3]

Hartmann, the reporter turned government official, saw it differently. TerHorst, he said, "had no instincts that had in any way been conditioned to the differences between a press officer and a member of the press."[4]

Ford had made it clear in advance that if he became president he would fire Ziegler, whose slighting remarks and condescending habit of referring to the vice president of the United States as "Jerry Ford" did not sit well with him.[5]

On August 9, Ziegler telephoned Hartmann to say he was flying to San Clemente with Nixon. If he could be of any help to the new press secretary, it would have to be that day. Hartmann passed the word to terHorst, and the outgoing and incoming spokesmen met for twenty minutes. As terHorst recalled the session, it was "here's the office, the men's room is around the corner, the safe is under my desk, here's the combination, if you need me give me a call in California—they're calling the helicopter now."[6]

The meeting set the tone for a hectic transition. Larry Speakes, a lowly press aide on the Nixon staff who was picked by terHorst as an assistant press secretary, likened the next thirty days to "standing by a railroad track and watching a freight train go by while trying to read the words on the box-cars." Speakes remembered that the staff worked from August 9 to September 9, weekends and all, without a day off.[7]

The calm, pipe-smoking newsroom veteran at the center of this turmoil moved quickly to try to demonstrate that the Ford administration would be open and aboveboard with the press. "I thought I could help straighten out the miserable climate between one side of the podium and the other," he said. At his first briefing, just after Ford was sworn in, terHorst was understandably nervous, his hands shaking throughout. The next day, he was more at ease. Asked whether Ford was still opposed to granting Nixon immunity from prosecution for Watergate offenses, as he had said at his vice presidential confirmation hearing, terHorst replied crisply, "Yes, I can assure you of that."[8]

Trying to put a new stamp on the new administration, terHorst outlawed use of the term "photo opportunity," first used in the Johnson White House and formalized under Nixon. His ruling did not last.

The term, meaning a brief chance for photographers and reporters to have a crack at the president at the beginning of an otherwise closed meeting, became a permanent piece of White House jargon.[9]

There were other changes that were more long-lasting. Reversing rules established during the Johnson and Nixon administrations, terHorst and his staff decreed that the pool of reporters accompanying the president in his motorcade would continue onto the White House grounds instead of being left at the gate, and that reporters would be admitted onto the South Lawn to witness the arrival and departure of the presidential helicopter.[10]

The new boss of the press office was considerate of his subordinates. When Ford decided to go to church on the first Sunday of his presidency, terHorst volunteered to handle the travel pool himself, accompanying reporters in the press van as the presidential motorcade made its way to and from the church. Assistant Secretary Bill Roberts manned the office while terHorst was gone, but terHorst took over the duty for the rest of the day. "Really very thoughtful and I appreciate it," thought Roberts.[11]

On Monday, August 26, it was decided that Ford would hold his first presidential news conference that Wednesday in the East Room. But terHorst wanted to change the format. "I did *not* want Jerry Ford standing behind a huge, bullet-proof podium with his back to the wall and that blue curtain, as Richard Nixon and Lyndon Johnson did. That setup made them look like caged men." At a meeting in the East Room, the new press secretary proposed taking down the curtain and turning the chairs around, so that the president would enter by walking down a spacious red-carpeted corridor that would then be the backdrop for his appearance.

Roberts, assigned to supervise television aspects of the press office operation, objected. "To me it looked like something for the coronation of a king or a queen," he said. "The long shot from the East Room down the hall made it look regal. It is . . . foreign to what President Ford represents." Someone else said it would be a great setting for a wedding. TerHorst still liked it, and decided to make a videotape and show it to the president on Tuesday. Instead of looking at the video, Ford went to the East Room, examined the setup, and approved it, along with terHorst's suggestions to use a smaller podium and move the front row of seats closer to it. The *Washington Post* noted the changes without comment in a generally favorable analysis of Ford's appearance, and other press comments were enthusiastic.[12]

The setting would become familiar to television viewers in succeeding administrations.

Ford's news conferences got mixed reviews. After his sixth, on January 21, 1975, Assistant Press Secretary Tom DeCair said in an internal memo, "A dry run would have helped him overcome some of the mid-sentence and mid-answer pauses he experienced. If he doesn't want to or doesn't seem to have time for a dry-run, someone should have the balls to tell him that he absolutely MUST." [13]

At a meeting before the first press conference, Ford's advisers peppered him with questions. "We would ask him the damnedest questions," Hartmann said. "Staffers would present embarrassing questions to the president to see how well he could handle those questions off the cuff." Ford assumed most of the questions would be on the economy, troubled as he took office. Hartmann disagreed. Reporters would be interested chiefly in what the president was going to do about Nixon. He was right. Although some reporters did ask about the economy, eight of the twenty-nine questions dealt with the former president's legal jeopardy.

Helen Thomas led off, asking, "Would you use your pardon authority, if necessary?" The president seemed nervous, shuffling through cue cards before answering that "until any legal process has been undertaken, I think it is unwise and untimely for me to make any commitment." Back in the Oval Office, he asked advisers how long this sort of questioning would go on. They said it would continue as long as Nixon's legal status remained unclarified. "I simply couldn't believe that the press would focus entirely on these matters," said Ford. "I was wrong." [14]

On August 30, Ford summoned Hartmann, Buchen, and Presidential Counselor John Marsh to the Oval Office. When they arrived, Haig was with him. In his usual calm, unemotional tone of voice, the president said he was inclined to grant Nixon immunity from prosecution. For moments, nothing was heard but the ticking of an antique clock on the office wall. Then Buchen suggested it was not the right time for such an announcement. Hartmann pointed out that only two days earlier, Ford had said he would let the legal process take its course before making any decision. But nobody raised any strong objection. [15]

The president's press secretary was not at the meeting. Ford and Buchen had discussed whether to fill him in on the pardon plan, but had decided against it. "If I informed him of the decision and reporters asked him whether or not a pardon was in the works, he would either have to lie and violate the pledge of openness and honesty he'd given his former colleagues, or have had to tell the truth," said Ford.[16]

Benton Becker, a Miami lawyer assisting in the Ford transition as a volunteer, was dispatched to San Clemente to confer with Herbert J. Miller Jr., a former assistant attorney general retained by Nixon. David Kraslow, Washington bureau chief for the Cox newspapers, learned that Becker and Miller were registered at the San Clemente Inn. He asked terHorst if the two were negotiating a possible pardon for Nixon. The press secretary checked with Buchen and told Kraslow that the lawyers were negotiating the transfer of the former president's papers and tapes. Kraslow accepted the explanation and did not write a story.[17]

The next afternoon, Saturday, September 7, terHorst was finally told what was going on. He immediately started preparing for the announcement. He also decided to resign—not, he said, because he had been kept in the dark, although he was piqued about this, but because he could not in conscience support the president's action.

Ordinarily, reporters received mimeographed copies of White House announcements. But terHorst thought making advance stencils would risk having the news leak. He got approval that night from Hartmann, Buchen, Marsh, and Haig for a tight security plan.

Beginning at 6 A.M. Sunday, two secretaries made copies of four documents on a machine in the White House basement, with a uniformed Secret Service officer guarding the door. The documents were the text of the pardon proclamation, the statement Ford was making on television, an opinion by Attorney General William B. Saxbe declaring Nixon the rightful owner of Watergate tapes and papers, and an agreement between Nixon and the government covering access to the tapes. Speakes and DeCair carried the copies to terHorst's private office. There the material was assembled behind drawn curtains.[18]

Reporters gathered on the lower level of the press room, alerted by telephone that a presidential announcement was forthcoming. "What is it?" they asked. "Is it foreign or domestic?" Always the answer was the same. "I'm sorry, I can't tell you." No, nobody could even give them a hint. In the Oval Office, Roberts set up a single camera for pool coverage.[19]

The night before, terHorst had broken the news to his family that he would have to be at work at 6 A.M. the next day, Sunday. When he had a chance, he told his wife why. Mrs. terHorst, who was active in

14. Jerald terHorst, his calm, pipe-smoking demeanor masking initial nervousness, spoke to journalists after being named press secretary by the new president, Gerald R. Ford. TerHorst resigned in protest when Ford pardoned Richard Nixon. *Courtesy Gerald R. Ford Library.*

Democratic politics in Washington's Virginia suburbs, asked, "What are you going to do about that?" TerHorst said he would do his job, and then resign. He wrote his letter of resignation at home, finishing about 3:30 A.M. before getting an hour or so of sleep. "It wasn't a very long letter, but it was a difficult one to write," he said. In his office that morning, he retyped it on a single piece of White House stationery, stuffed it into a manila envelope, and wrote on the envelope in red ink, "The President—Eyes Only." As he learned that morning that Nixon's response to the pardon would express no contrition, his resolve hardened. "I had been reared in the belief that forgiveness can be extended only after admission of wrongdoing," he said.

"It is with a heavy heart that I hereby tender my resignation as press secretary to the president, effective today," he had written. "My prayers nonetheless remain with you, sir."[20]

A few minutes before 10 A.M., a little more than an hour before the president was to make his announcement, terHorst entered the Oval Office. "Mr. President, I wanted to see you for a few moments before you went on the air," he said. Ford sensed that something was bothering his old friend, but nevertheless brought up some technical matters regarding the broadcast. TerHorst cut him short. "Mr. President, I have something here that you need to see." He opened the manila envelope and removed the letter. As Ford finished reading it, he spun his chair part way around and looked past terHorst to the windows opening onto the Rose Garden. He said he was sorry that terHorst felt as he did, and hoped he would reconsider. "My decision is final," said terHorst. Ford said his was, too. He walked around his desk, shook hands with the departing aide, and put his arm around his shoulder. As the president answered a telephone call, terHorst walked from the room, closing the door behind him. He had become the first press secretary ever to resign in protest over a presidential policy decision.[21]

Sitting in his high-backed chair in the Oval Office, Ford was troubled. He knew that terHorst's resignation would cast a shadow on his act of pardon. He summoned Marsh, a former Virginia congressman known for his tact, and asked him to try to persuade terHorst to withdraw his letter, at least for a day.[22]

TerHorst was delayed by negotiations with the television crews over coverage arrangements, and Marsh caught up with him on his way back to the press office. "Jerry, you can't do it," the Virginian pleaded. "Please reconsider . . . even for twenty-four hours." TerHorst agreed to think about it, but added, "I'm not changing my mind, Jack. I just have to do this." Marsh handed him the resignation letter, and he placed it in the inside breast pocket of his jacket.

After the television announcement, terHorst returned to his office and jotted a personal note to Ford saying he was committed to resigning that day despite Marsh's intercession. He attached the note to the letter and put both into a white envelope, again addressed to the president with the bureaucratic proviso "Eyes Only."[23]

In the whirl of activity surrounding Ford's bombshell announcement, most of the staff had missed their lunch. TerHorst called some of them together in his office late in the afternoon and they joined him over sandwiches. They talked about their handling of the story, and then terHorst fumbled in his desk drawer and pulled out an onionskin copy of the letter. Deputy Press Secretary Jack Hushen's response was much like Marsh's. "Jerry, you can't do this," he said. TerHorst was unmoved. "I'm going to clean out my desk and fade away," he said. He said he would withhold any public statement, allowing Ford to announce the resignation Monday on his return from a speaking engagement in Pittsburgh.[24]

But the story was too good to hold. Tom De Frank, White House correspondent for *Newsweek,* called and asked if there had been any staff resignations because of the pardon. Rather than deceive a reporter, terHorst told him the truth. The magazine put out a news release on its exclusive story, and it was picked up by the wire services and networks. To reporters who called him at his home in Alexandria that evening, terHorst said he had resigned for the "good conscience reasons" that he had expressed to Ford. Bill Roberts, handling the story at the White House, called the president and got a statement, saying, "I wish that Jerry could appreciate how difficult this decision was for me." Before reaching Ford, Roberts talked with Hartmann who "railed against . . . the rat, the dirty rat that would do a thing like that." On Monday morning, terHorst spent fifteen or twenty minutes in the office, cleaned out his desk, and left. He returned to the *Detroit News* as a columnist, and resumed the book he was writing before he joined the White House staff—a biography of Gerald Ford.[25]

Predictably, the resignation was the second line in many stories about the pardon in the Monday morning papers. Critics said the press secretary's action intensified the storm of criticism that followed the pardon, and that was blamed by many for Ford's defeat at the polls two years later. Maybe so. But even before terHorst's resignation became known, the flood of telephone calls to the White House switchboard was running 8 to 1 against the pardon.[26]

Some doubted the reason terHorst gave for resigning. They said he objected, not so much to the pardon, as to the fact he was not told about it sooner, and thus misled reporters. Nearly a quarter of a century later, Ford would say, "It probably was a combination of both." TerHorst said, "My basic reason was that I didn't want to spend my time as press secretary defending something with which I so vehemently disagreed. The fact I misled some people was also true, but it was secondary." If he had been advised from the start, he said, he would have done his job as press secretary until the announcement was made, and then resigned.

At the time, some at the White House believed that terHorst had found the job more grueling than he expected, and was looking for a way out. To such skeptics, Ford said, "You just don't understand these evangelical Michigan Dutchmen."[27] To his boss, terHorst had acted out of conscience.

A more basic question was whether it was a good reason. To Helen Thomas, terHorst's resignation "set a standard of integrity . . . and established the principle that you can say 'NO' to a president and walk away from a White House job." But Hushen, stepping in as acting press secretary after terHorst left, told reporters, "You should know that I do not share Jerry's belief that an individual should resign this position when he differs with a major policy matter. The person on this podium is communicating the president's views, not his own." Another White House staffer put it more succinctly, telling terHorst that "nobody cares what you think. People want to know what the president thinks. You're just a mouthpiece." Said terHorst: "I never presumed to be more than a voice to the media on behalf of the president, but at the same time I was not a robot either."[28]

•   •   •

The search for a new mouthpiece began immediately. Hartmann sent Ford a list of five names: David Broder of *The Washington Post;* Bonnie Angelo of *Time;* Bill Roberts, who had been the deputy press secretary to Ford as vice president before becoming an assistant in terHorst's operation; Jerry Friedheim, the Pentagon spokesman; and Ron Nessen of NBC, who covered Ford both as vice president and president. Roberts, asked for his own suggestions, mused, "I doubt they'd pick anybody from the media . . . since they got burned so badly with terHorst." Ford felt the same way at first. "Look what happened," he told Hartmann. "Why risk it again?" Hartmann believed picking another spokesman from the press room "would show Ford was not down on the White House press corps because terHorst had given him the business." Ford struck some names out and marked the remainder in order of preference. He asked Hartmann to sound them out. Angelo turned down the possible chance to be the first female press secretary. She had also declined an offer to be First Lady Betty Ford's spokeswoman.

When he called Nessen, Hartmann pretended to be asking advice and posing a hypothetical question: If the correspondent were being offered the job, would he accept? Nessen lived only a block and a half from the Hartmann home, and the president's chief of staff "could almost hear his eagerness without the phone."[29]

Ford liked Nessen. He had attended a party at the Nessen home two weeks after becoming president and had been noticed to dance "a long dance" with the correspondent's wife at a state dinner at the White House.[30] He asked Hartmann to double-check. "Nessen was the only person to whom I offered the post," he said.

When Hartmann brought Nessen to the Oval Office on September

24, the president raised a question: "Suppose a repeat of the terHorst-Nixon pardon situation occurred. If he knew everything and was asked about a sensitive issue, would that embarrass or compromise him before his former colleagues?" Nessen said it was no problem. "He recognized the potential conflict, but would trust our judgment." According to Nessen, Ford mentioned terHorst "with some anger" and said he "badly needed . . . someone who would not quit on him."[31]

Leaving the White House, Nessen was asked if he was going to be the new press secretary. "Not that I know of," he replied. When he got home, he received a call from Hushen. He had got off to a bad start by misleading reporters. He should tell them he was under consideration, but any announcement would have to come from the White House. He was on the telephone until nearly midnight correcting his mistake.[32]

After Nessen's appointment was announced a few days later, Hushen heard snickers as the new press secretary assured reporters he would never knowingly lie to the White House press corps or mislead its members. "Ron got off to a real rocky start," the deputy said.[33]

Nessen would be the first electronic journalist to become White House press secretary. Gone were the days when Truman's J. Leonard Reinsch was hounded out of the job before he even got it because his background was in radio.

In many ways, Ford had chosen a spokesman very different from his old friend terHorst. Where terHorst was calm and judicious, Nessen was volatile and loquacious. Where most reporters found terHorst congenial, some considered Nessen arrogant. Where the "evangelical Michigan Dutchman" was quick to resign on principle, Nessen told reporters at an early briefing that his views on the issues were irrelevant.

Nessen was also the first press secretary born and raised in the nation's capital. He went to American University in Washington for a year, then "got itchy to go to work" and took a job as a newscaster for a small radio station in Martinsburg, West Virginia. "I knew that I needed to end up with a college degree so while I worked at the station there I went to Shepherd College [in nearby Shepherdstown, West Virginia]," Nessen said. In 1954, at the age of twenty, he returned to the Washington area as a newscaster for a larger station in Arlington, Virginia, and then spent a year with a suburban newspaper in Rockville, Maryland, and six years with UPI in Washington. For most of these years, he was a part-time student at American University, from which he graduated in 1959. For NBC, his assignments included the war in Vietnam and the Johnson White House.

Reflecting the continuing growth of the federal bureaucracy, the press office now had a professional staff of seventeen. Five were presidential appointees. There were Nessen, two deputies, and six assistant press secretaries. The others included two photographers, two television advisers, three staff assistants, and a United States Information Agency officer assigned to the White House to deal with foreign policy news.

Counting nonprofessional personnel, the press office staff had increased to fifty-six in the Nixon administration. Ford's chief of staff, Donald Rumsfeld, ordered it reduced to forty-five. In April, DeCair told a reporter that it was down to fifty at the most. Privately, the assistant press secretary told Nessen, "I think if someone dug into it, they'd find that your staff is fully as big as Ziegler's."[34]

The administrative duties of the press secretary had increased greatly since the one-man operations of Hoover's George Akerson and Theodore Joslin. There were sensitive personnel matters to be dealt with.

Paul Miltich had been Ford's press secretary in the House of Representatives and as vice president. But as Nixon's troubles mounted and news coverage of Ford intensified, some reporters thought he was not up to the job. A *Chicago Tribune* article on the vice president's staff said the press secretary rated a C-minus with the enlarged number of reporters now covering Ford. When the time came to pick a presidential spokesman, the new president decided that his longtime aide was "hard-working and competent," but not "up to so major a responsibility." Miltich was downcast at being passed over, especially because a sister in Minnesota had told friends that her brother would be the presidential press secretary. "What can I tell them?" the embarrassed aide asked. He was heartened when Ford announced that Miltich would stay on as an assistant. But Hushen, director of information at the Justice Department, became terHorst's No. 1 aide as deputy press secretary, and Miltich was shunted into a job across the street in the Old Executive Office Building.[35]

After Nessen's advent, Miltich wanted to be head of the Communications Office, but was downgraded from assistant to the president to assistant press secretary and assigned to speechwriting and helping the president prepare for press conferences. In January 1975, Nessen was complaining that "the Paul Miltich problem" was still unsolved and "somebody is going to have to ask the president to ask Paul to take another job in the administration." In February, Miltich left to accept an appointment to the Postal Rate Commission.[36]

And then there were John McLaughlin, the Jesuit priest who had been one of Nixon's last defenders, and Ken Clawson, the former *Washington Post* reporter who had been a Nixon propagandist as director of communications. "They worked for Al Haig, or for the Republican party, or someone else, but they . . . were attached to the White House press office for salary purposes," terHorst said. In an August 24 memo, both were listed as "termination date unknown." In Hartmann's less bureaucratic language, "they simply refused to be fired."

On September 4, terHorst asked for McLaughlin's resignation, effective September 30. On September 10, the day after terHorst cleared out his desk, Hushen said McLaughlin was leaving, but he did not know when. On September 30, Nessen reported in a personnel memo that McLaughlin had "absolutely no place . . . in my operation, and he must go as soon as possible." Two days later, by Nessen's account, McLaughlin agreed to announce the next day that he was leaving on October 14. He later became a popular television talk show host.

As for Clawson, Nessen said in an internal memo that the holdover communications director "should leave the White House in the very near future." Clawson had been told by Haig that he might be detailed to Nixon until February 9 or retained at the White House until December 1. After a meeting with Nessen on October 7, Clawson agreed to take a month's vacation and officially leave on November 7.[37]

Relations between Nessen and Sheila Weidenfeld, the television producer hired by Betty Ford to be her press secretary, were rocky. They did not improve after Weidenfeld launched an ambitious plan to reorganize the East Wing press office and make it "easy and exciting" for reporters to cover the first family. Among other things, the plan called for two additions to her staff, a loudspeaker in the office so nobody would have to go to the trouble of attending West Wing briefings, and room service when there wasn't time to make it to the White House mess for lunch.[38]

Although 149 people received transcripts of the press secretary's briefings, it had long been the policy not to broadcast them to offices outside the press area, including those of presidential assistants. The fear was that a reporter might be listening and be able to circumvent the rule against filing a story before the briefing was over. Nessen pointed this out and suggested she send somebody to attend his briefings. Weidenfeld persisted and an exception to the rule was made for her office—"against my better judgment," said Nessen. As for the proposed increase in staff, he said, "Frankly I'm not aware that Sheila's operation does enough to require two extra people." Besides, he added, "with more people there is a greater chance of more mischief." He asked Chief of Staff Dick Cheney to leave his name out of it in turning down Weidenfeld's request, as she "tends to be aggressively resentful when she feels her requests are unjustly rejected."[39]

In July 1975, the White House Correspondents Association by-passed Weidenfeld and went directly to the president's press secretary after Ford decreed that official presidential receptions would be closed to coverage. In a letter to the president, given to Nessen for delivery, Helen Thomas complained that the policy would result in "distorted reports from third-hand sources after the event." Nessen argued that the administration had gone far enough by resuming the invitation of reporters as guests and permitting open coverage of formal remarks. The president, he said, should be allowed "a few brief minutes now and then to chat privately with his guests without reporters listening in to every word." Ford instructed Nessen to arrange for a pool of reporters to circulate at the receptions on a trial basis, without tape recorders or notebooks, and "with the understanding the pool reporters will respect the privacy of personal conversations."[40]

The short-tempered Nessen had flare-ups with reporters, but received good marks for accurate and detailed reporting of the president's meetings. Sitting in on a cabinet session, he saw himself as "a reporter inside the White House," scribbling notes on subjects ranging from extra long staple cotton to antitrust legislation and relaying lengthy quotes that were in the next day's papers.[41]

In foreign policy, Nessen was more at sea. He attended all major domestic policy meetings, on the president's orders, but few meetings of the National Security Council, although he had the required security clearances.[42]

In November 1974, he accompanied Ford on his first presidential trip abroad and got himself into what he himself described as "a full-fledged mess." The final stop on the president's Far Eastern tour was Vladivostok, where he reached an arms control agreement with the Soviets' Leonid Brezhnev. After the meeting, Kissinger told Nessen

15. President Ford's second press secretary, Ron Nessen, slouches in a chair at an Oval Office meeting. *Left to right:* Nessen, Robert Hartmann, Max Friedersdorf, Dick Cheney, John Marsh, the president. *Courtesy Gerald R. Ford Library.*

that he found Ford better than Nixon at face-to-face talks with the Russians. On a train to the airport, after a few drinks of vodka, Nessen translated this as "Richard Nixon could not achieve this in five years. President Ford has achieved it in three months." In ensuing days, newspapers ridiculed his remark as "gushing" and "puffery." Donald Rumsfeld, United States ambassador to the North Atlantic Treaty Organization, cabled Cheney strongly suggesting that Ford call Nixon and say that "Nessen was speaking for himself, not President Ford." Henry Kissinger, who had left for a stop in China after the Vladivostok meeting, also wired suggesting that Nessen back off from his statement. Ford said he was content to let the statement stand, but concurred when Nessen said a few days later, "I think it was probably a hasty and oversimplified remark." Taking a cue from Rumsfeld, Nessen said the agreement "was really a kind of a culmination of steps that have been taken over the years." Barely beneath the surface of all this was Kissinger's habit of talking to reporters on "deep background," not for attribution to anybody. Some writers bent the rules to say that the secretary of state had been the source of stories that Ford was the more willing of the two presidents to look his adversary in the eye. The reports sent Kissinger scurrying on a public mission to San Clemente to make his amends to the former president. "Kissinger was about as good as anybody at using information for his own purposes," said Nessen.[43]

Nessen soon learned that his foreign policy answers were heard farther away than San Clemente. After a January 1975, briefing, his national security aide, Les Janka, told him he thought he had closed the door too firmly on any future U.S. intervention in Vietnam. Nessen replied that he didn't think Hanoi devised its strategy according to what he said at the podium. "Oh, yes," said Janka. "The North Vietnamese know what you say at your briefings." Foreign Minister le Duc Tho, during talks with Kissinger, had once quoted an answer by Ziegler.[44]

On April 1, 1975, at the vacation White House in Palm Springs, California, Nessen told reporters that Ford had mentioned that morning "that there have been, and are, ongoing diplomatic efforts to have a negotiated settlement" between North and South Vietnam. Secretary of State Kissinger, reading at the State Department an URGENT Reuters story on the statement, was said to have exclaimed, "Bullshit!" and called Brent Scowcroft at the White House, his deputy in his other role as national security adviser. "Does Ron Nessen know something that I don't know?" he asked. Nessen said that after hearing Ford's remark he had checked with the NSC press aide, Margaret Vanderhye, and understood her to say there were new initiatives under way. Vanderhye said she had been misunderstood. Nessen, enraged, called Kissinger and Scowcroft and got their approval for a statement he gave out six hours after the original briefing. The press secretary told reporters, "I was misinformed on the subject today by a member of the National Security Council staff and as a result you were given some inaccurate information."[45]

On April 6, Nessen reportedly said at a press staff meeting that Kissinger might lose his NSC post. Gerald Warren, the Nixon holdover Nessen had picked as his deputy, is said to have warned him, "If that word gets out, Kissinger will make you walk the plank." Nessen was more guarded at his briefing, saying only that Ford was broadening the spectrum of people from whom he sought foreign policy advice. The statement had been approved by Rumsfeld, by now White House chief of staff. When CBS newsman Bob Schieffer asked him if this meant Kissinger was falling from favor at the White House, Nessen nodded in the affirmative. The next morning, Schieffer reported on

CBS radio that Kissinger might indeed be on his way out at the NSC. At his briefing that day, Nessen denied the story. Over lunch, Schieffer told Louis Thompson, Nessen's assistant in charge of administration, that Nessen was his source.

The next evening, at a briefing before the State of the Union speech, a reporter asked Kissinger, "Hey, Henry, who's going to replace you in the NSC?" To Nessen's obvious discomfiture, Kissinger replied, "Well, it might be Ronald Nessen."

(Ford did relieve Kissinger of his NSC duties in November 1975. Years later the former president said Nessen had known nothing in advance about the change in Kissinger's status "so how could he leak it?")

On April 11, Nessen fired Thompson, saying he was being let go because his task of reorganization was done, and told Kissinger he had solved the problem of the leak. Thompson told the *Des Moines Tribune* that he was a "fall guy" and that Nessen was widely known to be the source himself. Schieffer told the AP that he wouldn't say who the source was, but it was not Thompson.

Nessen, although he did suspect Thompson of leaking some anti-Kissinger stories, said later his action was "something I'm not proud of." Meanwhile, rumors circulated that Nessen might be replaced by one of his deputies, William Greener. No wonder that speechwriter John J. Casserly mused in his diary, "Where do they get the time for all the intrigue?"[46]

Intrigue there was plenty of, as usual at the White House. Even before Nessen's appointment was announced, Hartmann had moved to bring the press secretary under his control, advising Ford, "You'd better tell him, Mr. President, that I have a lot of experience in the field and that I'm going to be looking over his shoulder a lot." The president squelched his longtime aide, reminding both him and Nessen that Hartmann's field was speechwriting, but Hartmann still looked over Nessen's shoulder. Hartmann was disappointed in his ambition to be White House chief of staff, but Donald Rumsfeld, who got the job, kept a tight rein on the press secretary.[47]

Tension continued to simmer between the press office and Kissinger's National Security Council. In June 1975, an assistant press secretary who dealt with the foreign press in Washington resigned, citing what Nessen called "the demeaning position he felt he was in as a result of the NSC's refusal to allow him any role in foreign policy news guidance."[48]

Nessen's general policy, apparently dictated by Kissinger and others, was to provide information only when asked. Too often, he said, he wasn't asked. He came into the press room each day with a briefing book of two hundred pages containing prepared answers to anticipated questions. Each day there was a rehearsal in his office in which staff members played reporter and shot questions at him. Each day, many of these questions failed to come up at the briefing.[49]

What did come up was Nixon. In Nessen's first month as press secretary, according to one compilation, there were 1,074 questions asked in his briefings, and 477 of them dealt with the former president or his holdovers in the White House. Eight months after he moved in, he complained, "It is going to take me six months to get the smell of Watergate out of the press room. It's a snake pit." At a briefing in June, 1975 he scolded reporters for "cynical thinking habits" and "blind and irrational mistrust."

There were sharp exchanges in which the press secretary was called a liar and accused of covering up news. Speechwriter Casserly said Nessen "unnecessarily antagonized newsmen with games of oneupmanship. . . . He takes tough questions personally." When one reporter, after a particularly heated fifty-five minute session asked, "Ron, did you anticipate getting into this free-for-all when you came out here today?," Nessen shot back, "What, you feel I was not prepared? . . . What is it that you feel I was not prepared for?" The press secretary admitted he had to work to control his temper.[50]

The press office also spent time on the president's press conferences. Procedures for preparing his question-and-answer briefing book were gradually refined. For his November 26, 1975, conference, Ford had a book of seventy-eight pages including questions and answers, transcripts of press office briefings, memos, presidential statements, overviews of subjects, and a sheet headed "Things Possibly to Stay Away From."[51]

As the 1976 presidential election neared, *Newsweek* broached a politically sensitive matter that had previously been the subject of press room speculation and rumor. The campaigning Ford, the magazine said, "enjoys a pre-prandial drink with the boys, like any politician on the road, and occasionally shows it in his post-prandial speeches." Ford was not a heavy drinker. When he had two or three drinks after a round of golf, Bill Roberts thought it so exceptional that he made a point of it in his diary. Nevertheless, *Newsweek* was not alone in noticing that the president did sometimes fumble his words after a drink or two. "I'm still not prepared to say it publicly," a radio newsman was quoted as saying. The subject did not come up in any of the briefings after the magazine piece, but Nessen was aware of the problem. In April 1975, en route to New Orleans to speak at Tulane University, Ford had decided to insert in his speech a statement that the war in Vietnam "is finished as far as America is concerned." Nessen realized the importance the passage would have to young people. He also realized that his boss was having a tiring day and had sipped a cocktail. In a hotel elevator as they departed for the campus, he urged the president to read the speech slowly. Ford did, and the inserted line was greeted with tumultuous applause.[52]

By the end of 1975, Nessen's operation was coming under increasing criticism. On a presidential trip to China, correspondents complained the press secretary was frequently absent from the press room and often seemed poorly informed. Some said they were better off relying on the Chinese for information. Casserly, noting that reporters had laid off the press secretary for a few months after he accused them of "mindless arrogance," said they were "back sniping at him hot and heavy now." In the *Washington Post,* Lou Cannon wrote charitably that many reporters considered Nessen's most serious fault was "his willingness, out of a desire to seem helpful, to give information about subjects on which he is uninformed."[53]

But Nessen hung on. On election night, 1976, he ripped from his Teletype printer a UPI flash declaring Jimmy Carter the winner and Ford the loser in the battle for the presidency. He rushed to the office of Dick Cheney, who had succeeded Rumsfeld as chief of staff. Learning that Cheney had gone to the residence to brief the president, he followed with the wire service flash in his hand. When he saw Ford, he didn't have the heart to show it to him. He could see that the president had already been receiving bad news.[54]

On November 22, Carter met with the outgoing president. It was a long sad day for Nessen, answering questions about the trivia of Ford's last days in the White House, which were also his own. At times, he seemed close to breaking down. A couple of days later, for the first time, he skipped holding a briefing because he had nothing to say.[55]

The last question at his last White House briefing, on inauguration day, 1977, came from Frances Lewine of the Associated Press. It was simply, "Do you have anything else, Ron?" Ron didn't. He hesitated at the podium for a moment, thinking people might wish him luck, or even applaud. They didn't.[56]

Nessen went on to be Washington bureau chief for Mutual Radio News and public-relations director for a trade association.

What if it had been he, not terHorst, who faced being grilled by reporters about a presidential decision he could not find it in his heart to support?

"I don't think I would have had a problem doing that," said Nessen. "It would be his decision, and my job to give his reasons and his explanation for doing it, whether I agreed with him or not.

"The press secretary is not an elective official. In many ways he is a technician, a conveyor belt for information. Who could possibly care what my view of the issue is?" [57]

12

The Fine Hand

WHEN JIMMY CARTER BECAME PRESIDENT in January, 1977, Jody Powell had already been his press secretary for six years.

Not since the inception of the modern press office had a White House spokesman had so long and close a relationship with the chief executive he served. One had to go back to Woodrow Wilson's Joe Tumulty to find a parallel.

Just as Tumulty was Governor Wilson's private secretary in Trenton, Powell was Governor Carter's press secretary in Atlanta. And, unlike Tumulty, he remained a trusted adviser to Carter throughout his presidency.

"Jody Powell probably knows me better than anyone else except my wife," Carter said.[1]

Powell was one of the "key advisers" Carter convened to discuss strategy for dealing with the Iranian hostage crisis.[2] Powell was one of those urging the president to put pressure on Israel for accommodation with the Arabs.[3] Powell spoke up along with the president's economic advisers in talks on tax policy.[4] Powell took part in foreign policy discussions with the vice president, the national security adviser, and the secretaries of state and defense.[5]

"The press over there knows that when they deal with Jody they are dealing with somebody whose fine hand is very much in the policy decisions," said State Department spokesman Thomas Reston.[6]

Powell was born in 1943 in Vienna, Georgia, thirty-six miles east of Carter's home town of Plains on Georgia highway 27. From there, he went to Emory University in Atlanta, where he earned a degree in political science in 1966 and did graduate study. Carter by then was embarked in politics as a state senator and had made one unsuccessful campaign for governor. As he was gearing up for his second try in 1970, Powell came knocking on his door and found Rosalynn Carter fixing food for a meeting of student volunteers. He told her he was planning to write his thesis on a political campaign and wanted to get involved in one, so she sent him to the place in town where the group was meeting.[7]

Some months later, getting tired of driving himself from town to town on the campaign trail, Carter thought of Powell. He remembered that he was older than the other students and seemed to know more about politics, so he brought him aboard. But it was a driver he wanted, not an adviser. He already had a campaign press secretary, Bill Pope, who was wise in the ways of Georgia politics. It was not long before Carter was relying on his chauffeur to "present my views to the news reporters when the issue was not too important."[8]

Powell found himself intrigued by the reporters and their world. After Carter's upset victory in the Democratic primary, it was assumed the senator from Plains would be the next governor, and Powell began to "hope privately that if there was a place for me in the new administration it might be one that would allow me to continue to work with the press." Pope did not want to stay on. Carter searched for a press secretary among Georgia journalists but found none that satisfied him. On election night he offered the job to Powell, who gleefully accepted.[9]

In 1975, as the Georgia governor began his quest for the Democratic nomination to stand against President Ford, he and Powell traveled the country in rented cars and single-engine airplanes, sleeping on couches or in spare rooms of supporters—just the two of them for many months. "We had long talks, and sometimes fierce arguments, hammering out decisions together," said Carter. Powell critiqued Carter's speeches and helped him formulate answers to questions he would face. After Carter began winning primaries, the traveling staff grew, but "Jody remained the one closest to me." Reporters came to know that he spoke for the candidate.[10]

On election night, Powell, chain-smoking cigarettes and drinking Cokes, waited out the election returns with campaign manager Hamilton Jordan and the Carter family in a suite in Atlanta's Omni Hotel. At 3 A.M., Mississippi put Carter over the top. He had become the first candidate to defeat an incumbent president since Franklin D. Roosevelt in 1932.[11]

A few days later, the subject of a White House press secretary came up. Powell, now thirty-three, asked Carter whether he did not want someone who was older and had experience in Washington journalism. Greatly to Powell's relief, Carter said he had already thought about it, and he wanted Powell—"he was the natural choice."[12]

During the transition, Powell operated out of a Best Western Hotel in Americus, Georgia, the largest city anywhere near Plains, and held press briefings in the auditorium of an agricultural research cooperative. He met with his predecessors as White House press secretary, but found that things had changed so much that the value of their advice was limited. "Talking to Pierre Salinger about how he organized the press operations makes nice cocktail party gossip or history but it doesn't apply too much to what you're trying to do."[13]

With Powell in Americus were two associates who became his deputies in the White House. Rex Granum, a former political writer for the *Atlanta Constitution,* had joined the Carter campaign staff after his editors declined to spend the money to cover what they considered a quixotic venture.[14] Walt Wurfel, formerly with the *St. Petersburg Times* in Florida, had joined the campaign after Carter won the nomination.[15] They recruited Jim Purks, a former AP reporter in the South who had been Florida state press secretary for the campaign. He drove from Tallahassee to Americus and had an interview with Powell after waiting an hour and a half.[16]

The ninety-minute delay was typical of Powell. "I often grew exasperated with him when he came to work late, missed an appointment, procrastinated about a decision, or forgot to carry out my orders," said Carter.[17] Nobody ever said Jody Powell was efficient. After Powell came to the White House, reporters grew used to waiting more than an hour for a scheduled appointment with him. Even members of his forty-four-person staff had trouble getting in a word with him. His briefings seldom began at the appointed hour.[18]

Reporters who traveled with the Carter campaign were apprehensive about the future of White House press relations now that the man with the toothy grin and the ice-blue eyes had been elected. On New Year's eve, they placed a call to Gerald Ford at his Vail, Colorado, condominium and soon received a cheery call back from the former president. Then they tried the same thing with Carter. No call back, no message. "Anybody who has covered him knows he doesn't like reporters," said one correspondent.[19] Or, said veteran Richard L. Strout, "maybe he doesn't particularly care whether reporters like him or not."[20]

Carter came to office promising an open administration—to the extent of having open cabinet meetings. Even reporters doubted this would be possible, and within three weeks of taking office, Carter was instructing Powell, "No press in Cabinet meetings except on special occasions approved by me." For a while reporters were briefed on the sessions, but the briefings provided so little information that they were dropped.[21]

The new president did better on his promise to hold news conferences about every two weeks, or at least twenty times a year. Herb Klein, now a media consultant, thought this was a mistake, because it did not give the president time to think through the questions. In retrospect, Powell also considered the promise foolish. Nevertheless, in his first year, Carter held twenty-two formal meetings with reporters in Washington, all of them televised. He met with out-of-town editors and broadcasters nearly as often. In line with his pledge to forswear the more imperial trappings of the presidency, he moved the conferences from the ornate East Room to a workmanlike auditorium on the fourth floor of the Old Executive Office Building. It was, said a White House summary of press conference procedures, "easy to use, spacious, and convenient."[22]

Carter held his first presidential news conference at 2:30 P.M. on February 8, 1977. He said he looked forward to his "confrontations with the press to kind of balance up the nice and pleasant things that come to me as president." "I don't have any earth-shaking announcements," he said. "I want to spend a maximum amount of time each press conference to answer your questions." With that, he called on Frank Cormier, having been supplied in advance with a note saying the AP correspondent's name was pronounced "Core-mear." While not making earth-shaking news, the conference went well. Carter admitted his new administration had already made some mistakes in its dealings with Congress, and said he would speak out for personal freedoms in the Soviet Union and didn't think this would hurt the chances for arms control agreements. In the next day's *New York Times,* James Reston wrote that the conference showed "Carter at his best—open and honest, apologetic and hopeful."[23]

Meanwhile, journalists watched warily as Powell took control over the speechwriting, photography, and research staffs—all independent of the press office in previous administrations. They wondered if this were just a little empire building or part of a government-wide propaganda effort reminiscent of the Nixon years. They were distressed by

Powell's hints during the transition period that he might eliminate daily White House press briefings because they too often turned into snarling matches over trivial matters.[24]

Once the new team moved in, Powell scheduled briefings for 11:30 A.M. or 1:30 P.M. each day, although he was usually late for them. For the most part, they provided welcome relief from the contentious Nixon and Ford period. Powell gave up a traditional perquisite of the press secretary. Although he had the use of a White House car and driver to take him around town during the day, he drove himself to and from work.[25] Slouching over the lectern with his vest unbuttoned and his shirtsleeves rolled up, Powell delighted reporters with irreverent and sometimes barely printable quips. In his office, the door was often open. "The bitter taste is gone," said ABC's Ann Compton. But, said Powell, "I very well realize that I haven't been tested yet."[26]

He didn't have long to wait. In September 1977, the Senate Governmental Affairs Committee was investigating past business and banking practices of Budget Director Bert Lance, an old Georgia friend of the president. Some of the sharpest questioning came from Sen. Charles Percy of Illinois, the senior Republican on the committee. Two days before Lance was scheduled to testify, Powell called Loye W. Miller, Washington bureau chief of *The Chicago Sun-Times*, to pass on a rumor that the senator made regular flights on an aircraft owned by Bell and Howell, which he once headed, and that he had failed to reimburse a Chicago bank for facilities used in his reelection campaign.

Powell said he expected his call to Miller to be treated as background information, without his name being disclosed. Miller said he did not believe Powell had placed any restrictions on use of his call. He wrote a story about Powell's "apparent guerrilla offensive" against Lance's detractors. The story also reported that Bell and Howell had never owned an airplane and that Percy did reimburse the bank, and had a canceled check to prove it.

In an hour-long briefing the next day, Powell was not his usual chipper self. He apologized to Percy, described his action as "irresponsible, stupid, and wrong," and said the president agreed with that assessment. The incident, and the investigation that led to it and culminated in Lance's resignation, marked the point when "our relations with the press began to fray," Powell said.[27]

By early 1978, Powell was telling reporters that the atmosphere in the press room was turning ugly.[28] Reporters, in turn, were increasingly

16. Reporters found seats where they could as President Carter's shirt-sleeved Jody Powell entertained and informed them. Four years later, President Reagan furnished the room with rows of theater seats. *Courtesy Jimmy Carter Library.*

critical of Powell. Eventually, Carter's press secretary would come to describe the lower press office, the area next door to the briefing lounge, as "the first line of defense between the leader of the free world and the barbarians in the press room."[29] "There never was a honeymoon with the press," he told Carter, "but just a one-night stand."[30] A poll of thirty-seven print and broadcast journalists a year after Carter took office found 89 percent of them saying Powell served the president notably well, but only 29 percent saying the same about how well he served the press.[31]

The office of media liaison, part of Powell's domain in the Carter administration, had been established under Nixon as an arm of Herb Klein's communications office. Its main job was dealing with the out-of-town press. Wurfel remembered how impressed he had been, as a working journalist in Florida, to receive speech texts in big White

House envelopes. He also remembered that the editors of the *St. Petersburg Times* were invited to the Oval Office for an exclusive interview with President Ford. "He didn't make any news at all. But he got a six-column color photo in the paper, he got a banner headline, he got a sidebar article about the mood of the president in the Oval Office, and an analysis piece the next day." There was also a Sunday column and an editorial. Wurfel was struck by the fact that "a hardbitten news organization will succumb to this when the motive is obvious," and he brought the lesson with him to the White House.[32]

It paid off, for a while at least. After Carter met in the Oval Office with thirty journalists representing news outlets from Maine to Texas, a San Antonio broadcaster went on the air and praised the president in the words of eighteenth-century poet Oliver Goldsmith's description of the village schoolmaster: "Still the wonder grew and grew / How one small head held all he knew." Wurfel told Carter media adviser Jerry Rafshoon that such responses to a media liaison briefing were "typical—not a fluke."[33]

The president also held briefings for African American and Hispanic journalists. The office arranged briefings by other administration officials on agriculture, business, urban policy, and civil service reform.[34] Carter soon sounded a note of caution. In a handwritten note "To Jody" a month after his inauguration, he asked, "Have you figured up the enormous time which will be taken up by 20 visits of editors with administration leaders? It's excessive."[35]

Jim Purks was the principal writer for the media liaison office, preparing background papers on administration policies for editorial writers and columnists, as well as short pieces designed to be printed as received by African American and other ethnic publications. "The idea of those was to be as objective as possible and not sound like a propaganda machine, but to explain our side," said Purks. Pat Bario, a former Detroit journalist who ran the office, said, "The basic philosophy was that if we did our job very well as a press operation . . . if we answered the questions quickly and sincerely and honestly, that this would create such a nice impression of the president across the land that he would be re-elected."

"Anyway, that didn't happen," she conceded in 1980.

"Sometimes," said Purks, "we would have to resist the enthusiast who would want us to really turn it into propaganda." Nonetheless, some editors thought propaganda was what it was.[36]

Their objections were nothing compared to the hue and cry that arose when the office ventured into radio. Wurfel learned of a service sponsored by the Democratic National Committee in which a former Chicago disc jockey named Rich Nelson prepared recorded spots for use by radio stations in the districts and states of members of Congress who were up for reelection. "I suggest that we explore the possibility of setting up a radio actuality service within the White House," said Wurfel. In 1978, Nelson began doing twenty-second and forty-second taped pieces for distribution by Media Relations to about six hundred radio stations. Journalists criticized the program as propagandistic, arguing that Nelson was nowhere identified as a White House employee and therefore stations could present the spots as the work of an independent reporter. Radio freelancers in Washington also felt it threatened their livelihood. Wurfel stood his ground. The spots were of statements made in public meetings by the president or other administration officials. "We do not do fake interviews the way they do on Capitol Hill," said Wurfel. "All the stuff has been accessible to broadcasters who wanted to cover it." Powell dismissed the complaints as examples of "the press at its most juvenile."[37]

One of Powell's most heated arguments with his boss came over coverage arrangements for the Egyptian-Israeli summit held in September 1978 at Camp David. The president first angered his press secretary by refusing to make the initial announcement of the summit before television cameras or to answer questions. Later, when Carter wanted the press excluded from the presidential retreat in Maryland, Powell and Rafshoon complained bitterly and proposed alternate plans to allow the news media more access to the U.S., Israeli, and Egyptian representatives. Carter rejected them all in what he described as "an unpleasant confrontation." He wanted to minimize posturing and avoid "public statements, which would become frozen positions that could not subsequently be changed."[38]

The president won the argument, convincing his press secretary that "public negotiations through the press . . . could wreck the summit." Overcoming initial resistance by the Egyptians and Israelis, Powell became the only official source of information about the meetings. Each day, he held deliberately uninformative briefings at the American Legion Hall in nearby Thurmont, Maryland. American reporters soon complained that Egyptian and Israeli sources were giving background briefings to the Egyptian and Israeli press corps. Powell was particularly suspicious that the Israelis were beginning to leak and to manipulate the news. In response, he began talking more freely on a not-for-attribution basis.[39]

Throughout the thirteen days of meetings, Powell was part of a small group that met periodically with the president. Others were Secretary of State Cyrus Vance, Secretary of Defense Harold Brown, National Security Adviser Zbigniew Brzezinski, and Hamilton Jordan, now the White House chief of staff.[40]

By Sunday, September 17, the way appeared to be clear for agreement on a framework for peace, but Powell had to order plans for an announcement shelved after a snag developed over the treatment of holy sites in East Jerusalem. This problem and a procedural dispute delayed settlement, and Powell and Rafshoon had less than four hours to prepare for a late-night signing ceremony in the East Room of the White House.[41]

The framework agreement was accomplished, but negotiations for the signing of the treaty dragged on for months. By March 1979, Carter was considering a trip to Israel and Egypt to attempt again to mediate. Powell—"generally the most timid in the whole group on almost every issue," said Carter—was worried about the public-relations impact if Egypt's Anwar Sadat or Israel's Menachem Begin rejected a final U.S. proposal. He was also worried about "innocent mistakes on both sides of the podium" during such a quickly prepared and frantic trip. "I did not want my concerns about press relations to become a dominant factor, but I thought they should be put on the table," he said. Within a few days, Carter and his advisers, including Powell, were off to the Middle East.

The first stop was Cairo, where an atmosphere of "welcome, warmth and friendship" raised expectations.[42] In Jerusalem, the presidential party found Begin unyielding. The farthest the Israeli prime minister would go was to say that "great progress" had been made and the parties had agreed on "the ongoing need to continue the negotiations." On March 12, a few minutes before giving a briefing at press headquarters in the Jerusalem Hilton, Powell learned that Israeli Foreign Minister Moshe Dayan was meeting with Vance. He knew that Dayan was often more flexible than Begin, but did not know what the meeting was about.

Powell told reporters there was always the possibility that the remaining issues were going to be resolved, but added, "I think you know enough about the process to know that that has not usually been the case in these discussions." He refused to deny that he was "unhappy" with the outcome, and declined to comment on Begin's statement about "great progress." In later, less formal meetings in a private room, he told correspondents essentially the same thing, but advised them, in the indelicate jargon of the trade, to "cover your ass" by qualifying any pessimistic stories they wrote.

Most writers for morning newspapers followed this advice. Wire service reporters, however, have to turn their stories around and file overnight copy that can be set in type for early editions of the next day's afternoon newspapers. Having two stories to write instead of one, they often do not have time to attend private sessions such as those Powell was holding. The AP's Cormier, reluctant to write an inconclusive story for papers that would be hitting the streets while Carter was heading back to Washington, wrote that the president's mission had failed.[43]

The next morning, Carter flew to Cairo with good news. With the aid of Dayan's intervention, proposals had been worked out that Begin said he was willing to accept. But the news was still secret. "I had been tipped off that in fact things were moving, but of course couldn't say anything," said Deputy Press Secretary Granum.[44]

During a brief stop at the Cairo airport, Carter outlined the proposed agreement to Sadat, who accepted. He then called Begin. At that moment, Anne Edwards, an assistant in the press office, entered the airport VIP lounge escorting a press pool. Jordan ushered them out and told Edwards that the president was on the telephone with the Israeli leader. On the ramp outside, the thought struck Edwards: "Wait a minute. If they were talking to Begin, we got it. They did it."[45]

A few moments later, Carter walked to a podium to announce that an agreement had been reached. He then boarded *Air Force One* for the return flight to Washington, accompanied by the usual small pool of reporters. The main body of the traveling press boarded a chartered press plane after a briefing by Powell that he later described as "a model of double-talk and non information." Aboard the plane, Cormier, seated across the aisle from Powell, said, "My press secretary has lied to me. I trusted him, and he lied to me."[46]

CBS reporters also let Carter know that they thought they had been misled. The Voice of America's Philomena Jurey, on the other hand, thought that the impression conveyed to reporters by Powell in Jerusalem "was an accurate portrayal of the American perception at the time." Carter agreed. When Powell was making his pessimistic statements, the president said, "We all thought we had failed."[47]

Powell later said that in retrospect he would not change anything he said in his briefings that night, but he wished he had made a phone call to check on the Vance-Dayan meeting. He said he did not do so for three reasons. He did not think anybody would still be awake at the King David Hotel, where Carter and most of his senior staff were quartered. He saw little hope of success, anyway. And there was a surprise birthday party being given that night for ABC correspondent Sam Donaldson. Tired and discouraged, Powell said, "I went partying instead of finishing my job."[48]

The next international crisis to confront the Carter White House and its press office began on November 4, 1979, with a 3 A.M. telephone call to the brightly lighted Operations Center on the seventh floor of the State Department, a short walk from Secretary Vance's office. Political Officer Elizabeth Ann Swift in Teheran reported that the United States Embassy there had been overrun by about three thousand young Iranian militants, who had surrounded the chancery and were breaking into other buildings. In the tense hours that followed, fifty to sixty of the embassy staff, including Swift, were taken hostage. It would be fourteen months, and Carter would be leaving Washington in defeat, before they were released. Iran's fundamentalist government was backing the militants' demand that the deposed shah, undergoing medical treatment for cancer in the United States, be returned from his refuge to face Iranian justice. Before the crisis was resolved, the shah did leave the United States for Panama, and then fly to asylum in Egypt, where he died.[49]

In the days immediately after the seizure, Powell was among those urging the president to impose economic sanctions against Iran. The president followed the advice, overruling objections of the Justice, State, and Treasury departments. On November 23, at a National Security Council meeting at Camp David, Powell backed Carter's decision to seek the hostages' release through political means, but to warn the Iranians that the United States would retaliate if the captive diplomats were put on trial. Vice President Walter Mondale and Vance argued that any public warning might so antagonize the Iranians that their resistance would stiffen, so the message was sent privately.

In mid-March of 1980, Brzezinski informed Powell that there was a contingency plan for a rescue mission and filled him in on some of the details. On March 22, Powell attended a five-hour jeans-and-sweaters meeting of the national security high command at Camp David at which the president authorized a reconnoitering mission into Iran.[50]

A week later, Powell was awakened in the early hours of the morning by a call from the press office duty officer—the staff member whose turn it was that day to take calls from reporters out of office hours. There was a story from Teheran that Carter had apologized to Iran's Ayatollah Khomeini for American offenses against the Iranian people.

Arriving at the White House, the press secretary was confronted with a swarm of reporters. Some of them thought maybe there had been such a message and Powell had not been told about it. Powell thought so, too. "If that's true, I need to know about it," he told Jordan. The chief of staff told him the letter was a fabrication, and he passed this word to reporters. "No such message has been sent to anyone anywhere by the president or anyone else in this government," he said.

Aware in the back of his mind of Carter's confidential message warning of possible retaliation, he avoided a direct answer to the question of whether any message at all had been sent. Because the Swiss government confirmed it had relayed messages from the United States to Iran, some reporters remained skeptical of Powell's denial. The next day, Iranian President Albohassan Bani-Sadr announced that he had received a letter from Carter. It was described as threatening, not conciliatory, but reporters asked why Powell had not told them about it. He said he hadn't been asked, and saw no reason to volunteer information about a message that had been kept confidential for policy reasons.[51]

Carter got a bad press again on April 1, when he called reporters into the Oval Office and told them of a message he had just received from Bani-Sadr, a relative moderate with whom the administration had been negotiating. In what the president described as "a positive step," Bani-Sadr had told him the militants would transfer the hostages to Iranian government control provided no further economic sanctions were imposed. Carter told the reporters that if Bani-Sadr carried out his commitment, there would be no need for additional sanctions, although those in effect would be continued. In Teheran, Bani-Sadr claimed the United States had not carried out its part of the deal, and the deal collapsed.

What aroused press suspicions was that Carter, challenged for renomination by Sen. Edward M. Kennedy, had made the announcement at 7:20 A.M., twenty minutes after the polls opened in that day's Wisconsin primary. Kennedy accused the president of manipulating the news, and the *New York Times* headlined a front-page analysis, "Iran's Shadow on the Primary." The *Washington Post* took a similar line in a page-one analysis saying the "unusual early morning presidential appearance was more an exercise in domestic politics than international diplomacy." Also on the front page of both papers was another story: Carter had won the Wisconsin primary by a landslide, establishing a commanding lead over Kennedy. "We are about to have an enormous credibility problem," Powell told Jordan.[52]

One reason the impact of the coverage was so great is that the hostage crisis continued to be a big, big story, dominating the news. On CBS, Walter Cronkite signed off his dinner-hour broadcast each evening with a running count of how many days the hostages had been confined. On ABC, there was an entire program devoted to the hostage crisis. Entitled *America Held Hostage*, it was renamed *Nightline* and given a broader scope after the hostages were freed.

Powell was kept fully informed of developments, receiving regular guidance from the Iran Working Group at the State Department. He took an active part in the April 11 Oval Office planning session at which Carter declared that "it was time for us to bring our hostages home."[53]

The plan called for a ninety-member rescue team to be flown to a remote area code-named Desert One aboard six C-130 transport planes and be met by eight helicopters from American aircraft carriers in the Gulf of Oman. The rescue team would transfer to the helicopters and fly under cover of darkness to a mountain hiding place. The next night, trucks already purchased by U.S. undercover agents would be removed from a warehouse on the outskirts of Teheran and driven to a site near the hideaway. The rescue team would be driven to the compound where the hostages were held, overpower the guards, and free the hostages. Helicopters would pick up the hostages and rescuers and fly them to an abandoned airstrip outside Teheran, where C-141s would pick them up and fly them to Saudi Arabia.[54]

The original plan did not provide air cover for the C-141s, on the theory that the Iranians did not have the capability to intercept the planes at night. "Well, that's your judgment," Powell remembered saying. "I hope to hell you're right." He had a horror of the operation succeeding up to its final stages, then ending with the transports being shot down by enemy fighters. Air cover was provided in a later plan.[55]

Powell's role contrasted sharply with the way Pierre Salinger was kept in the dark about the Bay of Pigs and Cuban missile crises, but the position of the two men in the White House was also very different. Salinger, never a Kennedy insider, was specifically instructed by the president to deal with press policy only.[56] Powell contended that his role in the policy field had been exaggerated,[57] but others in the White House said the president consulted him on a wide range of issues.[58] Jordan felt that Powell "was inaccurately perceived as playing the traditional and limited role of mouthpiece."[59]

As a presidential adviser, Powell was at the heart of an effort to solve a nagging problem of humanitarian, political, and patriotic concern. As a spokesman, he knew more than he could tell about a big story. The conflict led him to falsely deny to reporter Jack Nelson, at the very time of the rescue mission, that any such effort was contemplated. As he said, he was placing his obligation to the national interest and the lives of the hostages above his obligation to tell the truth. Some reporters said he had destroyed his credibility, but most, including Nelson, agreed that his action was justified.

The mission failed when one of the helicopters crashed into one of the C-130s and burst into flames, killing eight American servicemen. It could be argued that publicity about the rescue plans would have prevented what turned out to be a disaster. But it also would have destroyed what the president and the officials of his administration honestly believed was their best chance of freeing the hostages. It is hard to criticize the decision Jody Powell made.

13

Staging the News

JODY POWELL'S ROLE in keeping the hostage rescue mission secret was literally a matter of life and death.

In November 1985, there was another example of a presidential press secretary's conflicting responsibilities that seems on the surface trivial, but is not.

As President Ronald Reagan and Soviet leader Mikhail Gorbachev met in Geneva to explore prospects for nuclear arms reduction, White House spokesman Larry Speakes feared that Gorbachev was getting the better of Reagan in the give-and-take with reporters.

Speakes had aide Mark Weinberg draft some remarks, polished them up, and told reporters they were things the president had said. One was "The world breathes easier because we are talking together." The other was even less earth-shattering.

Because the remarks were so inconsequential, it might be argued that counterfeiting them did not matter. Who cares? Speakes himself dismissed his action as "taking a bit of liberty with my P.R. man's license" to "spruce up the president's image."[1] The trouble with this argument is that no one had issued Larry Speakes any public-relations man's license.

The president does not, of course, originate all the words that pour forth from the White House under his name. Skilled writers craft his speeches, bureaucrats draft his veto messages, and diplomats labor over the toasts he offers to visiting heads of state. Their words, however, are at least adopted by the president. Speakes did not consult Reagan. Journalists reported, on the press secretary's authority, that the president had said things he could not even have known about. If Speakes had not boasted about the incident in his memoirs, the apoc-

ryphal quotations could have made their way from newspaper files
into history books. Conceivably, they still could. The conflict was not
between the press secretary's obligation to the press and his obligation
to the national interest and people's lives. It was between his obligation
to the press and, as Speakes put it, sprucing up the president's image.
Image making won. It should not have.

The White House newsroom where Speakes worked was much
changed from the one Jim Hagerty entered three decades before. By
conservative estimates, the Washington press corps had tripled since
the end of World War II. About forty-five hundred journalists had
access to the White House, including the seventeen hundred who had
passes with their pictures on them permitting regular admittance.

With the meteoric rise of television, "the press" had become "the
media," and Washington was its capital. The print media relied increasingly on news analysis, labeled as such, instead of just reporting what
the government was saying. A new generation of reporters, disillusioned by Vietnam and Watergate, saw themselves not as detached
observers but as active participants. Journalists said the more analytical
approach was needed to cope with increasingly complex problems of a
fast-growing society. Critics said the old rules of impartiality were
crumbling.

"Columnists are asked to know more than they can possibly
know," wrote Thomas Griffith, the news media reporter for *Time*
magazine.[2] In the Carter White House, Jody Powell made much the
same point. Sitting in his office, looking out over the North Lawn, he
could see the television correspondents doing their pieces for the evening news and know that "somewhere right at the end they were
going to try to tell the American people what it all really meant." The
trouble was, as Powell saw it, that "I knew and they knew, and they
knew that I knew, that they didn't know what it all really meant."[3]

Into this environment, Ronald Reagan moved with sweeping pro-
nouncements that admirers called visionary and detractors considered
simplistic. Looking for a spokesman to explain his policies to the press,
aides sounded out a number of reporters and speculated publicly that
the president might have four official spokesmen, instead of one. He
chose one—Jim Brady, a former teacher of government who had la-
bored off and on in the congressional and executive vineyards of Washington for two decades.

Like Pierre Salinger, Brady was jovial, irreverent, and an outsider.
He started the 1980 presidential campaign as press secretary to one of

Reagan's rivals, Texas governor John Connally. After Connally dropped out, Brady switched to the Reagan camp. Lyn Nofziger, a longtime California ally of Reagan, was press secretary, and Brady was named director of public affairs and research. He became chiefly known as the campaign joker. Early in the race, Reagan drew criticism from environmentalists when he said that trees are a major source of impure air; as the campaign plane flew over a Louisiana forest fire, Brady sang out, "killer trees, killer trees." Reagan's top aides were not amused. They also blamed him for leaking information to the press, although many reporters said he was not the source of the leaks.

After Reagan's victory, Brady became the spokesman for the transition team. Reagan insiders pressed their public search for a White House press secretary, and denied Brady the information he needed to function effectively. Unable to answer reporters' questions about Reagan's cabinet selection process, the transition spokesman quipped that the Internal Revenue Service had come up with a new ruling: "Lunches with me as a source are no longer deductible."[4]

Brady's Washington experience had begun in 1961 when he left teaching and doctoral study at Southern Illinois University to become a junior aide to his home state's Republican senator, Everett Dirksen. After leaving Dirksen's staff, he served as an aide to several officials in the Nixon and Ford administrations and then returned to Capitol Hill as an executive assistant to Republican Sen. William V. Roth Jr. of Delaware.

Now, at the age of forty, he became the president's press secretary, and he proposed to shake things up. For one thing, he wanted to whittle down the number of people with White House press credentials. Of the more than seventeen hundred, only about two hundred covered the beat regularly. Brady found, however, that under a court decision that came down in the Carter administration it was extremely difficult to lift a reporter's credentials for anything but security reasons. The United States Court of Appeals in Washington ruled in 1977 that even when the Secret Service cited security it must spell out the reason in detail and give "notice, opportunity to rebut, and a written decision . . . because the denial of a pass potentially infringes upon First Amendment guarantees."[5]

Balked in this effort, Brady turned to establishing a dress code for the press corps. He was particularly concerned about TV technicians, one of whom reportedly turned up at an Oval Office photo opportunity with a T-shirt asking, "Did you get yours today?" The Brady code

17. From FDR's casual chats in the Oval Office, the presidential press conference grew to Ronald Reagan's carefully staged extravaganzas in the elegant East Room. *Courtesy Ronald W. Reagan Library.*

was never precisely spelled out, but one aide described it as "something between white tie and T-shirt." It foundered after it was pointed out that the technicians would find it difficult to handle their equipment in a coat and tie.

Brady was more successful at introducing a modicum of decorum at presidential news conferences. Instead of seeing who could jump to his or her feet the fastest, reporters were asked to raise their hands and be recognized. It pretty much worked, but didn't stop five or six journalists from rising en masse if the president pointed in their general direction. "My finger must not aim right," said Reagan. The president had a diagram to show who was sitting where, but didn't always get it right. Once, he called on Bob Thompson of the Hearst newspapers while Thompson was watching the news conference on television at home. At Reagan's first news conference, a Brady plan to choose questioners by lottery was tried, but it met so much resistance that the press secretary said, "I think we'll go back to just raising your hand."

When Brady came up with the idea of having Reagan meet weekly with a small group of reporters, the White House inner circle bought it, hoping for headlines about the economy. Instead the stories focused on the president's criticisms of the Soviets and of Carter's hostage negotiations. An aide said Brady was admonished not to schedule any more such interviews "until he gets his act together." Nobody explained how he was supposed to control what questions the reporters asked, what answers the president gave, or how the reporters wrote their stories.[6]

Although he appeared not to have gained the confidence of Reagan intimates, the 6-foot, 235-pound former high school football player from Centralia, Illinois, who liked to call himself "the Bear," had the affection and respect of reporters. He also had the undying loyalty of his boss. Sadly, his active role at the White House was cut short on March 30, 1981, when he and Reagan both received bullet wounds in an assassination attempt as they left the Washington Hilton Hotel after a presidential speech. Reagan had a near brush with death, but quickly recovered. Brady was left paralyzed. Reagan announced that Brady would officially be White House press secretary "as long as I was living there."[7]

"Had he not been debilitated, Brady probably would have been ranked with the best White House spokesmen," said Joseph C. Spear in a study of presidential press relations.[8] "The Bear" resisted efforts by Reagan's inner circle to limit the press office to routine announcements and leave it to senior aides to interpret them. "Brady had no intention of being a weak press secretary," said a high-ranking White House communications aide. "He cared about his turf . . . and he was always questioning."[9] He did not stop. He and his wife, Sarah, became the nation's leading advocates of gun control, pushing through a reluctant Congress a firearms registration measure that became known as the Brady Bill.

18. Jim Brady (standing) took notes in the Oval Office as President Reagan conferred with top aides Edwin Meese (left) and Jim Baker (right) on his first day in office. *Courtesy Ronald W. Reagan Library.*

Larry Speakes, then a deputy press secretary, had lunch with Brady in the White House dining room on the day of the attempted assassination. He asked his boss if he wanted to go with the president to the Washington Hilton, or have his deputy do it. "I guess I'll go," said Brady. The next word Speakes had was a telephone call from David Prosperi, a press aide who had gone with Brady. "Shots have been fired," said Prosperi. "Brady is down. I don't know about the president." Very soon, they knew about the president. He was on his way to George Washington University Hospital. Speakes, along with top White House aides, headed there too.

After checking on Reagan's condition, and Brady's, Speakes returned to his office. It was full of reporters, clamoring for information. He suggested they move to the briefing room, which would be less crowded. He told the reporters that the president had been wounded in the left side and was undergoing surgery, and that the outlook was good.[10]

The questioning went on.

"Has the U.S. military been placed on any higher alert readiness?"

"Not that I'm aware of . . ."

Would Vice President George Bush assume the president's powers, or would there be a division of labor between them?

"Not that I'm aware of. We just haven't crossed those bridges yet. . . ."

Who was running the government, and would Bush become acting president if the president went under anesthesia?

"I cannot answer that question at this time."

Who would determine whether the vice president should become acting president?

"I don't know the details on that." [11]

Later, Speakes's briefings while the president lay wounded won him an award from the National Association of Government Communicators for "outstanding performance at a time of grave national crisis." [12]

Watching television, downstairs in the Situation Room, however, Alexander Haig was upset because Speakes "couldn't answer anything." Reagan's temperamental secretary of state had gathered with other top administration officials around a long table in the basement room where the National Security Council staff keeps track of the world's crises. National security adviser Richard Allen sat in the center seat on one side of the table, presiding. On the other side, Haig sat alone at one end, separated by empty chairs from Caspar Weinberger, the secretary of defense, and William Casey, the head of the CIA. Weinberger was asked the same question Speakes had been asked. Had he changed the alert status of the armed forces? He said he had not. [13]

Immediately behind Haig, a small color television set was recessed into the wall. Haig said later he noticed Allen gazing at it in consternation, and wheeled around in his chair. Listening to Speakes's understandably uninformed responses, Haig said, "We've got to get him off." The two men left the room, with Haig in the lead, and raced up a flight of stairs, down a short ramp, and through a corner of the lower press office. At this moment, Speakes was handed a note saying "Come to the Situation Room." As he reached the lower press office door, he was brushed aside by the out-of-breath and agitated Haig. [14]

Downstairs, Domestic Policy Adviser Martin Anderson, seated at the end of the table to Allen's left, did not notice Haig and Allen leave. Anderson remembered someone asking, "Where's Al?" Then, "My God, there he is, it's Al!" He had showed up on the television screen, telling reporters that no alert measures were contemplated and that

Bush was flying back to Washington from Texas. Next, he was asked who was making decisions for the government. He said:

> Constitutionally, gentlemen, you have the president, the vice president, and the secretary of state, in that order, and should the president decide he wants to transfer the helm, he will do so. He has not done that as of now. I am in control here, in the White House, pending the return of the vice president, and in close touch with him. If something came up, I would check with him, of course.[15]

At the words "I am in control," someone at the table downstairs said, "That's a mistake." Helene Von Damm, the president's secretary, who had joined the group, thought Weinberger "looked taken aback" by the words.[16]

When Haig returned, Weinberger told him he was wrong. Haig said to check the Constitution.[17]

Originally, the secretary of state was next in line of succession to the presidency after the vice president, but Congress had changed this in the mid-1960s to put the speaker of the House and president pro tempore of the Senate ahead of him. Under a separate military chain of command, the secretary of defense was next in line after the vice president. Weinberger assumed that Haig was referring to the out-dated law.[18] Haig said later he made "a poor choice of words," but merely meant that he was the senior cabinet officer present. Chief of Staff James Baker said he had told Haig that as such he was the person to be contacted at the White House if anything came up that needed action.[19]

After Speakes had a chance to confer with the senior officers in the Situation Room, it was decided that he would give another briefing after the vice president returned. It had been unclear who would step in for the disabled Brady, because Nofziger was giving briefings at the hospital and Speakes at the White House, but Baker told Speakes to take over. Nofziger told him he didn't want the job anyway. One of Speakes's first tasks was to deny a false rumor, which had made it onto television, that Brady had died. For the time being, Speakes did not feel comfortable moving into Brady's office, so he worked in his smaller deputy's office. After a couple of months, as it became clear Brady could not return to the hectic job of press secretary, Baker told Speakes to make the move. He could not be press secretary, under

Reagan's order, but he would be principal deputy. It was a distinction without a difference. He was suddenly the president's spokesman.[20]

The new de facto press secretary, forty-one, grew up in Merigold, Mississippi, a sawmill town in the Delta with a 1980 population of 574, where he wrote for the high school newspaper and became the part-time Merigold correspondent for the weekly in nearby Cleveland, Mississippi.

At the University of Mississippi, he became campus correspondent for the Memphis *Commercial-Appeal*. Summers, he worked in the Memphis bureau of United Press International and for the *States-Times* in Jackson, the Mississippi capital. In his senior year, he left without graduating and went through a series of jobs on Mississippi weeklies, writing editorials about potholes and about weed cutting on vacant lots. He sold office supplies and job printing on the side.

Speakes also put in a stint as a county civil defense official. In his spare time, he was a part-time correspondent for the *Commercial Appeal* and a twice-a-day newscaster on a country music radio station. In 1968, he moved to Washington as press secretary to Democratic Sen. James Eastland of Mississippi.[21]

He had been in Washington once before, on the Merigold High School senior class trip. The students toured the White House, visited veteran Senator Eastland's office and sat in the Senate visitor's gallery, where Speakes decided he wanted someday to cover the Senate as a reporter. Flacking for Eastland was the closest he ever got, but soon he had another ambition. Someday, maybe, he could be the White House press secretary.[22]

He got his foot on the ladder in 1974 with the aid of Ken Clawson, who in his days with the *Washington Post* had been a favorite of Eastland's. Now, as Nixon's communications director, Clawson gave Speakes a lowly press aide's job with an office in a far corner of the Old Executive Office Building. In a few months, he was made press secretary to James D. St. Clair, the Boston lawyer heading Nixon's Watergate defense team. From their offices in the old EOB, St. Clair and Speakes soon became disillusioned with Nixon. After the "smoking gun" tape, St. Clair saw that the president had deceived him. Speakes wrote in his memoirs that as he watched the former president leave for San Clemente, he promised never again to represent anyone in whom he did not believe.[23]

When Jerry terHorst became Ford's press secretary, he asked Speakes to be an assistant. The Mississippi high school boy who had visited the White House now had an office there. In the 1976 Republican presidential campaign, Speakes worked for President Ford's running mate, Sen. Robert Dole of Kansas. In the 1980 campaign, he was on the margin, serving part-time as liaison between Ford and Reagan's campaign committee. Between campaigns, he had become a vice president of a Washington public-relations firm, Hill and Knowlton. After Reagan's election, he joined the transition team.

When Brady was named press secretary, he told Speakes he wanted him for deputy. "My God," Speakes thought. "I'm really on my way back to the White House."[24]

Even after Brady's wounding thrust Speakes into the press secretary's seat, Communications Director David Gergen shared the daily briefing duty with him—Speakes on Mondays, Wednesdays, and Fridays, Gergen on Tuesdays and Thursdays. Gergen's answers to questions tended to be fuzzy and philosophical, and by early 1982, Baker decided to leave the briefings to Speakes. Gergen operated behind the scenes, holding background sessions with reporters on long-range strategy. "Larry's style is more popular with some of the powers that be around here," he said. Speakes denied then that there was personal tension between them, but confirmed in his memoirs what one reporter said at the time, that "they're pretty much at each other's throats." Speakes, below Gergen in the White House hierarchy and pay scale, fought for advancement and in August of 1983 was promoted to the top rank of assistant to the president. When Gergen left in 1984 to teach at Harvard, the press office gained more autonomy.[25]

Speakes decorated the press secretary's office with primitive art from the Mississippi Delta and a handmade quilt from Merigold. In his folksy southern manner, he urged reporters, "Tell me what you want, and I will try to get it."[26] He had his home telephone number listed in the directory.[27] A newspaper reporter writing a profile of Speakes in 1982 had difficulty finding anyone in the White House press corps who didn't like him.[28] Although some reporters still grumbled that he was uninformed, Lou Cannon of the *Washington Post* said in a 1983 interview, "Larry is underrated. He can be very helpful, and he's generally honest."[29] This attitude did not last. When he came to summing up the Reagan administration, Cannon wrote rightly that Speakes was "widely distrusted by the White House press corps."[30]

Like all presidential press secretaries, Speakes had a hard job. It began each day when he woke to the news on Washington's WETA

19. Larry Speakes had the title of principal deputy press secretary after he took over the disabled Jim Brady's duties. After leaving the White House, he disclosed that he attributed made-up quotations to President Reagan. *Courtesy Ronald W. Reagan Library.*

radio. While reading the *Washington Post* in the kitchen of his Annandale, Virginia, split-level, he divided a piece of yellow legal paper into columns headed "foreign" and "domestic" and listed the stories on which he could expect questions at his briefing. Arriving at the White House at 7:30, he read the *New York Times* and the White House news summary, and attended staff meetings before the first of his twice-a-day meetings with reporters. Afterward, he conferred with the president, read foreign cables in the situation room, perhaps attended a cabinet meeting, and got back to his office about 11:30 primed for the noon session with the press corps.[31]

Four days after Gergen's departure, what came to be known as the "line of the day" meeting was added to the routine. At these sessions, convened each morning by Deputy Chief of Staff and chief image maker Michael Deaver, Reagan's aides decided which meetings would be open to the press and which would not.

The reporters, however, had their own "line of the day," which didn't always follow rules laid down by the White House. One day, in

February 1982, Egyptian president Hosni Mubarak was visiting Reagan at the White House. The big news that day was a shipment of Soviet-made MIG23 fighter planes to Cuba. At a photo opportunity in the Oval Office, that's what ABC's Sam Donaldson asked about. Speakes, who had decreed that no questions could be asked by the pool of reporters at meetings with foreign heads of state, cut off the questioning and threatened to bar all questions at photo opportunities. It didn't work, partly because Reagan seemed to enjoy matching wits with reporters.[32]

When Reagan appeared in the briefing room with a group of congressmen to announce a compromise on the MX missile, reporters were urged to ask "specific questions on the subject of the day." When the press was allowed into the Oval Office for an impromptu news conference with the president, Speakes warned: "You screw it up and it doesn't happen anymore. . . . I can guarantee you that." The words were in the soft tones of the Mississippi Delta, but sounded disturbingly like Brian Donlevy as the French foreign legion sergeant in the 1939 movie *Beau Geste* who ends his warnings to recruits with an ominous "I promise you."[33]

"You don't tell us how to stage the news, and we won't tell you how to cover it," Speakes announced in the briefing room on October 12, 1982. The words raised reporters' hackles, but Speakes seemed proud of them. They were reproduced on a small sign on his desk.[34]

More and more, the news was staged for television. At one Oval Office session, a White House press aide asked print and radio reporters to move back so television reporters could stand in front of the president's desk. Only the TV correspondents got to ask questions.[35]

During his first year in office, Reagan's news conferences were scheduled for afternoon hours, giving journalists time to dissect his sometimes fumbled answers. Aides then decided to put him on in the evening, where the old master could perform unedited in the splendor of the East Room. His March 31, 1982, conference was acclaimed as his best yet.[36]

In his early days as spokesman, Speakes held morning briefings in his office and met with reporters at noon in the briefing room, still outfitted with the informally arranged deep leather couches and chairs installed in the Nixon era. Later, he also began holding the morning session in the briefing room, which was refurnished with sixty theater seats, arranged in rows and each bearing the name of a news organization. Now, said journalist James Deakin, reporters "would have to sit in assigned seats, like ladies and gentlemen, while the president's spokesmen made announcements and dodged questions." The remodeling, along with repairs to the roof of the press quarters, cost $166,000.[37]

The press office negotiated with television networks each week on which administration officials would appear on which Sunday interview shows. "The White House doesn't dictate, it coordinates," said Speakes. But he conceded that his office sometimes did ask cabinet members not to appear because "this is not an issue that we want to talk on."[38]

Speakes still was excluded from important meetings, such as Monday issues lunches with Reagan, a February 1982 strategy session at Camp David, and a regular Friday meeting of communications aides across the street at Blair House.[39]

His access to information became a vital issue on October 24, 1983. Bill Plante of CBS News was told by a source he had known for many years that the United States planned to invade Grenada, which was in the grip of a bloody uprising. Plante was dubious, thinking the most that might be in the works was a mission to evacuate a group of American medical students from the Caribbean island. When he asked Speakes, the press spokesman had his foreign affairs deputy, Bob Sims, check with Adm. John Poindexter, the deputy national security adviser. Poindexter told Sims the story was "preposterous" and to "knock it down hard."

Sims relayed Poindexter's words to Speakes, who told Plante, "Preposterous. Knock it down hard." Plante passed this on to colleagues in Washington and New York, and the story was not pursued. Twelve hours later, U.S. Marines and Army Rangers began the invasion of Grenada. From then on, Speakes said, when he got information from Poindexter, he passed it on in Poindexter's name, not his own. Most reporters believed that Speakes was relaying what he believed to be the truth.[40]

He came off less well a few months later when Reagan visited Blackwater National Wildlife Refuge on Maryland's Eastern Shore. The White House had just announced the appointment of Anne Burford, a Colorado lawyer, to an advisory committee on the environment. The committee didn't amount to much, but Burford's background did. First, she had been a vociferous critic of the Environmental Protection Agency as a Colorado state legislator. Second, Reagan had appointed her to head the agency she despised. And third,

she had been forced to resign under withering criticism from environmentalists. As Reagan finished watching a presentation about eagles,
television correspondents began shouting questions about possible
damage done by the appointment. Speakes, in turn, shouted
"Lights!," the signal for the television lights to be turned off. When
they didn't go off fast enough, he stuck his outspread hand in front of
the camera lens. "My guardian says I can't talk," said Reagan. But as
the questioning continued, the ever-obliging president talked anyway.
"I don't think there should be any thought of damage," he said. Then
the lights went out. The whole thing was shown on the evening news
—the splayed hands, Reagan's answer, and then darkness. It was not
the image the image makers wanted. Nancy Reagan, in particular, was
displeased.[41]

It was not the only time. Ten days after Reagan's successful surgery
for colon cancer in July 1985, he developed a scab on his nose that
turned out to be skin cancer. Mrs. Reagan, afraid the press would con-
nect the relatively minor affliction with the much more serious colon
cancer, tried to keep the whole thing secret. But when Reagan spoke at
an open meeting of evangelical broadcasters, reporters noticed a scar
on his nose where tissue had been taken for a biopsy. Under instructions from the first lady, Speakes told them it was irritation from a tube
attached to his nose after surgery. Would there be a biopsy? "There'll
be a routine check of it, yes," Speakes answered. Was it a test for
cancer? "I don't know. Just a routine examination, as you would if you
had a piece removed from your face." After dozens of questions,
Speakes acknowledged that what was being done was, in fact, a biopsy.

Speakes wrote a note to Mrs. Reagan saying press inquiries would
"only become worse if we seek to avoid the obvious question." He
suggested they announce that the irritation had been determined to
be an early skin cancer, unrelated to the colon cancer, and no treatment
was necessary. The first lady was not satisfied. At her suggestion, a
statement was issued saying the infected tissue had been "submitted
for routine studies for infection, and it was determined no further
treatment is necessary." The statement was headed "The White
House, Office of the Press Secretary." Speakes would not put his name
on it.

That Monday, when the Reagans returned from Camp David, the
president took the matter into his own hands. He invited six reporters
into the office and when one of them asked him about his nose, he
said a "basal cell carcinoma," a relatively harmless malignant growth,

had been removed. The next day, there were rancorous exchanges in the briefing room over whether the president's press secretary had lied. Helen Thomas came closest to getting it right when she said, "By omission, you left a big hole in the truth." In her memoirs, Mrs. Reagan said, "I shouldn't have done that to Larry."[42]

Like his predecessors, Reagan was given a briefing before each press conference. Rehearsals, two hours a day for two days, were held in the presidential family theater. So many White House aides thought their presence was necessary that the rehearsals were practically standing room only. On one occasion, Speakes told the briefers that their perceptive questions had left the president "cocked and ready for everything the press could throw at him."[43]

On November 19, 1986, badgered with questions about arms shipments to Iran, Reagan was less cocked and less ready. It was not for want of trying. At both of his rehearsals, the president was asked whether any third party, and in particular Israel, was involved in the arms shipments. Both times, he said no. Both times, Poindexter corrected him. Administration officials had acknowledged already that Israel had made shipments to Iran. The United States, which was seeking the release of hostages held by Iranian-backed terrorists in Lebanon, had promised to replenish Israeli arsenals. Still, when Bill Plante asked the president in the East Room about shipments from Israel, he said, "We did not condone, and do not condone, the shipment of arms from other countries." By the time the press conference ended, Speakes and Poindexter were ready with a "clarifying" statement saying that a third country was involved. Reagan, embarrassed by his misstep, approved the statement immediately and it was handed out in the pressroom within minutes.

Speakes had been kept in the dark about dates and other details of the arms transfers. He said he wanted the information so that he would know the facts, not to disclose them to the press. Poindexter, by now promoted to national security adviser, said no. An aide said it would probably be necessary to "stroke Larry."[44] The transactions became known as the Iran-Contra affair when it was disclosed, five days after the president's news conference, that proceeds from the shipments had been used to finance rebellion against Nicaragua's left-wing government.

Speakes left the White House at the end of January 1987 to become vice president of communications for Merrill Lynch Pierce Fenner and Smith in New York. In a swan song speech to the National

Press Club, he urged the White House to "make good on the age-old promise of less secrecy in government, not more."

"Let's not write a TV script and then create an event designed for the evening news," he said. "Let news truly be news. . . . If government engages in theatrics to convey its ideas, then don't blame television if they cover it with comic strip graphics."

His words rang hollow when the publication of his White House memoirs in 1988 disclosed that he had twice fabricated quotes for the president—at Geneva and after a Soviet plane shot down a Korean Air Lines jet in 1983, killing 269 people. In that case, he attributed to Reagan remarks actually made by George Shultz, who had succeeded Haig as secretary of state.

The disclosures created a furor. Speakes's successor as press secretary, Marlin Fitzwater, called his actions a "damn outrage." Reagan said he had not been aware that quotes were being made up, and he didn't like "kiss and tell" books.

Speakes, left with little alternative, resigned from Merrill Lynch three days after the story broke.[45] Later, he became chief spokesman for the United States Postal Service.

14

The Picture

AS A BOY, JIM HAGERTY MET THEODORE ROOSEVELT on the front porch at Sagamore Hill.

He never forgot it.

As a man, he sat on the steps of a Colorado cottage with Dwight Eisenhower while a White House photographer took their picture.

As a boy, Marlin Fitzwater saw that picture, blown up to great size on a wall of the Dwight D. Eisenhower Library in Abilene, Kansas.

He would never forget it.

Fitzwater, like Hagerty, would sit in the big office looking out on Pennsylvania Avenue. He would be a press secretary, not to one president like Hagerty, but to two.

Theodore Roosevelt, James Campbell Hagerty, Dwight David Eisenhower, Max Marlin Fitzwater. A continuity of sorts, from Long Island Sound to the Rockies.

Like all American continuities, it came wrapped in differences.

Fitzwater's Kansas plains were as different from Hagerty's streets of New York as Hagerty's streets were from the tidal currents of Oyster Bay. As far as you could see in Max Marlin's country, nothing broke the horizon line but the occasional tower of dust from a passing truck on a farm road.

The man who would explain two such different people as Ronald Reagan and George Bush to the world was born in 1942 and grew up on a rented farm in wheat-growing country south of Abilene.

He came to the Eisenhower Library, not as a tourist, but as a high school student planting tulip bulbs for a landscaping contractor the summer between his junior and senior years.

Because he had to go inside to make a telephone call, he saw the picture and felt "a curiosity about the man with the president, a curiosity about how to get there, impossible as it must be."

Curiosity and ambition led Fitzwater to student journalism on the Abilene High School *Booster* and at Kansas State University. He worked his way through school as editor of the weekly *Lindsborg News-Record,* columnist for the *Abilene Reflector-Chronicle,* and advertising salesman for the *Manhattan Mercury.* Manhattan, Kansas, that is.

Then it was off to Washington and the big time. But Washington didn't seem to want him. He tried the *Washington Post,* the *Washington Star,* the Washington bureau of the *Wall Street Journal,* United Press International, and the Bureau of National Affairs, which publishes newsletters. They all turned him down. Finally, he landed a job with the Appalachian Regional Commission, one of the first battalions of Lyndon Johnson's War on Poverty. Marlin Fitzwater was a spokesman. The idea intrigued him, being "one person who reconciled views through words, and used words to convey group action." He was to do it for three decades.

From the Appalachian commission, he went to the Department of Transportation, the Environmental Protection Agency, and the Treasury Department. In 1983, Dave Gergen called him and then Larry Speakes called him. Reagan White House Personnel Director John Herrington had spent a few days in the press office to determine whether it needed more help. Unaccustomed to the hectic pace of a newsroom, Herrington decided that it definitely did. Fitzwater became deputy press secretary for domestic policy, effective September 1.[1]

He soon became known as somebody to turn to for the details, a source new reporters on the beat were advised to get acquainted with. He was becoming bald. He was ruddy. He was rotund. He was proper in demeanor but quick with a quip, often aimed at himself. He was courteous, calm, and collected, with dark eyes always on the alert. He struck speechwriter Peggy Noonan as a man who "does not expect the right thing to happen."[2] Whenever he walked into the briefing room, he felt fear.[3]

In 1985, Fitzwater moved across the street into the Old Executive Office Building to become press secretary to Vice President George Bush. The vice president was gearing up for his 1988 presidential run, and wanted people who had White House experience. Fitzwater was destined not to become a part of the campaign, however. After Speakes resigned as Reagan's acting press secretary, Fitzwater was approached about that job. He later learned that Nancy Reagan originally wanted Sheila Tate, who had been her press secretary in Reagan's first term, and Chief of Staff Don Regan wanted Ann McLaughlin, who had been Regan's assistant for public affairs when he was secretary of the treasury. Fitzwater was the compromise candidate.

He felt qualms of guilt at the thought of leaving amid preparations for the Bush campaign, but the vice president said he should accept the position. He also advised Marlin that he should be sure he was guaranteed access to the president. It was the first issue Fitzwater raised when he met with Regan. From his days at the Treasury Department, he had reason to know that the former Marine Corps officer and Wall Street tycoon ran a tight ship. Many White House aides complained that it was difficult to get to see the president.

Fitzwater also told Regan he wanted Brady to continue as press secretary, but he wanted to be assistant to the president for press relations, not principal deputy. Regan said he would talk to the president. As it turned out, however, he left it to the somewhat nervous Fitzwater to raise the matter himself when he was called to the Oval Office for the final interview on January 12, 1987. Reagan said he could have both the access and the title that he wanted. It became Fitzwater's policy to simply show up at any meeting he thought he should attend, without waiting for an invitation. He was never asked to leave.[4]

After their meeting in the Oval Office, Reagan walked with Fitzwater into the briefing room and announced his appointment. Reporters, happy to see the old pro back among them, applauded. Some even stood. As time went on, the good feelings would become frayed.

Fitzwater's first problem was with the podium. It was too small for him, so he ordered one that could hold the loose sheets of paper he liked to use as notes. He did research for the top story of the day himself, keeping in mind the aim of "influencing the story so it reflected the president's viewpoint." He also wanted to know five basic facts about five other stories that the press corps would be interested in, reasoning that if he did this he would be ahead of the reporters. These five stories he parceled out to his assistants.[5]

Far more days than not, the big story was the seething Iran-Contra controversy. Two and a half weeks into his job, Fitzwater got a call from Nancy Reagan. He had already, as Speakes's deputy, acquired a shrewd awareness of the first lady's influence. In a memo written at

20. Marlin Fitzwater of the Ronald Reagan and George Bush administrations was the first press secretary to serve two presidents, except for Pierre Salinger's brief stint as a holdover for Lyndon Johnson. *Courtesy Ronald W. Reagan Library.*

Regan's request when his old boss was seeking advice on how to be chief of staff, he wrote. "Don't underestimate the first lady's role . . . Probably through someone on your own staff, you must find a way to manage her requirements."

Now, with the administration's Iran-Contra troubles deepening, stories had been appearing in the press that the president wanted a new chief of staff in place of Regan. "You know those stories about Don Regan?" the first lady asked. Yes, he certainly did. He had just read the third one in a row. "Well, you should just stay out of them," said Mrs. Reagan. Fitzwater got the message that he had been too firm in defending the chief of staff. Mrs. Reagan had told her husband repeatedly that Regan should be fired, but the president was reluctant to take action. When Fitzwater talked to Regan about her telephone call, the chief of staff suggested he "stand back out of the way."[6]

Meanwhile, Fitzwater was reassuring Mrs. Reagan of his efforts to play down the impact of the Iran-Contra stories. On February 24, he sent her a transcript of his briefing that day and pointed out his remarks that "the Iran situation takes up very little of our time" and that "the President's mood is very high and very upbeat and determined." He also pointed out his response to a question by Chris Wallace of NBC, a favorite of the first lady's, concerning the president's memory. Wallace asked, "Is he—is his memory up to snuff? Does he remember key facts? Is there a problem there?" Fitzwater responded, "That's outrageous, Chris. I won't deal with it. It's nonsense."[7]

On February 27, a presidentially appointed board headed by Sen. John Tower of Texas concluded that Reagan's lax management style and misdeeds by his subordinates had led to the error of trying to trade arms for hostages. The president replaced Regan with Howard Baker of Tennessee, the former Senate majority leader, on March 2. The man responsible for hiring Fitzwater had been fired. And Baker wanted the president to name Tom Griscom, who had been his press secretary on Capitol Hill, as White House spokesman. Reagan refused. Marlin was his press secretary, and would remain. On March 4, the president conceded on national television that the arms-for-hostages deal had been a mistake. At a briefing a few days later, Fitzwater was asked whether the president endorsed all the Tower Board's conclusions. Yes, he said, the president accepted the entire report. Did that mean Reagan agreed with the board's conclusion that Secretaries Shultz and Weinberger could have done more to stop the arms-for-hostages transaction? Yes, the president accepted the entire report.

As far as Weinberger was concerned, that was the wrong answer. The secretary of defense had been pressing Reagan to acknowledge that he had opposed the deal. He put in an angry call to Baker. Fitzwater, encountering the chief of staff in the hallway, asked if he had heard from Weinberger and what Weinberger wanted. "He wants a presidential retraction and he wants you," said Baker. "He wants me fired?" asked Fitzwater. "Yes, he does, but I don't think we'll do it."

Back in his office, Fitzwater dashed off a note to Weinberger expressing regret over "the stories involving my comments." It was, he said wryly, in line with one of his basic rules: "Grovel if you have to." In his Saturday radio address that week, Reagan said, "In the case of the Iranian arms sale matter, both Secretary Shultz and Secretary Weinberger advised me strongly not to pursue the initiative . . . it turned out they were right and I was wrong."[8]

When a Senate committee began televised hearings on the Iran-Contra affair, the tension increased. Standing at the sturdy podium he had imported to fit his sturdy frame, Fitzwater would grip its sides as he fended off sharp questions. Generally, he kept his sense of humor and avoided the testiness that marked Speakes's tenure. "You know, it's important not to get too excited here," he said. "It's going to be with us for a long time." He cut back his briefing schedule from two a day to one a day. Asked if he would go back to holding two briefings on busy days, he said, "Do you think I'd volunteer for this twice in one day? You're out of your tree."[9]

In July, the press secretary sent Mrs. Reagan a copy of an AP story quoting him as saying that the president was following the hearings "with interest and . . . concern to get answers to those questions that we didn't have answers on before." He was attempting, he told the first lady, "to show a greater degree of satisfaction with the course of the hearings." "I was very sensitive to her interests," said Fitzwater. "She made enough calls to me about what was being said and what was in the papers and so forth that I felt it made good sense to apprise her of what was going on in the briefings."[10]

The U.S.-Soviet summit in Washington in December 1987 gave Reagan a chance to focus attention on his efforts for arms control and improved relations with the Soviets and away from his shipments of arms to Iran. Five days before the summit was to convene, the administration released a report, required by Congress, on violations of arms-control treaties. The report contained harsh criticism of the Soviets at a time when the White House had been encouraging Soviet leader Mikhail Gorbachev and his reforms. Reporters asked why the administration was running hot and cold at the same time in its approach to the Soviets. Fitzwater sought to settle the seeming contradiction with the formula: "This is not a summit or a session to be taken lightly between friends. This is a summit between old enemies." "Old enemies" was too good a quote for the press to pass up, and Fitzwater knew it immediately. "I was aghast with myself . . . my slip of the tongue would be used to anger Gorbachev." As usual, the privately operated Federal News Service quickly had a transcribed text of the White House spokesman's remarks humming into government offices, newsrooms, and embassies. The Soviet ambassador sent a cable to Moscow. Advisers debated whether to show the offending phrase to Gorbachev, and decided they would. Fitzwater and Soviet spokesman Gennadi Gerasimov had agreed to hold an unprecedented joint briefing for the opening of the summit, and it went off without incident. The next day, at a photo opportunity in the Oval Office, a pool reporter called out the question: "Old friend or old enemies?" Reagan said, "Well, I think you can judge for yourselves." Gorbachev said nothing, but was staring straight at Fitzwater. Fitzwater thought maybe the president had saved him. Then, just before the Soviet delegation left, he was introduced to Gorbachev. "This is Marlin Fitzwater," said interpreter Pavel Plazchenko. "He's the one who said we are old enemies." The Soviet leader pulled his hand from Fitzwater's grasp, raised it in a fist, and said, "If you had said that in my country, I would scold you." "Sometimes, I get scolded in my country," said Fitzwater.

One of the first controversies of 1988 was of an entirely different nature. Six years earlier, Mrs. Reagan had promised to stop borrowing clothes from fashion designers and had been cautioned by the White House counsel's office that any such loans should be disclosed. Despite this, *Time* magazine reported, the first lady had continued to borrow thousands of dollars worth of designer gowns. Her press secretary, Elaine Crispen, said that although there was no legal requirement that the loans be reported, the first lady regretted not heeding the counsel's advice. Fitzwater told reporters the president was "very upset about the attacks on the first lady."

In November, George Bush became the first sitting vice president since Martin Van Buren to be elected to the presidency. Sheila Tate had handled the press for Bush in the campaign and was widely expected to be the first woman to head the White House press office. Although reporters had found Tate helpful when she was Mrs. Reagan's press secretary, the campaign press corps complained that she was too inaccessible. Bush offered Fitzwater the job and asked him if he had any questions. Fitzwater remembered the advice Bush had given him before he accepted Reagan's offer two years earlier. He also remembered that Bush was given to secrecy. "Will I have access to you, and to all meetings?" he asked. The president-elect said he thought that could be worked out. How about National Security Council meetings? "Well, I don't know" said the former CIA director. "Some of those may not be appropriate." Fitzwater wanted the job, and didn't want Bush putting an obstacle in the path by saying no, so he headed him off. "Let's wait and see how it works out," he said. Nevertheless, he saw trouble ahead.[11]

Knowing Bush's low-key style, Fitzwater advised Bush not to try to compete with former movie star Reagan at prime-time news conferences in the awesome setting of the East Room. Bush, heeding the advice, met with reporters in the workaday briefing room. He held

280 news conferences in his four years in office, far more than Reagan
—so many that only CNN regularly carried them on television and
even some White House correspondents occasionally skipped them.[12]

As he had with Reagan, Fitzwater confined his briefings to one a
day, held at 11 A.M. or "as soon after as possible." He felt Speakes's
morning briefings were "a disaster because we didn't have enough
news to support two briefings a day, and all it did was result in arguments." The theory had been that the morning briefing was confined
to the president's schedule for the day. It didn't work, because reporters asked about whatever was on their minds.

Fitzwater resisted the increasing pressure from TV journalists to
televise the briefings, as the ones at the State Department already were.
He argued that this would make them as stilted as the ones at the State
Department, where the spokesman tended to turn to the appropriate
page in his briefing book and read the prepared guidance. Privately,
Fitzwater said, "I enjoyed the briefing process and I didn't want to
assume the risk of saying something wrong and having it repeated on
camera every night for six weeks. I knew my reaction to that risk would
be that I would be willing to venture less on what the president was
thinking about and what he really wanted to do."[13]

Fitzwater's fondness for colorful if seemly language sometimes got
him into trouble. Once, responding to a question about a Danish
political controversy with which he was unfamiliar, he said that to him
Danish was something you sent out for along with coffee. When his
words reached Copenhagen, he had to apologize to the Danes.

A more serious problem arose after only a few months in his new
job. The Soviets' Gorbachev had sprung a series of surprises in a
seeming battle with the United States over which was the most zealous
about curbing the arms race. In the fall of 1988, Gorbachev marched
into the United Nations and announced dramatic unilateral arms cuts.
In the succeeding spring, it was an announcement of short-range missile reductions. Then, in May 1989, came a letter to Bush saying the
Soviets had stopped arms shipments to Nicaragua at the end of the
previous year.

When asked how the United States would respond, Fitzwater contrasted the administration's "very careful and methodical" approach
to arms reduction with the Soviets' strategy "of throwing out in a
kind of drugstore-cowboy fashion one arms control proposal after
another." His words sent reporters scurrying for the precise definition
of "drugstore cowboy." One dictionary gave it as a person who makes

promises he can't keep. It was once widely used to characterize young men who had nothing better to do than hang around drugstores.

Whatever it meant, it was not diplomatic language. Nor was it spontaneous. Fitzwater had thought of it in advance, and his staff tried to talk him out of it. The response was electric. First there were the reporters, coming outside his door after he had retreated to the office. "Where'd you get that drugstore cowboy?" cried Helen Thomas. Others were also in full cry. Knowing he had made a bad mistake, Fitzwater headed for the Oval Office. "Mr. President," he said, "I'm terribly sorry. I'll do whatever it takes to help make this right. Apologize to Gorbachev. Whatever. And if it gets bad, I'll resign immediately." Bush said he didn't think that would be necessary. Nevertheless, the furor continued. Senate Majority Leader George Mitchell commented stiffly, "It's narrow, shortsighted and not in anyone's interests to simply respond to an initiative by what I think can fairly be described as name-calling." *Pravda* said the remark showed the administration's "poverty of ideas." Soviet Ambassador Yuri Dubinin asked, "What are we to make of this? Our foreign ministers have a positive meeting, and now there's this abuse." Assistant Secretary of State Lawrence Eagleburger exclaimed, "Some cowboy! For that matter, some drugstore!"

It blew over, with no formal response from the Soviets, no apologies, and no resignation. "It was my fault for being too glib," said Fitzwater.[14] Ironically, Bush's passion for secrecy worked in his press secretary's favor in the fall of 1989. Listening to Fitzwater's briefings, which were piped into his study, the president heard reporters ask over and over, "When is Bush going to meet with Gorbachev?" One day in late October, he called Fitzwater in and told him. "I'm going to meet with Gorbachev later in the year. We don't have a date yet." He had approached Gorbachev three months earlier. There was nothing to announce, but he wanted Fitzwater to know so that he would not say something such as "They haven't discussed it" and then be in trouble for misleading reporters. Secretary of State James Baker and National Security Adviser Brent Scowcroft were the only others he had told. Neither Secretary of Defense Dick Cheney nor CIA chief William Webster knew of his plans.

"It was really kind of a turning point in my relationship with the president because it told me that, regardless of his own penchant for secrecy in many areas, he fully understood how the press operated and what my needs were."[15]

Six months later, the White House announced that the two leaders would meet in December aboard U.S. and Soviet ships anchored in Malta harbor. The day before the announcement was made, the story appeared in the *Washington Post*. Fitzwater said the leak didn't matter, but Bush was so angry that he never again gave an interview or answered a question for the reporter who wrote it. Aboard the USS *Belknap* at Malta, Fitzwater was pleased that Gorbachev greeted him warmly and said nothing about drugstore cowboys.[16]

The most outspoken challenge Fitzwater faced in the briefing room came in the aftermath of an abortive coup in Panama in 1989. Manuel Noriega, the Panamanian dictator who had once been supported by the CIA, was now out of favor as an indicted international drug smuggler. Noriega was defeated in a Panamanian election, but voided the results. Americans were outraged by television pictures of the winner, Guillermo Endara, and one of his elected vice presidents being beaten over the head by Noriega's troopers. Bush went so far as to say Panamanians should "do everything they can to get Mr. Noriega out of there." At the end of September, troops led by Moises Giroldi, a rebellious army major, appealed for U.S. aid in seizing Noriega and forcing him from office. The rebels' key request was that U.S. forces stationed in Panama to protect the Panama Canal be used to close two roads by which loyalist troops might rescue Noriega. Top military leaders concluded the plot was half-baked and recommended that the United States not get involved. They did agree to block one of the routes, a causeway, by stationing armed troops in a commanding position alongside it. They declined to block the Bridge of the Americas, which crosses the canal into Panama City, because it would require giving open assistance to the rebels.

On Tuesday, October 3, sitting in the president's study while Bush attended an unrelated meeting in the Oval Office, Fitzwater was watching CNN on television. The set was turned so low it was scarcely audible, but what came through loud and clear to the president's spokesman was that there was a coup in Panama, and he hadn't heard anything about it.

Fitzwater told reporters the administration had never been directly informed of a coup plot. "If we were," he said, "the president doesn't know about it, the secretary of state doesn't know about it and the secretary of defense doesn't know about it." Even in his 1995 memoirs, Fitzwater said there had been no presidential briefing. He later said that he was not sure of this and that the president may have been informally briefed. In fact, White House records showed that Secretary of State James A. Baker III, Secretary of Defense Dick Cheney, newly designated Joint Chiefs of Staff Chairman Colin L. Powell, and others met with the president in the Oval Office from 9:00 A.M. to 9:30 A.M. on Monday, October 2, to discuss the coup.

On Tuesday afternoon, troops loyal to Noriega freed the dictator and began rounding up the rebels. By now, reporters were lined up outside Fitzwater's office and wanted to know why, if the president was so anxious to see an end to Noriega's rule, he had not acted. "Was the U.S. called on to help? Did we offer military help?" the spokesman was asked. "We were not asked to help," Fitzwater said. But he was uneasy. "The press had a whiff of something we didn't have, but we didn't know what."

The next day, Roman Popadiuk, deputy press secretary for foreign affairs, told Fitzwater he had just learned that the CIA station chief in Panama had met Sunday night with Giroldi. The leader of the rebellion informed the station chief of the coup and asked that the Bridge of the Americas be blocked. Popadiuk said Robert Gates, the deputy national security adviser, told him that CIA officials in Washington had not informed the president because they hadn't been told themselves.

That night, Fitzwater accompanied the president to a speaking engagement in Chantilly, Virginia. As they flew back to the White House in the helicopter, Bush asked him if he had heard anything new on Panama. Fitzwater repeated what he had been told. "I sure didn't know about it," said Bush. Fitzwater concluded that everybody was covering up for "not coordinating properly, not reading the right reports, not making the right phone call, not telling the president, not demanding better information, not something."

The episode raised questions both of the administration's credibility and its competence. *Newsweek* headed its account of the affair "Amateur Hour." Republican Sen. Jesse Helms likened the American role to that of the Keystone Kops of the silent movie era.

At his October 10 briefing, Fitzwater was asked whether he was aware that his assertions "that there was no contact directly with the U.S. or indirectly with the U.S. . . . were lies." He said calmly that the United States closed the causeway to protect lives, and the president did not know that the action had been requested by the coup leader. He said everything he told the press was exactly what the president had been told. "My guiding principle" he said later, "was that it was better for me to be accused of lying than for the president and Cheney to be accused of incompetence." [17]

In December, after Noriega's forces shot and killed an off-duty

Marine lieutenant, the United States invaded Panama. At a meeting in the Oval Office, Fitzwater told Bush he thought most public and press response to the invasion would be positive, although "of course, you're going to have that element in the press that will criticize you." Noriega was taken into custody on January 3, 1990, and brought to Florida to face drug charges. Losses in the operation were officially reported at 23 U.S. military personnel killed, along with 314 Panamanian military and 202 Panamanian civilians. The Pentagon came under heavy criticism in the press for not allowing U.S. reporters to cover the operation while it was under way. There was, if anything, even stronger criticism when the Pentagon came up with a pool system for coverage of the lightning war touched off by Iraq's invasion of Kuwait in 1990. In both cases, the contention centered on the Pentagon, with the White House on the periphery.[18]

Fitzwater's first brush as White House spokesman with presidential health problems came on a day at the races. On May 4, 1991, Bush suffered shortness of breath and an irregular heartbeat while jogging at Camp David. His spokesman and a friend had decided that day to attend the annual Gold Cup steeplechase race near Middleburg, Virginia. They were in his car and just leaving when Fitzwater's beeper went off. Like Jim Hagerty's telephone call from Denver, it was a constant ring, not intermittent. Fitzwater knew what that meant. Quickly, he read the message: "CALL HERRICK. CAMP DAVID. EMERGENCY." He found a restaurant in a nearby town and asked the bartender for a phone.

From a narrow hallway outside a men's room, Fitzwater dialed the White House operator. The operator put him through to press aide John Herrick, who had drawn the Camp David duty that weekend. The president was being taken to Bethesda Naval Hospital, Herrick told him. Fitzwater dictated a statement and told Herrick to call it to the wire services just before he got on the helicopter with the president. The key sentence said that Bush "was taken to the Camp David medical facility and was examined by Dr. Michael Nash, one of the president's physicians, and determined to have . . ." He told Herrick to fill in the blank with the correct medical term as he got it from the doctor. He then sped to the White House.

Chief of Staff John Sununu, meanwhile, called Camp David, and Herrick read him the statement, filling in the blank with the term Nash had given him, "atrial fibrillation." According to Fitzwater, Sununu said something like, "Whoa. We don't want to say atrial fibrillation.

We don't need to get people scared of a heart attack." Looking back at the incident later, Sununu said he favored waiting for tests at Bethesda before saying anything. "I don't think we should be speculating, especially when the doctors caution us that it's a preliminary conclusion," he said.

At this point, Herrick saw the president walking from the infirmary to the helicopter with a heart monitor and intravenous fluid bottle attached to him and the doctor holding his arm. Aboard the helicopter, Bush wanted to make sure the press was being told that he was going to the hospital. Herrick read Fitzwater's statement to him, not mentioning his conversation with Sununu. He did not have time to telephone the wire services before leaving, but did so as soon as the helicopter reached Bethesda.

At the White House, Fitzwater worked on a further statement, but again faced arguments from Sununu. "My feeling is you don't jump into news releases before you know where you're going," the chief of staff said. As Hagerty had done at the time of Eisenhower's heart attack, the president's spokesman pointed out the political harm that would come from lying about the president's health. After getting Sununu's approval, he read a statement covering Bush's condition, medication, and tests and saying he was "relaxed, comfortable, and having dinner with Mrs. Bush." The doctors had told the presidential spokesman there was no chance it could be a heart attack, but he left this out of the statement to avoid further argument with Sununu, who he felt didn't want the words mentioned. Fitzwater figured that reporters would ask anyway, as they did.

Another argument arose when doctors said the president might need electrical cardioversion, a procedure used to shock the heart back into its normal rhythm if medicine didn't do the trick. If needed, it was to be done early in the morning of May 6. Because it would require a general anesthetic, there would be a temporary transfer of presidential power to Vice President Dan Quayle. Fitzwater reasoned that the American people should be told about this possibility the night before, rather than learning on the morning news that Quayle was acting president. Sununu argued that they should wait until the doctors decided that the procedure was necessary before saying anything. "I just thought that if anybody had a responsibility not to be putting speculative possibilities into press reports, it was the White House," he said. Fitzwater wrote a statement of which the fifth paragraph said, "We remain hopeful that the medication will return his heart to normal rhythm. If by morning that is not the case, the doctors will consider electrical cardioversion. . . . During the short time the president would be under anesthesia, the vice president would be acting president under the Twenty-Fifth Amendment." At Bethesda, it was shown to the president, who said to go ahead with it. As it turned out, the procedure was not needed, and the president quickly returned to work.[19]

The Bush administration had abandoned the Reagan era "line of the day" meetings for what David Demarest, the White House communications director, called "a more open, two-way relationship with the press." In other words, said Demarest, it was left to the press "to decide what it was going to cover as the most important message or theme of the day."[20]

Ironically, this fed criticism that Bush lacked "vision"—that he did not, in fact, have an important message or theme. The perception was a major factor in Bush's defeat at the polls by Arkansas governor Bill Clinton in 1992.

"The president used to complain, 'we're not getting our message out,' " Fitzwater said. "Well, the fact was, there wasn't a strong message on the economy to get out. . . . There is no such thing as a president not getting his message out . . . something is being communicated. In our case, it was that President Bush was out of touch with the economy."[21]

Fitzwater's journey from Abilene to the White House may have begun with a glimpse of Jim Hagerty's picture, but there was a vast difference between the two press secretaries.

Hagerty advised Eisenhower to slash spending, to travel abroad, to be the "Tribune of the People."

Fitzwater said, "My value to reporters was greatest if they thought everything I said was reflecting the president's thinking, not my own thinking."

He avoided appearing on television talk shows because "every time I did that it tended to imbue me with a set of ideas or opinions about presidential activities and policies."

"I thought a good press secretary should be reflective of the president," he said.[22] The press secretary was the messenger; only the president could provide the message.

15

The Door

ON JANUARY 20, INAUGURATION DAY, 1993, reporters coming to work at the White House found the door between the lower and upper presidential press offices locked.

The resulting furor must have struck many Americans as about the silliest of all inside-the-beltway uproars. What difference did it make if the door was locked or unlocked?

To the White House press corps it made a big difference, and it spelled the beginning of troubled press relations for the new administration of President Bill Clinton.

Movement within the West Wing, where the president and his senior staff have their offices, is severely limited for journalists covering the White House. To interview anyone outside the press office area, either in the West Wing or the Old Executive Office Building across an enclosed street, they must get an appointment and be escorted.

This means that for coverage of breaking news their best bet is the press secretary's office in the upper of the two press office areas. The lower press office, right next door to the briefing room, is the domain of lower-ranking press assistants who can often offer little but routine guidance.

When reporters could not move freely through the door from the lower office into the hallway that leads to the office of the press secretary, they were cut off from what was often their only source of information.

"This is an act of war," exclaimed UPI's redoubtable Helen Thomas.[1] When the new administration experimented with televising its briefings, Thomas seized the opportunity to make a case to the

public, loudly demanding on national television that reporters be allowed access to the press secretary.[2]

George Stephanopoulos, the former congressional aide recruited
by Clinton to be his communications director, later conceded that the
move was "stupid" and said, "I can't defend it."[3] Others reported
that the rule was imposed by Clinton and his activist first lady, Hillary.[4]

Marlin Fitzwater, keeping an eye on his successors from a getaway
on the Chesapeake Bay, thought the president's press officers as well as
the reporters were losing out on information they needed. Specifically,
Fitzwater believed a more open press office could have alerted Clinton
and his staff to the dangers of their assault on the White House travel
office.

For years, the travel office had chartered airplanes to transport
media personnel, at the expense of their employers, on trips with the
president. On May 19, the Clinton administration fired most of the
employees of the office. Officials cited financial mismanagement, but
reporters noted that Catherine Cornelius, who had been placed
in charge of the operation, was a distant cousin of the president.
Friends of Clinton had expressed interest in bidding on the charter
business.[5]

In preparing talking points for the press office to use in announcing the change, the White House director of administration, David
Watkins, reportedly anticipated that the announcement would be
greeted with enthusiasm in the press room.[6]

The response was far otherwise. The travel office emloyees were
the people who made sure that reporters got where they needed to be
and got there on time, who saw that their luggage was there when
they arrived, who got up early in the morning to put the luggage back
on the bus.

Even Clinton was said to have realized that his inexperienced staff
had erred. The press office had failed to properly gauge the response
of journalists to a story involving both political patronage and an arm
of the White House that had so often been of help to them. It struck
Fitzwater that reporters hanging around outside either Stephanopoulos' office or that of Press Secretary Dee Dee Myers would have
provided early warning signals.[7] The door eventually was unlocked,
but the press office remained awry.

Myers, a thirty-one-year-old Californian who wore dangly earrings
and made flip remarks, was both the youngest presidential press secretary in history and the first woman to hold the job. An admiring profile

21. President Bill Clinton named Dee Dee Myers as his press secretary, the first woman to hold the position. *Courtesy AP/Wide World.*

in *Vogue* saluted the "toughness and cool" with which she dealt with the White House press corps.[8]

Among reporters, her reception was less enthusiastic. Personally, they liked her, finding her buoyant personality a welcome relief from the more astringent manner of Stephanopoulos and others in Clinton's inner circle. But, said one veteran Washington newsman, "I never knew a reporter over there who felt Dee Dee was much help to them." Others echoed his view, although some thought the blame was not hers.[9]

"I thought Dee Dee was first rate and tried very hard to do a job within the limits that were put on her," said Mark Knoller of CBS News. "She wasn't always well informed, but that just wasn't her fault."[10]

Certainly it wasn't. Clinton did not give her the authority and stature that normally went with the job. She didn't even get the office. Stephanopoulos sat where press secretaries had sat before him; Myers was shunted to a small office two doors away formerly occupied by a succession of deputies. Stephanopoulos gave the newsmaking afternoon briefings while Myers handled the morning sessions on the president's schedule. Stephanopoulos was in effect the president's spokesman. Sometimes, he was even referred to as the press secretary, and Myers as his deputy.

Clinton and his advisers, anxious to get credit for naming a woman as press secretary, threw Myers to the lions. She had none of the experience that is most important for success in the job. She had never worked as a reporter. She was not a close associate of the president. Although she had worked in Democratic campaigns in California and as Clinton's campaign press secretary, she was inexperienced in government public relations. Her lack of journalistic experience, along with the restrictions on her access, made it difficult for her to get the information reporters needed. She was in over her head.

On top of this, Clinton, coming off a campaign in which he was hounded with questions about his private life and his draft record, came to the White House with more than the usual animosity toward the press corps. Reporters found this reflected in the attitude of Myers and her staff, who often failed to return telephone calls and responded curtly to press queries. "They came in with a chip on their shoulder," said one. "They had no real respect for the press." [11]

Some in the White House and the press corps, particularly women, saw Myers as a victim of discrimination by an all-male establishment. There was truth to this. When she blurted out to a reporter that the FBI was investigating the travel office, not yet having been told that this was supposed to be kept under wraps, Director of Administration Watkins complained that it was "typical of the haphazard way the press office operated." [12] One male writer, kindly disposed toward Myers personally, detected a lack of gravitas in her conduct. [13] Perhaps Pierre Salinger's Bermuda shorts had been all right, but dangly earrings were too much.

"I was given responsibility that exceeded my authority, and it has put me in a continually difficult position," said Myers. "I think this happens to women a lot."

"Dee Dee didn't have all the tools she needed," said her successor, Mike McCurry. [14]

Whatever the reasons for her difficulties, Myers did not, to her credit, accept them without a fight. She campaigned for more information, for the right to give the main briefings, and for the press secretary's office.

In May 1993, David Gergen, a White House aide to both Nixon and Reagan and now a columnist who had written glowingly of Clinton, was brought in to bolster the president's public image. Myers was aghast. Playing the role of a reporter in a practice session for Gergen's first meeting with the press, she asked, "What are you doing here? You're the engineer and the spokesman for what Clinton ran against and was elected on." Gergen took the blow in good sort, and Myers was soon advised that she would take over briefing duties from Stephanopoulos.[15]

But she did not get the big office. It went to Mark Gearan, a popular deputy chief of staff who was replacing Stephanopoulos as communications director. Nor did she get greater access to information. In June, former president Bush was reported to have been the target of an assassination attempt by Iraqi leader Saddam Hussein during a visit to the Middle East. When Myers was asked the status of an FBI report on the allegation, she replied, "We hear that it's in its final stages, but it's not complete." The report had been given to the president the night before, but no one had told her. She complained to Gergen and to Anthony Lake, the national security adviser, and Gergen promised to try to keep her better informed. He also counseled her she should step up her own checking with White House sources. At her next briefing, Myers was grilled mercilessly by reporters about her misstep.[16]

Things did not get better. In July, Clinton's old school friend Mack McLarty was replaced as chief of staff by Leon Panetta, a California congressman who was chairman of the House Budget Committee. That night, on television's *Larry King Live,* Panetta was asked if he planned to install his own press person at the White House. "It's likely, obviously," Panetta said. "I'm going to be bringing in some of my own people to try to assist me in that effort, sure."

Shortly after the late-night broadcast, Panetta got one of his first orders from his new boss. The president told him to telephone Myers immediately and tell her it was all a mistake. Myers was glad to get the midnight call but nevertheless felt Panetta had "left me hanging out there a little bit." The next morning, Panetta repeated his apology at a senior staff meeting. Reporters still wanted to know when she was leaving. "People are watching me too closely," she said. "I don't think you can argue things are going well."[17]

From her standpoint, she was right. Without her knowledge, Panetta was talking with McCurry, then the spokesman for the State Department, about the job.[18] McCurry, like Myers, had never been a reporter. He knew Clinton less well than she did. In the 1992 primary campaign, he worked for one of Clinton's opponents, Sen. Bob Kerrey of Nebraska. Unlike Myers, however, he had a record as a government spokesman in Washington. He had been press secretary to a succession of Democratic senators and then spokesman for the Democratic National Committee before going to Foggy Bottom with Secretary of State Warren Christopher. He also had a reputation as an advocate of openness. Working for former Arizona governor Bruce Babbitt in the 1988 Democratic primary season, it had been his idea to let reporters watch Babbitt prepare for a television debate.[19]

On September 22, Myers read a story on the Reuters news service wire headed "State Department Aide to Become Clinton Spokesman." At an angry meeting in the chief of staff's office, she told Panetta, "I don't think I'm asking too much not to read about my replacement on Reuters." Panetta wanted to divide the job between the two of them, much as had been done with Stephanopoulos. Myers said that would not do. That night, she met with the president in the Oval Office and, later, had another meeting with Panetta. She remained as press secretary and moved into the spacious office that her predecessors had enjoyed. But she would leave by the end of the year.[20]

On January 5, 1995, Clinton made it official, introducing McCurry in the briefing room. His appointment was welcomed by reporters. The *Washington Post,* tossing aside the rule against opinions in news stories, exclaimed, "He certainly seems like a jolly fellow."[21]

McCurry, forty, began private off-the-record sessions with White House correspondents to get their views on how to improve the working relationship. He instructed his staff to deal courteously with reporters and return their telephone calls.[22] "The over-all atmosphere became much kinder and gentler," said one correspondent.[23]

After McCurry had held the job for more than a year, Jack Nelson of the *Los Angeles Times* ranked him with Jody Powell and Marlin Fitzwater among press secretaries "who will really tell you things that will help you understand what is going on."[24] Knoller said, "I think he is one of the best press secretaries I have ever encountered in the 20 years I have covered the White House on and off."[25]

In October 1995, McCurry, like many press secretaries before him, got into trouble with his glib tongue. Clinton was engrossed in budget negotiations with the new Republican majority in Congress, and Medicare was a key issue. Responding to a question at a briefing, McCurry said Republicans would like to see Medicare "just die and go away" and then added, "That's probably what they'd like to see happen to seniors too, if you think about it." House Speaker Newt Gingrich and Senate Majority Leader Bob Dole called upon Clinton to fire his press secretary and apologize. McCurry apologized, kept his job, and told reporters the president agreed with him that he had said the wrong thing.[26]

A month later, McCurry ruffled the water again with a flip remark. Gingrich had said he had complained of being snubbed by the president during a trip on *Air Force One,* and the press secretary said, "Maybe we can send him some of those little M&Ms with the presidential seal" that are handed out to guests on the presidential airplane. With budget negotiations still going on, the president made it clear he was not amused. McCurry found pictures of Clinton talking with Gingrich and Dole on the plane and had them reproduced and distributed.[27]

It got worse. In January, *Time* magazine ran a White House photograph of Clinton, looking for all the world like a college professor at the blackboard, lecturing Dole, Gingrich, and others on the budget. Gingrich said he had been promised that the pictures would not be released, but the White House press office had released them anyway. Once more, McCurry was treated to a sample of Clinton's famous rage.[28]

Seeking always to build bridges between the president and the press, McCurry tried in March of the campaign year of 1996 what he called "psych-background." He encouraged Clinton to drop by the press area of *Air Force One* on a trip home from Israel and hold forth in what was supposed to be a background session, attributable only to "the highest authority."

The president had done this once before, but with no restrictions. On a return flight from California in September, he had visited with reporters for about an hour. McCurry tried to cut it off, but the voluble president returned to the press table and proclaimed, to his press secretary's dismay, that he was "also trying to get people out of their funk." The remark created such a furor that the president had to pull back three days later, saying he was really optimistic and didn't think Americans were in a funk.

This time, the results were no better. Although the president's comments were made only to a small pool of reporters, they wrote a report, as was their duty, that was circulated to other news organizations. The Associated Press, part of the pool, accurately reported that he made "no ground-breaking news." Topics ranged from his current reading to Russia's problems to his worries about daughter Chelsea's dating. Inevitably, the identity of the "highest authority" became known. There was no more "psych-background." [29]

Later in the year came an occasion when what the president was saying didn't jibe with what his press secretary was saying. Billy Dale, the fired head of the travel office, had been charged with fraud and acquitted. Congress was considering a bill to reimburse Dale's legal expenses. McCurry, asked if Clinton supported the bill, said, "Yes, he would sign it." During the first week of August, McCurry was on vacation, but his deputy, Barry Toiv, repeated the same claim. That afternoon, at an appearance in the Rose Garden, Clinton was asked whether he would support the bill. Will you, a reporter asked him, "keep your word"? Angrily, the president shot back, "I never gave my word on that." He said he didn't see why Dale should be reimbursed while many of his own aides, called to testify before investigating committees of Congress, had to pay their own legal fees. White House aides were dismayed by Clinton's outburst, and Toiv said McCurry had been "perhaps a little bit forward leaning in his description of the president's position." [30]

After Clinton's victory over Dole in the 1996 presidential election, McCurry was quoted as saying his objective in the second term would be to improve Clinton's relations with the press. He was noncommittal about how successful he would be.

"Intellectually, he knows it's the right thing to do, but to do it well, he has to feel it in his heart," he said of Clinton. [31]

In their hearts, though, few presidents have been very fond of reporters. Grover Cleveland spoke of their "colossal impertinence." Woodrow Wilson called them "contemptible spies." Herbert Hoover refused to break bread with them. Lyndon Johnson said, "I think they want to hurt me." Richard Nixon considered them "part of my political opposition." Jimmy Carter complained that they had "absolutely no interest in issues at all." George Bush attacked them in front of his staff. Even FDR and Kennedy, notably convivial with journalists in public, excoriated them in private.

Clinton had been dogged throughout his 1992 campaign by questioning about sexual escapades and his avoidance of the draft during the Vietnam war. In his first term, both Congress and a special prosecutor investigated his involvement in the failed Whitewater real estate venture that had resulted in criminal prosecutions in his native Arkansas. To this, in the second term, were added allegations of improper solicitation of political campaign money, some of it from foreign sources. It was enough to make any president dislike aggressive questioning by reporters.

By the time Clinton took office, the press had changed greatly from the days of Cleveland and Wilson, or even Roosevelt and Kennedy. McCurry estimated that a third to half of every story written about the 1996 campaign contained "some level of analysis" by the reporter.[32] This was probably an overstatement in the heat of a campaign, but it was true that factual reporting was increasingly supplemented by analysis, both in columns labeled as such and in the background portions of news stories. In writing what the late *Washington Post* publisher Philip Graham once called "the first rough draft of history," journalists more and more felt a responsibility to put the facts in perspective.

Sometimes, they seemed to forget that it was only a first draft.

As reporters changed, so did the technology with which they worked. Gone were the days of two clear-cut news cycles—one for morning papers and one for afternoon papers. Time was that presidential announcements were alternated between cycles, and press secretaries guarded carefully against leaks in advance. Now it was "all the news all the time."[33]

"We basically don't let presidents make announcements any more," said McCurry. Reporters were briefed the night before "to get the story moving overnight."[34] That way, the early morning stories would begin, "President Clinton is to announce today. . . ." "The headlines will only linger for a very brief period unless you find a way to keep it in front of the American people for a longer period of time," McCurry said.[35]

In 1948, wire service correspondent Merriman Smith foresaw the day when microphones and television cameras would be admitted to at least some presidential news conferences, but did not envision the possibility of their entry into the press secretary's briefings.[36] Television inched its way into the briefing room, however, first for just a few shots at the beginning of the briefing, then for the first five minutes of it during the Dee Dee Myers era. With McCurry's arrival, television cameras were allowed to be on for the entire briefing, just as at the State Department. Live televising could be done only by request, and sometimes was denied. But reporters no longer had to wait until the briefing was over to file their stories. Wire services stationed a reporter

22. Mike McCurry came from the State Department to be Bill Clinton's second presidential spokesman. *Official White House photograph.*

in their booths, listening to an audio feed, who could file the news as it broke.

Although past press secretaries had usually shunned on-camera interviews with television reporters, McCurry gave them frequently on the North Lawn outside his office and on out-of-town trips. "He does it as often as he is asked," said Knoller, "probably because he is very good at it." [37]

Some of McCurry's predecessors worried that the position was becoming too visible.

"In some cases, those briefings are treated more importantly than they ought to be," said Jody Powell. "In an ongoing crisis, the press secretary may be on the air every night for weeks, maybe months, and that to me is not the way it ought to be. That's a role that in most cases is best reserved for the president. To me, it runs the risk of diminishing the impact of his speaking if his spokesman is speaking on television every night of the week." [38]

"I think it started going downhill when Ziegler was forced to deal with Watergate every day," said George Christian. [39]

Marlin Fitzwater cited the example of Stephanopoulos: "He was on every talk show in America. Within a matter of weeks he had his own set of ideas and priorities and opinions about issues, recognizable to the press and public, so that he no longer was that valuable as a direct reflection of the president."[40]

McCurry, however, did not seem to have eclipsed Bill Clinton. "Nobody cares what Mike McCurry thinks," he said. "It is what the president thinks and believes that is important."[41]

·   ·   ·

As George Bruce Cortelyou looked back on his tenure as President McKinley's private secretary, he wrote a memo for the guidance of the new hands in Theodore Roosevelt's White House on the duties of a presidential aide. Among the duties he listed was the care of the White House stables. He said nothing about the White House press corps.[42]

In this and in other ways, the change from McKinley to Clinton was profound. President Hoover's press secretaries worked in anonymity, and few Americans had any idea what they looked like. Mike McCurry's words and image could be flashed around the world by satellite. As the White House and its press contingent geared up for a new century, however, one thing remained unchanged.

In the end, it was the president who spoke for the president.

Notes
Bibliography
Index

Notes

1. The Game

1. C. C. Buel, "Our Fellow-Citizen of the White House: The Official Cares of a President of the United States," *The Century*, Mar. 1897, 647–48.

2. Marlin Fitzwater, *Call the Briefing! Bush and Reagan, Sam and Helen: A Decade with the Presidents and the Press* (New York: Random House, 1996), 339.

3. Betty Houchin Winfield, *FDR and the News Media* (Urbana, Ill.: Univ. of Illinois Press, 1990), 79.

4. Hamilton Jordan, *Crisis: The Last Year of the Carter Presidency* (New York: G. P. Putnam's Sons, 1982), 271; Powell, *The Other Side of the Story* (New York: Morrow, 1984), 225–32.

5. Jack Nelson, author's interview, by telephone, May 28, 1946; Powell, author's interview, Washington, D.C. Feb. 29, 1996.

6. Powell, exit interview with David Alsobrook of Presidential Papers Staff, Washington, D.C., Dec. 2, 1980, 5.

7. James E. Pollard, *The Presidents and the Press* (New York: Macmillan, 1947), 10.

8. Arthur M. Schlesinger, Jr., *The Age of Jackson* (New York: Book Find Club, by arrangement with Little, Brown, 1945), 71.

9. Pollard, 80, 235, 292; Stewart Alsop, *The Center: People and Power in Political Wahington* (Harper and Row, 1968), 192.

10. Benjamin Temple Ford, *A Duty to Serve: The Governmental Career of George Bruce Cortelyou*, unpublished doctoral diss., Columbia Univ., 1903, 46.

11. Donald R. Burkholder, *The Caretakers of the President's Image*, unpublished doctoral diss., Wayne State Univ., 1973, 37, in Harry S Truman Library; Allan L. Damon, "Presidential Accessibility," *American Heritage*, Apr. 1974, 62.

12. *Budget of the United States, Fiscal Year 1996: Appendix* (Washington, D.C.: Government Printing Office, 1995), 55.

13. Pollard, 133.

14. Thomas Jefferson to Francis Hopkinson, Mar. 13, 1789, quoted by Pollard, 66.

15. Henry Wise, quoted by Schlesinger, 72–73.

16. Helen Nicolay, *Lincoln's Secretary: A Biography of John G. Nicolay* (New York: Longmans, Green, 1949), 9, 13, 329.

17. Nicolay, 305.

18. L. A. Gobright, *Recollections of Men and Things at Washington During the Third of a Century* (Philadelphia: Claxton, Remsen and Heffelfinger, 1869), 334.

19. Robert S. Harper, *Lincoln and the Press* (New York: McGraw-Hill, 1951), 95.

20. Gobright, 319, 335–37; David Homer Bates, "Lincoln in the Telegraph Office," *The Century,* May 1907, 127.

21. Gobright, 337–39; Nicolay, 185.

22. Benjamin Perley Poore, *Perley's Reminiscences of Sixty Years in the National Metropolis* (Philadelphia: Hubbard Brothers, 1886), 1:142–43.

23. Gobright, 318; Harper, 130–33.

24. F. B. Marbut, *News from the Capital: The Story of Washington Reporting* (Carbondale: Southern Illinois Univ. Press, 1971), 167; George Turnbull, "Some Notes on the History of the Interview," *Journalism Quarterly,* No. 3, 272–79; Poore, 1:399, 2:525.

25. Marbut, 167.

26. *Editor & Publisher,* Oct. 31, 1931.

27. *Public Opinion,* June 19, 1886, 197–98; Pollard, 290; Nicolay, 329.

28. Allan Nevins, *Grover Cleveland: A Study in Courage* (New York: Dodd, Mead, 1933), 305–7; Rexford G. Tugwell, *Grover Cleveland* (New York: Macmillan, 1968), xvi; *Public Opinion,* June 12, 1886, 173–75; Poore, 2:492–93; John Tebbel and Sarah Miles Watts, *The Press and the Presidency: From George Washington to Ronald Reagan* (New York: Oxford Univ. Press, 1985), 270–71.

29. Arthur Wallace Dunn, *Gridiron Nights* (New York: Frederick A. Stokes, 1915; reprint, New York: Arno Press, 1974), 18–19.

30. Richard V. Oulahan, *Presidents and the Press,* chap. 10, Unpublished Manuscripts folder, Richard V. Oulahan papers, Hoover Library.

31. Buell, 662; Tugwell, 191.

32. Edward B. MacMahon, M.D., and Leonard Curry, *Medical Cover-ups in the White House* (Washington, D.C.; Farragut, 1987), 38–55.

33. Delbert Clark, *Washington Dateline* (New York: Frederick A. Stokes, 1941), 53; *Editor & Publisher,* Oct. 31, 1931; Earl Godwin, "White Housekeeping," *Goldfish Bowl,* July 1937.

2. The Confidential Stenographer

1. Lily Cortelyou, *Reminiscences,* 5, unpublished manuscript in George Bruce Cortelyou papers, box 72, manuscript division, Library of Congress.

2. Cortelyou papers, box 72, folder containing items removed from Cortelyou's wallet at the time of his death.

3. Ford, 1–25.

4. Lily Cortelyou, 7.

5. Arthur Wallace Dunn, *From Harrison to Harding: A Personal Narrative, Covering a Third of a Century* (Fort Washington, N.Y.: Kennicat Press, 1971), 209-10.

6. Margaret Leach, *In the Days of McKinley* (New York: Harper, 1959), 231.

7. Dunn, *From Harrison to Harding,* 210.

8. Lily Cortelyou, 18.

9. Ford, 44; Dunn, *From Harrison to Harding,* 209–10.

10. George Cortelyou, handwritten diary entries for July 1, 1898; Jan. 23, 1900; and Feb. 4, 1900, Cortelyou papers, box 53.

11. Ida Tarbell, "President McKinley in War Time," *McClure's,* July 1898, 213–14; Godwin.

12. Leach, 126.

13. *New York Times,* May 26, 1907, cited in Ford, 47.

14. George Cortelyou, transcribed shorthand notes for Mar. 23, Apr. 20, Apr. 22, Apr. 23, Apr. 25, and June 2, 1899, Cortelyou papers, box 52.

15. Albert Halstead, "The President at Work—A Character Sketch," *The Independent,* Sept. 5, 1901, 2081.

16. *The Work of the President's Office,* unattributed typescript dated Feb. 20, 1908, 13, Cortelyou papers.

17. Ford, 45–46; Lewis L. Gould, *The Presidency of William McKinley* (Lawrence, Kans.: The Regents Press of Kansas, 1980), 38; Donald A. Ritchie, *Press Gallery: Congress and the Washington Correspondents* (Cambridge, Mass.: Harvard Univ. Press, 1991), 202.

18. *Budget Appendix,* 55.

19. George Cortelyou, transcribed shorthand notes for Mar. 18, 1898, Cortelyou papers, box 52.

20. Lyndon Orr, "Great Secretaries to the President," *The Scrap Book,* Nov. 1907, cited in Ford, 51–52. (Ford speculates that Orr was a pseudonym for Richard Harding Davis.)

21. Tarbell, 214.

22. Charles G. Dawes, *A Journal of the McKinley Years,* edited and with a foreword by Bascom N. Timmins (Chicago: Lakeside Press, 1950); Ford, 56.

23. H. Wayne Morgan, *William McKinley and His America* (Syracuse, N.Y.: Syracuse Univ. Press, 1963), 509; George Cortelyou, handwritten diary entries for July 13, 1899, and Jan. 4, 1900, Cortelyou papers, box 53.

24. Ford, 59; Dawes, 276.

25. George Cortelyou, memorandum to Rudolph Forster, Jan. 26, 1903, Cortelyou papers.

26. Lily Cortelyou, 8.

27. Charles Penrose, *George B. Cortelyou (1862-1940): Briefest Biography of a Great American* (New York: The Newcomen Society, 1955), 12–13; David S. Barry, *Forty Years in Washington* (Boston: Little, Brown, 1924), 286–88.

28. William Howard Taft to William Allen White, quoted in George Juergens, *News from the White House: The Presidential-Press Relationship in the Progressive Era* (Chicago: Univ. of Chicago Press, 1981), 95.

29. Juergens, 14.

30. Clark, 54–55.

31. Henry Fairlie, "The Rise of the Press Secretary," *The New Republic,* Mar. 18, 1978, 21; Barry, 266–67.

32. *Charleston News and Courier,* reprinted in *The Journalist,* Nov. 22, 1902, 54; Bascom N. Timmins, "This Is How It Used to Be," in *Dateline: Washington—The*

Story of National Affairs Journalism in the Life and Times of the National Press Club, ed. Cabell Phillips et al. (New York: Greenwood Press, 1968), 50.

33. David McCullough, *The Path Between the Seas: The Creation of the Panama Canal, 1870–1914* (New York: Simon and Schuster, 1977), 248.

34. Oulahan, under the pseudonym Victor Proud, "Roosevelt, the Politician," *Saturday Evening Post,* Sept. 21, 1907; Juergens, 65; Richard V. Oulahan to Ray Stannard Baker, Mar. 15, 1929, 2, Baker papers, reel 81.

35. Oulahan, *Presidents and the Press,* chap. 13, 1.

36. Blaire Atherton French, *The Presidential Press Conference: Its History and Role in the American Political System* (Lapham, Md.: Univ. Press of America, 1982), 3.

37. Archibald Willingham Butt, *Taft and Roosevelt: The Intimate Letters of Archie Butt, Military Aide* (Garden City, N.Y.: Doubleday, Doran, 1930), 1:30.

38. Oulahan, *How the Rough Riders Were Named,* chap. 25 of unpublished manuscript, 2–4, Oulahan papers; Barry, 281.

39. Oulahan, *Presidents and the Press,* chap. 13, 11–12.

40. Juergens, 46–47.

41. Juergens, 48.

42. McCullough, 248.

43. Albert E. Smith in collaboration with Phil A. Koury, *Two Reels and a Crank* (Garden City, N.Y.: Doubleday, 1952), 148–49.

44. Juergens, 95.

45. Oulahan, *Presidents and the Press,* chap. 14, 1.

46. Oscar King Davis, *Released for Publication: Some Inside Political History of Theodore Roosevelt and His Times, 1898–1918* (Boston: Houghton Mifflin, 1925), 126–27.

47. Dunn, *From Harrison to Harding,* 101.

48. Davis, 157.

49. Dunn, *From Harrison to Harding,* 101.

50. Davis, 178.

51. Butt, 1:19.

52. Oulahan, *Presidents and the Press,* chap. 14, 1; "Gathering News at Washington," *The Quill,* Apr. 1921, "Articles and Speeches," Oulahan papers.

53. Timmins, 50.

54. Butt, 1:26.

55. Ibid., 1:31.

56. Fairlie, 21.

57. Oulahan, *Presidents and the Press,* chap. 14, 2–3.

58. Butt, 1:319.

59. Walter Lord, *A Night to Remember* (New York: Bantam Books, 1956), 73–77.

60. John P. Eaton and Charles A. Haas, *Titanic: Destination Disaster—The Legends and the Reality* (New York: W. W. Norton, 1987), 46–47.

61. Butt, 1:vii–x.

3. The Inexhaustible Font

1. August Heckscher, *Woodrow Wilson* (New York: Scribner's, 1991), 125–27.

2. Joseph P. Tumulty, *Woodrow Wilson as I Know Him* (Garden City, N.Y.: Doubleday Page, 1921), 7–8; John M. Blum, *Joe Tumulty and the Wilson Era* (Archon Books, 1969), 11.

3. Heckscher, 11–19.

4. Blum, 4–5, 9.

5. Heckscher, 150–51.

6. Tumulty, *Woodrow Wilson*, 2.

7. Blum, 9–12.

8. Tumulty, *Woodrow Wilson*, 10–13; Heckscher, 151.

9. Tumulty, *Woodrow Wilson*, 28; Blum, 22; Arthur Walworth, *Woodrow Wilson, 2: World Prophet* (New York: Longmans, Green, 1958), 187.

10. Announcement printed in Jersey City *Jersey Journal*, Jan. 13, 1911, in Arthur S. Link, ed., *Papers of Woodrow Wilson* (Princeton, N.J.: Princeton Univ. Press, 22, 1976), 328–29.

11. Blum, 26, 31–32; Tumulty, *Woodrow Wilson*, 362; Woodrow Wilson to Mary Allen Hulbert Peck, Feb. 19, 1911, *Wilson Papers, 22*, 438–39.

12. Woodrow Wilson to Edith Bolling Galt, Aug. 7, 1915, *Wilson Papers, 34*, 126; George Creel, "Woodrow Wilson, the Man Behind the President," *Saturday Evening Post*, Mar. 28, 1931, 37; Woodrow Wilson to Edith Bolling Galt, Aug. 9, 1915, *Wilson Papers, 34*, 139; Woodrow Wilson to W. J. Stone, Mar. 28, 1924, quoted in Ray Stannard Baker, *Woodrow Wilson: Life and Letters—Volume Four, President, 1913–14* (Garden City, N.Y.: Doubleday, Doran, 1931), 234; Woodrow Wilson to Edith Bolling Galt, Aug. 7, 1915, *Wilson Papers, 34*, 126.

13. Blum, 47–48.

14. Tumulty, *Woodrow Wilson*, 125.

15. George Juergens, "Woodrow Wilson," in Kenneth W. Thompson, ed., *Ten Presidents and the Press* (White Burkitt Miller Center of Public Affairs at the Univ. of Virginia, 1983), 6–7; *New York Times*, Feb. 4, 1913, *Wilson Papers, 27*, 96; press conference, Mar. 19, 1914, *Wilson Papers, 39* (1979), 353–54.

16. Raymond Clapper, diary entry for June 3, 1932, Raymond Clapper papers, manuscript division, Library of Congress; Heckscher, 161–62, 185; Woodrow Wilson to Mary Allen Hulbert Peck, Jan. 13, 1911, and Peck to Wilson, same date, *Wilson Papers, 22*, 329–30, 332.

17. Blum, 49; Edward House, diary, Jan. 8, 16, and 24, 1913, *Wilson Papers, 27*, 24, 57, 71.

18. Robert C. Hilderbrand, *Power and the People: Executive Management of Public Opinion in Foreign Affairs, 1897–1921* (Chapel Hill, N.C.: Univ. of North Carolina Press, 1981), 94–95.

19. Baker, 229–30.

20. Timmons, 51.

21. Hilderbrand, 95; James David Barber, *The Presidential Character: Predicting Performance in the White House* (Englewood, N.J., Prentice Hall, 1992), 50.

22. Press conference, Mar. 22, 1913, *Wilson Papers, 27*, 210–12; Oulahan, *Presi-*

dents and the Press, chap. 11, 1–3; Woodrow Wilson to Edith Bolling Galt, Aug. 23, 1915, *Wilson Papers, 34* (1980), 302.

23. Oulahan, *Presidents and the Press,* chap. 11, 9–10; Oulahan to Ray Stannard Baker, Mar. 15, 1929, Ray Stannard Baker papers, Library of Congress Manuscript Division, reel 81; unpublished interview, June 23, 1913, *Wilson Papers, 27,* 565.

24. Hilderbrand, 97.

25. Press conference, Jan. 29, 1914, *Wilson Papers, 17,* 201.

26. Hilderbrand, 103; Oulahan, *Presidents and the Press,* chap. 11, 9.

27. Heckscher, 284.

28. Joseph P. Tumulty, "In the White House Looking Glass," 26, *New York Times,* Dec. 31, 1921.

29. *Literary Digest,* Jan. 17, 1920.

30. Tumulty, "In the White House Looking Glass."

31. Blum, 105.

32. Tumulty, *Woodrow Wilson,* 152–53; Heckscher, 298–300, 328–30.

33. Tumulty, *Woodrow Wilson,* 214–15.

34. Ibid., 218–21; Blum, 120.

35. Blum, 120; Juergens, *Woodrow Wilson,* 7; Edith Bolling Wilson, *My Memoir* (Indianapolis: Bobbs-Merrill, 1938), 275; Edith Bolling Galt to Woodrow Wilson, Aug. 25, 1915, and Wilson's reply, Aug. 28, 1915, *Wilson Papers, 34,* 327–28, 352.

36. "The Hon. Joseph Tumulty"; Blum, 120–21; *Wilson Papers 27* (1978), xv; John Sharp Williams to Woodrow Wilson, Jan. 31, 1914, *Wilson Papers, 29,* 208; Edward House, diary, Sept. 24, 1915, *Wilson Papers, 34,* 513–16.

37. Blum, 121–22.

38. Mark Sullivan, typed diary entry for Aug. 3, 1923, copy of Mark Sullivan papers from Hoover Institution Archives, Hoover Library.

39. Blum, 123.

40. Woodrow Wilson to Charles W. Eliot, quoted by Hilderbrand, 109.

41. Ibid.

42. Walworth, 112–13.

43. Blum, 133–34; Tumulty, "In the White House Looking Glass."

44. Blum, 134–36; Walworth, 113.

45. Blum, 135–36; Walworth, 113–14.

46. Blum, 170; Tumulty, *Woodrow Wilson,* 341; Joseph P. Tumulty to Woodrow Wilson, Nov. 21, 1918, *Wilson Papers, 53* (1986), 156; Ray Stannard Baker, "Interview with Joseph P. Tumulty," manuscript in Baker papers, reel 83.

47. Martin Schram, *The Great American Video Game* (New York: Morrow, 1987), 73–74; Heckscher, 502; Blum, 171.

48. Heckscher, 517; Blum, 172–73; to Joseph P. Tumulty, received Dec. 9, 1918, *Wilson Papers, 53,* 440; telegram from Joseph P. Tumulty, Jan. 14, 1919, *Wilson Papers, 54,* 53; Ray Stannard Baker to Cary Grayson, Jan. 14, 1919, *Wilson Papers, 54,* 59; Joseph P. Tumulty to Cary Grayson, and Woodrow Wilson to Joseph P. Tumulty, Jan. 16, 1919, *Wilson Papers, 54,* 105; Woodrow Wilson to Joseph P. Tumulty, Jan. 20, 1919, *Wilson Papers, 54,* 158.

49. Juergens, *News from the White House,* 254.

50. Joseph Jefferson O'Neill, quoted in Gene Smith, *When the Cheering Stopped:*

The Last Years of Woodrow Wilson (New York: William Morrow, 1964), 89; David Lawrence, cited in G. Smith, 91; MacMahon and Curry, 69.

51. G. Smith, 95–96, 124.

52. Ibid., 157, 160; Essary, 50; Heckscher, 634.

53. Blum, 171; G. Smith, 187; Joseph P. Tumulty to Cary Grayson, Jan. 16, 1919, *Wilson Papers, 54,* 106; *Life,* Jan. 16, 1919.

54. Charles Willis Thompson, *Presidents I've Known and Two Near Presidents* (Indianapolis: Bobbs-Merrill, 1929), 340.

55. Francis Russell, *The Shadow of Blooming Grove: Warren G. Harding in His Times* (New York: McGraw-Hill, 1968), 460; Columbia, Mo., *Tribune,* May 25, 1921; Book Drafts folder, chap. 16, Oulahan papers, Hoover Library; Thomas L. Stokes, *Chip off My Shoulder* (Princeton, N.J.: Princeton Univ. Press, 1940), 107–8.

56. Book Drafts folder, Oulahan papers, chap. 15; Raymond Clapper, "White House Spokesman Mystery Stirs Senate Curiosity at Last," *Editor & Publisher,* Jan. 15, 1927.

57. Eben A. Ayers, letter to Earl O. Ewan, Mar. 3, 1945, Ayers paper, Truman Library; Associated Press, quoted in "Paragraphs from the Life of Steve T. Early," *The Carbuilder,* Oct. 1951, 12, Stephen Early folder, Walter Trohan papers, Hoover Library; MacMahon and Curry, 78, 84–86.

58. Louis Ludlow, *From Cornfield to Press Gallery: Adventures and Reminiscences of a Veteran Washington Correspondent* (Washington, D.C.: W. F. Roberts, 1924), 369; John L. Blair, Coolidge, the Image-Maker: The President and the Press, 1923–1929," *New England Quarterly,* Dec. 1973, 499–500.

59. Ludlow, 372, 378; Blair, 502; Donald R. McCoy, *Calvin Coolidge: The Quiet President* (New York: Macmillan, 1967), 166–67; Harold Brayman, "Hooverizing the Press," *Outlook and Independent,* Sept. 24, 1930, 124, Oaki-Owen 29–31 folder, George Akerson papers, Hoover Library; Raymond Clapper, typescript, 3, Harding 1923 folder, Clapper papers.

60. Charles G. Ross, "The Washington Correspondent," 10–11, clipping in Ross papers, Truman Library; Clapper, "Spokesman Mystery"; Blair, 509–10.

61. Clapper, "Spokesman Mystery"; Blair, 516.

62. Raymond Fielding, *The American Newsreel: 1911–1967* (Norman: Univ. of Oklahoma Press, 1972), 130; Blair, 521.

63. McCoy, 151, 284–85; Blair, 509–10.

64. *Washington Star,* Feb. 24, 1929; Oulahan, chap. 4, "Book Manuscript," Oulahan papers; Leo Rosten, quoted in Craig Lloyd, *Aggressive Introvert: A Study of Herbert Hoover and Public Relations Management, 1912–1932* (Columbus: Ohio State Univ. Press, 1972), 68; Theodore G. Joslin, *Hoover off the Record* (New York: Doubleday, Doran, 1934), 68.

4. The Public Relations Secretary

1. "Chosen by Hoover as His Assistant," clipping, HH's Assistant folder, George Akerson papers, Hoover Library; David Burner, *Herbert Hoover: A Public Life* (New York, Knopf, 1979), 197; "Secretaries of Efficiency," clipping, Lawrence Richey papers, Hoover Library; George Akerson, letters to Herbert Hoover, Akerson papers.

2. Transcript, George Akerson Jr. oral history interview, Mar. 11, 1969, 14–15,

Hoover Library; Thomas Carens, "Hoover's Right Hand Man," *New York Herald Tribune,* undated clipping, Biographies of George Akerson folder, Akerson papers; McCoy, 383–84; typescript tentatively dated January 1931, 9–10, HH's Secretary folder, Akerson papers.

3. *Outlook,* Oct. 1, 1930, Richey papers.

4. Carens.

5. "The Secretariat," *American Mercury,* Dec. 1929, 385–95, reprint file, Hoover Library; Herbert Hoover, *The Memoirs of Herbert Hoover: The Cabinet and the Presidency, 1920–1933* (New York: Macmillan, 1952), 43; Harold Brayman, *New York Evening Post,* Sept. 26, 1931, Clippings folder, Richey papers; "Secretaries of Efficiency"; Akerson oral history transcript, 9.

6. Carens; "The Secretariat," 387.

7. Ibid., 386–87.

8. News conference, Mar. 5, 1929, *Public Papers of the Presidents of the United States: Herbert Hoover, Containing the Public Messages, Speeches, and Statements of the President, 1929* (Washington, D.C.: Government Printing Office, 1974), 12–14.

9. George H. Manning, "Hoover's Press System Best Instituted by Any President, Capital Writers Say," *Editor & Publisher,* Mar. 16, 1929, 1, HH's Secretary folder, Akerson papers; Mark Sullivan, *Press Conferences,* memo tentatively dated Mar. 1929, 2, "Sullivan," President's Personal file, Hoover Library; Harold Brayman, "Hooverizing the Press," *Outlook and Independent,* Sept. 24, 1930, 124, clipping in "Oaki-Owen 29–31" folder, Akerson papers; news conference, Mar. 8, 1929, *Public Papers, 1929,* 16–20; Theodore Joslin, *The President and the Press,* 16–20, Unpublished Manuscripts folder, Joslin papers, Hoover Library; Robert S. Allen and Drew Pearson, *Washington Merry-Go-Round* (New York: Blue Ribbon Books, 1931), 330.

10. Manning, "Hoover's Press System," 1; Hard; Richard Oulahan, radio address, Feb. 19, 1929, 3, Articles and Speeches folder, Oulahan papers, Hoover Library; Brayman, "Hooverizing the Press," 124–25; "The Secretariat," 388; Allen and Pearson, 331.

11. News conferences, Mar. 12, 15, and 19, and Apr. 30, 1929, *Public Papers, 1929,* 21–23, 25–29, 30–33, 127; Brayman, "Hooverizing the Press," 124; Allen and Pearson, 330–31.

12. Brayman, "Hooverizing the Press," 124; news conference, June 2, 1931, *Public Papers, 1931,* 282-83; Press Relations folder, Herbert Hoover papers, presidential period, Hoover Library.

13. George H. Manning, "White House Best Source for Rapidan Camp 100 Miles Away," *Editor & Publisher,* July 13, 1930; Charles G. Ross, "The Press Conference," undated handwritten memo, 2, Charles G. Ross papers, Truman Library.

14. Brayman, "Hooverizing the Press," 124; "The Secretariat," 389; Ross, untitled typed memo, July 10, 1931, 1, Ross papers.

15. "The Secretariat;" Akerson oral history, 34–35.

16. Hoover, *Memoirs,* 327; Brayman, "Hooverizing the Press," 155.

17. Akerson oral history, 5–6; transcript, Loren R. Chandler oral history interview, Jan. 23, 1970, 26; Raymond Clapper memo on White House interview, Feb. 27, 1931, 5, Raymond Clapper papers, box 7, Manuscript Division, Library of Congress.

18. *Outlook,* Oct. 1, 1930; *Time,* Jan. 12, 1931, 11; Burner 154, 255–56; news conference, Jan. 2, 1931, *Public Papers, 1931,* 1; typescript tentatively dated Jan. 1931,

1, HH's Secretary folder, Akerson papers; Akerson oral history, 14–15; Allen and Pearson, 323–24.

19. Theodore G. Joslin, "Hoover's First Year," *World's Work,* Mar. 1930, reprint file, Hoover Library.

20. Theodore G. Joslin, diary, Mar. 17, 1931, and Jan. 7, 1933, "Diary 1931" and "Diary 1933," Theodore G. Joslin papers, Hoover Library.

21. *Public Papers, 1931,* 164; Joslin, diary, Apr. 6, Apr. 30, 1931, Joslin papers.

22. *Outlook,* undated clipping, Richey papers, Hoover Library; Brayman, "4 Secretaries."

23. Joslin, *The President and the Press,* 9; Joslin, diary, Feb. 28 and June 27, 1932, Joslin papers.

24. News conference, June 20, 1931, *Public Papers, 1931,* 321; Mark Sullivan to Lawrence Richey, June 20, 1931, "Sullivan," President's Personal file, Hoover Library; Joslin, diary, June 20, 1931; Clapper, diary, June 20, 1931, Clapper papers, box 7; Joslin, *The President and the Press,* 10.

25. Clapper diary, July 6, 1931, Clapper papers; Manning, "Best News Source"; Joslin, diary, July 6, 1931, Joslin papers; Herbert Hoover to F. T. Birchell, June 7, 1929, Turner Catledge folder, President's Personal file, Hoover Library; news conference, July 6, 1931, *Public Papers, 1931,* 337–41; Ross diary, July 10, 1931, Ross papers; *New York Times,* July 6, 1931, 1, July 10, 1931, 10.

26. Manning, "Best News Source"; A. H. Kirchhofer to Herbert Hoover, Sept. 1, 1931, 3–4, Newspapers—*Buffalo Evening News* folder, President's Personal file, Hoover Library; Joslin, diary, June 27, 1932, Joslin papers; Allen and Pearson, 346.

27. Clapper diary, Sept. 1, 1931, Clapper papers.

28. Clapper diary, July 9–10, 1931, Clapper papers, box 7; Ross diary, July 10, 1931, Ross papers; *New York Times,* July 10, 1931, 10, July 18, 1931, 21.

29. Clapper diary, July 15 and July 25, 1931, Clapper papers.

30. News conference, Aug. 7, 1931, *Public Papers, 1931,* 376; Joslin diary, Aug. 7, 1931, Joslin papers.

31. Joslin diary, Aug. 25, 1931, Joslin papers.

32. Transcript, Byron Price oral history interview, Mar. 21, 1969, 4–5, Hoover Library; Joslin, diary, Aug. 8, 1932, Joslin papers; Allen and Pearson, 32.

33. Clapper diary, Sept. 15, 1931, Clapper papers.

34. Joslin diary, Sept. 22, 1931, Joslin papers; Joslin, *The President and the Press,* 16.

35. News conference, Oct. 6, 1931, *Public Papers, 1931,* 462–63; Clapper diary, Oct. 6, 1931, White House Banking Conference folder, Clapper papers; George H. Manning, "White House News Ban on Bank Parley Upset by Correspondents," *Editor & Publisher,* Oct. 10, 1931, 1.

36. Raymond Clapper, "Talk with Coolidge Northampton 9:30 A.M.–12 Nov. 13, 1931," 2, Clapper papers, box 7.

37. Folder of written questions, Public Relations folder, Herbert Hoover papers, Hoover Library; transcript, Edward T. Folliard oral history interview, Aug. 6, 1968, 4–5, Hoover Library; telegram, United Press to Raymond Clapper, Oct. 6, 1920, and handwritten statement, Clapper papers, box 66.

38. News conferences, June 16, 22, and 24, 1932, presidential statements, July

28 and 29, 1932 *Public Papers, 1932–33*, 261–63, 267–70, 276–78, 339–40, 348–50; Joslin diary, June 19, 1932, Joslin papers; Burner, 306–12; Edgar Robinson and Vaughn Davis Bornet, *Herbert Hoover: President of the United States* (Stanford, Calif.: Hoover Institution Press, 1975), 234.

39. Clapper to "Karl," Aug. 15, 1932, Clapper papers; presidential address, *Public Papers, 1932–33*, 357–76; Burner, 198, 258, 308.

40. Joslin diary, Aug. 20, 1932, Joslin papers; index, *Public Papers, 1932–33*, 1315–16.

41. Clapper diary, Aug. 24, 1932, Clapper papers.

42. Joslin, "Memoranda," facing date of Nov. 1, 1932, in diary.

5. *"The Early"*

1. Betty Houchin Winfield, *FDR and the News Media*. (Urbana: Univ. of Illinois Press, 1990), 71–72.

2. *New York Herald Tribune*, Dec. 1, 1940.

3. Steven E. Schoenherr, *Selling the New Deal: Stephen T. Early's Role as Press Secretary to Franklin D. Roosevelt* (diss., Univ. of Delaware, 1976, in Franklin D. Roosevelt Library, hereinafter cited as FDRL), 29–31; letter, Stephen Early to Robert E. Sherwood, Jan. 16, 1948, Early papers, Personal folder, FDRL, 1.

4. S. J. Woolf, "Up the Ladder with F. D. R.," *New York Times Magazine*, Aug. 27, 1939, 9.

5. Schoenherr, 35; Early to Sherwood, 2; Geoffrey C. Ward, *A First-Class Temperament: The Emergence of Franklin Roosevelt* (New York: Harper and Row, 1989), 529.

6. Schoenherr, 35–36.

7. Ibid., 20; Paul W. Ward, "Roosevelt Keeps His Vow," *The Nation*, Sept. 25, 1935, 348; Betty Houchin Winfield, *Roosevelt and the Press: How Franklin D. Roosevelt Influenced Newsgathering, 1933–1941* (diss., Univ. of Washington, 1978), 165–66; Early to Sherwood, 2.

8. Schoenherr, 40–41; Franklin D. Roosevelt, *The Public Papers and Addresses* (New York: Random House, 1938), 2:39.

9. Letter, Raymond Clapper to "Bob," Mar. 1, 1933, Clapper papers, manuscript division, Library of Congress, hereinafter cited as LC; Schoenherr, 45; *U.S. News*, Sept. 3, 1934.

10. Schoenherr, 40, 43, 46; Clapper to "Bob"; Theodore Joslin, diary, Jan. 19, 1933, Joslin papers, Herbert Hoover Presidential Library, hereinafter cited as HHPL; Early to Sherwood, 2.

11. Schoenherr, 43–44.

12. Franklin D. Roosevelt, *Public Papers*, 30–31.

13. *New York Times*, Mar. 9, 1933; Raymond P. Brandt, "The President's Press Conference," *Survey Graphic*, July 1939, 449.

14. Joseph Alsop, *FDR, 1882–1945: A Centennial Remembrance* (New York: Viking, 1982); "Assistant Secretary Acts"; Patrick Anderson, *The President's Men: White House Assistants of Franklin D. Roosevelt, Harry S. Truman, Dwight D. Eisenhower, John F. Kennedy, and Lyndon B. Johnson* (Garden City, N.Y.: Doubleday, 1968), 59.

15. Winfield, *FDR;* Walter Trohan, oral history interview, HHPL, 25; Drew Pearson and Robert S. Allen, "How the President Works," *Harpers,* June 1936, 2.

16. Richard L. Strout, oral history interview, Feb. 5, 1971, Truman Library.

17. Winfield, *FDR,* 55; Raymond Clapper, "Why Reporters Like Roosevelt," *Review of Reviews & World's Work,* June 1934; James J. Butler, "Truman's First Press Conference," *Editor & Publisher,* Apr. 21, 1945, 9.

18. Brandt, 4.

19. John Gunther, *Roosevelt in Retrospect* (New York: Harper, 1950), 22–23.

20. Oulahan, "9, Wilson Press Conferences," *Presidents and the Press.*

21. Schoenherr, 89–90, 92, 94–95; Ward, 348; Winfield, "Franklin D. Roosevelt's Efforts to Influence the News During his First Term Press Conferences," *Presidential Studies Quarterly,* 1981, 189–90.

22. Schoenherr, 44–45.

23. *U.S. News,* Sept. 3, 1934.

24. Schoenherr, 73; Allan L. Damon, "Presidential Accessibility," *American Heritage,* Apr. 1974, 63.

25. Winfield, *FDR,* 86–87.

26. Ward, 349.

27. *Chicago Tribune,* Oct. 13, 1934.

28. Theodore G. Joslin, speech before the National Republican Club, Jan. 26, 1935, Joslin papers, Addresses folder, HHPL, 2, 4–5; "Federal Publicity," *Editorial Research Reports,* 1940, Clapper papers, Censorship folder, LC, 209.

29. *New York Times,* Jan. 16, 1935, clipping in Early papers, Scrapbook folder, FDRL.

30. Raymond Clapper, diary, Mar. 5, 1933, Clapper papers, LC.

31. Winfield, *FDR,* 61–63; Arthur Krock, oral history interview, HHPL, 57–58.

32. *New York Times,* Mar. 19, 1933, 10:8.

33. Raymond Clapper, diary entry, Mar. 5, 1933, Clapper papers, LC; Schoenherr, 111.

34. George E. Akerson Jr., oral history interview, Mar. 11, 1969, Hoover Library.

35. *New York Times,* July 3, 1933, 10:10.

36. J. Leonard Reinsch, *Getting Elected: From Radio and Roosevelt to Television and Reagan* (New York: Hippocrene, 1988), 13; Samuel I. Rosenman, *Working with Roosevelt* (New York: Harper, 1952), 453.

37. Winfield, *FDR,* 108; *Broadcast Merchandising,* quoted in Winfield, diss., 206.

38. Schoenherr, 77–78; Stephen Early, diary, Sept. 7, 1937, Early papers, Diary folder, FDRL.

39. Delbert Clark, " 'Steve' Takes Care of It," *New York Times Magazine,* July 27, 1941, 11; *Washington Post,* Oct. 9, 1934; *Chicago Daily Times, Look,* and *St. Louis Post-Dispatch,* clippings in Early papers, Scrapbook folder, FDRL; Jim Bishop, *FDR's Last Year: April, 1944–April, 1945* (New York: William Morrow and Co., 1974), 13.

40. Graham J. White, *FDR and the Press* (Chicago: Univ. of Chicago Press, 1979), 18; Betty H. Winfield, "Mrs. Roosevelt's Press Conference Association: The First Lady Shines a Light," *Journalism History,* Summer 1981, 63; Winfield, *FDR and the News Media,* 55–56; letter, Stephen Early to Eleanor Roosevelt, Feb. 10, 1941, Early papers, Mrs. Roosevelt folder, FDRL.

41. *Time,* Nov. 11, 1940, 17–18; *Editor & Publisher,* Nov. 16, 1940, 4.

42. Anderson, 60–61; newspaper clippings, Reference file, Stephen Early folder, Clapper papers, LC; Samuel Rosenman papers, Stephen Early folder, FDRL; Harold L. Ickes, *The Secret Diary of Harold L. Ickes, Vol. 3: The Lowering Clouds, 1939–1941* (New York: Simon and Schuster, 1954), 52.

43. Johnny Thomson, quoted in Winfield, *FDR,* 114.

44. Loring in the *Providence Evening Bulletin,* Orr in the *Chicago Tribune,* reprinted in *Time,* Nov. 4, 1940, 17.

45. Raymond Clapper, diary, Oct. 31, 1932, Clapper papers, Roosevelt Trip folder, LC.

46. Winfield, diss., 114; Schoenherr, 149.

47. Rosenman, 453.

48. Winfield, *FDR,* 116.

49. Raymond Fielding, *The American Newsreel, 1911–1967* (Norman: Univ. of Oklahoma Press, 1972), 201.

50. Stephen Early, diary, Sept. 28, 1938, Early papers, FDRL).

51. Stephen Early, diary entries, Aug. 26 to Sept. 1, 1939, Early papers, Diary folder, FDRL; Roosevelt, *Public Papers, 1939 Volume* (New York: Macmillan, 1941), 457.

52. Memo, "dj" to Early, President's file, Early folder, FDRL.

53. Winfield, *FDR,* 54.

54. Roosevelt, *Public Papers, 1941 Volume* (New York: Harper, 1950).

55. *Washington Daily News,* Feb. 24, 1941; letter, Clapper to Cranston Williams, Feb. 24, 1941, Clapper papers, Censorship folder, LC.

56. Clippings from the *New York Herald Tribune,* Apr. 8 and 9, 1941, and *PM,* Dec. 17, 1941, Clapper papers, Censorship folder, LC.

57. Clark, 11; memo, Mellett to the president, July 18, 1941, and president's reply, July 21, 1941, Mellett papers, office correspondence, White House folder, FDRL.

58. Lowell Mellett to president, Nov. 28, 1941, Mellett papers, White House Correspondence folder, FDRL.

59. Stephen T. Early and Richard Eaton, "Behind the White House, Condensed from an Interview over WMCA," *News Digest, Your Radio Magazine,* June 1944, 99.

60. Schoenherr, 189–90; Early papers, Press Conferences folder, FDRL; White House Usher Diary, Dec. 7, 1941, FDRL.

61. Schoenherr, 203.

62. Kenneth G. Crawford, "The Nation," *PM,* Dec. 17, 1941, Early papers, Ken Crawford folder, FDRL.

63. Schoenherr, 203–4.

64. Ibid., 205; letter, Stephen Early to John Boettiger, Boettiger papers, FDRL.

65. Schoenherr, 209–10; Ickes, 351.

66. Letter, John H. Crider, Thomas F. Reynolds, William C. Murphy, Bert Andrews, and Joseph A. Fox to Stephen Early, Mar. 31, 1941, Early papers, White House Corps folder, FDRL.

67. Telegram, Stephen Early to William Hassett, Sept. 1, 1944; memo, Terry Lorenz to Tom Blake, Sept. 2, 1944, Early papers, Hassett Memos folder, FDRL; Schoenherr, 210.

68. Letters, Henry M. Stimson to the president, Dec. 28, 1944, president to Stimson, Jan. 1, 1945, President's Secretary's file, Early folder, FDRL.

69. Harry C. Butcher, *My Three Years with Eisenhower: The Personal Diary of Captain Harry C. Butcher, USNR—Naval Aide to General Eisenhower, 1942 to 1945* (New York: Simon and Schuster, 1946), 775–76.

70. Eben Ayers, diary, Jan. 18 and Mar. 22, 1945, Ayers papers, Early file, Harry S. Truman Library; Rosenman, 454; letter, Early to Marguerite LeHand, Apr. 6, 1939, Early papers, Below the Belt folder, FDRL.

71. Eben Ayers, diary, Mar. 22 and Mar. 24, 1945, Ayers papers, Early folder, FDRL; Ickes, 52.

72. William Hassett, "The President Was My Boss: Part Seven," *Saturday Evening Post,* Nov. 21, 1953.

73. Harry S. Truman, *Memoirs by Harry S. Truman: Volume One—Year of Decisions* (Garden City, N.Y.: Doubleday, 1955), 4–5.

6. Scholar in the Press Office

1. Charles G. Ross, typescript, July 10, 1931, Presidential Press Secretaries folder, Charles G. Ross papers, Harry S. Truman Library, hereinafter cited as HSTL.

2. Roland T. Farrar, *Reluctant Servant: The Story of Charles G. Ross* (Columbia: Univ. of Missouri Press, 1969), 79.

3. *St. Louis Post-Dispatch,* Aug. 3, 1923, cited in Farrar, 79–80.

4. Charles G. Ross, "The St. Louis Post-Dispatch," in fiftieth anniversary edition, Dec. 1928, reprinted in book form,, as revised and supplemented by Carlos F. Hurt, in June 1940, Mar. 1944, and Sept. 1949, 46.

5. Walter Trohan, oral history interview, Washington, D.C., Oct. 7, 1970, 67, HSTL.

6. Eben A. Ayers, oral history interview, Jan. 12, 1967–June 30, 1970, 21, HSTL; Robert J. Donovan, *Conflict and Crisis: The Presidency of Harry S. Truman, 1945–1948* (New York: Norton, 1977), 23.

7. Lorena A. Hickok, "We Always Looked Up to Charlie," *Saga,* June 1951, 20.

8. Merle Miller, *Plain Speaking: An Oral Biography of Harry S. Truman* (New York: Putnam's, 1974), 35–36.

9. Christopher Ricks, ed., *The Poems of Tennyson in Three Volumes, Second Edition Incorporating the Trinity College Manuscripts,* 3 (Berkeley: Univ. of California Press, 1987), 205–10.

10. Farrar, 11–21; Alonzo L. Hamby, *Man of the People: A Life of Harry S. Truman* (New York: Oxford Univ. Press, 1995), 14–19.

11. *St. Louis Republic,* May 29, 1905, clipping, General News Clippings folder, Charles G. Ross papers, HSTL; James W. Markham, *Boyard of the Post-Dispatch,* 36 ff., cited in Farrar, 35.

12. Charles G. Ross, *The Writing of News: A Handbook* (New York: Henry Holt, 1911), 22.

13. Farrar, 69–70.

14. Charles G. Ross, diary, Feb. 24, 1919, Charles G. Ross papers, HSTL.

15. Charles G. Ross, "The Washington Press Gallery," address at the Univ. of Missouri School of Journalism during journalism week, 1926, *The University of Missouri Bulletin Journalism Series,* No. 42, 11–13; *St. Louis Post-Dispatch,* Jan. 13, 1925.

16. Farrar, 84–85, 89; Ross, "The St. Louis Post-Dispatch."

17. Robert S. Allen and Drew Pearson, *Washington Merry-Go-Round* (New York: Blue Ribbon, 1931), 349.

18. Ross, "The Washington Press Gallery," 10–14.

19. Ross, diary, Feb. 24, 1919, Ross papers, HSTL.

20. *St. Louis Post-Dispatch,* Oct. 30, 1932, quoted in Farrar, 98.

21. Farrar, 101–2, 105.

22. Charles G. Ross, telegram to Joseph Pulitzer Jr., July 25, 1934, Joseph Pulitzer Jr. papers, box 95, manuscript division, Library of Congress, hereinafter cited as LC.

23. Joseph Pulitzer Jr., telegram to Charles G. Ross, July 26, 1934, Pulitzer papers, LC.

24. Charles G. Ross, telegram to Joseph Pulitzer Jr., July 28, 1934, Pulitzer papers, LC.

25. *St. Louis Post-Dispatch,* quoted in Jonathan Daniels, *The Man of Independence* (Philadelphia: Lippincott, 1950), 85.

26. Hamby, 198; Harry S. Truman, *Memoirs of Harry S. Truman, Volume One —Years of Decisions* (Garden City, N.Y.: Doubleday, 1955), 141, 159.

27. Joseph Pulitzer Jr., memo to Charles G. Ross, July 24, 1935, 3, Pulitzer papers, box 95, LC.

28. Charles G. Ross, memo to Joseph Pulitzer Jr., Pulitzer papers, box 95, LC.

29. Charles G. Ross, *Introduction to Report,* 1, 51, Pulitzer papers, box 95, LC.

30. *St. Louis Post-Dispatch,* Sept. 27, 1936, quoted in Farrar, 125–27.

31. *St. Louis Post-Dispatch,* Aug. 5, 1940, quoted in Hamby, 238.

32. *Time,* Jan. 23, 1939; Farrar, 134.

33. *St. Louis Post-Dispatch,* Apr. 18, 1940, and Charles G. Ross, memo to Joseph Pulitzer Jr., quoted in Farrar, 140–41.

34. Farrar, 148.

35. *Christian Science Monitor,* Apr. 20, 1945, 3; Farrar, 223; Margaret Truman, *Harry S. Truman* (New York: Pocket Books, 1974), 5, 39, 247; *Time,* Apr. 30, 1945, 19.

36. Hickok, 85–86.

37. Farrar, 154–55; *Editor & Publisher,* Apr. 21, 1945, 71; *Christian Science Monitor,* Apr. 20, 1945, 3; J. Leonard Reinsch, *Getting Elected: From Radio and Roosevelt to Television and Reagan* (New York: Hippocrene, 1988), 4, 12–13, 24–32; *Broadcasting,* Apr. 23, 1945, 13.

38. Hickok, 86; Harry S. Truman, *Memoirs,* 60; Farrar, 155–56.

39. Farrar, 156–57; *Christian Science Monitor,* Apr. 20, 1945, 1, 3; Scott Hart, "Truman and Ross: America's No. 1 Team," *Coronet,* Jan. 1946, 10; president's news conference, Apr. 20, 1945, *Public Papers of the Presidents of the United States: Harry S. Truman, April 12 to Dec. 31, 1945* (Washington, D.C.: Government Printing Office, 1961), 16–19.

40. Farrar, 161–207; Hart, 9; Walter Davenport, "The New White House Boys," *Colliers,* Nov. 17, 1945, 14; Hamby, 301; *New York Times,* Dec. 6, 1950, 1.

41. Robert H. Ferrel, ed., *Truman in the White House: The Diary of Eben A. Ayers* (Columbia: Univ. of Missouri Press, 1991), 18; *Baltimore Sun,* Feb. 12, 1948, 1; Carleton Kent, oral history interview, Washington, D.C., Dec. 21 and 29, 1970, 33–34, HSTL.

42. *Editor & Publisher,* Apr. 21, 1945, 9, 71.

43. Strout, oral history interview, 2.

44. Ross, diary, Feb. 21, 1946, 16, diary 1946 Typed folder, Ross papers, HSTL.

45. Robert S. Allen and William V. Shannon, *The Truman Merry-Go-Round* (New York: Vanguard, 1950), 55.

46. Hart, 9.

47. Cabell Phillips, *The Truman Presidency: The History of a Triumphant Succession* (New York: Macmillan, 1966), 115–17.

48. Phillips, 87; H. S. Truman, 335–36; Farrar, 165-66; William M. Rigdon and James Dereiux, *White House Sailor* (Garden City, N.Y.: Doubleday, 1962), 294; A. Merriman Smith, *Thank You, Mr. President: A White House Notebook* (New York: Harper and Brothers, 1946), 241–42; memo, Eben A. Ayers to Charles G. Ross, July 6, 1945, and letter, July 20, 1945, Ross papers, HSTL.

49. *Mr. Ayers' Press and Radio Conference,* Aug. 6, 1945, Eben Ayers papers, Letterhead folder, HSTL.

50. Undated note, Eben A. Ayers papers, Censorship folder, HSTL.

51. Hickok, 86.

52. Farrar, 170–72.

53. Edward T. Folliard, oral history interview, 69, HSTL; Reinsch, 37–38.

54. Memo with no heading, Jan. 11, 1946, Eben A. Ayers papers, White House Eexecutive Office folder, HSTL; Charles Roberts, memo to "nation (kosner)," Feb. 16, 1965, Charles Roberts papers, Herbert Hoover Presidential Library, hereinafter cited as HHPL.

55. William Seale: *The President's House: A History* (Washington, D.C.: White House Historical Association, 1986), 1008–11; Lorenzo S. Winslow, radio address, station WOL, Jan. 2, 1946, Charles G. Ross papers, White House Extension folder, Ross papers, HSTL.

56. Kent, 33–34.

57. Ayers, oral history interview, 21.

58. Donovan, 23.

59. Hamby, 301.

60. James L. Butler, "Capital Writers Ired by News Blockade," *Editor & Publisher,* Mar. 30, 1946, 28.

61. Allen and Shannon, 56.

62. Charles G. Ross, reply to July 20, 1945, letter from Eben Ayers, Ross papers, HSTL.

63. Edward T. Folliard, oral history interview, Washington, D.C., Aug. 20, 1970, 25–26, HSTL; handwritten notes, June 25, 1948, Personal Diary notes folder, Ross papers, HSTL.

64. Phillips, 150–51; Ross, diary, Sept. 21, 1946, 44, Diary 1946 Typed folder, Ross papers, HSTL.

65. Ross, diary, Sept. 21 and 23, 1946, 45–48, Diary 1946 Typed folder, Ross papers, HSTL; Phillips, 152; Robert H. Ferrel, *Harry S. Truman: A Life* (Columbia: Univ. of Missouri Press, 1994), 225.

66. Farrar, 181.

67. B. H. R. memo to Joseph Pulitzer Jr., Nov. 8, 1946, Pulitzer papers, LC.

68. The president's press conference, Nov. 11, 1946, *Public Papers of the Presidents 1946* (Washington, D.C.: Government Printing Office, 1962), 480.

69. Hamby, 301; M. Truman, 4.

70. Farrar, 181, 233.

71. Phillips, 439; David McCullough, *Truman* (New York: Simon and Schuster, 1992), 626.

72. Trohan, 67.

73. Donovan, 397.

74. John Hersey, "The Wayward Press: Conference in Room 474," *The New Yorker,* Dec. 16, 1950, 80–88; Charles G. Ross, undated typed and handwritten notes, Ross papers, Atomic Bomb folder, HSTL; Ferrel, *Truman in the White House,* 383–85.

75. Hersey, 89–90; Hickok, 87.

76. Farrar, 222–25; handwritten notes, Dec. 5, 1950, Last Notes folder, Ross papers, HSTL; Hickok, 88.

77. Farrar, 225–36.

78. "Charles G. Ross Collapses," *New York Times,* Dec. 6, 1950.

79. M. Truman, 544–46.

80. Farrar, 227.

7. *"Tell Jim to Take Over"*

1. The reminiscences of James C. Hagerty (Mar. 2, 1967) in the collection of the Columbia Univ. Oral History Research Office, hereafter COHO, 289; *Airmen,* Oct. 7, 1955, 8, clipping in Charles Roberts papers, Denver Trip Heart Attack folder, Herbert Hoover presidential Library, hereinafter cited as HHPL; *Knickerbocker News,* July 10, 1961, B-3.

2. Gordon Ames Moon II, *James Campbell Hagerty's Eight Years in the White House,* unpublished thesis, Univ. of Wisconsin, 1962, 256–61.

3. Merriman Smith, "White House Front Man: James C. Hagerty, the President's Press Secretary," *New York Times Magazine,* Oct. 4, 1953, 88–89.

4. Moon, 256.

5. Ferrel, *Truman in the White House,* 387–88; Robert H. Ferrel, *Harry S. Truman: A Life* (Columbia: Univ. of Missouri Press, 1944), 188.

6. Roger Tubby, oral history interview, Washington, D.C., Feb. 10, 1970, 8–11, Harry S. Truman library, hereinafter cited as HSTL.

7. Mrs. Joseph H. Short, oral history interview, 18, HSTL.

8. Irving Perlmeter, oral history interview, 11, HSTL.

9. Perlmeter, 39; Robert Nixon, oral history interview, 716, HSTL.

10. Roger Tubby, diary, Sept. 17, 1952, quoted in David McCullough, *Truman* (New York: Simon and Schuster, 1992), 910.

11. COHO, 7.

12. *Knickerbocker News,* July 10, 1961, B-3.

13. *Houston Post,* Feb. 5, 1956, 1.

14. COHO, 8, 73–74.

15. James Hagerty, memo to Sherman Adams, Dec. 20, 1952, 1–2, 4–5, Hagerty papers, box 10, Subject series, Transition folder, Dwight David Eisenhower Library, hereinafter cited as DDEL; Henry F. Pringle, "President's Voice: James C. Hagerty," *Nation's Business,* July 1953, 40.

16. David Lawrence, letter to William E. Robinson, with handwritten notation "To Haggerty" [*sic*] and extract from letter, Lawrence to President Truman, Feb. 17, 1950, Hagerty papers, Press Conference Material series, DDEL.

17. *Mr. Hagerty's Press and Radio Conference Jan. 21, 1953,* 2, Hagerty papers, box 39, Hagerty Press Conference series, First Conference folder, DDEL.

18. Hagerty press conference Jan. 21, 1953, 1–2.

19. James C. Hagerty, diary, Jan. 13, 1954, Hagerty papers, box 1, Diary series, DDEL; *Public Papers,* Dwight D. Eisenhower, "News conferences" in index, 1953 and 1954 volumes.

20. "Suggested Schedule for First Conference" and "President Eisenhower's Press and Radio Conference #1," Hagerty papers, boxes 59 and 68, Press Conference Material series, DDEL.

21. Hagerty memo to Adams, 2.

22. Mrs. Joseph H. Short, 59–60; Robert Nixon, 439.

23. *Times Picayune,* Aug. 3, 1966.

24. Robert Nixon, 427–28; *New York Times,* Mar. 11, 1956, 15.

25. COHO, 946.

26. COHO, 441–46; Ann Whitman, diary, "Pre-press," Mar. 16, 1960, Whitman papers, DDEL.

27. *Public Papers,* Dwight D. Eisenhower, 1958, 95; *Time,* Jan. 17, 1958, 13.

28. Hagerty, memo to Adams, 4.

29. Hagerty press conference, Jan. 21, 1953, 1.

30. Frank Stanton, telegram to James C. Hagerty, Jan. 21, 1953; Hagerty, letter to Stanton, Jan. 22, 1953; Hollis M. Seavey, memo to Hagerty, Feb. 13, 1953, Hagerty papers, DDEL.

31. Paul R. Leach, letter to James C. Hagerty, Jan. 21, 1953; Charles J. Lewis, letter to President Eisenhower, Jan. 24, 1953, with attachment, Hagerty papers, Press Conference Material series, DDEL.

32. *Broadcast by Ray Scherer,* Dec. 16, 1953, radio station WRC, Hagerty papers, DDEL.

33. *Evening Star,* July 5, 1956, A-16; *New York Times,* Mar. 1, 1956, 18.

34. COHO, 79–81, 176; David Halberstam, *The Powers That Be* (New York: Knopf, 1979), 244–45; Robert H. Ferrel, ed., *The Diary of James C. Hagerty: Eisenhower in Mid-Course, 1954–1955* (Bloomington: Indiana Univ. Press, 1983), 168.

35. *Public Papers,* Dwight D. Eisenhower, 1955, 185–99; *New York Times,* Jan. 20, 1955, 1, 13.

36. Ferrel, *Hagerty Diary,* 168–69; *New York Times,* Jan. 20, 1955, 13, 30, 39.

37. COHO, 84.

38. Halberstam, 25.

39. James Reston, "Dilemma of the White House Q & A," *New York Times Magazine,* June 1, 1958.

40. *Public Papers,* Dwight D. Eisenhower, 1955, 185; Robert Montgomery, *Open Letter from a Television Viewer* (New York: Heineman, 1968), 64.

41. Smith, "White House Front Man," 89; COHO, 503.

42. Smith, "White House Front Man," 89.

43. "Jim Hagerty Remembers Ike's Best Golf Scores as Follows," Charles Roberts papers, Ike's Golf folder, HHPL.

44. Unnamed journalist quoted in Douglass Cater, *The Fourth Branch of Government* (Boston: Houghton Mifflin, 1959), 162.

45. Quoted in Moon, 261–62.

46. Milton MacKaye, "Ike's Man Friday," *Saturday Evening Post,* May 21, 1960, 52, 54; COHO, 183; Patrick Anderson, *The President's Men* (Garden City, N.Y.: Doubleday, 1968), 182.

47. COHO, 44.

48. "White House Staff Notes from Hagerty and Snyder," Mar. 1, 1955, Charles Roberts papers, HHPL; Strout, 6; *Department of State Bulletin,* May 11, 1953, July 20 and 21, 1953, and index for Jan. 4 to June 28, 1954.

49. Robert A. Rutland, "President Eisenhower and His Press Secretary," *Journalism Quarterly,* Fall 1957, 452; *Department of State Bulletin,* Dec. 21, 1953, 851.

50. James Hagerty to President Eisenhower, memo Dec. 9, 1958, Hagerty papers, box 9, Subject series, The President—Memoranda folder, DDEL.

51. Dwight D. Eisenhower, *The White House Years: Waging Peace, 1956–1961* (Garden City, N.Y.: Doubleday, 1965), 561–62.

52. Anderson, 186.

53. MacKaye, 57; Hagerty, 289; Ann Whitman diary, quoted in Robert T. Ferrel, ed., *The Eisenhower Diaries* (New York: Norton, 1981), 302–3; Ferrel, *Hagerty Diary,* 233; Howard Snyder, letter to Maj. Gen. Wilton B. Persons, quoted in Sherman Adams, *Firsthand Report: The Story of the Eisenhower Administration* (New York: Harper and Brothers, 1961), 184; Edward B. MacMahon and Leonard Curry, *Medical Cover-ups in the White House* (Washington, D.C.: Farragut, 1987), 104.

54. Ferrell, *Hagerty Diary,* 233–34; COHO, 289.

55. COHO, 289–302; Richard M. Nixon, *Six Crises* (Garden City, N.Y.: Doubleday, 1962), 132.

56. COHO, 289–304; Nixon, *Six Crises,* 144.

57. COHO, 289–304; Ann Whitman, diary, quoted in Ferrel, *Eisenhower Diaries,* 303; Dwight D. Eisenhower, *The White House Years: Mandate for Change, 1953–1956* (Garden City, N.Y.: Doubleday, 1963), 538; Ferrel, *Hagerty Diary,* 237; Stephen E. Ambrose, *Eisenhower: Volume Two—The President* (New York: Simon and Schuster, 1984), 272.

58. *Airmen,* Oct. 7, 1955, clipping in Charles Roberts papers, Denver Trip Heart Attack folder, HHPL; COHO, 289–304; Anderson, 186; Eisenhower, *Mandate for Change,* 538.

59. Anderson, 188.

60. Ferrel, *Eisenhower Diaries,* 327; *New York Times,* June 25, 1961, 13; Cater, 163.

61. Anderson, 189; *New York Times,* June 25, 1961, 13; Cater, 163.

62. Eisenhower, *Waging Peace,* 277–79; *New York Times,* Nov. 27, 1957, 10.

63. MacMahon and Curry, 115; "Statement by Mrs. Wheaton," Nov. 26, 1957, and "News Conference," Nov. 26, 1957, Charles Roberts papers, Ike's Health folder,

HHPL; typed notes, undated, Charles Roberts papers, Speech Notes folder, HHPL; *New York Times,* Nov. 26, 1957, 10; "Medical Bulletins," 10.

64. Adams, 189.

65. MacMahon and Curry, 115; *New York Times,* Nov. 27, 1957, 1; *New York Times,* Nov. 28, 1957, 34.

66. *New York Times,* Jan. 1, 1958.

67. Frederick W. Collins, *Providence Journal,* quoted in Cater, 164.

8. Entertaining the Press

1. Bill Wilson, memo to Pierre Salinger, Jan. 14, 1961, box 11, Presidential Press Conferences folder, Salinger papers, John F. Kennedy Library, hereinafter cited as JFKL; John F. Kennedy, *The Kennedy Presidential Press Conferences* (New York: Earl M. Coleman Enterprises, 1978), 67–69; Mary McGrory, Peter Lisagor, George Herman, oral history interview, Washington, D.C., Aug. 4, 1964, JFKL 53; Charles Roberts, memo to "Press or Radio-TV," Jan., 1961, Kennedy Press Relations folder, Roberts papers, Herbert Hoover Presidential Library, hereinafter cited as HHPL; *New York Times,* Jan. 26, 1961.

2. McGrory, Lisagor, Herman, oral history interview, 79–80; Barbara Coleman, oral history interview, Washington, D.C., Jan. 19, 1968, 42, JFKL; Ernest G. Warren, oral history interview, Whitestone, Va., Feb. 29, 1968, 23, JFKL; "Salinger's Drawbacks (or Complaints of Newsmen)," undated typescript in Kennedy Press Relations folder, Charles Roberts papers, HHPL; *Time,* May 1, 1961, 3; Patrick Anderson, 231; undated typed notes in Kennedy Press Relations folder, Roberts paper, HHPL; William H. Lawrence, oral history interview, Washington, D.C., Apr. 22, 1966, JFKL; Arthur M. Schlesinger Jr., *A Thousand Days: John F. Kennedy in the White House* (Boston: Houghton Mifflin, 1965), 207; *Time,* Jan. 20, 1961, 26; Jack Anderson, "Pierre Salinger," *Parade,* Apr. 21, 1963; Patrick Anderson, 231; *New York Times,* Mar. 20, 1964, reprinted in *Congressional Record,* vol. 110—Part 5, 5774–75.

3. *Washington Star,* July 25, 1961; *The Globe and Mail,* Dec. 25, 1960; *New York Herald Tribune,* Nov. 12, 1960, box 109, News Clippings folder, Pierre Salinger papers, JFKL; Pierre Salinger, *With Kennedy* (Garden City, N.Y.: Doubleday, 1966), 16–18; Patrick Anderson, 230–33.

4. Pierre Salinger, *With Kennedy,* 29–32; Coleman, oral history interview; *Washington Star,* Dec. 29, 1960, News Clippings Dec. 1960 folder, box 109, Salinger papers, JFKL.

5. Salinger, *With Kennedy,* 54; Robert Shaplen, "Meet the New Press Secretary," *Saturday Review,* Jan. 14, 1961, 45.

6. Salinger, *With Kennedy,* 56; Salinger, oral history interview, Los Angeles, Aug. 10, 1965, 108, JFKL.

7. Dean Rusk, as told to Richard Rusk, *As I Saw It,* ed. Daniel S. Papp (New York: Norton, 1990), 334; Salinger, *With Kennedy,* 56; excerpt from Salinger press briefing, Dec. 27, 1960, Kennedy Press Relations folder, Roberts papers, HHPL.

8. Salinger, *With Kennedy,* 57–58.

9. Theodore C. Sorensen, *Kennedy* (New York: Harper and Row, 1965), 322–23; Charles Roberts, "Image and Reality," in Kenneth W. Thompson, ed., *The Kennedy*

Presidency: Seventeen Intimate Perspectives of John F. Kennedy (Lanham, Md.: Univ. Press of America, 1985), 178; "TV-Radio," undated clipping from *Newsweek,* 56, in Kennedy Press Relations folder, Roberts papers, HHPL.

10. Charles Roberts, memo to "Press or Radio-TV," Kennedy Press Relations folder, Roberts papers, HHPL; Salinger, oral history interview, 54; Wilson, memo to Salinger, 1.

11. Wilson, memo to Salinger, 2; McGrory, Lisagor, Herman, oral history interview, 54; Salinger, *With Kennedy,* 59.

12. Wilson, memo to Salinger, 1; Robert J. Donovan, *New York Herald Tribune,* Mar. 12, 1961, sec. 2, 4.

13. Salinger, *With Kennedy,* 62, 75–78, 108–9; Richard Reeves, *President Kennedy: Profile of Power* (New York: Simon and Schuster, 1993), 39; Associated Press, "Press Aide Hatcher 'Stays Out of News,' " clipping in Kennedy Staff folder, Charles Roberts papers, HHPL; Coleman, oral history interview, 69.

14. Salinger, *With Kennedy,* 78; Salinger, oral history interview, 114.

15. Salinger, *With Kennedy,* 127–28; McGrory, Lisagor, Herman, oral history interview, 82; Peter Lisagor, second oral history interview, Washington, D.C., May 12, 1966, 70, JFKL; undated typescript, 5, box 11, Relationship of the President and the Press folder, Pierre Salinger papers, JFKL.

16. "TV-Radio" clipping; Salinger, *With Kennedy,* 138; Kennedy, *Press Conferences,* 1–11; *New York Times,* Jan. 26, 1961.

17. Salinger, *With Kennedy,* 136–38; Sorensen, 323–24; Schlesinger, 716; Rusk, 334; Charles Roberts, memo to "Press (and Nation)," Kennedy Press Relations folder, Roberts papers, HHPL.

18. Salinger, *With Kennedy,* 77–78, 131–32; Salinger, oral history interview, 105, 147–48; Robert T. Hartmann, "Kennedy's Press Secretary," *The Quill,* Jan. 1961, 18; Lewis L. Gould, "There's History to Role of First Lady," *The Quill,* Mar., 1966, 29; Liz Carpenter, *Ruffles and Flourishes: The Warm and Tender Story of a Simple Girl Who Found Adventure in the White House* (Garden City, N.Y.: Doubleday, 1970), 113.

19. Salinger, *With Kennedy,* 78; McGrory, Lisagor, Herman, oral history interview, 80; undated typed notes on Western Union press message paper, and "Salinger's Drawbacks," Kennedy Press Relations folder, Charles Roberts papers, HHPL; *Time,* Jan. 20, 1961, 26; Coleman, oral history interview, 36; Edward T. Folliard, oral history interview, Washington, D.C., Mar. 30, 1967, 23, JFKL.

20. Donald R. Burkholder, *The Caretaker of the President's Image,* unpublished diss., Wayne State Univ., 1973; *Editor & Publisher,* Feb. 4, 1961, 6; Salinger, *With Kennedy,* 136, 153; Kennedy, *Press Conferences,* 8.

21. *Editor & Publisher,* Feb. 4, 1961, 6; Kennedy, *Press Conferences,* 1; Salinger, *With Kennedy,* 140.

22. Salinger, *With Kennedy,* 58; *Editor & Publisher,* Feb. 4, 1961, 6; Salinger, author's telephone interview, Jan. 3, 1997; Salinger, *P.S.: A Memoir* (New York: St. Martin's, 1995), 290.

23. Salinger, *With Kennedy,* 145–47; Salinger, *P.S.,* 109; Salinger, author's interview; *Time,* May 1, 1961, 63.

24. Kennedy, *Press Conferences,* 83–85; Salinger, *With Kennedy,* 154–55.

25. *New York Times,* Apr. 14, 1961; *Time,* Apr. 28, 1961, 65.

26. Salinger, *With Kennedy*, 155–57; Kennedy, "Address, 'The President and the Press' Before the American Newspaper Publishers Association," New York, Apr. 27, 1961, *Public Papers*, 1961, 337.

27. Salinger, *With Kennedy*, 156–59; *Washington Post*, May 10, 1961, 3; Earl R. Hutchinson, "Kennedy and the Press: The First Six Months," *Journalism Quarterly*, Fall 1961, 456–57.

28. Burkholder, 70; *Time*, Mar. 3, 1961, 17.

29. *New York Times*, June 1, 1961, 1, 14; Robert Smith Thompson, *The Missiles of October: The Declassified Story of John F. Kennedy and the Cuban Missile Crisis* (New York: Simon and Schuster, 1992), 232.

30. Salinger, *With Kennedy*, 172; Salinger, author's interview.

31. Salinger, *With Kennedy*, 173; Rusk, 368; Salinger, author's interview.

32. "Stenographic Transcript of Conversation Between President Kennedy and NBC Correspondent Ray Scherer for the NBC Television Network Program *JFK#2*," 14, Kennedy Staff folder, Charles Roberts papers, HHPL; Merriman Smith, undated note to Charles Roberts, Kennedy Staff folder, Roberts papers, HHPL.

33. Salinger, *P.S.*, 139–43; Salinger, *With Kennedy*, 176–77, 219–37; Patrick Anderson, 234–38; Kennedy, *Press Conferences*, 201.

34. Salinger, *With Kennedy*, 249–52; R. S. Thompson, 232; Reeves, 385.

35. Salinger, *With Kennedy*, 252–53; O'Donnell, 322.

36. Salinger, oral history interview, 141–42; Salinger, *With Kennedy*, 255.

37. *The Annals of America, Volume 18, 1961-1968: The Burdens of World Power* (Chicago: Encyclopedia Britannica, 1976), 140–42.

38. *Washington Post*, Oct. 25, 1961, A6; *New York Times*, Oct. 25, 1961, 21; R. S. Thompson, 308–9; Salinger, *With Kennedy*, 288–89; Wes Gallagher, author's telephone interview, Jan. 5, 1997.

39. Salinger, *With Kennedy*, 293–94; Robert F. Kennedy, *Thirteen Days: A Memoir of the Cuban Missile Crisis* (New York: Norton, 1969), 75.

40. Salinger, *With Kennedy*, 257.

41. Salinger, messages to Wes Gallagher, James C. Hagerty, et al., Nov. 3 and 7, 1962; Hagerty folder, Salinger papers, JFKL; Kennedy, *Press Conferences*, 406; Charles Roberts, memo to "Press (and Nation)," Nov. 23, 1962, 3–4, Kennedy Press Relations folder, Roberts papers, HHPL.

42. Salinger, *With Kennedy*, 1–8; Walter W. Heller, *Chronology of Events on Board the Aircraft Carrying the Cabinet Group to Japan on Friday, November, 22, 1963, the Day of President Kennedy's Death*, typescript with notation "drafted 11/23/63," box 1, Chronology of Events on Board Aircraft folder, Aides—Pierre Salinger collection, Lyndon Baines Johnson Library, hereinafter cited as LBJL; Rusk, 296.

43. Garamekian, oral history interview, 88–89.

44. Jerald F. terHorst and Col. Ralph Albertazzie, *The Flying White House: The Story of Air Force One* (New York: Coward, McCann and Geoghegan, 1979), 216.

45. Folliard, oral history interview, 33.

46. Garamekian, oral history interview, 89–93.

47. Salinger, *P.S.*, 158.

9. The Disposable Press Secretary

1. Salinger, *P.S.*, 160.

2. Frank Cormier, James Deakin, and Helen Thomas, *The White House Press on the Presidency: News Management and Co-Option* (Lanham, Md.: Univ. Press of America, 1983).

3. Salinger, *P.S.*, 165.

4. Ibid., 160.

5. Ibid., 160, 165; Harry David Latimer, *The Press Secretaries of Lyndon Johnson*, unpublished diss., Brown Univ., 1973, 76.

6. Lyndon Baines Johnson, *The Vantage Point: Perspectives of the Presidency, 1963–1969* (New York: Holt, Rinehart and Winston, 1971), 181–82.

7. Carpenter, 112–13.

8. McGeorge Bundy, memo to president, Dec. 7, 1963, Aides—Pierre Salinger collection, box 1, Press Conference #1 folder, Lyndon Baines Johnson Library, hereinafter cited as LBJL; Douglass Cater, memo to Bill Moyers, Office Files Bill Moyers collection, box 51, Press Conference Material 1964 folder, LBJL.

9. *Newsweek*, Jan. 1, 1968, 11; *Public Papers of the Presidents of the United States: Lyndon B. Johnson, 1963–64*, 34–35, A-51.

10. Salinger, *P.S.*, 160, 165.

11. Ibid., 165–69; Eleanor Fowle, *Cranston: The Senator from California* (San Rafael, Calif.: Presidio, 1980), 170; *Congressional Record, 88th Congress, Second Session* (Washington, D.C.: Government Printing Office, 1964), 5774; Joseph Barr, oral history interview, Pittsburgh, June 10, 1969, LBJL.

12. Fowle, 171–83; Salinger, *P.S.*, 169–72; *Congressional Record* 19396–413; Lou Cannon, *President Reagan: The Role of a Lifetime* (New York: Simon and Schuster, 1991), 45–46.

13. *Congressional Record*, 5774.

14. Salinger, *P.S.*, 160; Latimer, 100–101.

15. Latimer, 101; Charles Roberts, typed notes, Feb. 19, 1965, Johnson Press Relations folder, Roberts papers, HHPL; George Reedy, author's telephone interview, Jan. 23, 1997.

16. Latimer, 100; Samuel Houston Johnson, ed. Enrique Hank Lopez, *My Brother Lyndon* (New York: Cowles, 1970), 152; Reedy, author's interview.

17. Latimer, 103; James Deakin, *Lyndon Johnson's Credibility Gap* (Washington, D.C.: Public Affairs Press, 1968), 15; Robert Baskin, oral history interview, Dallas, Mar. 16, 1974, LBJL; Reedy, author's interview.

18. Latimer, 102; Stewart Alsop, oral history interview, Washington, D.C., July 15, 1969, LBJL; Dan Rather, oral history interview, Washington, D.C., Apr. 16, 1973, LBJL; Charles Roberts, memo to "Press (Pollak)" re "LBJ and the Press," 4, Johnson Press Relations folder, HHPL; Carpenter, 104.

19. Roberts, Feb. 19, 1965, notes.

20. George Reedy, undated memo to president; Douglass Cater, memo to president, Aug. 18, 1964, 1, files of Douglass Cater, box 13, Memos to White House Staff folder, LBJL; Reedy, *Lyndon B. Johnson*, 64–65; Reedy, author's interview; *Time*, Nov. 6, 1965; Charles Boatner, oral history interview, Fort Worth, Texas, June 1, 1976, LBJL; Alsop, oral history interview.

21. *Editor & Publisher,* Dec. 5, 1964; Baskin, 47.

22. Reedy, author's interview; Warren Rogers, "The Truth about LBJ's Credibility," *Look,* May 2, 1967, 75; Fred Panzer, memo to Marvin Watson, Nov. 29, 1967, with attached clipping, office files of Marvin Watson, box 19, Credibility Gap folder, LBJL.

23. William McGaffin and Erwin Knoll, *Anything but the Truth: The Credibility Gap—How the News Is Managed in Washington* (New York: Putnam's, 1968), 32; Roberts, memo to "Press (Pollak)," 3; Reedy, author's interview.

24. McGaffin, 19, 32; Deakin, 42; Roberts, memo, 4.

25. Reedy, *Lyndon B. Johnson,* 60–61; Bill Moyers and president, recorded telephone conversation K66.02, 10:17 A.M. Dec. 22, 1966, LBJL.

26. Reedy, *Lyndon B. Johnson,* 4, 65–66, 69, 148.

27. Reedy, *Lyndon B. Johnson,* 69; *Time,* July 16, 1965, 16.

28. Charles Roberts, memo to "Press," Jan. 13, 1966, Johnson Press Relations folder, Roberts papers, HHPL; *Time,* Oct. 29, 1965, 25; Evans and Novak, 299, 508–9; Sam Johnson, 156; Latimer, 124–25.

29. *Life,* Sept. 10, 1965, 48.

30. Charles L. May, oral history interview, Washington, D.C., May 6, 1969, 26, LBJL; Booth Mooney, oral history interview, Apr. 8, 1969, 41–42, LBJL; *Newsweek,* Dec. 26, 1966, 19.

31. Latimer, 123; Don Oberdorfer, "The Man Who Speaks for LBJ," *Saturday Evening Post,* Oct. 23, 1965, 32–33; *Time,* Oct. 29, 1965, 26.

32. *Newsweek,* Dec. 26, 1966, 18; Henry Brandon, "The New Press Secretary," *Saturday Review,* Aug. 7, 1965, 10; Evans and Novak, 343n; Latimer, 124; Bromley Smith, oral history interview, Washington, D.C., July 29, 1969, 37; Anderson, 347.

33. Chester R. Huntley, oral history interview, 15, Univ. of Texas Oral History Project, May 12, 1969, LBJL.

34. Carpenter, 105; *Time,* Oct. 29, 1965, 25; George Christian, *The President Steps Down: A Personal Memoir of the Transfer of Power* (New York: Macmillan, 1970), 13; Latimer, 126; Booth Mooney, oral history interview, Apr. 8, 1961, 41–42.

35. Reedy, *Lyndon B. Johnson,* 67–68; *Public Papers,* 1965, 917–27; Reedy, author's interview; McGaffin, 60–61; *Washington Post,* Aug. 26, 1965, A19.

36. Deakin, 46–47; Herbert Read, memo to Jack Valenti, May 9, 1966, office files of Bill Moyers, box 134, State Department Press Contacts folder, LBJL.

37. Carpenter, 105.

38. Associated Press, "Moyers Kept Surgery under Wraps," Nov. 4, 1966, clipping in Johnson Press Relations folder, Charles Roberts papers, HHPL.

39. Undated clipping, source not identified, Johnson Press Relations folder, Roberts papers, HHPL.

40. McGaffin, 30–31; Sidey, 181; Reedy, author's interview.

41. McGaffin, 33.

42. Charles Roberts, "LBJ's Credibility Gap," from *Newsweek,* Dec. 19, 1966, © 1966, Newsweek, Inc. All rights reserved. Reprinted by permission.

43. Packard to Mel Elfin and Charles Roberts, Dec. 16, 1966, Credibility Gap folder, Roberts papers, HHPL.

44. *New York Times,* Feb. 20, 1966.

45. Bromley Smith, oral history interview, 37; Anderson, 341.

46. Charles Bartlett, oral history interview, Washington, D.C., May 6, 1969, 26, LBJL.

47. Sam Johnson, 156; Lady Bird Johnson, *A White House Diary* (New York: Holt, Rinehart and Winston, 1970), 306.

48. Bill Moyers and president, taped telephone conversation, Dec. 26, 1966, LBJL; William Manchester, *The Death of a President, November 20–November 25, 1963* (New York: Harper and Row, 1967), 317, 666.

49. Bartlett, oral history interview, 26; Oberdorfer, 33; Walter Trohan, *Political Animals: Memoirs of a Sentimental Cynic* (Garden City, N.Y.: Doubleday, 1975), 349; *New York Times,* Dec. 16, 1966, 46.

50. Charles Roberts, memo to "Press," Jan. 13, 1966, 2–4.

51. *Newsweek,* Dec. 26, 1966, 18.

52. Latimer, 150; George Christian, oral history interview, 2, Nov. 11, 1968, LBJL.

53. Christian, oral history interview, 7–8.

54. Christian, oral history interview, 6; Christian, author's interview, Austin, Tex., Oct. 22, 1996; George Christian, memos to the president, Aug. 3, 9, 15, 31, 1967, Aides—Christian collection, box 3, Press Contact Report folder, LBJL.

55. Christian, oral history interview, 7–8; Christian, author's interview.

56. Christian, oral history interview, 9; Christian, author's interview.

57. Christian, author's interview.

58. Deakin, 49; Rogers, 70; Christian, author's interview.

59. Christian, author's interview; Christian, memo to the president, May 12, 1967; George Christian and Tom Johnson, memo to Liz Carpenter, May 12, 1967; Christian, memo to Liz Carpenter, May 16, 1967; Carpenter, Christian et al., memo to president, May 16, 1967; Carpenter, memo to Mrs. Johnson, Apr. 25, 1967, Aides —Christian collection, box 4, Memos folder, LBJL.

60. Christian, author's interview; *Newsweek,* Nov. 27, 1967, 23, and Jan. 1, 1968, 11–12.

61. Hugh Sidey, *A Very Personal Presidency: Lyndon Johnson in the White House* (New York: Atheneum, 1968), 192–93; Deakin, 49.

62. Lyndon Johnson, 428–29; Lady Bird Johnson, 616.

63. Lyndon Johnson, 430; Joseph A. Califano Jr., *The Triumph and Tragedy of Lyndon Johnson: The White House Years* (New York: Simon and Schuster, 1991), 269.

64. Califano, 269; Lyndon Johnson, 431.

65. Lyndon Johnson, 435; Lady Bird Johnson, 646; President's daily diary, box 14, Mar. 16–31, 1968.

66. Carpenter, 110.

10. No Longer Operative

1. Stanley I. Kutler, *The Wars of Watergate: The Last Crisis of Richard Nixon* (New York: Knopf, 1990), 197.

2. Elizabeth Drew, *Washington Journal: The Events of 1973–74* (New York: Random House, 1974), 323.

3. Burkholder, 72.

4. Theodore White, *The Making of the President, 1968* (New York: Atheneum, 1969), 169.

5. Jeb Stuart Magruder, *An American Life: One Man's Road to Watergate* (New York: Atheneum, 1974), 61.

6. J. Anthony Lukas, *Nightmare: The Underside of the Nixon Years* (New York: Viking, 1976), 392; Dan Rather and Gary Paul Gates, *The Palace Guard* (New York: Harper and Row, 1974), 152; James M. Naughton, "How the 2nd Best-Informed Man in the White House Briefs the 2nd Worst-Informed Group in Washington," *New York Times Magazine,* May 30, 1971, 25; Ronald Ziegler, author's telephone interview, Apr. 1, 1997.

7. H. R. Haldeman, *The Haldeman Diaries: Inside the Nixon White House* (New York: Putnam's, 1994), 58.

8. Charles Roberts, undated memo to *Periscope* and *Nation,* Roberts papers, HHPL.

9. Tom Wicker, *One of Us: Richard Nixon and the American Dream* (New York: Random House, 1991), 398.

10. Lukas, 392; William Safire, *Before the Fall: An Inside View of the Pre-Watergate White House* (New York: Random House, 1991), 398; Ziegler, author's interview.

11. Herbert G. Klein, interview, July 17, 1973, 31–32, exit interview files, Nixon Presidential Materials Project, Archives 2, hereinafter cited as NP (unless otherwise noted, materials are in White House Special files, Staff Member Office files).

12. Herbert G. Klein, interview by A. James Reichley, Jan. 6, 1968, 3, GRFL.

13. Jules Witcover, "Focusing on Nixon," *Columbia Journalism Review,* Winter 1968–69, 16; Rather, 151; *Washington Post,* Jan. 9, 1973, A1, A7.

14. Ronald Ziegler, Reichley interview, Nov. 15, 1977, 2, GRFL; Ziegler, author's interview.

15. Helen Thomas, *Dateline: White House* (New York, Macmillan, 1975), 129; Gerald L. Warren, interview, Oct. 24, 1974, 2, 8, exit interview files, NP; Philomena Jurey, *A Basement Seat to History: Tales of Covering Presidents Nixon, Ford, Carter, and Reagan for the Voice of America* (Washington, D.C.: Linus Press, 1995), 61; Ziegler, author's interview.

16. Thomas, 72, 129, 130–32; Naughton, 25–26.

17. *Wall Street Journal,* July 3, 1970, 4.

18. Safire, 352.

19. "The White House: Proposed EOB Press Facilities and Connecting Tunnel to the West Wing," Apr. 10, 1969, H. R. Haldeman box 289, NP; Memorandum of Record, June 23, 1969, Haldeman box 288, West Wing Underground Press Facilities folder, NP; Ziegler, author's interview.

20. Haldeman, *Diaries,* 89; Luther A. Huston, "Nixon Puts Newsmen in Lap of Luxury," *Editor & Publisher,* Apr. 18, 1970, 18.

21. Naughton, 9.

22. Dwight Chapin, memo to Ronald Ziegler, Apr. 14, 1970, NP.

23. Don Rumsfeld, memo to Ron Nessen, Oct. 16, 1975, with reply, same date, Nessen papers, box 133, GRFL.

24. H. R. Haldeman, memos to Patrick Buchanan, Jan. 25 and 29, 1969, Haldeman box 49, Memos for Pat Buchanan folder, NP; Martin F. Nolan, "The Reselling of the President," *Atlantic,* Nov. 1972, 80.

25. Bruce Oudes, ed., *From the President: Richard Nixon's Secret Files* (New York: Harper and Row, 1989), 34.

26. H. R. Haldeman, memo to Herb Klein and Ron Ziegler, Jan. 23, 1970, Haldeman box 56, Memos Ron Ziegler folder, NP.

27. Dwight Chapin, memo to William Safire, Dec. 15, 1970; Stephen Bull, memo to H. R. Haldeman, Jan. 16, 1971; Alexander Butterfield, memo to Pat Buchanan and others, Feb. 2, 1972; John Andrews, memo to David Hoopes, Mar. 31, 1972; John Andrews, memo for the president's file, June 16, 1972; Stephen Bull, memo to H. R. Haldeman, Mar. 7, 1973, and reply, same date, all in Bull box 3, Anecdotalist folder, NP.

28. Patrick J. Buchanan, memo to the president, May 3, 1971, with undated clipping from *Wall Street Journal,* Buchanan box 4, Presidential Memos folder, NP.

29. Ziegler, author's interview; Kutler, 174; Oudes, 125–26; Haldeman, *Diaries,* 403.

30. Ronald L. Ziegler, memo to H. R. Haldeman, Oct. 31, 1969, Haldeman box 53, Memos Ron Ziegler folder, NP.

31. Oudes, 262.

32. Ron Ziegler, memo to Bob Haldeman, Jan. 9, 1971, Haldeman box 72, Safire—Ziegler folder, NP.

33. Rowland Evans Jr. and Robert D. Novak, *Nixon in the White House: The Frustration of Power* (New York: Random House, 1971), 315.

34. Ron Ziegler, memo to H. R. Haldeman, Nov. 20, 1969, with attached speech draft, Ziegler box 1, Agnew Speech folder, NP.

35. Haldeman, *Diaries,* 109.

36. Jon M. Huntsman, memo to Ron Ziegler, Mar. 18, 1971, with attached extract from White House News Summary, Mar. 17, 1971, and Ziegler reply, Mar. 20, 1971, Haldeman box 76, Ziegler folder, NP.

37. Naughton, 9.

38. Kutler, 433.

39. Warren, exit interview, 8.

40. Naughton, 9, 24, 25.

41. Ziegler, author's interview; J. Bruce Whelihan, memo to Ron Ziegler, Apr. 16, 1973, Ziegler box 1, Basic Reorganization folder 3, NP.

42. Richard Nixon, *RN: The Memoirs of Richard Nixon* (New York: Grosset and Dunlap, 1978), 354; H. R. Haldeman, memo to Alex Butterfield, Dec. 22, 1970, and Ron Ziegler, memo to H. R. Haldeman, Jan. 9, 1971, Haldeman box 72, Safire—Ziegler folder, NP.

43. Alexander P. Butterfield, memo to Ronald Ziegler, Aug. 7, 1969, Haldeman box 51, Memos Ron Ziegler folder, NP.

44. H. R. Haldeman, memo to Ronald Ziegler, Feb. 6, 1969, Haldeman box 49, Ronald Ziegler folder, NP.

45. Dwight Chapin, memo to Ron Ziegler, June 20, 1970, Chapin box 10, NP.

46. Dwight Chapin, memo to Ron Ziegler, Nov. 16, 1971, Chapin box 15, NP; Don Oberdorfer, "The China Press Scenario," *The Nation,* Mar 27, 1972, 397; Haldeman, *Diaries,* 403.

47. Haldeman, *Diaries,* 26.

48. H. R. Haldeman, memo to Ron Ziegler, Dec. 31, 1970, Haldeman box 272, Safire—Ziegler folder, NP.

49. John Ehrlichman, *Witness to Power: The Nixon Years* (New York: Simon and Schuster, 1982), 68.

50. *Washington Daily News,* Nov. 18, 1970, and *Washington Sunday Star,* Nov. 29, 1970, Ziegler box 20, Press File folder, NP.

51. Jon M. Huntsman, memo to Ronald Ziegler, Feb. 23, 1971, and reply, Feb. 26, 1971, with attached clip from *Wall Street Journal,* Feb. 19, 1971, Haldeman box 74, Ziegler folder, NP.

52. Peter Lisagor, letter to the president, Jan. 4, 1971, with attached memorandum on relationship between president and newsmen; *New York Times,* June 19, 1972, Ziegler box 21, Press File folder, NP.

53. *New York Times,* Jan. 21, 1971, C3.

54. *Washington Post,* Mar. 18, 1971, A21.

55. Stephen Bull, memo to David Parker, Dec. 2, 1971, with schedule for "A Day in the Life of the President"; Stephen Bull, memo to John Connally, Dec. 2, 1971; Stephen Bull, memo to H. R. Haldeman, Dec. 5, 1971, all in Bull box 3, "A Day in the Life of the President" folder, NP.

56. Constance Stuart, interview, Mar. 15, 1973, 13–14, exit interview file, NP.

57. Marie Smith, letter to Constance Stuart, Nov. 20, 1969, and Constance Stuart, memo to H. R. Haldeman, Nov. 24, 1969, Haldeman box 54, Memos Connie Stuart folder, NP.

58. Thomas, 154.

59. Dwight Chapin, memo to Ron Ziegler, White House Central files, Chapin box 10, NP; Thomas, 155.

60. *Washington Post,* Dec. 18 and 19, 1972, B1.

61. *Washington Post,* June 20, 1972, A14; John W. Dean III, *Blind Ambition: The White House Years* (New York: Simon and Schuster, 1976), 107.

62. Ron Ziegler, transcript of briefing, June 19, 1972; Pat Buchanan and Ron Ziegler, memos to the president, June 20 and 22, 1972, Buchanan box 23, Domestic Briefing Book Backup folder, NP; Nixon, *RN,* 638.

63. Haldeman, *Diaries,* 514–32; John J. Sirica, *To Set the Record Straight: The Break-in, the Tapes, the Conspirators, the Pardon* (New York: Norton, 1979), 130.

64. Haldeman, *Diaries,* 564, 568; Walter Isaacson, *Kissinger: A Biography* (New York: Simon and Schuster, 1992), 480.

65. Haldeman, *Diaries,* 571; *Washington Post,* Jan. 23, 1973, A1, 13; *Washington Post,* Jan. 25, 1973, A1.

66. Haldeman, *Diaries,* 597–611.

67. Kutler, 271–72.

68. Robert Walters, "What Did Ziegler Say, and When Did He Say It?" *Columbia Journalism Review,* Sept.–Oct. 1974, 35; Safire, 352.

69. Carl Bernstein and Bob Woodward, *All the President's Men* (New York: Simon and Schuster, 1974), 292; Thomas, 195; Nixon, *RN,* 857; James Cannon, 160; Ehrlichman, 331–32.

70. Haldeman, *Diaries,* 652; Nixon, *RN,* 836.

71. Haldeman, *Diaries,* 654–55; Nixon, *RN,* 839; Ehrlichman, 386–87.

72. Haldeman, *Diary,* 671–72; Nixon, *RN,* 848; H. R. Haldeman with Joseph Di Mona, *The Ends of Power* (New York: Times Books, 1978), 291–92.

73. *Public Papers, Richard Nixon, 1973,* 134.

74. James Cannon, 160.

75. Ehrlichman, 331–32.

76. Lukas, 4.

77. Isaacson, 594; *Christian Science Monitor,* Dec. 17, 1973, 5.

78. Nixon, *RN,* 962; Haig, 362; Thomas, 199; Ziegler, author's interview.

79. Nixon, *RN,* 934–35; Lucas, 440.

80. Nixon, *RN,* 1051.

81. Ibid., 1053.

82. Thomas, 217.

83. Haig, 478; Nixon, *RN,* 1057.

84. Drew, 409; Thomas, 222.

85. Robert T. Hartmann, *Palace Politics: An Inside Account of the Ford Years* (New York: McGraw-Hill, 1980), 158.

11. A Matter of Conscience

1. Gerald R. Ford, *A Time to Heal: The Autobiography of Gerald R. Ford* (New York: Harper and Row, 1979), 31; Jerald terHorst, author's telephone interview, Feb. 11, 1997.

2. J. W. Roberts, transcript of taped diary, Aug. 8, 1974, Gerald R. Ford Library, hereinafter cited as GRFL.

3. Helen Thomas, *Dateline: White House* (New York: Macmillan, 1975), 259–60.

4. Robert Hartmann, interview by Mark J. Rozell, Dec. 15, 1989, 8, GRFL.

5. Hartmann, *Politics: An Inside Account of the Ford Years* (New York: McGraw-Hill, 1980), 116–17; Gerald Ford, 168–70.

6. Hartmann, *Politics,* 161; terHorst, interview by Mark Rozell, June 27, 1990, 1, GRFL.

7. Larry Speakes, interview by Mark J. Rozell, Feb. 6, 1990, 1, GRFL.

8. J. W. Roberts diary, Aug. 10, 1974, GRFL; James Cannon, *Time and Chance: Gerald Ford's Appointment with History* (New York: Harper Collins, 1994), 355–56; terHorst, author's interview.

9. Roberts diary, Aug. 10, 1974, GRFL; Reedy, author's interview.

10. Roberts diary, Aug. 13, 18, 19, 1974, GRFL.

11. Ibid., Aug. 14, 1974, GRFL.

12. Ibid., Aug. 26–28, 1974; terHorst, interview by Rozell, 6; G. Ford, 156–58; *Washington Post,* Aug. 29, 1974, A19.

13. Tom DeCair, memo to Dick Cheney, Jan. 21, 1975, Nessen papers, box 133, GRFL.

14. Gerald Ford, 156–58; Hartmann, Rozell interview, 14, GRFL; *Washington Post,* Aug. 29, 1974, A19.

15. Hartmann, *Politics,* 257–61; Alexander M. Haig Jr. with Charles McCarry, *Inner Circles: How America Changed the World—A Memoir* (New York: Warner, 1992), 514.

16. G. Ford, 173–74.

17. Ibid., 174–75; Jerald F. terHorst, *Gerald Ford and the Future of the Presidency* (New York: The Third Press, 1974), 235.

18. terHorst, *Ford,* 228–29.

19. Ibid., 229–30; Speakes, *Speaking Out,* 65–66.

20. terHorst, *Ford,* 225–27; G. Ford, 175–76.

21. terHorst, *Ford,* 226–27; G. Ford, 175–76.

22. Hartmann, *Politics,* 265–66.

23. terHorst, *Ford,* 230–33.

24. Ibid., 233; Speakes, *Speaking Out,* 66–67.

25. terHorst, *Ford,* 233–34; Roberts diary, Sept. 8 and 9, 1974, GRFL; Speakes, Rozell interview, 7, GRFL.

26. terHorst, *Ford,* 233.

27. John Osborne, *White House Watch: The Ford Years* (Washington, D.C.: New Republic, 1977), 7; Gerald Ford, author's telephone interview, Feb. 11, 1977; terHorst, author's interview.

28. Thomas, 259–60; Jack Hushen, news conference at the White House, Sept. 10, 1974, 2, Ron Nessen files, box 1, GRFL; terHorst, author's interview.

29. Hartmann, *Politics,* 288–90; Roberts diary, Sept. 12, 1974, GRFL; Hartmann, Rozell interview, 10–11, GRFL.

30. Roberts diary, Aug. 16 and 25, GRFL.

31. G. Ford, 184; Ron Nessen, *It Sure Looks Different from the Inside* (Chicago: Playboy Press, 1978), 10–13.

32. Nessen, *It Sure Looks Different,* 13.

33. Mark J. Rozell, *The Press and the Ford Presidency* (Ann Arbor: Univ. of Michigan Press, 1992), 201.

34. Jerald terHorst, memo to Alexander Haig, Aug. 24, 1974, undated list of White House press office salaries, Ronald Nessen papers, box 135, Press Office Staff folder, GRFL; Tom DeCair, memo to Ronald Nessen, Apr. 24, 1975, Nessen papers, box 135, DeCair folder, GRFL; John Osborne, "White House Watch," *New Republic,* Mar. 1, 1975, 10.

35. Roberts diary, July 25, Aug. 9, 10, 16, GRFL; G. Ford, 156–58, 184; terHorst, Rozell interview, 4, GRFL.

36. Talking Paper, Subject Paul Miltich, Oct. 24, 1974, Miltich memo to Nessen, Oct. 25, 1974, Ronald Nessen papers, box 135, Press Office Staff folder, GRFL; Ron Nessen, memo to Dick Cheney, Jan. 16, 1975, Nessen papers, box 127, Cheney folder, GRFL; Nessen, memo to Miltich, Feb. 15, Nessen papers, box 135, Miltich folder, GRFL.

37. terHorst, Rozell interview, 4, GRFL; Hartmann, *Politics,* 280; terHorst, memos to John McLaughlin, Sept. 4 and Oct. 1, 1974, Nessen papers, box 135, McLaughlin folder, GRFL; Hushen, news conference, Sept. 12, 1974, Nessen files, box 1, GRFL; Nessen, memo to Donald Rumsfeld Sept. 30, 1974, Nessen papers, box

132, Rumsfeld folder, GRFL; Osborne, 20; Nessen, memo to Ken Clawson, Oct. 7, 1974, Nessen papers, box 135, Clawson folder, GRFL.

38. Sheila Weidenfeld, memo to Mrs. Ford, Dec. 4, 1974, Nessen papers, box 127, Cheney folder, GRFL.

39. Ron Nessen, memo to Sheila Weidenfeld, Nov. 4, 1974, Sheila Weidenfeld memo to Ron Nessen, Nov. 1, 1974, Louis Thompson, memo to Brig. Gen. Adams, Dec. 10, 1974, Nessen papers, box 134, Weidenfeld folder, GRFL; Nessen, memos to Cheney, Jan. 31, 1975, and Nov. 16, 1974, Nessen papers, box 127, Cheney folder, GRFL; Nessen, author's telephone interview, Feb. 12, 1997.

40. Helen Thomas, letter to President Ford, July 8, 1975, and Ron Nessen, memo to Don Rumsfeld, July 14, 1975, Nessen papers, box 133, GRFL; Gerald R. Ford, letter to Helen Thomas, Aug. 7, 1975, Nessen papers, box 134, Weidenfeld folder, GRFL.

41. Ron Nessen, handwritten notes, Oct. 30, 1974, Nessen papers, box 294, Notes folder, GRFL; *Washington Post,* Oct. 31, 1974.

42. Lou Cannon, "Nessen's Briefings: Missing Questions (and Answers)," *Columbia Journalism Review,* May 1975, 16.

43. Nessen, *It Sure Looks Different,* 50–51; Rumsfeld, message to Scowcroft for Cheney, Nov. 1974, Nessen papers, box 127, Cheney folder, GRFL; Walter Isaacson, *Kissinger: A Biography,* 627; *New York Times,* Feb. 17, 1975; Nessen, author's interview.

44. Nessen, *It Sure Looks Different,* 92.

45. L. Cannon, "Nessen's Briefings," 16.

46. Osborne, "White House Watch," *New Republic,* Apr. 26, 1975, 8; *Newsweek,* Apr. 28, 1975, 35; John J. Casserly, *The Ford White House: The Diary of a Speechwriter* (Boulder: Colorado Associated Univ. Press, 1977), 74–75; Louis M. Thompson Jr., interview by Mark Rozell, Nov. 20, 1990, 13–14; Isaacson, 605; Nessen, *It Sure Looks Different,* 133–34.

47. G. Ford, 184; *Newsweek,* Nov. 24, 1975, 27.

48. Ron Nessen, memo to Dick Cheney, June 11, 1975, GRFL.

49. L. Cannon, "Nessen's Briefings," 13.

50. Casserly, 104–6; Nessen, news conference, June 6, 1975, Nessen files, box 9, GRFL.

51. Briefing book, Nov. 26, 1975, press conference, Nessen papers, GRFL.

52. *The Media Report,* Nov. 21, 1975; Nessen, author's interview; Nessen, *It Sure Looks Different,* 108; Roberts diary, Sept. 8, 1974, GRFL; *Public Papers,* Gerald Ford, 1975, 208.

53. *Washington Post,* Dec. 14, 1975, A1; Casserly, 218.

54. Nessen, *It Sure Looks Different,* 314–15.

55. Osborne, 441.

56. Nessen, *It Sure Looks Different,* 333.

57. Nessen, author's interview.

12. The Fine Hand

1. *New York Times,* Feb. 28, 1977, 12.

2. Jimmy Carter, *Keeping Faith: Memoirs of a President* (Toronto: Bantam Books, 1982), 466.

3. Zbigniew Brzezinski, *Power and Principle: Memoirs of the National Security Adviser, 1977–1981* (New York: Farrar, Straus, Giroux, 1983), 88, 239.

4. J. Carter, 541.

5. Cyrus Vance, *Hard Choices: Critical Years in America's Foreign Policy* (New York: Simon and Schuster, 1983), 337.

6. Kenneth W. Thompson, ed., *The Virginia Papers on the Presidency, Volume 4* (Charlottesville, Va.: The White Burkett Miller Center, 1980), 59.

7. Rosalynn Carter, *First Lady from Plains* (Boston: Houghton Mifflin, 1984), 67.

8. J. Carter, 42–44.

9. Jody Powell, *The Other Side of the Story* (New York: Morrow, 1984), 28.

10. J. Carter, 42–44.

11. R. Carter, 141.

12. Powell, 28; J. Carter, 44.

13. Jody Powell, Miller Center interview, Carter Presidency Project, Vol. 10, Dec. 17–18, 1981, 6, 8.

14. Rex Granum, exit interview tape, side 1, Jimmy Carter Presidential Library, hereinafter cited as JCPL.

15. Walt Wurfel, exit interview, Washington, D.C., May 10, 1979, JCPL.

16. Jim Purks, exit interview, Dec. 2, 1980, JCPL.

17. J. Carter, 44.

18. *New York Times,* Feb. 28, 1977, 12; John Osborne, "In Jody's Shop," *New Republic,* Mar. 8, 1978, 18–19.

19. *Washington Post,* Jan. 20, 1977, E1.

20. Richard L. Strout, "TRB," *New Republic,* Nov. 20, 1976, 4.

21. Helen Thomas, "Carter Still Accessible," *Editor & Publisher,* Jan. 21, 1978, 42; Jimmy Carter, memo to Jody Powell, Feb. 7, 1977, Office of Staff Secretary Handwriting file, box 226, JCPL; Powell, 305.

22. Thomas, "Carter Still Accessible"; *New York Times,* Feb. 9, 1978, A21; "Presidential News Conferences," Anne Edwards Advance, box 11, Press Conferences Background folder, JCPL; Powell, 305.

23. *Public Papers, Jimmy Carter, 1977,* 92–100; *New York Times,* Feb. 9, 1977, A28.

24. Reid, "Reporters See."

25. Jody Powell and Ray Jenkins, Miller Center interviews, 99, 100, JCPL.

26. *New York Times,* Feb. 28, 1977, 12; Cormier, "Powell Still Credible," *Editor & Publisher,* Jan. 21, 1978, 42.

27. *New York Times,* Sept. 15, 1977, A1, B20; Powell, 50.

28. John Osborne, "In Jody's Shop (II)," *New Republic,* Mar. 15, 1978, 10.

29. Powell, Miller Center interview, 2.

30. J. Carter, 127.

31. Cormier, "Powell Still Credible," 43.

32. Walt Wurfel, exit interview, Washington, D.C., May 10, 1979, JCPL.

33. Walt Wurfel, handwritten note to Jerry Rafshoon, June 20, 1978, with attached commentary by Logan Stewart, KTSA-KTFM, San Antonio, Tex., June 12, 1978, Rafshoon communications, box 4, Office of Media Liaison folder, JCPL.

34. Walt Wurfel, memo to Jerry Rafshoon, May 30, 1978, Rafshoon communications, box 4, Office of Media Liaison folder, JCPL.

35. Jimmy Carter, handwritten note to Jody Powell, Feb. 24, 1977, Staff Secretary Handwriting, box 226, Jody Powell folder, JCPL.

36. Wurfel memo to Rafshoon; Purks exit interview; Pat Bario exit interview, Carter Presidency Project, JCPL.

37. *New York Times*, Dec. 2, 1978, 12; Jody Powell, author's interview, Washington, D.C., Feb. 29, 1996; Wurfel, exit interview, JCPL.

38. J. Carter, 317–18; Brzezinski, 252–53.

39. Powell, 65, 69–70; Brzezinski, 258.

40. Brzezinski, 252–53.

41. Powell, 85–86; Vance, 26; William B. Quandt, *Camp David: Peacemaking and Politics* (Washington, D.C.: Brookings, 1986), 254.

42. J. Carter, 415–16; Powell, 91–92.

43. Powell, 94–97.

44. J. Carter, 423–25; Granum, exit interview tape, side 2, JCPL.

45. J. Carter, 425; Anne Edwards, exit interview tape, Washington, D.C., Sept. 5, 1980, JCPL.

46. Powell, 97–98.

47. Powell, 99; Philomena Jurey, *A Basement Seat to History: Tales of Covering Presidents Nixon, Ford, Carter, and Reagan for the Voice of America* (Washington, D.C.: Linus Press, 1995), 180; J. Carter, 426.

48. Powell, 95–101.

49. Harold H. Saunders, "The Crisis Begins" in *American Hostages in Iran: The Conduct of a Crisis* (New Haven, Conn.: Yale Univ. Press, 1985), 36–37; J. Carter, 457–58; Pierre Salinger, *America Held Hostage: The Secret Negotiations* (Garden City, N.Y.: Doubleday, 1981), 52.

50. Brzezinski, 479, 483, 487, 490.

51. Powell, 210–13; Hamilton Jordan, *Crisis: The Last Year of the Carter Presidency* (New York: Putnam's 1982), 240–42; *New York Times,* Mar. 31, 1980, A1.

52. J. Carter, 503–4; Powell, 215–18; Jordan, 248; Jimmy Carter, remarks to reporters, Apr. 1, 1980, *Public Papers, Jimmy Carter, 1980,* 576; *Washington Post,* Apr. 2, 1980, A1.

53. Saunders, 70.

54. J. Carter, 506–7.

55. Powell, author's interview.

56. William S. White, "Kennedy's Seven Rules for Handling the Press," *Harper's,* Apr. 1961, 94.

57. Jody Powell, exit interview, Washington, D.C., Dec. 2, 1980, 4.

58. Osborne, "In Jody's Shop," 18.

59. Jordan, 171.

13. Staging the News

1. Larry Speakes with Robert Pack, *Speaking Out: The Reagan Presidency from Inside the White House* (New York: Avon Books, 1989), 169–70.

2. Dom Bonafede, "The Washington Press—Competing for Power with the Federal Government," *National Journal,* Apr. 17, 1982, 664–74; John Herbers, "The President and the Press Corps," *New York Times Magazine,* May 9, 1982, 74; Karna

Small, letter to Edward Schaefer, July 29, 1982, Public Relations box 28, Ronald Reagan Library, hereinafter cited as RRL.

3. Kenneth W. Thompson, ed., *Three Press Secretaries on the Presidency and the Press* (Lanham, Md.: Univ. Press of America, 1983), 14.

4. Bill Peterson, "Brady, the Good-Humored Outsider," *Washington Post,* Jan. 7, 1981, A23.

5. *Newsweek,* Feb. 23, 1981, 81; 569 Federal Reporter, 2d series, at 124.

6. *Public Papers, Ronald Reagan, 1984,* 248.

7. Ronald Reagan, *An American Life* (New York: Simon and Schuster, 1990), 489.

8. Joseph C. Spear, *Presidents and the Press: The Nixon Legacy* (Cambridge, Mass.: MIT Press, 1984), 7.

9. Dick Kirschten, "Communications Reshuffling Intended to Help Reagan Do What He Does Best," *National Journal,* Jan. 28, 1984, 156.

10. Speakes, 7–12.

11. Alexander M. Haig Jr., *Caveat: Realism, Reagan, and Foreign Policy* (New York: Macmillan, 1984), 158.

12. *Washington Post,* Jan. 29, 1983, A8.

13. Martin Anderson, *Revolution: The Reagan Legacy* (Stanford, Calif.: Hoover Institution, 1990), 314; *Washington Post,* Mar. 7, 1982, H1.

14. Haig, 159; Speakes, 12.

15. Anderson, 315; Haig, 159–60; Speakes, 2.

16. Helene Von Damm, *At Reagan's Side* (New York: Doubleday, 1989), 193–94.

17. Donald T. Regan, *For the Record: From Wall Street to Washington* (San Diego: Harcourt Brace Jovanovich, 1988), 167.

18. Caspar W. Weinberger, *Fighting for Peace: Seven Critical Years in the Pentagon* (New York: Warner Books, 1990), 90.

19. Haig, 167.

20. Speakes, 14–21.

21. Ibid., 22–37.

22. Ibid., 38–49.

23. Ibid., 50–64.

24. Ibid., 65–80.

25. Herbers, 97; Kirschten, 156; Bumiller, H12.

26. Herbers, 96.

27. *Washington Post,* Aug. 15, 1982.

28. Bumiller, H1.

29. Spear, 255.

30. Lou Cannon, *President Reagan: The Role of a Lifetime* (New York: Simon and Schuster, 1991), 569.

31. *Washington Post,* Mar. 7, 1982, H12.

32. Kirschten, 153–54; Herbers, 75; Sam Donaldson, *Hold On, Mr. President!* (New York: Random House, 1987), 125–26.

33. *Washington Post,* Jan. 29, 1983, A2.

34. Donaldson, 123.

35. *Washington Post,* Jan. 29, 1983, A2.

36. Herbers, 46.

37. *Washington Post,* Jan. 29, 1983, A2; Herbers, 75; James Deakin, *Straight Stuff: The Reporters, the White House, and the Truth* (New York: William Morrow, 1984), 201.

38. *Chattanooga Times,* Feb. 12, 1987, Z1.

39. Kirschten, 155–56; *Washington Post,* Mar. 7, 1982, H1.

40. Speakes, 187–92; Donaldson, 132; Mark Hertsgaard, *On Bended Knee: The Press and the Reagan Presidency* (New York: Farrar Straus Giroux, 1988).

41. Donaldson, 127; Speakes, 307–8.

42. Speakes, 240–47; Nancy Reagan with William Novak, *My Turn: The Memoirs of Nancy Reagan* (New York: Random House, 1989), 282.

43. Herbers, 46; Speakes, memo to Mike Baroody and Bob Sims, Feb. 23, 1984, RRL, author's freedom of information request; Marlin Fitzwater, *Call the Briefing! Bush and Reagan, Sam and Helen: A Decade with Presidents and the Press* (New York: Random House, 1995), 195.

44. Speakes, 359–61; Tom Blanton, ed., *White House E-Mail: The Top Secret Computer Messages the Reagan/Bush White House Tried to Destroy* (New York: The New Press, 1995), 209–10.

45. *Washington Post,* Jan. 31, 1987, A3; Speakes, 148–52, 397–400.

14. The Picture

1. Fitzwater, 38–71.

2. Peggy Noonan, *What I Saw at the Revolution: A Political Life in the Reagan Era* (New York: Random House, 1990), 206.

3. Fitzwater, 95.

4. Ibid., 74–79, 144; N. Reagan, 315.

5. Fitzwater, 92, 95.

6. Ibid., 168; Regan, 92; N. Reagan, 62, 320, 322.

7. Marlin Fitzwater, memo to the first lady, Feb. 24, 1987, with enclosed transcript, Office of the Press Secretary file, box 18643, Role of the First Lady folder, RRL.

8. Fitzwater, 101–4.

9. *Montgomery Journal,* May 18, 1987, 2; Fitzwater, 95.

10. Marlin Fitzwater, note to Mrs. Reagan, July 10, 1987, with enclosed wire story, Office of the Press Secretary file, box 18643, Role of the First Lady folder, RRL; Fitzwater, author's interview.

11. Fitzwater, 172–74.

12. Mark J. Rozell, *The Press and the Bush Presidency* (Westport, Conn.: Praeger, 1996), 149, 170.

13. Marlin Fitzwater, author's telephone interview, Apr. 2, 1997.

14. Fitzwater, 229–43; *Newsweek,* May 9, 1989, 48; Michael R. Beschloss and Strobe Talbott, *At the Highest Levels: The Inside Story of the End of the Cold War* (Boston: Little, Brown, 1993), 72–73.

15. Fitzwater, 247–48; Beschloss and Talbott, 126; Fitzwater, author's interview.

16. Fitzwater, 248–49, 256–57.

17. Ibid., 210–11; Bob Woodward, *The Commanders* (New York: Simon and

Schuster, 1992), 119–22; Dan Quayle, *Standing Firm: A Vice Presidential Memoir* (New York: Harper Collins, 1994), 142; *Newsweek,* Oct. 16, 1989, 26–31; president's daily diary, Oct. 2, 1989, George Bush Presidential Library.

18. Woodward, 171, 193, 195.

19. Fitzwater, 274–80, 284–91; John Sununu, author's telephone interview, Apr. 4, 1997.

20. Rozell, *Bush Presidency,* 151.

21. Ibid., 163.

22. Fitzwater, author's interview.

15. The Door

1. Kenneth T. Walsh, *Feeding the Beast: The White House Versus the Press* (New York: Random House, 1996), 9.

2. Helen Thomas, author's telephone interview, Apr. 9, 1997.

3. Fred Barnes, "The Importance of Being George," *New Republic,* Sept. 6, 1993, 20.

4. Elizabeth Drew, *On the Edge: The Clinton Presidency* (New York: Simon and Schuster, 1994), 175.

5. *Washington Post,* May 22, 1993, A1, A10.

6. James B. Stewart, *Blood Sport: The President and His Adversaries* (New York: Simon and Schuster, 1996, 263–64.

7. Drew, 184; Fitzwater, 240.

8. Julia Reed, "Admiring Myers," *Vogue,* Apr., 1993, 276.

9. Conversations with author.

10. Mark Knoller, author's telephone interview, Apr. 10, 1997.

11. Author's conversation.

12. Stewart, 264.

13. Walsh, 124.

14. Jeffrey H. Birnbaum, *Madhouse: The Private Turmoil of Working for the President* (New York: Random House, 1996), 175; Michael McCurry, speech to National Press Club, Feb. 29, 1996.

15. Bob Woodward, *The Agenda: Inside the Clinton White House* (New York, Simon and Schuster, 1994), 231; Birnbaum, 163; Walsh, 148.

16. Birnbaum, 163–64.

17. Ibid., 171–75, 181.

18. Ibid., 184.

19. McCurry, Press Club.

20. Birnbaum, 184–88; *New York Times,* Sept. 24, 1994, 9.

21. *Washington Post,* Jan. 6, 1975, A7.

22. Walsh, 205–6.

23. Author's conversation.

24. Jack Nelson, author's interview.

25. Knoller, author's interview.

26. *Washington Post,* Oct. 28, 1995, A14.

27. Bob Woodward, *The Choice* (New York: Simon and Schuster, 1996), 323.

28. Ibid., 359–60.

29. Ibid., 314; *Washington Post,* Mar. 16, 1996, A1, A8; Ken Auletta, "Inside Story," *The New Yorker,* Nov. 18, 1996, 59.

30. *Washington Post,* Aug. 2, 1996, A4.

31. Auletta, 59–60.

32. Ibid., 51.

33. McCurry, Press Club.

34. Auletta, 60.

35. *Washington Post,* July 14, 1996, A16.

36. Smith, *Many Men,* 93.

37. Knoller, author's interview.

38. Powell, author's interview.

39. Christian, author's interview.

40. Fitzwater, author's interview.

41. McCurry, Press Club.

42. George Cortelyou, memorandum to Rudolph Forster, Jan. 26, 1903, George Bruce Cortelyou papers, LC.

Bibliography

Archives

Gerald R. Ford Library, Ann Arbor, Mich.
Herbert Hoover Library, West Branch, Iowa
Dwight D. Eisenhower Library, Abilene, Kans.
Harry S. Truman Library, Independence, Mo.
Jimmy Carter Library, Atlanta, Ga.
Ronald Reagan Library, Simi Valley, Calif.
Lyndon Baines Johnson Library, Austin, Tex.
George Bush Library, College Station, Tex.
Library of Congress Manuscript Division, Washington, D.C.
Nixon Presidential Materials Project, National Archives 2, College Park, Md.

Government Publications

Budget of the United States Government, Fiscal Year 1996. Washington, D.C.:
    Government Printing Office, 1995.
Congressional Record, 88th Congress, Second Session. Washington, D.C.: Gov-
    ernment Printing Office, 1964.
Department of State Bulletin. May 11, 1953, July 20, 1953, Dec. 21, 1953,
    and index for Jan. 4 to June 28, 1954.
Public Papers of the Presidents of the United States. Washington, D.C.: Govern-
    ment Printing Office.

Books

Adams, Sherman. *Firsthand Report: The Story of the Eisenhower Administra-
    tion.* New York: Harper and Brothers, 1961.

Allen, Robert S., and Drew Pearson. *Washington Merry-Go-Round*. New York: Blue Ribbon Books, 1931.

Allen, Robert S., and William V. Shannon. *The Truman Merry-Go-Round*. New York: Vanguard, 1950.

Alsop, Joseph. *FDR, 1882–1945: A Centennial Remembrance*. New York: Viking, 1982.

Alsop, Stewart. *The Center: People and Power in Political Washington*. New York: Harper and Row, 1968.

Ambrose, Stephen E. *Eisenhower: Volume Two—The President*. New York: Simon and Schuster, 1984.

Anderson, Martin. *Revolution: The Reagan Legacy*. Stanford, Calif.: Hoover Institution, 1990.

Anderson, Patrick. *The President's Men: White House Assistants of Franklin D. Roosevelt, Harry S Truman, Dwight D. Eisenhower, John F. Kennedy, and Lyndon B. Johnson*. Garden City, N.Y.: Doubleday, 1968.

Baker, Ray Stannard. *Woodrow Wilson, Life and Letters: Volume Four, President, 1913–14*. Garden City, N.Y.: Doubleday, Doran, 1931.

Beschloss, Michael R., and Strobe Talbott. *At the Highest Levels: The Inside Story of the End of the Cold War*. Boston: Little, Brown, 1993.

Bernstein, Carl, and Bob Woodward. *All the President's Men*. New York: Simon and Schuster, 1974.

Birnbaum, Jeffrey H. *Madhouse: The Private Turmoil of Working for the President*. New York: Random House, 1996.

Bishop, Jim. *FDR's Last Year: April, 1944–April, 1945*. New York: Morrow, 1974.

Blanton, Tom, ed. *White House E-Mail: The Top Secret Computer Messages the Reagan/Bush White House Tried to Destroy*. New York: The New Press, 1995.

Blum, John M. *Joe Tumulty and the Wilson Era*. Archon Books, 1969.

Brzezinski, Zbigniew. *Power and Principle: Memoirs of the National Security Adviser, 1977–1981*. New York: Farrar, Straus & Giroux, 1983.

Burner, David. *Herbert Hoover: A Public Life*. New York: Knopf, 1967.

Butcher, Harry C. *My Three Years with Eisenhower: The Personal Diary of Captain Harry C. Butcher, USNR—Naval Aide to General Eisenhower, 1942 to 1945*. New York: Simon and Schuster, 1946.

Butt, Archibald Willingham. *Taft and Roosevelt: The Intimate Letters of Archie Butt, Military Aide*. Two vols. Garden City, N.Y.: Doubleday, Doran, 1930.

Califano, Joseph A., Jr.: *The Triumph and Tragedy of Lyndon Johnson: The White House Years*. New York: Simon and Schuster, 1991.

Cannon, James. *Time and Chance: Gerald Ford's Appointment with History*. New York: HarperCollins, 1994.

Cannon, Lou. *President Reagan: The Role of a Lifetime.* New York: Simon and Schuster, 1991.

Carpenter, Liz. *Ruffles and Flourishes: The Warm and Tender Story of a Simple Girl Who Found Adventure in the White House.* Garden City, N.Y.: Doubleday, 1970.

Carter, Jimmy. *Keeping Faith: Memoirs of a President.* Toronto: Bantam Books, 1982.

Carter, Rosalynn. *First Lady from Plains.* Boston: Houghton Mifflin, 1984.

Casserly, John J. *The Ford White House: The Diary of a Speechwriter.* Boulder: Colorado Associated Univ. Press, 1977.

Cater, Douglass. *The Fourth Branch of Government.* Boston: Houghton Mifflin, 1959.

Christian, George. *The President Steps Down: A Personal Memoir of the Transfer of Power.* Macmillan, 1970.

Clark, Delbert. *Washington Dateline.* New York: Frederick A. Stokes, 1941.

Cormier, Frank, James Deakin, and Helen Thomas. *The White House Press on the Presidency: News Management and Co-Option.* Lanham, Md.: Univ. Press of America, 1983.

Daniels, Jonathan. *The Man of Independence.* Philadelphia: Lippincott, 1950.

Davis, Oscar King. *Released for Publication: Some Inside Political History of Theodore Roosevelt and His Times, 1898–1918.* Boston: Houghton Mifflin, 1925.

Dawes, Charles G. *A Journal of the McKinley Years,* edited and with a foreword by Bascom N. Timmins. Chicago: Lakeside Press, 1950.

Deakin, James. *Lyndon Johnson's Credibility Gap.* Washington, D.C.: Public Affairs Press, 1986.

————. *Straight Stuff: The Reporters, the White House, and the Truth.* New York: Morrow, 1984.

Dean, John W. III. *Blind Ambition: The White House Years.* New York: Simon and Schuster, 1976.

Donaldson, Sam. *Hold On, Mr. President!* New York: Random House, 1987.

Donovan, Robert J. *Conflict and Crisis: The Presidency of Harry S Truman, 1945–1948.* New York: Norton, 1977.

Drew, Elizabeth. *On the Edge: The Clinton Presidency.* New York: Simon and Schuster, 1994.

————. *Washington Journal: The Events of 1973–1974.* New York: Random House, 1974.

Dunn, Arthur Wallace. *From Harrison to Harding: A Personal Narrative, Covering a Third of a Century, 1888–1921.* Port Washington, N.Y.: Kennikat Press, 1971.

————. *Gridiron Nights: Humorous and Satirical Views of Politics and Statesmen as Presented by the Famous Dining Club.* New York: Frederick A. Stokes, 1915. Reprint. New York: Arno Press, 1974.

Eaton, John, and Charles A. Haas. *Titanic: Destination Disaster—The Legends and the Reality*. New York: W. W. Norton, 1987.

Ehrlichman, John. *Witness to Power: The Nixon Years*. New York: Simon and Schuster, 1982.

Eisenhower, Dwight D. *The White House Years: Mandate for Change, 1953–1956*. Garden City, N.Y.: Doubleday, 1963.

———. *The White House Years: Waging Peace, 1956–1961*. Garden City, N.Y.: Doubleday, 1965.

Evans, Rowland Jr., and Robert D. Novak. *Nixon in the White House: The Frustration of Power*. New York: Random House, 1971.

Farrar, Ronald T. *Reluctant Servant: The Story of Charles G. Ross*. Columbia: Univ. of Missouri Press, 1969.

Ferrel, Robert H. *Harry S. Truman: A Life*. Columbia: Univ. of Missouri Press, 1994.

———, ed. *The Diary of James C. Hagerty: Eisenhower in Mid-Course, 1954–1955*. Bloomington: Indiana Univ. Press, 1983.

———, ed. *The Eisenhower Diaries*. New York: Norton, 1981.

———, ed. *Truman in the White House: The Diary of Eben A. Ayers*. Columbia: Univ. of Missouri Press, 1991.

Fielding, Raymond. *The American Newsreel: 1911–1967*. Norman: Univ. of Oklahoma Press, 1972.

Fitzwater, Marlin. *Call the Briefing! Bush and Reagan, Sam and Helen: A Decade with the Presidents and the Press*. New York: Random House, 1996.

Ford, Gerald R. *A Time to Heal: The Autobiography of Gerald R. Ford*. New York: Harper and Row, 1979.

Fowle, Eleanor. *Cranston: The Senator from California*. San Rafael, Calif.: Presidio, 1980.

French, Blaire Atherton. *The Presidential Press Conference: Its History and Role in the American Political System*. Lanham, Md.: Univ. Press of America, 1982.

Gobright, L. A. *Recollections of Men and Things at Washington During the Third of a Century*. Philadelphia: Claxton, Remsen and Haffelfinger, 1869.

Gould, Lewis L. *The Presidency of William McKinley*. Lawrence, Kans.: The Regents Press of Kansas, 1980.

Gunther, John. *Roosevelt in Retrospect*. New York: Harper, 1950.

Haig, Alexander M. Jr. *Caveat: Realism, Reagan, and Foreign Policy*. New York: Macmillan, 1984.

Haig, Alexander M., Jr., with Charles McCarry. *Inner Circles: How America Changed the World: A Memoir*. New York: Warner, 1992.

Halberstam, David. *The Powers That Be*. New York: Knopf, 1979.

Haldeman, H. R. *The Haldeman Diaries: Inside the Nixon White House*. New York: Putnam's, 1994.

Haldeman, H. R., with Joseph Di Mona. *The Ends of Power.* New York: Times Books, 1978.

Hamby, Alonzo L. *Man of the People: A Life of Harry S. Truman.* New York: Oxford Univ. Press, 1995.

Harper, Robert S. *Lincoln and the Press.* New York: McGraw-Hill, 1951.

Hartmann, Robert. *Palace Politics: An Inside Account of the Ford Years.* New York: McGraw-Hill, 1980.

Heckscher, August. *Woodrow Wilson.* New York: Scribner's, 1991.

Hertsgaard, Mark. *On Bended Knee: The Press and the Reagan Presidency.* New York: Farrar, Straus & Giroux, 1988.

Hilderbrand, Robert C. *Power and the People: Executive Management of Public Opinion in Foreign Affairs, 1897–1921.* Chapel Hill, N.C.: Univ. of North Carolina Press, 1981.

Hoover, Herbert. *The Memoirs of Herbert Hoover: The Cabinet and the Presidency, 1920–1933.* New York: Macmillan, 1952.

Hoxie, R. Gordon, ed. *The White House: Organization and Operations.* New York: Center for the Study of the Presidency, 1971.

Hoyt, Edwin P. *Grover Cleveland.* Chicago: Reilly and Lee, 1962.

Ickes, Harold L. *The Secret Diary of Harold L. Ickes, Vol. 3: The Lowering Clouds, 1939–1941.* New York: Simon and Schuster, 1954.

Isaacson, Walter. *Kissinger: A Biography.* New York: Simon and Schuster, 1992.

Johnson, Lady Bird. *A White House Diary.* New York: Holt, Rinehart and Winston, 1970.

Johnson, Lyndon Baines. *The Vantage Point: Perspectives of the Presidency, 1963–1969.* New York: Holt, Rinehart and Winston, 1971.

Johnson, Sam Houston. Ed. Enrique Hank Lopez. *My Brother Lyndon.* New York: Cowles, 1970.

Jordan, Hamilton. *Crisis: The Last Year of the Carter Presidency.* New York: G. P. Putnam's Sons, 1982.

Joslin, Theodore G. *Hoover off the Record.* New York: Doubleday, Doran, 1934.

Juergens, George. *News from the White House: The Presidential-Press Relationship in the Progressive Era.* Chicago: Univ. of Chicago Press, 1981.

Jurey, Philomena. *A Basement Seat to History: Tales of Covering Presidents Nixon, Ford, Carter, and Reagan for the Voice of America.* Washington, D.C.: Linus Press, 1995.

Kennedy, John F. *The Kennedy Presidential Press Conferences.* New York: Earl M. Coleman Enterprises, 1978.

Kennedy, Robert F. *Thirteen Days: A Memoir of the Cuban Missile Crisis.* New York: Norton, 1969.

Kreisberg, Paul H., ed. *American Hostages in Iran: The Conduct of a Crisis.* New Haven, Conn.: Yale Univ. Press, 1985.

Kutler, Stanley I. *The Wars of Watergate: The Last Crisis of Richard Nixon.* New York: Knopf, 1990.

Leach, Margaret. *In the Days of McKinley.* New York: Harper and Bros., 1959.

Link, Arthur S., ed. *Papers of Woodrow Wilson.* Princeton, N.J.: Princeton Univ. Press.

Lloyd, Craig. *Aggressive Introvert: A Study of Herbert Hoover and Public Relations Management, 1912–1932.* Columbus: Ohio State Univ. Press, 1972.

Lord, Walter. *A Night to Remember.* New York: Bantam Books, 1956.

Ludlow, Louis. *From Cornfield to Press Gallery: Adventures and Reminiscences of a Veteran Washington Correspondent.* Washington, D.C.: W. F. Roberts, 1924.

Lukas, J. Anthony. *Nightmare: The Underside of the Nixon Years.* New York: Viking, 1976.

McCoy, Donald R. *Calvin Coolidge: The Quiet President.* New York: Macmillan, 1967.

McCullough, David. *The Path Between the Seas: The Creation of the Panama Canal, 1870–1914.* New York: Simon and Schuster, 1977.

———. *Truman.* New York: Simon and Schuster, 1992.

McGaffin, William, and Erwin Knoll. *Anything but the Truth: The Credibility Gap—How the News Is Managed in Washington.* New York: Putnam's, 1968.

MacMahon, Edward B., M.D., and Leonard Curry. *Medical Cover-ups in the White House.* Washington, D.C.: Farragut, 1987.

Magruder, Jeb Stuart. *An American Life: One Man's Road to Watergate.* New York: Atheneum, 1974.

Manchester, William. *The Death of a President, November 20–November 25, 1963.* New York: Harper and Row, 1967.

Marbut, F. B. *News from the Capital: The Story of Washington Reporting.* Carbondale: Southern Illinois Univ. Press, 1971.

Miller, Merle. *Plain Speaking: An Oral Biography of Harry S. Truman.* New York: Putnam's, 1974.

Montgomery, Robert. *Open Letter from a Television Viewer.* New York: Heineman, 1968.

Morgan, H. Wayne. *William McKinley and His America.* Syracuse, N.Y.: Syracuse Univ. Press, 1963.

Nessen, Ron. *It Sure Looks Different from the Inside.* Chicago: Playboy, 1978.

Nevins, Allan. *Grover Cleveland: A Study in Courage.* New York: Dodd, Mead, 1933.

Nicolay, Helen. *Lincoln's Secretary: A Biography of John G. Nicolay.* New York: Longmans, Green, 1949.

Nixon, Richard M. *RN: The Memoirs of Richard Nixon.* New York: Grosset and Dunlap, 1978.

————. *Six Crises.* Garden City, N.Y.: Doubleday, 1962.

Noonan, Peggy. *What I Saw at the Revolution: A Political Life in the Reagan Era.* New York: Random House, 1990.

Osborne, John. *White House Watch: The Ford Years.* Washington, D.C.: New Republic, 1977.

Oudes, Bruce, ed. *From the President: Richard Nixon's Secret Files.* New York: Harper and Row, 1989.

Penrose, Charles. *George B. Cortelyou (1862–1940): Briefest Biography of a Great American.* New York: The Newcomen Society in North America, 1955.

Phillips, Cabell, et al., eds. *Dateline: Washington—The Story of National Affairs Journalism in the Life and Times of the National Press Club.* New York: Greenwood, 1968.

————. *The Truman Presidency: The History of a Triumphant Succession.* New York: Macmillan, 1966.

Pollard, James E. *The Presidents and the Press.* New York: Macmillan, 1947.

Poore, Benjamin Perley. *Perley's Reminiscences of Sixty Years in the National Metropolis.* Two vols. Philadelphia: Hubbard Brothers, 1886.

Powell, Jody. *The Other Side of the Story.* New York: William Morrow, 1984.

Quandt, William B. *Camp David: Peacemaking and Politics.* Washington, D.C.: Brookings, 1986.

Quayle, Dan. *Standing Firm: A Vice Presidential Memoir.* New York: Harper-Collins, 1994.

Rather, Dan, and Gary Paul Gates. *The Palace Guard.* New York: Harper and Row, 1974.

Reagan, Nancy, with William Novak. *My Turn: The Memoirs of Nancy Reagan.* New York: Random House, 1989.

Reagan, Ronald. *An American Life.* New York: Simon and Schuster, 1990.

Reeves, Richard. *President Kennedy: Profile of Power.* New York: Simon and Schuster, 1993.

Regan, Donald T. *For the Record: From Wall Street to Washington.* San Diego: Harcourt Brace Jovanovich, 1988.

Reinsch, J. Leonard. *Getting Elected: From Radio and Roosevelt to Television and Reagan.* New York: Hippocrene, 1988.

Rigdon, William M., with James Derieux. *White House Sailor.* Garden City, N.Y.: Doubleday, 1962.

Ritchie, Donald A. *Press Gallery: Congress and the Washington Correspondents.* Cambridge, Mass.: Harvard Univ. Press, 1991.

Robinson, Edgar, and Vaughn Davis Bornet. *Herbert Hoover: President of the United States.* Stanford, Calif.: Hoover Institution, 1975.

Roosevelt, Franklin D. *The Public Papers and Addresses of Franklin D. Roosevelt, with a Special Introduction and Explanatory Notes by President Roosevelt: 1939 Volume—War and Neutrality.* New York: Macmillan, 1941.

————. *1941 Volume—The Call to Battle Stations, Compiled with Special Material and Explanatory Notes by Samuel I. Rosenman.* New York: Harper and Brothers, 1950.

Rosenman, Samuel I. *Working with Roosevelt.* New York: Harper and Brothers, 1952.

Ross, Charles G. *The Writing of News.* New York: Henry Holt, 1911.

Rozell, Mark J. *The Press and the Bush Presidency.* Westport, Conn.: Praeger, 1996.

————. *The Press and the Ford Presidency.* Ann Arbor: Univ. of Michigan Press, 1992.

Rusk, Dean, as told to Richard Rusk. *As I Saw It.* Ed. Daniel S. Papp. New York: Norton, 1990.

Russell, Francis. *The Shadow of Blooming Grove: Warren G. Harding in His Times.* New York: McGraw-Hill, 1968.

Safire, William. *Before the Fall: An Inside View of the Pre-Watergate White House.* Garden City, N.Y.: Doubleday, 1975.

Salinger, Pierre. *America Held Hostage: The Secret Negotiations.* New York: Doubleday, 1981.

————. *P.S.: A Memoir.* New York: St. Martin's, 1995.

————. *With Kennedy.* Garden City, N.Y.: Doubleday, 1966.

Schlesinger, Arthur M. Jr. *The Age of Jackson.* New York: Book Find Club, 1945.

————. *A Thousand Days: John F. Kennedy in the White House.* Boston: Houghton Mifflin, 1965.

Schram, Martin. *The Great American Video Game: Presidential Politics in the Television Age.* New York: Morrow, 1987.

Seale, William. *The President's House: A History.* Washington, D.C.: White House Historical Association with the Cooperation of the National Geographic Society, 1986.

Sidey, Hugh. *A Very Personal Presidency: Lyndon Johnson in the White House.* New York: Atheneum, 1968.

Sirica, John J. *To Set the Record Straight: The Break-in, the tapes, the Conspirators, the Pardon.* New York: Norton, 1979.

Smith, A. Merriman. *A President Is Many Men.* New York: Harper and Brothers, 1948.

————. *Thank You, Mr. President: A White House Notebook.* New York: Harper and Brothers, 1946.

Smith, Albert E., in collaboration with Phil A. Koury. *Two Reels and a Crank.* Garden City, N.Y.: Doubleday, 1952.

Smith, Gene. *When the Cheering Stopped: The Last Years of Woodrow Wilson.* New York: William Morrow, 1964.

Sorensen, Theodore C. *Kennedy.* New York: Harper and Row, 1965.

Speakes, Larry, with Robert Pack. *Speaking Out: The Reagan Presidency from Inside the White House.* New York: Avon Books, 1989.

Spear, Joseph C. *Presidents and the Press: The Nixon Legacy.* Cambridge, Mass.: MIT Press, 1984.

Stewart, James B. *Blood Sport: The President and His Adversaries.* New York: Simon and Schuster, 1996.

Stokes, Thomas L. *Chip off My Shoulder.* Princeton, N.J.: Princeton Univ. Press, 1940.

terHorst, Jerald F. *Gerald Ford and the Future of the Presidency.* New York: The Third Press, 1974.

terHorst, Jerald F., and Col. Ralph Albertazzie. *The Flying White House: The Story of Air Force One.* New York: Coward, McCann and Geoghegan, 1979.

Thomas, Helen. *Dateline: White House.* New York: Macmillan, 1975.

Thompson, Charles William. *Presidents I've Known and Two Near Presidents.* Indianapolis: Bobbs-Merrill, 1929.

Thompson, Kenneth W., ed. *The Kennedy Presidency: Seventeen Intimate Perspectives of John F. Kennedy.* Lanham, Md.: Univ. Press of America, 1985.

———. *Ten Presidents and the Press.* Charlottesville, Va.: White Burkett Miller Center of Public Affairs at the Univ. of Virginia, 1983.

———. *Three Press Secretaries on the Presidency and the Press.* Lanham, Md: Univ. Press of America, 1983.

———. *The Virginia Papers on the Presidency, Volume 4.* Charlottesville, Va.: The White Burkett Miller Center, 1980.

Thompson, Robert Smith. *The Missiles of October: The Declassified Story of John F. Kennedy and the Cuban Missile Crisis.* New York: Simon and Schuster, 1992.

Trohan, Walter. *Political Animals: Memoirs of a Sentimental Cynic.* Garden City, N.Y.: Doubleday, 1975.

Truman, Harry S. *Memoirs by Harry S. Truman: Volume One—Year of Decisions.* Garden City, N.Y.: Doubleday, 1955.

Truman, Margaret. *Harry S. Truman.* New York: Pocket Books, 1974.

Tugwell, Rexford G. *Grover Cleveland.* New York: Macmillan, 1968.

Tumulty, Joseph P. *Woodrow Wilson as I Know Him.* Garden City, N.Y.: Doubleday Page, 1921.

Vance, Cyrus. *Hard Choices: Critical Years in America's Foreign Policy.* New York: Simon and Schuster, 1963.

Von Damm, Helene. *At Reagan's Side.* New York: Doubleday, 1989.

Walsh, Kenneth T. *Feeding the Beast: The White House Versus the Press.* New York: Random House, 1996.

Walworth, Arthur. *Woodrow Wilson, 2: World Prophet.* New York: Longmans Green, 1958.

Ward, Geoffrey C. *A First-Class Temperament: The Emergence of Franklin Roosevelt.* New York: Harper and Row, 1989.

Weinberger, Caspar W. *Fighting for Peace: Seven Critical Years in the Pentagon.* New York: Warner Books, 1990.

White, Graham J. *FDR and the Press*. Chicago: Univ. of Chicago Press, 1979.

White, Theodore. *The Making of the President, 1968*. New York: Atheneum, 1969.

Wicker, Tom. *One of Us: Richard Nixon and the American Dream*. New York: Random House, 1991.

Wilson, Edith Bolling. *My Memoir*. Indianapolis: Bobbs-Merrill, 1938.

Winfield, Betty Houchin. *FDR and the News Media*. Urbana: Univ. of Illinois Press, 1990.

Woodward, Bob. *The Agenda: Inside the Clinton White House*. New York: Simon and Schuster, 1994.

———. *The Choice*. New York: Simon and Schuster, 1996.

———. *The Commanders*. New York: Simon and Schuster, 1992.

Articles

Anderson, Jack. "Pierre Salinger." *Parade*, Apr. 21, 1963.

Auletta, Ken. "Inside Story." *New Yorker*, Nov. 18, 1996.

Barnes, Fred. "The Importance of Being George." *New Republic*, Sept. 6, 1993.

Bates, David Homer. "Lincoln in the Telegraph Office." *The Century*, May 1907.

Blair, John L. "Coolidge, the Image-Maker: The President and the Press, 1923–1929." *New England Quarterly*, Dec. 1973.

Bonafede, Dom. "The Washington Press—Competing for Power with the Federal Government." *National Journal*, Apr. 17, 1982.

Brandon, Henry. "The New Press Secretary." *Saturday Review*, Aug. 7, 1965.

Brandt, Raymond P. "The President's Press Conference." *Survey Graphic*, July 1939.

Brayman, Harold. "Hooverizing the Press." *Outlook and Independent*, Sept. 24, 1930.

Buel, C. C. "Our Fellow-Citizen of the White House: The Official Cares of a President of the United States." *The Century*, Mar. 1987.

Butler, James J. "Capital Writers Ired by News Blockade." *Editor & Publisher*, Mar. 30, 1946.

———. "Truman's First Press Conference." *Editor & Publisher*, Apr. 21, 1945.

———. "White House Spokesman Mystery Stirs Senate Curiosity at Last." *Editor & Publisher*, Jan. 15, 1927.

———. "Why Reporters Like Roosevelt." *Review of Reviews & World's Work*, June 1934.

Clark, Delbert. " 'Steve' Takes Care of It." *New York Times Magazine*, July 27, 1941.

Cormier, Frank. "Powell Still Credible." *Editor & Publisher*, Jan. 21, 1978.

Crawford, Kenneth G. "The Nation." *PM,* Dec. 17, 1941.

Creel, George. "Woodrow Wilson, the Man Behind the President." *Saturday Evening Post,* Mar. 28, 1931.

Damon, Allan L. "Presidential Accessibility." *American Heritage,* Apr. 1974.

Davenport, Walter, "The New White House Boys." *Collier's,* Nov. 17, 1945.

Early, Stephen T. "Below the Belt." *Saturday Evening Post,* June 10, 1939.

Early, Stephen T., and Richard Eaton. "Behind the White House, Condensed from an Interview over WMCA." *News Digest, Your Radio Magazine,* June 1944.

Fairlie, Henry. "The Rise of the Press Secretary." *The New Republic,* Mar. 18, 1978.

Godwin, Earl. "White Housekeeping." *Goldfish Bowl,* July 1937.

Gould, Lewis L. "There's History to Role of First Lady." *The Quill,* Mar. 1966.

Halstead, Albert. "The President at Work—A Character Sketch." *The Independent,* Sept. 5, 1901.

Hart, Scott. "Truman and Ross: America's No. 1 Team." *Coronet,* Jan. 1946.

Hartmann, Robert T. "Kennedy's Press Secretary." *The Quill,* Mar. 1966.

Hassett, William. "The President Was My Boss: Part Seven." *Saturday Evening Post,* November 21, 1953.

Herbers, John. "The President and the Press Corps." *New York Times Magazine,* May 9, 1982.

Hersey, John. "The Wayward Press: Conference in Room 474." *The New Yorker,* Dec. 16, 1950.

Hickok, Lorena. " 'We Always Looked Up to Charlie.' " *Saga,* June 1951.

Huston, Luther A. "Nixon Puts Newsmen in Lap of Luxury." *Editor & Publisher,* Apr. 18, 1970.

Hutchinson, Earl R. "Kennedy and the Press: The First Six Months." *Journalism Quarterly,* Fall 1961.

Joslin, Theodore G. "Hoover's First Year." *World's Work,* Mar. 1930.

Kirschten, Dick. "Communications Reshuffling Intended to Help Reagan Do What He Does Best." *National Journal,* Jan. 28, 1984.

MacKaye, Milton. "Ike's Man Friday." *Saturday Evening Post,* May 21, 1960.

Manning, George H. "Hoover's Press System Best Instituted by Any President, Capital Writers Say." *Editor & Publisher,* Mar. 16, 1929.

———. "White House Ban on Bank Parley Upset by Correspondents." *Editor & Publisher,* Oct. 10, 1931.

———. "White House Best Source for Rapidan Camp 100 Miles Away." *Editor & Publisher,* July 13, 1930.

Naughton, James M. "How the 2nd Best-Informed Man in the White House Briefs the 2nd Worst-Informed Group in Washington." *New York Times Magazine,* May 30, 1971.

Nolan, Martin F. "The Reselling of the President." *Atlantic,* Nov. 1972.

Oberdorfer, Don. "The China Press Scenario." *The Nation,* March 27, 1972.
———. "The Man Who Speaks for LBJ." *Saturday Evening Post,* Oct. 23, 1965.
Orr, Lyndon. "Great Secretaries to the President." *The Scrap Book,* Nov. 1907.
Osborne, John. "In Jody's Shop." *New Republic,* Mar. 8, 1978.
———. "In Jody's Shop (II)." *New Republic,* Mar. 15, 1978.
———. "White House Watch." *New Republic,* Mar. 1, 1975, Apr. 26, 1975.
Oulahan, Richard V. "Gathering News at Washington." *The Quill,* Apr. 1921.
———, [Victor Proud, pseud.]. "Roosevelt, the Politician." *Saturday Evening Post,* Sept. 21, 1907.
Pearson, Drew, and Robert S. Allen. "How the President Works." *Harpers,* June 1936.
Pollard, James E. "President Truman and the Press." *Journalism Quarterly,* Fall 1951.
Pringle, Henry F. "President's Voice: James C. Hagerty." *Nation's Business,* July 1953.
Reed, Julia. "Admiring Myers." *Vogue,* Apr. 1993.
Reston, James. "Dilemma of the White House Q & A." *New York Times Magazine,* June 1, 1958.
Roberts, Charles. "LBJ's Credibility Gap." *Newsweek,* Dec. 19, 1966.
Rogers, Warren. "The Truth about LBJ's Credibility." *Look,* May 2, 1967.
Shaplen, Robert. "Meet the New Press Secretary." *Saturday Review,* Jan. 14, 1961.
Smith, Merriman. "White House Front Man." *New York Times Magazine,* Oct. 4, 1953.
Strout, Richard L. "TRB." *New Republic,* Nov. 20, 1976.
Tarbell, Ida. "President McKinley in War Times." *McClure's,* July 1898.
Thomas, Helen. "Carter Still Accessible." *Editor & Publisher,* Jan. 21, 1978.
Turnbull, George. "Some Notes on the History of the Interview." *Journalism Quarterly,* No. 3.
Walters, Robert. "What Did Ziegler Say, and When Did He Say It?" *Columbia Journalism Review,* Sept.–Oct. 1974.
Ward, Paul W. "Roosevelt Keeps His Vow." *The Nation,* Sept. 25, 1935.
White, William S. "Kennedy's Seven Rules for Handling the Press." *Harper's,* Apr. 1961.
Winfield, Betty Houchin. "Franklin D. Roosevelt's Efforts to Influence the News During His First Term Press Conferences." *Presidential Studies Quarterly,* 1981.
———. "Mrs. Roosevelt's Press Conference Association: The First Lady Shines a Light." *Journalism History,* Summer 1981.

Witcover, Jules. "Focusing on Nixon." *Columbia Journalism Review,* Winter 1968–69.

Woolf, S. J. "Up the Ladder with F.D.R." *New York Times Magazine,* Aug. 27, 1939.

Unpublished Manuscripts

Burkholder, Donald R. *The Caretaker of the President's Image.* Diss. Wayne State Univ., 1973.

Cortelyou, Lily. *Reminiscences,* in George Bruce Cortelyou papers, manuscript division, Library of Congress.

Ford, Benjamin Temple. *A Duty to Serve: The Governmental Career of George Bruce Cortelyou.* Diss. Columbia Univ., 1963.

Joslin, Theodore G. *The President and the Press.* Unpublished Manuscripts folder, Joslin Papers, Hoover Library.

Latimer, Harry David. *The Press Secretaries of Lyndon Johnson.* Diss. Brown Univ., 1973.

Moon, Gordon Ames II. *James Campbell Hagerty's Eight Years in the White House.* Thesis. Univ. of Wisconsin, 1962.

Oulahan, Richard V. *Presidents and the Press.* Book draft in Richard V. Oulahan Papers, Hoover Library.

Schoenherr, Steven E. *Selling the New Deal: Stephen T. Early's Role as Press Secretary to Franklin D. Roosevelt.* Diss. Univ. of Delaware, 1976.

Winfield, Betty Houchin. *Roosevelt and the Press: How Franklin D. Roosevelt Influenced News Gathering, 1933–1941.* Diss. Univ. of Washington, 1978.

Author's Interviews

Christian, George. Austin, Tex., Oct. 22, 1996.

Fitzwater, Marlin. By telephone. April 2, 1997.

Ford, Gerald R. By telephone. Feb. 11, 1997.

Gallagher, Wes. By telephone. Jan. 5, 1997.

Knoller, Mark. By telephone. Apr. 10, 1997.

Nelson, Jack. By telephone. May 28, 1996.

Nessen, Ronald. By telephone. Feb. 12, 1997.

Powell, Jody. Washington, D.C., Feb. 29, 1996.

Reedy, George. By telephone. Jan. 23, 1997.

Salinger, Pierre. By telephone. Jan. 3, 1997.

Sununu, John. By telephone. Apr. 4, 1997.

terHorst, Jerald. By telephone. Feb. 11, 1997.

Thomas, Helen. By telephone. Apr. 9, 1997.

Ziegler, Ronald. By telephone. Apr. 1, 1997.

Oral History Interviews

Akerson, George Jr. Mar. 11, 1969. Hoover Library.

Alsop, Stewart. Washington, D.C., July 15, 1969. Johnson Library.

Ayers, Eben A. Jan. 12, 1967–June 30, 1970. Truman Library.

Barr, Joseph. Pittsburgh, June 10, 1969. Johnson Library.

Baskin, Robert. Dallas, Mar. 16, 1974. Johnson Library.

Boatner, Charles. Fort Worth, Tex., June 1, 1976. Johnson Library.

Chandler, Loren R. Jan. 23, 1970. Hoover Library.

Coleman, Barbara. Washington, D.C., Jan. 19, 1968. Kennedy Library.

Folliard, Edward T. Aug. 6, 1968. Hoover Library.

————. Washington, D.C., Mar. 30, 1967. Kennedy Library.

————. Aug 20, 1970. Truman Library.

Garamekian, Barbara. Washington, D.C., June 10, 1964. Kennedy Library.

Hagerty, James C. The Reminiscences of James C. Hagerty (Mar. 2, 1967). In the collection of the Columbia Univ. Oral History Research Office.

Huntley, Chester R. May 12, 1969. Univ. of Texas Oral History Project. Johnson Library.

Kent, Carleton. Washington, D.C., Dec. 21 and 29, 1970. Truman Library.

Krock, Arthur. Nov. 21, 1966. Hoover Library.

Lawrence, William H. Washington, D.C., Apr. 22, 1966. Kennedy Library.

Lisagor, Peter. Washington, D.C., May 12, 1966. Kennedy Library.

McGrory, Mary, Peter Lisagor, and George Herman. Washington D.C., Aug. 4, 1964. Kennedy Library.

May, Charles L. Washington, D.C., May 6, 1969. Johnson Library.

Mooney, Booth. Apr. 8, 1969. Johnson Library.

Perlmeter, Irving. Washington, D.C., May 24 and 29, 1967. Truman Library.

Powell, Jody. Dec. 2, 1980. Carter Library.

Price, Byron. Mar. 21, 1969. Hoover Library.

Rather, Dan. Washington, D.C., Apr. 16, 1973. Johnson Library.

Salinger, Pierre. Los Angeles, Aug. 10, 1965. Kennedy Library.

Short, Beth. Alexandria, Va., Feb. 16, 1971. Truman Library.

Smith, Bromley. Washington, D.C., July 29, 1969. Johnson Library.

Strout, Richard L. Feb. 5, 1971. Truman Library.

Trohan, Walter. Oct. 16, 1980. Hoover Library.

————. Oct. 7, 1970. Truman Library.

Tubby, Roger. Washington, D.C., Feb. 10, 1970. Truman Library.

Warren, Ernest G. Whitestone, Va., Feb. 29, 1968. Kennedy Library.

Warren, Gerald L. Oct. 24, 1974. Nixon Project.

Ziegler, Ronald. Nov. 15, 1977. By A. James Reichley. Ford Library.